THE BRITISH BOOK TRADE

AN ORAL HISTORY

THE BRITISH BOOK TRADE

AN ORAL HISTORY

Edited by Sue Bradley

THE BRITISH LIBRARY

First published in 2008 by
The British Library
96 Euston Road
London NW1 2DB

Paperback edition first published in 2010

British Library Cataloguing in Publication Data
A catalogue record for this book is available from The British Library

The views expressed in *The British Book Trade: An Oral History*
are not necessarily those of the editor or publisher.

ISBN 978 0 7123 5091 4

Designed by Andrew Shoolbred

Cover design by Andrew Barron

Typeset at The Spartan Press Ltd,
Lymington, Hants

Printed and bound in Great Britain
by MPG Books Ltd

CONTENTS

To everyone who made a *Book Trade Lives* recording,
and the others who contributed in different ways.

NOTE TO READERS

The accounts in this book are edited extracts from interviews recorded between 1997 and 2006 for *Book Trade Lives*, one of a number of oral history collections initiated by National Life Stories, an independent charity based at the British Library Sound Archive. The original full-length versions are accessible at the British Library, with content details available online at www.cadensa.bl.uk. Some interviews have been closed for a time by the speakers. Further information about National Life Stories and its collections can be found at www.bl.uk/nls. The aim of this book is to offer a flavour of what the *Book Trade Lives* collection holds and an invitation to explore it further.

The editor, Sue Bradley, was the interviewer responsible for *Book Trade Lives*. She has worked with oral history since the early 1990s. Previously she worked in second-hand bookselling and in publishing, when she was editor of *The British Library General Catalogue of Printed Books* and *Les Archives Biographiques Françaises*. She is now a research associate at the Centre for Rural Economy, Newcastle University.

FOREWORD

Oral history is the voice of the past: we hear the story told by those who experienced it at the time. We hear emotion, opinion – we can tell what sort of person is speaking. Some oral histories cry out for further expression; they ask to be read, as well as heard – they lend themselves to book form. *Book Trade Lives* is a prime instance. Here is a trade – industry, profession – which is concerned with the creation and dissemination of books. Those working in it are focused upon the ultimate product – that unique, compact, infinitely flexible form of communication. All the voices in the *Book Trade Lives* collection are testimony to this. Behind their stories and their comments hovers the ghost of the book – the ghosts of millions of books. Hence this book – the tale of the book trade in tangible form.

That said, here is a work from which voices ring out. Sue Bradley's skill has been to interweave her material so that each chapter gives us an aspect of the book business seen and reported by a group of disparate people, their individuality shining forth: Frank Stoakley of Heffer's in Cambridge on the purchase of the scientist Rutherford's books, which were found to be 'lousy with the radium'; David Whitaker reporting Alex Macmillan's description of Birch Grove, his family home, as 'built on Hall and Knight's *Algebra* and furnished on *Gone with the Wind*.' The voices sometimes correct one another – as in the various descriptions of Christina Foyle – or seem to respond to each other, which is of course an effect of the careful editorial process. It is the book form that makes it possible to bring this extra dimension to the original oral histories: instead of hearing one discrete account at length, we can now turn to themes – the life of a publisher's rep, the Net Book Agreement, the role of the bookseller – and see how different accounts throw light on each subject.

Oral history interviewing is qualitatively different from, say, press interviewing. The journalist tends to arrive with a set of questions. The oral history interviewer will indeed have a plan – a structure – in mind, but works much more on the hoof: the interview is a dialogue in which the interviewer, listening intently, responds to what has been said – picking up on something to raise a further question, returning to a previous point to suggest expansion. It is a fascinating process. The sympathetic interviewer can draw out material that the interviewee had half forgotten or had not thought of contributing. That is why oral history is often alive with stories: the subject is encouraged to enrich the narrative. An individual life story is at issue, but the telling of it is a dialogue, which prevents a featureless plod through the decades; the end product will have the colour and zest of conversation.

In the penultimate chapter, Mark Barty-King refers to the book trade as a cottage industry. It may be less so today, in the age of the conglomerates, but it certainly has been, and remains to a great extent, a world of persons, of personalities, of personal relationships. This quality leaps from the pages of *The British Book Trade*: people are remembering each other, describing one another, telling us how they interacted – and, in the process, how they made and sold books. The authors cease, at points, to be shadowy unmentioned presences and are conjured up from surprising angles – glimpses of T.S. Eliot at Fabers from Rosemary Goad and Anne Walmsley; the young Seamus Heaney encountered by bookseller Elizabeth McWatters.

Editors are candid about their dislikes – Marni Hodgkin turning down Roald Dahl on account of personal distaste, 'a latent nastiness . . . I didn't care for. A kind of malicious quality.' – and about their satisfactions – Judy Taylor pouncing on *Where the Wild Things Are*, which had been turned down by eight unresponsive publishers. Such anecdotes remind us that what we are able to read is determined, in the first instance, by a person pondering a manuscript, and by their reaction to it.

The story of a nation's books is an aspect of its history, and this account of their creation is a revealing social record. Changing attitudes and practices in the book business mirror in many ways changes in wider social *mores*. It is intriguing to read Tim Rix's memory of the assistant in Longman's production department who would reach out to put on his jacket when receiving a phone call from the managing director – knee-jerk deference. The gentlemen publishers of the early and mid-20th century seem archaic figures today, with their patronage of booksellers and the vague assumption that the women working for them would of course have private incomes to supplement their meagre wages. They seem as far removed from the publishing executive of today as the chain bookshops are from the patrician independent of fifty years ago, which I am old enough to remember, without too much affection. As a diffident twenty year old, you did not lightly enter Bumpus, or Truslove & Hanson, where some austere person would come up to you and enquire coldly if they could help. Bookshops have subsequently learned not to be daunting to the young, or to the browser, and I deeply regret the precarious situation of many independents today. The chains have their own merits. But they dictate what is on offer to the book buyer at any one time, at the expense of the quirky, the esoteric, the title with minority appeal.

I have been a trustee of National Life Stories since the archive was set up, and have always known that oral history is a vital complement to conventional history (interestingly, through my reading rather than through listening – back to the value of oral history in book form). As a writer, I am one of those skulking in the shadows here – off the page, as it were – but NLS now has its *Authors' Lives* project underway, in the service of which I have found myself on the receiving end of an oral history interview, and have thus gained further insights into the technique, and even greater admiration for its practitioners.

The contribution of *Book Trade Lives* to the archive created by National Life Stories represents a treasure trove for the future. Those misty figures, the publishers and booksellers of the next century (I am one of those who believe firmly that the book has a future) will now be able to wonder at the curious practices of their predecessors.

Penelope Lively

INTRODUCTION

What if we could hear the booksellers and publishers of centuries past describe their days? Their concerns, inspirations, and perceptions of the trade? What if, indeed. But suppose we asked their 20th-century counterparts? And so we did. We did not set out to make a book. The aim was to create a collection of oral histories to be preserved at the British Library Sound Archive so that listeners today and in the future could experience these live recordings for themselves. It was the voices that we started with.

National Life Stories (NLS) had been established in 1987 to 'record first-hand experiences of as wide a cross-section of present-day society as possible'. Artists, the financial sector, the steel industry, the food industry; theatre designers, Post Office employees, chefs, horticulturalists, architects . . . The archive continues to grow. And within each project the same brief applies: experiences across the board. For the book trade, we wanted to include the lives of secretaries, warehouse staff and sales assistants, as well as high-profile figures. We aimed to build a multi-dimensional picture that showed the business from many different angles and covered the grandest time scale. So name checkers will be disappointed: *Book Trade Lives* does not include all the leading lights. But everyone we interviewed had something extraordinary to say.

The results were more surprising than I anticipated. I began work as the interviewer in November 1998 with the assumption that, given the pace of change in the 20th century, the recordings would document significant shifts in working lives. And they certainly evoke a world barely recognisable today: one where publishers read unsolicited manuscripts, contracts gave the right to publish 'throughout the British Empire and elsewhere', and reps swapped gossip in Kardomah cafés. A world of deference and snobbery, of loyalty often rewarded by lifetime employment, if not a pension. A world where books were published and sold according to the instincts of individuals, and where a publisher's name on the spine of a book – John Murray, Harrap, Dent, Gollancz or André Deutsch – or a bookseller's over the shop front – James Thin, Heffer's, Dillon's, Foyle's – would often be that of the person or family still running the firm. What I had not expected was how long that world had endured, or how profoundly it would alter as a result of the changes that have swept through the industry from the 1980s onwards.

Most long-established independent businesses have now been absorbed by international publishing conglomerates or high street chains. New technologies have revolutionised production, distribution and sales. Historically, publishers controlled the economics of the trade, but today the balance of power has swung dramatically in favour of major book retailers. The ending of the Net Book Agreement in 1995 gave all book outlets the freedom to compete on prices. Chains, online booksellers and supermarkets now use their buying power to drive hard bargains with publishers, while smaller businesses find it harder to survive.

The personal dynamics of the industry have shifted as well. The old publishing houses were run by men and serviced by badly-paid women; today, two of the three largest publishing groups are headed by women executives. Gone are the days when publishers, cushioned by private incomes and with no shareholders to satisfy, published work on the basis of literary merit without first considering the bottom line. Booksellers, who felt – often correctly – that publishers condescended to them socially as well as economically, can no longer be treated as the poor relations. And whereas the trade once relied on face-to-face dealings and on 'gentlemen' keeping their word, sales data can now be revealed at the click of a mouse and the figures speak for themselves.

I may not have grasped the extent of these changes to start with, but I soon realised that others understood them very well indeed. The founders and trustees of NLS, who include the historians Asa Briggs and Paul Thompson, saw the British book trade as a priority for oral history. From its place at the heart of our culture, this business is a mirror of the wider world. It is also surprisingly small, and has always been shaped by the attitudes and personalities of those working inside it. To document its history through the medium of life stories would not only highlight the part that people played, but also show connections between the book trade and its times.

When Martyn Goff, administrator of the Booker Prize, became chairman of NLS in 1993, the idea gained momentum. Then one day, a friend, Ian Norrie, London bookseller and author of *Mumby's Publishing and Bookselling in the Twentieth Century*, happened to ask Martyn if he knew of an institution that would back a project he had in mind himself: an oral history of the book trade. Martyn was quick to see the benefit of getting him on board.

Encouraged by Ian, and by Eric de Bellaigue, NLS treasurer and an expert on the financial history of the book business, Martyn devoted himself to fundraising. The breakthrough came during lunch with a publisher friend, Rayner Unwin. As soon as Rayner heard the proposal, he offered support from the charitable trust established by his father, Sir Stanley, who had founded the family firm of Allen & Unwin in 1914. The first tranche of money was offered up front. The rest, which was matching funding, attracted donations from others. So behind *Book Trade Lives* is a typical book trade story: friends, lunch, finance, and the drive to make something substantial out of a great idea.

Rob Perks, director of NLS at the British Library, welcomed the newly-formed advisory committee, which Martyn would chair with unflagging optimism for the next seven years: Ian and Rayner; Michael Turner, a former director of Methuen and translator of *Tintin*; and David Whitaker, of the Whitaker's publishing dynasty and a key player in the technological development of the trade. The committee named the project *Book Trade Lives* and advertised for an interviewer.

I only heard about this by chance when, at the end of a telephone conversation about an oral history project I was trying to set up in Dorset, I asked Rob Perks for news of NLS. He hadn't known of my earlier work in second-hand books and reference publishing. The thought of combining my interests in oral history and books was compelling – there was no question of not applying for the job. When I met the committee several months later, they greeted me with a long and daunting list of recommended interviewees, which would be thoroughly reviewed at every future meeting. They also provided an ongoing education in the history of the trade – mainstream publishing and bookselling being a different world from the sheltered waters I had occupied – and enough rope to follow my personal biases even when at the expense of their own.

Two years later, when Rayner died shortly after becoming ill, we lost a shrewd and inspiring presence. Nevertheless, his vision has been an important influence on the *Book Trade Lives* collection. He had insisted on a series of recordings with Scottish booksellers and publishers – a reminder that London has never been the only hub of the British book trade. He had been adamant that recordings should not just include the great and the good. And he had stressed the importance of representing booksellers to the same extent as publishers. Rayner's prescription for this oral history project was a sound one, and it was one with which the committee unanimously agreed.

The result is a collection of life-story recordings that includes experiences of bookselling in the 1920s (Tommy Joy in Oxford, Frank Stoakley in Cambridge), publishing in the 1930s (Sir John Brown at Oxford University Press, Charles Pick at Victor Gollancz), and of working at Simpkin Marshall wholesalers before and after the Second World War. It contains recollections about T. S. Eliot at Faber & Faber (Rosemary Goad, Anne Walmsley), of trade with Eastern Europe during the Cold War (Tony Pocock, John Prime), of Collins (Ian Chapman), Blackie and Nelson (Martha van der Lem Mearns), of Penguin (Charles Clark, Peter Mayer) and Longman (Lynette Owen, Tim Rix), of Thames & Hudson (Peggy Bowyer, Sue Thomson), McGraw-Hill and Butterworths (Gordon and Betty Graham), of Odhams and Book Club Associates (Stan Remington), of Paul Hamlyn Publishing and Octopus (Sue Thomson), Jonathan Cape (Philippa Harrison, Trevor Moore), Hodder &

Stoughton, Hutchinson (various), and Virago (Carmen Callil). The histories of long-established family firms are told by members of the current generation, including Douglas Grant (Oliver & Boyd), Christopher Foyle, Nicholas Heffer, John Murray, Ainslie Thin and David Whitaker; while independent bookselling is described from Belfast (Elizabeth McWatters) and the Bahamas (Karl Lawrence), to Birmingham (Ian Miller), Grasmere (Margaret and Dan Hughes) and King's Lynn (Maureen Condon).

The crucial history of the Net Book Agreement is recalled by Clive Bradley (Publishers Association), Gerry Davies (Booksellers Association), Philippa Harrison (latterly of Little, Brown), and Terry Maher (Pentos bookselling chain). Figures such as André Deutsch and Max Reinhardt of the Bodley Head look back on their early days in publishing, and are recalled in turn by colleagues – secretaries, editors and publishers' representatives – who describe their own experiences of the trade, including impressions of each other as well as the events they shared. The result is a complex and revealing network of inter-related perspectives.

In 2000 Jenny Simmons joined us from Sussex University to make recordings with specialists in book production and design. This series, which includes Iain Bain (Bodley Head), Matthew Bourne (Phaidon, Harper-Collins, National Trust), Ron Costley and Giles de la Mare (Faber & Faber), Elizabeth Dobson (Victor Gollancz), Ronald Eames (Allen & Unwin), David Gadsby (A. & C. Black), Werner Guttmann (Hammond & Hammond, Thames & Hudson) and William Procter (Sidgwick & Jackson), constitutes a valuable contribution to book trade history in itself.

The following year, Penny Mountain, former deputy editor of *The Bookseller*, brought her experience to the committee. She championed recordings with younger members of the business – a policy which paid dividends. Not only have many younger contributors experienced the upheavals of conglomeration, but their accounts confound assumptions that values in the book world have changed across the board. Neil Astley (Bloodaxe), Andrew Franklin (Profile), Emma Hargrave (Tindal Street Press), Jessica Kingsley (Jessica Kingsley Ltd), Sylvia May (HarperCollins), Lynette Owen (Longman) and Diane Spivey (Methuen and elsewhere), are among those whose interviews extend the collection from the First World War – when the oldest interviewee (Reggie Last) began his career at W. H. Smith in Woburn Sands – into the 21st century.

Given the shift from family firms to international conglomerates, it is fitting that the final committee member should have been David Young, who began his career at Thorsons, the company established by his grandfather, and was chief executive of Time Warner when he joined us. We were glad of the chance to make a recording with him – and, indeed, with everyone on the committee with the sad exception of Rayner, who had always insisted that others be given priority. His memoir, *George Allen & Unwin: The Remembrancer* (Merlin Unwin Books, 1999), suggests that his contribution would have been remarkable. If only we had known there was so little time.

Perhaps Rayner felt there was nothing to add to his book, although other recordings – such as Max Reinhardt's – show how the live, interactive quality of oral history can bring a fresh dimension to a well-worked autobiography. Or maybe, having written it down, he just didn't want to 'go through it all again', as another prospective interviewee explained in one of the few 'no thank you' responses we received. In agreeing to make a recording, interviewees were embarking on a process that demanded energy and reflection, where questions that were stimulating to one, might feel frustrating or too exacting to another. It could also be time consuming. Several people chose not to finish their interviews. We are grateful for their willingness to give it a go, and for their clarity in stopping.

The recordings that we made are in-depth life stories. They include recollections of early life and education, of family and friends, personal interests and views, as well as precise and vivid descriptions of work. This complex biographical approach produces evidence that is intimate in detail, but set firmly in the wider context of its time. In the long term this will help to guard against meanings being lost with changes in the local landscape. It will also give listeners a broad field of references in which to find meanings we cannot envisage today. The vitality of those meanings will come from the reflective quality of the testimony, as it does from personal diaries written centuries ago.

The recordings often end with a discussion about the interview process and the type of material that it produced. I have included a few representative comments in the final chapter. They touch on questions that oral historians have debated for years, including the nature of memory, the collaborative nature of interviews, and the way that accounts of events can vary in different contexts. *The Oral History Reader* (*See* Suggestions for further reading) is a comprehensive selection of writings exploring these and other issues. Alessandro Portelli's essay *What Makes Oral History Different?*, reprinted there, first appeared in 1979. His influential argument, that the subjective nature of oral evidence should be understood as its essential strength, has invigorated the practice of oral history ever since. Personal testimony can convey truths about attitudes, values, aspirations and regrets. It may not always report the 'facts', but it excels in conveying what the past has come to mean.

However, as Portelli points out, this does not preclude such testimony from being factually correct. Here, it was striking how many of the most obscure details in recordings turned out to be accurate. I have wondered if this was due to the capacity, innate or acquired, which once enabled booksellers to cite bibliographical details for thousands of individual titles without consulting catalogues. Recalling his early days at John Menzies in Glasgow, Willie Kay mentioned what must otherwise be a long-forgotten book, *Sajo and Her Beaver People*: 'published by Peter Davies . . . a bestseller that Christmas . . . that would be 1936.' When I checked them at the British Library, these details were spot on.

Given that oral testimony is notoriously unreliable as a source of names and dates, this illustrates a point I often heard about the prodigious memories of older booksellers compared with their present-day counterparts who use computers to check whether or not a particular title is in stock. The development and adoption of the numerical ISBN (international standard book numbering) system by the British book trade in the early 1970s changed the basis on which bibliographical data is stored and, incidentally, allowed the industry to pioneer electronic applications that would transform the retail sector as a whole. But Willie Kay also recalled how he had been trained, as an apprentice in the 1930s, to arrange stock on the shelves. 'Remember, boy,' he was told by Mr Campbell, the head buyer, 'the alphabet is the best friend of the bookseller.' The link this suggests between the alphabet and memory is one reason for the title of the first chapter.

The original *Book Trade Lives* recordings are held at the British Library Sound Archive, where they are already consulted by biographers, book trade historians, students of publishing, researchers seeking the kind of contemporary historical details which the collection provides in abundance and, from time to time, by interviewees or their relatives. When depositing their recordings, contributors can close them to public access for a specified period. Some *Book Trade Lives* interviewees have decided to do so.

Recordings were transcribed when funds allowed. The benefits are obvious, despite the risk that transcripts may tempt researchers away from the primary source, which remains the spoken word. Written summaries are made of all recordings. These allow researchers to navigate the contents and make subject searches via the Sound Archive's online catalogue.

We enjoyed the freedom to record long interviews for *Book Trade Lives*. Their average length is fifteen hours, although some are shorter and others considerably longer. Many were made over months, and in some cases, several years; most in the homes of interviewees, others at the British Library or a combination of the two, and just a few were recorded in the interviewee's work place. Even by oral history standards, these recordings are long. To some extent this reflects my own desire for illustration, but it was also a response to two distinctive features of the book trade. The first is the frequency with which members moved between companies, and sometimes between bookselling and publishing. This meant that a single interview could cover an unusual amount of ground. Secondly, the book trade, which depends on speech to sell the written word, is full of gifted story tellers. Had the recordings been shorter we could have made a greater number, but this would have meant skimping on description in order to include essential facts, which is not the best use of oral history. From an archival perspective the choice can be a hard one – and, I have to confess, some recordings proved so engaging that it was hard to tear myself away.

A complete list of interviewees follows the acknowledgements below. There are notable absences, and the list of those we would have liked to ask, had circumstances allowed, is nearly as long again. The book trade is a broad church. How could a single project do justice to it all? *Book Trade Lives* focuses on mainstream publishing and bookselling, and on the everyday life of the business more than its literary side. I am pleased that NLS's current *Authors' Lives* project is helping to redress the balance.

As it stands, the *Book Trade Lives* collection holds around 1,600 hours of recorded oral history material. If the point of it all is the spoken word, why did we decide to turn some of it into a book? We wanted to let people know about the *Book Trade Lives* recordings. We had produced a CD of edited extracts in 2002, but the collection had grown considerably since then and the material seemed too good not to share. A book would offer the chance for it to reach a different, wider audience. And although this was essentially an oral history, given its subject, publication seemed a logical next step. It would complete the circle.

But working with the material presented particular challenges. How on earth do you represent 1,600 hours of speech in 300 pages? Choose one extract from each recording? Publish a limited number of edited life stories? Organise the material around specific themes? The first two arrangements could show the power of the first-person narratives and some outstanding moments in individual interviews. I wavered before deciding on the third. A thematic approach would enable the book to chart key developments in British publishing and bookselling, such as the growth of paperback publishing and the end of the Net Book Agreement. It could also offer snapshots of various subjects that had emerged from the recordings: publishers' representatives, British books abroad, women booksellers, and the way in which the social life of the trade underpinned the business. Above all, it would be a chance to show something of what oral testimony might bring to the written history of the book trade.

The life stories themselves are so multi-faceted that working with them felt like handling a kaleidoscope. This is how the pieces came together for me this time; each person who takes up the originals will discover different patterns. The material here consists of snippets, or longer passages composed of many snippets taken from different points in individual interviews and woven together. This process sometimes felt like severing life-connecting threads, so the fact that the original recordings remain intact at the British Library is reassuring. There has been no final cutting room floor. Others will be able to appreciate, and grapple with, the intricacies of the primary sources.

In representing this material, I have worried about losing the integrity of the life stories, about plundering them to furnish a narrative of my own, and about the risks of partial or mis-representation. I have used Chapter 4, which is about children's books, to include recollections about early lives because I wanted to give a sense of what these add to the interviews and they seemed to fit naturally here. The focus of each *Book Trade Lives* recording is the narrator's own trajectory, but the extracts published here might only describe a third party. A prime example is in Chapter 17, where Sue Thomson talks about Paul Hamlyn. If it gives the impression that the value of her recording rests in an association with this familiar name, it is misleading; the truth is that her own authority lends weight to what she says.

I promised the speakers that readers would be advised to treat these extracts as partial, subjective and fluid – views and opinions may have changed, or be inadequately represented – and to cross-check facts. In Chapter 19, Andrew Franklin recommends that researchers seek information to put the testimony in context from the trade press and books about the industry. The growth of the History of the Book as an independent academic field is producing an increasing number of rewarding and authoritative sources. Whether this history is recorded through the written or the spoken word, my hope is that an interest in one will lead to an appreciation of the other, and encourage the development of both.

Despite speakers' concerns, the *Book Trade Lives* recordings are remarkably corroborative of each other, and kinder to colleagues than some expect and others might deserve. This disarming bias – and anyone who doubts it is a bias should see Chapter 17 – is indicative of a business where word gets round and gossip is a powerful regulator. As Carole Blake explains in Chapter 18: 'There is very little breaking of faith in publishing, even these days. We all know that if we give our word on something and that turns out not to stick, then we will not only lose the trust of that particular person, but of others who will hear about it.' Word got round about these recordings as well, and the question I was asked most often was 'Who has closed theirs?' Secrets are an irresistible challenge to the book trade, and if the anticipation of gossip can act as a check on behaviour, it can also be a pleasure that helps to forge close bonds. This is reflected in the personal warmth that colours many *Book Trade Lives* recordings. 'What does it mean to have spent your life working with books?' I asked Willie Kay. 'It means,' he said, 'that I have been working with friends.'

When it came to themselves, interviewees spoke frankly: about their dreams, disappointments, beliefs, aspirations and values. These varied from person to person apart from the last. Trust, generosity and the ability to entertain were highly rated across the board – attributes which *Book Trade Lives* interviewees demonstrated in abundance, on and off the record, and especially in offering these personal accounts for others to make what they will of them in the future.

The way the extracts are juxtaposed might suggest that speakers are responding to each other. My excuse is that this reflects the sociability of the trade. Of course, the construction is entirely artificial; the recordings were made individually. The conversation, such as it is, happened in my head and on the page, as I arranged, cut and re-arranged the pieces. The one response which did occur is in Chapter 17 when Tim Rix follows Tony Pocock with: 'Tony slightly exaggerates the extent to which OUP was competing successfully with [Longman].' In the course of making Tim's recording, I had shown him that particular passage in Tony's transcript.

Also, as the collection grew, the interviews were increasingly influenced by my own recollections of previous ones. The process of arranging the material like this gave me a chance to explore correspondences, and revealed some I had not seen before, such as the two contrasting stories about Paul Hamlyn's coat at the end of Chapter 7. These are examples of the tale the book trade loves to tell of his 'rags to riches' success, but they say even more about the companies involved – W. H. Smith and John Menzies – and, maybe, something about differences between the book business in London and Glasgow. And I had no idea before starting on Chapter 17 how many different accounts there were of the book trade out-drinking all others. Stories are vehicles for meaning, and the ones that endure are often the most flexible. In the course of the recordings I was sometimes struck by parallels between publishing – editing in particular – and the production of oral history. The title of the final chapter: 'Are you working or are you just chatting?' refers to both.

The textures of speech – its hesitations and emphases, shifts in speed, pitch and tone – are impossible to translate onto the page. Written language needs a more formal structure. Working from verbatim transcriptions, I tried to edit the words in a way that conveyed a sense of the rhythm and style of the original. Where possible – as it was with seventy out of the eighty-three speakers in the book – I sent the results to the interviewees or surviving relatives for comments. Their amendments were mainly to spellings or facts, but sometimes they suggested changing the grammar, or occasionally a few words, to clarify meanings. I did this reluctantly at first, but as time went on I began to see the point. To remember the voices was not always a help. What makes sense to the ear may not be clear to the eye – irony, for example, or when verbatim transcription obscures the subject of a sentence. In those cases I re-wrote to make the meaning clear. Sometimes the written word is too bald. In one instance, the speaker and I agreed to replace a reference to 'that woman' with that woman's name; the effect was much closer to the original tone. When an adjective recurred too often, I tried to find an alternative – sometimes with help from the speaker, sometimes by searching for one they had used elsewhere. Occasionally I worked a name or a date into the text to avoid a footnote. Twice I added sentences substantially re-written by a speaker to ensure that the information was accurate, and once, a whole paragraph. Having done so, I felt I should agree to another interviewee's request to add a 'bloody' to some reported speech because, they argued, it was what that particular person had actually said to them. It made a change from the request I was familiar with from previous oral history projects to 'take the swear words out.' This is the book trade – so I removed 'quite' and 'very' as often as I could, but kept more expressive intensifiers. Overall, I found it impossible to apply blanket editing rules. I tried to make the meaning plain – which entailed considerable pruning – and I wanted the text, when read aloud, to sound like the speaker. That was one reason for retaining some of the interviewer's questions: this testimony was not produced through spontaneous combustion.

Only in three instances did I remove substantial material from the draft: once at the request of an interviewee, once at the request of a relative of an interviewee who had died, and once on the advice of an interviewee's friend. The first meant re-working a whole chapter, which felt hard at the time but I think they were right and that the book is better for it. The second meant relinquishing a passage I was attached to, but maybe the speaker would have wanted it deleted, and whose material is this anyway? In the third, I was obliged to the friend for pointing out a potential libel that I had not spotted. Above all, I have been grateful for the licence I was given to edit these words. If the speakers had done it themselves, they would have done it differently. All mistakes and infelicities are down to me.

I have tried to check the spellings of as many names as possible and apologise for any that are wrong. Inconsistencies in names of companies, such as Longman or Longmans, Faber & Faber, Fabers or Faber, reflect variations in written as well as spoken usage, and to have standardised them would often have meant changing the subsequent grammar to match.

Just as the collection as a whole is not a gallery of leading lights, neither is this book a showcase for the 'best of *Book Trade Lives*'. The collection includes outstanding recordings whose qualities could not have been easily presented here, or which have been omitted for specific reasons. Martyn Goff's interview recorded by Cathy Courtney, for example, is closed while he is writing his autobiography, due soon from Simon & Schuster. Tanya Schmoller and John Rolfe provided such evocative accounts of their time at Penguin that if Jeremy Lewis had not recently published his excellent biography of Allen Lane, to which they each contributed, I would have tried to build a chapter round them. Douglas Grant's and Nicholas Heffer's meticulous oral histories of their family companies could equally have occupied a chapter each, and it felt frustrating to be cherry picking fragments of the latter to make general points in the bookselling chapter, however apposite. Robin Alston's interview is invaluable in showing what reprographic processes, and those of the Scholar Press in particular, can contribute to scholarship. Tony Schmitz's recording provides an important account of bookselling under apartheid in Rhodesia, which needs a more specific context to do it justice, and Peggy Bowyer's acutely observed account of the challenges faced by women in the industry during the 1960s and '70s will be invaluable to whoever writes the history of the Women in Publishing organisation – as they must – so long as they heed her equally open reflections on the interview process.

The most striking absence here is that of material from the recordings made by Jenny Simmons with experts in production and design. These interviews merit attention in their own right and I hope that at some point funds will be available to transcribe them. Unfortunately I am not familiar enough with them to be able to home in on relevant passages from memory, as I could with untranscribed recordings that I made myself. They remain an untapped resource that is ready, with the rest of the unpublished collection, to inspire one of the further works I hope that *Book Trade Lives* might help to generate.

Sue Bradley

ACKNOWLEDGEMENTS

The *Book Trade Lives* oral history collection now held at the British Library would not have been possible without the generosity of many individuals. First and foremost, I would like to thank everyone who gave their time to make recordings, with special thanks to: Robin Alston, Iain Bain, Matthew Bourne, Peggy Bowyer, Ron Costley, Elizabeth Dobson, Brian Duffield, Carol Easton, Joan Fall, Douglas Grant, Werner Guttmann, Dan Hughes, Rosemary Ind, Giles de la Mare, Ajay Parmar, Kate Pocock, John Rolfe, Tony Schmitz, Tanya Schmoller, Liz Thomson and Elizabeth Young – key among the many whose contributions are waiting for another book.

I am indebted to the members of the *Book Trade Lives* advisory committee – Martyn Goff, Penny Mountain, Ian Norrie, Michael Turner, Rayner Unwin, David Whitaker and David Young – who provided professional, financial and moral support beyond the call of duty. Martyn chaired the committee with consummate diplomacy from start to finish. Ian Norrie also made a number of valuable *Book Trade Lives* recordings, including those with Christina Foyle and Ronald Whiting which I have drawn on here.

I would like to thank Rob Perks, director of National Life Stories, for managing the project so patiently and constructively over the last ten years, and my other colleagues at National Life Stories for sharing their experience and inspirations, especially Mary Stewart, administrator; Susie Cole, Cathy Courtney, Alex King, Elspeth Millar, Bre Stitt and Melanie Unwin, all of whom gave me practical help as well. Special thanks are due to: Jenny Simmons, my fellow interviewer early in the project, who made recordings with experts in production and design, Charlotte Benson, who made the recording with Rosemary Ind, Susan Hutton for her impeccable transcriptions, and Margaret Lally for timely and efficient help with documentation.

The project has benefited from the support of all the trustees of National Life Stories, and especially from the knowledge, enthusiasm and commitment of Eric de Bellaigue, Penelope Lively and Jennifer Wingate.

As an independent charity within the British Library Sound Archive, National Life Stories relies on donations in order to carry out its work. The *Book Trade Lives* recording programme was funded by bodies that include the Esmé Fairbairn Charitable Trust, the Unwin Charitable Trust and the Max Reinhardt Charitable Trust, as well as by much appreciated gifts from individuals. This support was essential. The personal interest taken in the project by Rayner Unwin and his family, and by Joan Reinhardt and Belinda McGill, has also meant a lot.

The book itself owes its existence to the continuing support of the Unwin Charitable Trust, and I am grateful to its trustees, John Taylor, Ainslie Thin and Merlin Unwin. The help of the advisory committee and staff of National Life Stories has also been vital. I would particularly like to thank Rob Perks and David Whitaker for their invaluable comments on the typescript, and David Way of British Library Publishing for his faith in the enterprise. Above all, I am indebted to Penny Mountain, whose sustained practical help, advice and encouragement have been crucial to the book's production.

Many others have helped, of course. They include (in alphabetical order) Alison Bennett, Michael Bott of the publishing archive at Reading University, Clive Bradley, Marion Donne of the Publishers Association, Simon Eliot and Ian Willison of the School of Advanced Study at the University of London, Claire Fons, David Hicks of the Book Trade Benevolent Society, Anne Liddon of the Centre for Rural Economy at Newcastle University, Mary Morris of Duckworth, John Parke of the Booksellers Association, Martin Pick, Paul Richardson of Oxford Brookes University, Tim Rix, Polly Russell of the British Library, Bill Samuel of Foyle's, Lynda Smith, John Trevitt who did the index, and Neil Ward of the University of East Anglia. During the recordings I frequently heard people say that the book world is a friendly place. I have been lucky enough to discover for myself that this is true.

Ultimately, of course, the book has depended on the generosity of its contributors and their relatives. They have allowed me to select these extracts and to edit them in a manner that I justified as 'retaining the flavour of the spoken word', even when the results went against the grain of their professional sensibilities. They took pains to check details in response to my numerous and always urgent queries, and were tactful when pointing out my errors. I hope they will forgive me for those that remain, and for representing their speech in ways they would not have chosen for themselves. I am immensely grateful to them all for making my work on this book such a pleasure.

The *Book Trade Lives* collection currently holds recordings with: Robin Alston, Neil Astley, Gloria Bailey, Iain Bain, Mark Barty-King, Elsie Bertram, Carole Blake, Anthony Blond, Matthew Bourne (JS), Peggy Bowyer, Clive Bradley, John Brown, Brigitte Bunnell, Elizabeth Burchfield, Margaret Busby, Sue Butterworth, Carmen Callil, Marcus Campbell, Ivan Chambers (IN), Ian Chapman, Charles Clark, Robert Clow, Peter Cochrane, Maureen Condon, Ron Costley (JS), Laurence Cotterell, Gwenda David, Gerry Davies, Giles de la Mare (JS), Stephen Dearnley, André Deutsch, Elizabeth Dobson (JS), Brian Duffield, Ronald Eames (JS), Carol Easton, Julian Fall, Joan Fall, Klaus Flugge, Christina Foyle (IN), Christopher Foyle, Andrew Franklin, Louie Frost, David Gadsby (JS), Michael Geare, Rosemary Goad, Martyn Goff (IN, and elsewhere by CC), Gordon Graham, Betty Graham, Douglas Grant, Alain Gründ, Werner Guttmann (JS), Emma Hargrave, Philippa Harrison, Nicholas Heffer, Alan Hill (IN), Marni Hodgkin, Dan Hughes, Margaret Hughes, Robin Hyman, Rosemary Ind (CB), Tommy Joy, Willie Kay, Ian Kiek, Jessica Kingsley, Reggie Last, Marjorie Last, Karl Lawrence, Cherry Lewis, Terry Maher, Sylvia May, Peter Mayer, Belinda McGill, Elizabeth McWatters, Ian Miller, John Milne, Trevor Moore, Victor Morrison (JS), Penny Mountain, Diana Murray, John R. Murray, Ian Norrie, Eric Norris, Lynette Owen, Ajay Parmar, Charles Pick, Tony Pocock, Kate Pocock, John Prime, William Procter (JS), Max Reinhardt, Stan Remington, Tim Rix, John Rolfe, Ruth Rosenberg (CC), Keith Sambrook, Per Saugman, Tony Schmitz, Tanya Schmoller, Michael Seviour, Diane Spivey, Frank Stoakley, Bert Taylor, Judy Taylor, Ainslie Thin, Edward Thompson, Liz Thomson, Sue Thomson, Michael Turner, Carol Unwin, Martha van der Lem Mearns, Nigel Viney (JS), Anne Walmsley, David Whitaker, Ronald Whiting (IN), Efric Wotherspoon, David Young, Elizabeth Young.

The interviewers were Charlotte Benson (CB), Cathy Courtney (CC), Ian Norrie (IN) and Jenny Simmons (JS). All other recordings were made by Sue Bradley.

1 | THE ALPHABET

In 1907 three British companies merged to form the largest book wholesaler in the world. Simpkin, Marshall, Hamilton, Kent & Co. carried the stock of almost every British publisher and distributed it to booksellers throughout the British Isles and overseas. Millions of books were held in their vast warehouse at Ave Maria Lane in the City of London. But on the night of Sunday 29 December 1940 the premises were destroyed in the bombing which devastated the area round St Paul's – the heart of London's book trade since the 16th century.

Bert Taylor I went up on the Monday morning and all the Simpkin Marshall staff were standing in Ludgate Hill, surveying the ruins. We had heard there'd been a heavy raid, and set out not knowing what we would find. But what we saw was indescribable. I had never seen such desolation in my life. Paternoster Row, Ave Maria Lane and bordering onto Ludgate Hill, was a scene of smouldering ruins, and what had been Simpkin Marshall's was just a heap of smoking rubble.

Ian Kiek Three million books went up in smoke on one night. Three million. I remember cycling up to have a look at the devastation.

Karl Lawrence Simpkin Marshall was critical to the trade at that time because it carried huge stocks of books, some of them long out of print. The warehouses of many publishers were bombed that night: Hutchinson's, Hodder & Stoughton, Longmans, Collins . . . That raid almost destroyed the British publishing trade.[1]

Bert Taylor had started work at Simpkin Marshall in 1920 at the age of fifteen.

Bert Taylor My father had no connection with books whatsoever. He worked at Kilburn for a firm of engineers, repairing and caring for stationary steam engines. But strangely enough, after I had written to *The Daily Chronicle* in response to an advert, and received a postcard asking me to go for an interview at Simpkin Marshall along with several other letters about jobs vacant, my father chose that one. He said, 'I've heard of Simpkin Marshall – they're good people.' I knew nothing about them, so on his word I took it. I had the interview and got the job.

---

1 In *The Truth About a Publisher*, Allen & Unwin, 1960, Sir Stanley Unwin states that six million books were lost from Simpkin Marshall alone.

The firm was actually Simpkin, Marshall, Hamilton, Kent & Company, but it was known to the trade as Simpkin's. They were the greatest wholesalers of books in the world at that time. Not only did they cover the whole of the British Isles, but they also had a big export business that sent books to Africa and India and other places overseas. They ran a fleet of Model T Fords – 'Simpkin Marshall Wholesale Booksellers and Newsagents' – because they also had a flourishing periodical business at Orange Street in Leicester Square. But the periodical business closed a few years after I joined, and Simpkin's devoted themselves entirely to books.

At first I worked in the receiving department, where the books arrived – a rambling place under Stationers' Hall Court and Ave Maria Lane. There were at least six of us down there, and we were kept fully occupied most of the day. An awful lot of books came in, so I got to know the various publishers – Blackie's, Nelson, Macmillan, Collins, Sidgwick & Jackson, Gerald Duckworth, just to quote a few. Many of those names have now disappeared from booksellers' shelves, I'm sorry to say. But when I first entered the trade, publishing was a gentleman's business. A publisher published a book, not to make a lot of money out of it, but because he thought it ought to be published. That was the motive of quite a few publishers in those days.

How did you know that? It's something I learnt from elder folk in the book trade. And I could see that they were absolutely right, because certain books hadn't a snowball's chance in Hades of selling in big numbers.

Can you describe the inside of the building in detail? Not in detail. It was a rabbit warren. Under Stationers' Hall Court was what they called the 'crown-sewed pie',[2] where books were kept on shelves, and lookers-out doing booksellers' orders would go round looking for books and take them up to the despatch department. But I spent the whole of my day in the receiving department, unpacking books and distributing them to various parts of Simpkin's. You would burrow underground through alleyways of books, then go upstairs to the fiction department – the 'stock hall' as they called it – where there were lookers-out coming round with order sheets from booksellers all over the country.

Was it noisy? There'd be the chatter of folks, and people moving ladders – that sort of thing – but I wouldn't say it was noisy in any degree.

I also had a short period in the stockroom, which was full of ledgers. Every book that Simpkin Marshall stocked was listed in those ledgers alphabetically, and when a looker-out got an order for six copies, he would find the title in the ledger, and if it read 'thirty-six copies in stock' he would alter it to 'thirty'. That's how they knew how much stock they had. A system that on balance worked very well. When you think that Simpkin

---

2 'Crown-sewed': alluding to size and binding of book. 'Pie': 'a mass of type mingled indiscriminately' (*Shorter Oxford English Dictionary*).

Marshall received an order from every bookshop in the country almost every day, it was fantastic.

What made Simpkin Marshall so important? In one day a bookseller might get orders for twenty titles. Instead of writing out twenty orders to twenty different publishers, he put them all on one order to Simpkin's. Later, he got the whole bill on one invoice, supplied from one wholesaler. That's the beauty of wholesale bookselling – if you can get the terms[3] right. There were educational terms and medical terms, which varied. But for general fiction it was twenty-five per cent off, or sometimes a third – if you could offer a bookseller a third off, they thought it was marvellous. But prior to my joining Simpkin's, there had been a system called discount bookselling, which meant that booksellers could offer discounts and one bookseller was competing against another. Then the Net Book Agreement had come in,[4] and no book could be sold for less than its published price. That stopped this business of cutting prices, until three years ago[5] when the Net Book Agreement went up the spout. It was a great protection for booksellers, the Net Book Agreement.

Can you describe a typical day at Simpkin's? In the receiving department it was comparatively simple: we were there at eight o'clock and finished at five thirty, with three quarters of an hour for lunch. Opposite Simpkin Marshall in Ave Maria Lane there was a Joe Lyons tea shop, which was quite handy. But most people brought their lunch and stayed on the premises.

What did you do? I went out. I preferred to be out than in. When the end of a day came, we would all gather round the exit, waiting for St Paul's to chime the half hour, and when old Tom struck – woosh! – you were out. I had to go to Liverpool Street – we knew the shortest route, which took about ten minutes – to get a train back home to Walthamstow.

I hadn't been at Simpkin's a year when I was summoned up to the secretary's office. 'We've been looking at your records, Taylor,' he said. 'We are very pleased with what you've done. We have decided to increase your salary.' I had started on twelve shillings and sixpence per week. 'We are going to put it up to fifteen shillings.' So I was walking on air. Later, there was some difficulty over wages, so we all came out on strike for six weeks, in association with W.H. Smith & Son who were in the same union.[6] We decided to start the strike in mid-November, which was the busiest time of the year for Simpkin's, with the Christmas trade coming up. But we never got anywhere with it. We were still out in January, and in the end we had to go back with our tails between our legs, beg for our jobs back, and surrender our union cards. That was the end of Simpkin Marshall as a closed union

---

3 The amount a retailer pays to the supplier (publisher or wholesaler), generally calculated as a percentage of the book's cover price.

4 The Net Book Agreement came into force on 1 January 1900.

5 The Net Book Agreement ended in October 1995.

6 Probably National Union of Printing, Bookbinding and Paper Workers.

house. That would have been around 1928, because by then I had been promoted to the remainder[7] showroom in Ave Maria Lane.

My immediate boss there was Charles Robertson – a short, stocky Scotsman and a trained bookman. It was from him that I learned my love of antiquarian books. I became a collector myself, eventually.

Where had he trained? James Thin of Edinburgh, one of the great bookshops of Scotland. Mr Robertson bought all the remainders that Simpkin's sold and he was well known in the trade. He was a good bookman.

What's a good bookman? One who knows a lot about books, as simple as that. And he had a good knowledge of the publishing trade. He was shown these books and had to visualise their sales potential. Which he did do, very ably.

I worked in the remainder department until I was asked, would I like a job on the road, as a country rep[8] for the remainder department of Simpkin Marshall? Would I not! I jumped at the chance. Then I was on the road for Simpkin's until they were blitzed in 1940.

Ian Kiek first joined Simpkin Marshall in 1932, at the age of sixteen, for a period of eighteen months before entering his father's bookselling business. He returned to Simpkin Marshall several years later.

Ian Kiek When I first went to Simpkin Marshall, I walked in wearing a Harris tweed suit. Someone said, 'Gorblimey, here comes the Turkish carpet.' One thing I learnt at Simpkin's – it taught me a great deal, actually – was that most people didn't talk like me. The others came from Walthamstow and parts of London where I had never been. I was particularly fond of two: one was called Albert and the other was Ken. When I married Eveline, they both came over on Albert's motorbike and watched us coming out of church. That was in 1940. Albert was killed in Crete in 1943. That kind of news often made me ask myself, 'Ian, are you doing the right thing?' I had plenty of doubts about being a conscientious objector, but I stuck to my decision.

Why did you go to work at Simpkin's? My father said, 'Before you come and work for me in Sidney Kiek & Son,[9] I think it would be good for you to get as much knowledge as you can from Simpkin Marshall.'

What did he think you would learn? To give you one little example: you remember the *Everyman Library*? I got to know the titles and authors of each of the thousand volumes.[10] That's the sort of memory I have. And I remember so much about my days at that place. My very first day I was sent to the trade counter by a Mr Bissex, to meet a Mr Pooley, who was in charge

7 A remainder is a book which is offered to booksellers and the public at a reduced price because its sales are not economically viable otherwise.
8 Wholesaler's or publisher's travelling sales representative, also called 'traveller'.
9 Non-conformist bookseller and publisher in Paternoster Row.
10 The *Everyman Library* was founded by Joseph Dent in 1906. The original collection of fifty titles reached 1,000 in the late 1950s.

of all the orders coming in from London booksellers. He told a young man, whose name was Frank, to take me round. Frank was a looker-out, and for three weeks I went round with him, learning where all the books were.

It was a terrific place – 300 staff and millions of books – but the atmosphere there was deplorable. You weren't allowed to speak to each other. There was a man called Mr Mills, who would walk round making sure that you were looking out orders and not stopping to have a chat. I still shudder when I think about him. And at twenty past five, when you were allowed to go down and wash your hands, you knew not to be first in the queue – always be a dozen back – because the names were ticked off on sheets which were taken upstairs, and if your name was continually early, they would have you up and say, 'Your name, Kiek, has appeared here several times. Make sure that you arrive at a later time.' This happened to me. Also, by Wednesday I had run out of money. I found a little J.P. restaurant in Newgate Street, but I was too frightened to go in. Eventually a waitress, whose name was Ethel, said, 'Do you want something to eat, Sonny Jim? Come in.' So I went into this restaurant and had sausages and chips. As I left she said to me, 'Always come here. And don't worry when you run out of money – pay us on Monday when you come again.'

Some of the boys at Simpkin Marshall heard that W.H. Smith Wholesalers got paid considerably more than we did, so they started to get a trade union going. I put my name down, because even then my tendencies were that way inclined. Mr W.T. Smith, the company secretary, found out about this. Then the chairman, Mr Evelyn Pugh, came back from his holiday. He walked through the remainder department to his office, wearing a black homburg – I remember it clearly – and within an hour, thirty staff – those who had joined the trade union – were sacked. But he didn't hear about me. I didn't come from Ilford or Romford, and perhaps I had the slight accent of a minor public schoolboy, so they didn't imagine I would ever join the trade union. About a fortnight later Mr W.T. Smith called me up to his office and said, 'We're putting your wages up, Kiek, to twenty-seven shillings and sixpence.' I said, 'Thank you very much, Sir.' Twenty-seven and sixpence may not seem much to you, but it did enable me to have jam doughnuts during the morning.

Roughly when did they start the trade union? About 1938. The top wage you could get when you were twenty-one was three pounds five shillings a week, which is what I was getting when I married Eveline. But that was the way things were for so many people then. I met a young man at Simpkin's who said, 'I'm writing a book to get out of this place.' The book that he wrote was *No Orchids for Miss Blandish*. It was a fabulous seller.

What was he doing there? Nothing very much. He worked in the showroom, and he was busy writing *No Orchids for Miss Blandish*, which was regarded as a very daring book indeed. I saw him take his manuscript over to Jarrolds, the publishers.

What was his name? James Hadley Chase. He quickly wrote one bestseller after another and then went to live in Paris. But I always remember him saying to me, 'I'm writing this book to get out of this place.' Little did he know that he was writing one of the biggest paperback sellers of the war years. *No Orchids for Miss Blandish*, followed by *The Dead Stay Dumb*.

I eventually moved to the remainder department, which was lovely after working in the bigger part of Simpkin Marshall. There weren't more than twelve of us, and we were all good friends. The remainder department stocked books which weren't selling – people from the publishers would bring them to the boss, Mr Robertson: 'We've got 1,000 of this title left. Can you take them?'

It was Mr Robertson who got me back to Simpkin's after the collapse of Sidney Kiek & Son, when Father sold the business to Doran, Hart.[11] The first thing they did was to shoot my father out, and I remember seeing him in tears as he left the shop he had owned since 1910. It wasn't entirely his fault that the business went; this was happening everywhere. Now my father was out of a job, my brother Stuart was out of a job, and I was out of a job. I had a terrible feeling of depression. But someone at Simpkin Marshall must have heard, because Mr Robertson sent a message, 'Ian, there's a place for you, if you want to come back to us.' So I returned the following Monday. Mr Robertson was a Scot. He just looked at me from under his beetling eyebrows and said, 'Hello, Kiek. Nice to see you back.'

Can you describe him? He looked very fierce, but if there was a girl around, he'd have a cuddle if he could. There was a nice girl called Olive Bacon, who was a typist upstairs, and we knew that he'd no sooner put his bowler hat on the rack than he would go in and have a cuddle, so we would all creep up the stairs and have a look. Pathetic, really, but it's the sort of thing young boys do. Then he would come down to see that everything was going smoothly. Mr Robertson was the best paid man in Simpkin Marshall, earning more than all the directors except for the chairman. We respected him for his terrific knowledge. But we were amused.

I married Eveline on the 23rd of March 1940. Three months later Mr W.T. Smith called me up and said, 'Kiek, have you had your calling up papers?' I said, 'Mr Smith, I'm waiting for a tribunal.'[12] He said, 'Well, leave at once, then.' I was sacked. So I said goodbye to my friends at Simpkin's. It was an incredible place. But in its way it left a mark on me.

What kind of mark? To love the world of books. Despite everything, I still at the end of it loved books.

11 Manufacturing stationers, 10 Paternoster Row.
12 To assess his application to serve as a conscientious objector.

After the Blitz, a group of publishers set up a new company called Simpkin Marshall (1941), which was run from Book Centre on the North Circular Road before moving to premises on the junction of Rossmore Road and Park Road, London NW8. In 1951 the business was sold to Robert Maxwell (born Jan Hoch) who also pursued a career as scientific publisher, newspaper owner, Labour MP and fraudster. In 1952 Karl Lawrence joined Simpkin's as a graduate trainee.

Karl Lawrence When I was given the first order to pick, I was told, 'Go out into the Alphabet and find these books.' I just stared – 'What's the Alphabet?' – and they told me, 'It's the shelves.' It was a name that was juggled around all day long: 'Where's Joe?' 'He's out in the Alphabet.' You knew that he was looking for a book and supposedly working if he was in the Alphabet. It wasn't necessarily the case, because there were always lots of out-of-work actors and out-of-work other people there as temps, and they would go out and bury themselves in the Alphabet, reading a book. The corridors were very long and you could easily get lost in there, so there were always dead spots where no one would ever see them, in between the aisles. Certainly I spent a fair amount of time reading books in the Alphabet.

Simpkin Marshall stocked nearly 200,000 titles – a copy of almost every book each publisher had in print. Hundreds of orders would come in every morning, and almost all of them would be picked, packed and despatched the same day. London booksellers could telephone an order through and have it delivered by lunchtime, or they could collect it immediately from the trade counter.

When the orders arrived, someone would sort them, then give them to the lookers-out, and off we would go round the shelves, finding the books. You needed to know who the publisher was in order to find the book, so if the bookseller hadn't written it on the order, you would look it up in the catalogues. But some men, who had been working there for years, could glance down the order and scribble the publisher's name beside each title, straight off the top of their heads. They worked with absolute economy: they wouldn't move from the bench until they had written in the names of all the publishers, then they would walk round the Alphabet in the right order, picking out the books. There were a few trolleys, but mostly you carried the books yourself. You would stretch out your arm to make a sort of shelf, with the palm of your hand forming a bookend, and stack the books along your arm, spine out. All these tricks, they knew. I still carry books like that from time to time.

One of the wheezes that lookers-out had: if they wanted a particular book for themselves or to give to somebody, they would get it off the shelf and mess it up – make it dusty, bend a corner or tear the dust jacket – then take it up to the trade counter and the man there would reduce it. You could get a fifteen-shilling book for a shilling because it was unsaleable. They would then go back to the bench and clean it up – everybody had a hand brush for cleaning. If they had bent the corner of the cover, they would bash the corner of the book to straighten it out. They used blotting paper to get the dust off the jacket and the sides of the book – you just rubbed it with a lot of white blotting paper and that would pull out the dust and the marks. Or you could use bread – that was better, but it left a mess and you had to get back with a brush to clean the crumbs off. Or you would take the good jacket off another book and put it on the one you'd bought.

The men were all members of the union – Natsopa,[13] I think. One of the union perks was to go on a Saturday night to pack the Sunday newspapers. Almost all the union members at Simpkin Marshall had their share of Saturday nights. They would come away with as much money as they had earned for the week at Simpkin Marshall, and it was paid in cash. There was great camaraderie among the union men; they looked after each other because they knew that their strength was in unity. If somebody looked out the wrong book, they didn't have a row about it, and there was never any attempt to score over another person or another department – not that I ever observed, anyway. It was like a team, but the team didn't have the goal of winning, they had the goal of having a nice life. And they succeeded. They didn't have any targets and nobody worked their fingers to the bone. The tea break was sacrosanct. People used to read the paper, smoke – people smoked all day long – drink their tea, eat a sandwich . . . Well, there weren't sandwiches in those days, there were just hard rolls with chunks of cheese shoved in them – that's all that was available.

After I'd been there a few months we moved to the Old Brewery on Marylebone Road, which we did during the night. It wasn't all that far away, the place was shelved already, and we carried all the books in our arms, down the road to the new warehouse. An incredible logistics exercise, but it worked – Simpkin Marshall moved in a weekend. There was more space in the new place, and there was light and air. It also had a canteen, which was a plus.

I did see Robert Maxwell a number of times. He used to go around handing out £5 notes. What it was in aid of, I don't know. He also used to walk around with his bankers. It always looked so peculiar, these suited gentlemen walking around this warehouse where everybody was in their working clothes. Maxwell himself was a very big person, so he dominated the others in this little posse. Certainly all the staff outside the 'top floor' offices felt that he was up to something, but they didn't know what it was. And he wasn't there all that much, because even in those days he was flitting round the world.

I eventually went to work for Vince Andrews, who ran Simpkin Marshall's overseas agency. This operation charged overseas booksellers a commission to buy books on their behalf from British publishers. Simpkin's supplied books to Australia, New Zealand, India and South Africa – we used

13 National Society of Operative Printers and Assistants.

to sell unbelievable quantities into the overseas markets. A Union Castle passenger liner sailed from London to Durban every Thursday morning, and on Wednesday lunchtimes we would send out 400 bags weighing sixty-six pounds each, plus some bulky stuff in wooden crates on pallets. Simpkin's overseas agency was important to publishers because of the huge quantity of books that it bought. We could almost make or break a book. *The Cruel Sea*[14] was published just before I joined Simpkin's; I think we supplied 3,000 of that to Foyle's in Cape Town.

Vince Andrews was a Mason, which he was particularly proud of, and I think he had established connections through his Masonry. But he did have a real nose for books. He read very quickly, he read a lot, and he had a good commercial eye for a title. It was like being the buyer for Waterstone's: he could subscribe 75,000 of a big book. Several of the buyers at W.H. Smith had similar power, but they didn't buy the quantities that Andrews bought. Although I read modern fiction – particularly D.H. Lawrence, Graham Greene and Huxley – I had never read mass-market or popular fiction. Vince Andrews certainly introduced me to that. He gave me books to read for my opinion as soon as I joined his department. The first was *The Silver Chalice* by Thomas Costain, and he wanted me to read it that night. It was 370-odd pages, published by Hodder. I didn't really care for it but I could see that it obviously was going to be a seller. I read lots of books for him after that. Cape, who rarely published thrillers, picked up the first James Bond – *Casino Royale* – and they printed some proof copies. Vince Andrews gave it to me because he didn't care for thrillers, so I read the first Bond before it was published. As a result of my enthusiasm, Vince read it, and we eventually bought 3,000 – which was incredible for an unknown thriller writer – and sent them out to these overseas bookshops.

What did Vince Andrews look like? Small and dapper – he always wore a smartly-cut suit with a collar and tie – and silver-haired even when I first met him, when he must have been quite young. If he was telling you something, he would talk a lot with his hands, moving them around on the table, and he spoke very quickly. He had worked all through the war, and he told me that one of the reasons he hadn't gone into the army was because he was in a reserved occupation, which was the exporting of books. He also said that his Masonic connections had allowed him access to paper when it was very much rationed. Presumably he could then offer it to a publisher to get particular reprints done – and Simpkin's did some publishing themselves at that time. But Vince Andrews was certainly respected in the trade for his buying nous. When Simpkin's went bust, W.H. Smith head-hunted Andrews – they took him, together with the whole of Simpkin's overseas agency business, because they knew how valuable it was.

I owe him a lot. Vince Andrews was the first man that I worked for in

14 Nicholas Monsarrat, *The Cruel Sea*, Cassell & Co., 1951.

the book business: he got me to read commercially, he got me to understand the buying, and he let me go into the admin systems – which was the first time I sensed that I had a talent for systems – and if I went into his office for some reason, he would chat for ten minutes about what was happening in the book trade.

And I probably owe as much to Simpkin Marshall itself. It wedded me to the book trade for the rest of my life. Most important of all, it was Simpkin Marshall and its senior management who introduced me to Alex Lofthouse from the Bahamas, who asked me if I would like to go out and run his bookshops. Part of the price for effecting the introduction was that we would become a customer of Simpkin Marshall – though it afterwards took some argument to get them to supply books on the terms we had agreed.

A year or so later, Simpkin Marshall went bankrupt. I wasn't in this country then, so I only know the stories. I do know that it nearly bankrupted several publishers. André Deutsch told me that he went in the night before and rescued all his stock. Many others never got their stock back and were owed a lot of money by Simpkin Marshall.

At this time, Michael Seviour was working in the warehouse of Chatto & Windus.

Michael Seviour When it looked as though Simpkin's was in big trouble, Piers Raymond[15] got hold of Bill, who was our delivery man. Bill had a plain van. Piers told us to go up to Simpkin's and collect all the Chatto stock which they held. He gave us a paper signed by him, and we drove up, saw the man in charge and said, 'We've come to collect all the Chatto stock.' He said, 'I don't know anything about this' and went away, so we hung about for an hour or so. Eventually he came back and said, 'Yes, all right, you can have it.' So we collected all the stock in Simpkin Marshall that belonged to Chatto. There was a great sigh of relief when we returned with all the books – Mr Piers was very pleased. Other publishers didn't get their stock out in time.

Karl Lawrence The debacle cost the publishing industry dear. And it cost individuals dear, because many publishing companies were individually owned at that time. I know that there were huge stocks in Marylebone Road that had not been paid for because they were held on some sort of consignment arrangement without having been invoiced, so they had to be treated as an asset of Simpkin Marshall when the firm went into liquidation, and the publishers were left with no books and no money.

The common gossip was that a number of Simpkin Marshall's buyers had working arrangements with salesmen at various publishers to buy a large reserve stock, even though it wasn't really needed. I knew the Simpkin's buyer who covered Hamish Hamilton and Michael Joseph, and if you ever

15 A director of Chatto & Windus.

asked him why there were so many copies of their books in the bulk store, he would have a twinkle in his eye. Huge quantities of books were sold within the book trade at that time, and there's all sorts of scurrilous gossip about how much pay-off in one form or another went to various buyers. When I was bookselling, I was certainly given a lot of books as part and parcel of my relationship with reps. But I didn't get bottles of whisky. Or cash.

2 | GETTING FIXED UP

Sir John Brown was born in 1916. He was known to his friends in the trade as Bruno.

Bruno Brown I had a very sensible and agreeable schoolmaster at Lancing, where I was at school. He was the biology master, and because of my country upbringing I enjoyed natural history and, indeed, biology. When he asked, 'What are you going to do when you're grown up?' I said firmly, 'I want to become a publisher.' Which rather shook him. He said, 'If you want to be a publisher you must take a science degree because all your rivals will have been reading history and English and other such useless subjects. Much better to have a degree in science.' So I took his advice and it worked like a charm – I got my first job simply because they wanted an assistant with a science degree.

Why did they want a science degree? Because publishers publish all sorts of books, and they have no difficulty in getting hold of bright, sensible young men and women who can edit English. But if somebody produces a science book, it's not so easy to find someone on the staff who understands it.

Bruno Brown graduated from Oxford in 1937, after reading zoology at Hertford College.

The university appointments committee told me that I hadn't a hope because everyone wanted to go into publishing. But in due course I received a circular from the Oxford Press,[1] saying, 'There is a vacancy. If you are interested, we can provide you with more information.' I said that I was and applied. I remember thinking it was the ideal job. I wanted to get out of England, I wanted to travel and, with the war coming, I thought it would be a good thing to get fixed up.

André Deutsch was born in Hungary in 1917. He moved to England shortly before the Second World War.

André Deutsch My family said I must learn a trade. All kinds of silly suggestions came up. I worked for a famous lady society photographer, and the other thing I learnt was to recite poetry in Hungarian – what an idiotic way to hope to earn money in England. But I loved it. I did that for about eighteen months and performed in two clubs for literary gatherings. My

---

1 Elsewhere referred to as Oxford University Press, OUP, or 'the Press'.

father thought I was an idiot – not for performing, but for polishing my ability to recite. It wasn't a very bright idea to try to earn a living somewhere abroad by reciting Hungarian poetry.

Is that what you had planned to do? No, no. I was a realist, knowing that I wouldn't make money out of it.

What kind of poetry was it? All Hungarian. I'm re-reading one volume. Is there a thick book on that table behind you? Have a look. I didn't have the talent to write good poetry, but I was deeply in love with verse and poetry.

Who is it that you've been reading recently? József Attila. When I learnt reciting, I concentrated as much as I was allowed on two poets: Karinthy and József Attila.

The only time I really used my ability to read poetry was when I was interned on the Isle of Man, after Hungary came into the war. I disliked practically every fellow Hungarian in the camp – they talked about business and nothing else – but there was a man in charge of the Hungarian section called Orczy, and he and I talked about different things from most of the other internees. He was very kind, and suggested that I give a sort of literary séance, which was unbelievable, because I was so young and ignorant. Most of the people who were in the audience had never read a line of poetry but, if I remember correctly, I got some claps, and I enjoyed it, and I was mighty proud.

I'm glad I was interned, because through internment I got to the world of publishing. In the camp was a very unpleasant Hungarian who did all kinds of things – selling salami, making films. When, after about two months in the camp, I was told that I would be out in a week or so, he asked what I was going to do when I got back. I said, 'I don't know. I will try to join the RAF.' In fact, they didn't take me. But he said, 'I've got a publishing company. Will you help me?' I said, 'My dear man, I had read more books by the time I was fifteen than you have ever read in your life, but that doesn't qualify me to run a publishing house.' But he insisted and offered me £8 a week, which in those days was not bad.

André Deutsch later went to work for the publishers Nicholson & Watson, where the managing director was John Roberts.

After about two years – before the end of the war – I thought perhaps I did have some hidden ability – I wouldn't say talent – to go into publishing. But it was very difficult to get a job in those days, and lots of English people were anti-foreigners because of the war. I told my boss my plans, and he said, 'Yes, my lad, you are right. But don't leave us and go into an unknown world and starve. Work with us, work hard and, in the evening, muck about publishing.' I did that for about two years. By that time it was post-war, and I was a wreck.

Laurence Cotterell They sent my regiment to Palestine in '39 and we didn't come back for five years, by which time this country had changed irrevocably, and my mother was living in Fulham, in a nice flat near Bishop's Park. I'd had no chance of getting in touch with her; she didn't know whether I was alive or dead. I presented myself to her door, rang the bell, hero returning. Down she came, opened the door: 'Oh, hello, dear. Bring the milk up with you.' Then she said, 'There's a message from a man at Lloyds Bank in Regent Street, who would like you to give him a ring if and when you get back.' We had no telephone, so I went out and found one and rang this fellow. He said, 'Oh, Mr Cotterell, yes. A client of ours, a Mr Siegfried Sassoon, would like to see you if you are still alive.' I promised him that I was. 'Could we make an arrangement for you to see him? By coincidence he's in London for a week or two at the Albany.' So I went along full of awe and trepidation on the afternoon appointed, and Sassoon opened the door himself. I said, 'You wanted to see me.' 'Oh, yes,' he said, 'Laurence Cotterell. Good.'

Why were you there? Harrap had published an anthology called *Poems from Italy* – they were really Eighth Army poems – which became a bestseller during the war. I had four alleged poems in that. Walter Harrap – one of the great publishers – had asked Sassoon to write the foreword. Sassoon said to me, 'Young man' – I was then, too – 'I like what you've written for this collection. I wanted to use four lines of yours to round off my introduction. Have I your permission to do so?' I stammered something about being flattered. 'That's good,' he said, 'because the book's been out for six months.'

What were your impressions of him? He was kind enough – he had somebody bring in tea or coffee, which was hospitable – but I felt I was only a sounding board for him to show off a little bit. I presume he did this with everybody. Oh, truly he faced up to reality in the trenches, but I think everything else was something of a pose.

How was he showing off to you? He was being noble and telling me how much he admired my stuff. The inference was, 'Yes, my boy, you obviously studied mine and have learned from it.' Didn't actually say it, but this was behind it. I think he personalised everything. Nothing wrong about that, nothing aggressive. He was a man of immense talent and didn't mind showing his appreciation of himself. Which is a good, honest thing to do, I imagine.

Why do you think he wanted to see you in person? It was no inconvenience to him, and it was another audience. I don't mean that in an unkind way. I found him charming. Charming, humourless, and always – even if he didn't show it physically – a furrowed mental brow, as if he was still puzzling about his ultimate role and the shape it should take – the shape he should be, in other words. I should think a lot of people are like that, aren't they?

Why do you say he was humourless? Oh, he had no humour at all, none, no, no. I tried one or two cracks on him, and he looked at me and you could see him puzzling them out literally. Nothing is more damning to the jokester than to have his jokes taken literally.

Do you remember what jokes you tried to make? What were we talking about, he and I? Somewhere along the line I used that phrase, 'Without cavalry, war is a mere vulgar brawl.' Which was supposed to be funny. 'Oh, yes,' he said. 'But you must remember that Alexander relied on his infantry, you know. He didn't need cavalry.' I thought, Oh, Christ, here we go. 'And of course,' he said, 'Xenophon. No cavalry there, you know.' Then we got onto naval power and I remarked on the mythical encounter between an American sailor and a British sailor. The American, thinking of the Royal Navy: 'How's the world's second largest navy?' 'Fine,' says the British sailor. 'How's the world's second best?' Sassoon had to analyse that, too. He said, 'I wouldn't say necessarily that our navy was better.' From that moment on, I stopped trying to make crude jokes.

As I was leaving he said, 'Cotterell, they'll call you a war poet. I am probably the foremost war poet myself' – no modesty, this was quite prosaically said – 'but in fact, there's no such thing as a war poet *per se*. A poet is a poet is a poet. It doesn't matter whether you are born to conditions of opulence or poverty, the quality of the poetry will be the same. The content will be different – it will be coloured by your experiences and background, your upbringing and birth. But the quality will be consistent. And I hope you will remember that.' I thought, well, gawd bless you, Mr Sassoon. And off I went.

Peter Cochrane Having got through the Italian campaign and been sent to the army staff college in India, I thought, now I have a sporting chance of getting back to Louise[2] in one piece. I'm not going to go to the Bar after all, because there is nobody to keep me while I'm eating the dinners, but I have always wanted to be involved in books, preferably in publishing.

Louise had an uncle, Frank Morley, who had been a director of Fabers. He had left before the war and gone to New York, where he worked at Harcourt Brace. I wrote to him for advice, and he gave me a letter of introduction to Harold Raymond at Chatto & Windus. So, after being demobbed, I went to Chatto's and was interviewed by Harold Raymond, Ian Parsons and Norah Smallwood.[3] They asked what qualifications I had. Well, nil. But I was able to say that I had found myself a temporary job at Batsford's to try to pick up this mysterious thing called experience. I think this amused them. Also, I'd had a fairly eventful war. Harold Raymond had been an infantryman in the First World War, and I think that softened his heart. I had acquired a DSO and an MC, and they were interested that I hadn't stayed on in the army. A fortnight later I got a letter saying that the nice woman who had held the fort during the war as their publisher's reader had decided she'd had enough. Would I like to come and join

2 Louise Morley, who had married Peter in 1943.
3 Directors of Chatto & Windus.

them? So I did. It was the happiest decision I could have made, except financially. After commanding troops on active service, it was very nice to be in civvy life and chatting to the packers in the warehouse without having to order them to do things. And it was fun being exposed to the wit and wisdom of Harold, Ian and Norah. But the real fun was getting a good book and – with the author's approval and consent – trying to make it even better. This, I thought, was the really magical part. And it was a small trade then. Publishers knew booksellers; agents knew publishers. And because the firms themselves were small, you became involved in the whole gamut of publishing.

Stephen Dearnley I was first lieutenant on *HMS Una*, one of the U-class submarines, working out of the training flotilla, *HMS Cyclops*, at Rothesay. The captain of submarines there was Teddy Young – Edward Young – who had the distinction of being the first reserved naval officer to have command of an operational submarine in the war, in the Mallaca Straits. A heck of good bloke. Young, in pre-war days, was production manager for Allen Lane at Penguin, and he would tell how Lane had sent him up to Regent's Park to draw penguins so they could work out their logo. When Teddy got a bit pissed, and if there were girls on board, he'd draw penguins all round the wardroom walls. He really was a delightful man – one of those very enthusiastic people. The war was coming to an end, we were talking about publishing, and it was he who got me interested in the idea of going into books.

My father had a parish south of London, near Banstead. One of his parishioners was a man named Harry Praed who owned The Map House, which dealt in maps and travel books at the corner of St James's Street and St James's Place. I told Harry Praed I had an idea of going into books – who should I see? He thought a bit, then said, 'Hutchinsons are good, but Colonel Hutchinson's quite mad. I think Gollancz is too difficult. I'd say it's a toss up between Macmillan and Collins.'

Collins were then in St James's Place. The first bloke I saw there was Sydney Goldsack, the sales director. In the interview, he said, 'Tell me, were you a prefect at school?' I had to say, 'I'm sorry, I can't remember.' There was almost total non-communication. But fortunately he said, 'I think you'd better see Ian Collins.' So I was given a railway ticket to Glasgow.

Peter Cochrane In 1946 Chatto & Windus linked up with the Hogarth Press,[4] and for a number of years Leonard Woolf would come into the office probably twice a week. My job was to sift through and read the typescripts that came in. Those from established authors went straight to whoever

---

4 The Hogarth Press was founded by Leonard and Virginia Woolf in 1917.

looked after them, then I sorted through the others and, if there seemed to be real merit in any of them, lobbied the senior partners. I got talking to Leonard in this way. I remember him as a kindly man, but he wouldn't let pass lazy comments. 'Well, Peter,' he would say, 'what exactly do you mean by that?' He was a very encouraging person, I found. And he would always, always, read all the submissions to the Hogarth Press. He threw out the rubbish without further say so, but if there was something he thought was interesting, he would say, 'Have a look at this, then come and tell me what you think.'

Leonard Woolf was a very good publisher – he had a good eye for a good book. He was enough of a businessman to know that you had to keep solvent, but he was never on the look-out for blockbusters. Well, blockbusters hardly existed in those days. Paper was rationed, so you didn't want to squander your precious paper ration on something that was going to be either dismissed as a trivial book or, literally, not worth the paper it was printed on. Another reason was because you couldn't push too many boats into the water at once: you wanted to be able to give your reps a chance to really sell the books you were publishing in a season. Also, you had to balance the printing of new books against reprints of books that sold steadily, because you didn't want to let the backlist die. The new books were the marmalade, but the backlist was your future bread and butter. This is why it was so difficult for a new publisher who started from nothing and had to live on the new books. Rupert Hart-Davis, a brilliant publisher, always said he was ruined by the fact that his first book and, I think, his second were both runaway bestsellers. The problem was that the cost of reprinting had to be paid long before the revenue from the sales came in.

André Deutsch Do you know who General Wingate was, in the Second World War? A very distinguished British soldier. I called my first firm Allan Wingate – it sounded English, of course – and started. Struggle, no money, or not enough money. Friends. Including a lady called Diana Athill, who became a very fine writer, and was then working at the BBC. I thought she should join me, because I loved her – we were great pals – and we talked about literature. She said yes. She knew as much about publishing as I did, perhaps less. We got some people together and two rooms in Great Cumberland Place. I met some writers, and we pushed the boat out.

People said we would last three months. But I had enormous luck. I read a wonderful review of *The Naked and the Dead* – an American review, because it was published first in New York. Then Diana read it and we both decided we should try to get the British rights, which was utterly ridiculous because there were so many famous publishers in London at the time. But I wrote to a man called Graham Watson, who was a director of Curtis Brown, which was a well-established, large literary agency with partners in America, one of whom had sent them *The Naked and the Dead*. By this time the book had received enormous publicity in the American press. Graham wrote back a sweet letter, saying, 'I have a list as long as my arm of British publishers;' – Chatto & Windus, Cape, Secker & Warburg, anybody who meant anything in those days – 'it's not worth putting your name down, because it will go soon.' I said, 'Look, don't be silly, put me down. It'll cost you nothing.' And every one of those illustrious, well-established, literary publishers turned it down. They were afraid of the sex, which, if you have read the book, you will be aware of. One day Graham rang me and said, 'This is idiotic, but you are next in the list. I'll send it to you, but will you have money to go through with it?' I assured him that somehow I would. And that book was published by Wingate and was an enormous success.

Do you remember how much you paid for the rights? Nothing, because he couldn't sell it anywhere – I think it was £750 – but I was surprised he accepted my offer.

I then had the problem of getting the paper, because paper was rationed. Publishers like Chatto and Oxford University Press had an allocation based on what they had used in the past, but I didn't have such a document, because Allan Wingate had only published about fifteen books. But I cajoled and screamed, and somehow we managed to find enough paper for the first printing, which was 10,000 copies. Lots of people thought that I was out of my mind. 'Who knows Norman Mailer?' In the end it sold about 80,000 copies. I was very triumphant. And Norman became a great friend. I met him in New York and we published another six or seven books of his, then we fell out with each other. We are back in friendship.

How did you get the £750? I begged and borrowed – I didn't steal.

Can you say more about how you managed to get enough paper? There was a girl, whose name I don't remember now. We didn't have any special relation-ship, but she was funny and I liked her. English. Somewhere in her family there was somebody who had access to paper.

The problem was that we were soon facing a demand. The first printing vanished within two weeks, although the book was expensive – thirty bob – and we printed another 15,000. It was nerve-racking to get the paper. It wasn't very good paper, but it was paper – and it was a big, thick novel. Very early on – I'm switching back – *The Sunday Times* said on its front page: 'This is a novel that shouldn't be published: it will be bad for youth, and bad for young women.' Scotland Yard then appeared at my door – a very silly man, who came twice, fiddling with a copy of *The Naked and the Dead*, which I am sure he hadn't read. But we won the game, and Allan Wingate, a totally unknown firm, was suddenly established in the publishing world.

Tim Rix When I was fifteen the warden of Radley[5] said, 'Well, Rix, what do you think you want to do?', and it just came out: 'I want to be in publishing.'

---

5 The headmaster of Radley College (boys' public school), who at that time was J.C. Vaughan Wilkes.

I still can't explain it. There was no publishing in the family, and I hadn't really thought about it much. He said, 'Oh, you must go and see Norrington. I will arrange it.' A.L.P. Norrington was Secretary to the Delegates of Oxford University Press,[6] no less. So I bicycled from Radley – which is about three miles from Oxford – to Walton Street, and was received by Sir Arthur Norrington, later vice-chancellor of Oxford and God knows what. He sat me down and said, 'You want to know about publishing?' I said, 'Yes please, Sir.' So he told me. He explained what he'd done at OUP and the sort of things that went on in a publishing house, for about an hour. I could hardly have expected more. I then bicycled back to school, even more convinced that I wanted to be in publishing.

What was it that left you more convinced? What I had instinctively realised, I think, when I said I wanted to be in publishing, was that if you were lucky enough to be an editor you were dealing with authors and different subjects. I saw myself as a jack of all trades. I knew it was no good trying to be an academic – I just didn't have the patience to stick with one thing. Publishing would give me the chance to get mixed up in a whole lot of different things, and of course in those days it did have – and I suppose still has to some extent – a lot of glamour about it.

After national service in the navy, Tim Rix read English Literature at Clare College, Cambridge, then took up a post-graduate fellowship at Yale. In 1958 he returned to Britain and looked for a job in publishing.

I wrote to about thirty publishers and three replied. Then I contacted Leo Cooper[7] – whom I had been at school with – who was working at Longman. Leo said, 'Come and have lunch', so we met at The Coach and Horses just round the corner from Longman, which was then in Clifford Street.

Leo was working in the publicity department for a man called Laurence Cotterell and the first thing he did was to persuade him to see me. Laurence Cotterell was a PR man through and through – he had an extraordinary capacity to make his number with people and could pick up the phone to the editor of *The Times Educational Supplement* as easily as to the editor of *Time* magazine. He had two interests in life: one was poetry – he later became secretary to the Poetry Society – and the other was the history of pugilism. He wasn't tall, but he was broad shouldered, with a boxer's face. He was extremely nice to me. He said, 'What you are, is a Rolls Royce without a gear box' – which didn't comfort me much – 'so somehow we've got to find you a gear box.' Then he sent me off to have an interview with Noel Brack, the general manager.

Noel Brack belonged to the gentlemanly school of publishing and it was a very straightforward interview: where had I been at school? What had I

6 OUP is governed by a university committee whose members are known as 'delegates'.
7 Leo Cooper later became an independent publisher specialising in military history.

done at school? I had gone on to Cambridge – he'd been at Cambridge as well – and I'd been in the navy. He didn't ask if I had been an officer, it was just assumed. And he didn't ask silly questions like, did I love books? You could see him thinking, this man might be useful to us, how can I fit him in? He said, 'I think you might fit in with the overseas educational publishing.' Whose director was abroad, as he often was. 'I'll take you on as a proof reader until John Chapple comes back from Africa, because I expect he would like to interview you. Then we can see whether there is a place for you in the overseas educational side of the business.' And that is exactly what happened.

Longman was a fairly old-fashioned family firm. The directors – the family – were still called Mr Mark, Mr Willie and Mr Michael, and there was an assistant in the production department who, if he was telephoned by the managing director, would put on his jacket to continue the phone call – I actually saw him do it. People who had worked for Longman for thirty or forty years were commonplace, so the company had this terrifically strong ethos of solidity and continuity. It was very paternalistic, which had its upside: despite being deferential, Longman was an extremely friendly firm, and nobody had ever been sacked unless they'd had their hand in the till. They had kept everybody on through the Depression, when salaries were reduced – including the directors'. It simply wouldn't have occurred to anybody at Longman to make staff redundant. The company made demands on you, but they were demands of loyalty in return for support, continuity and security.

What did the loyalty entail? That you would put everything you could into it – you would do whatever was needed. In overseas educational publishing you had to travel a tremendous amount, but you never complained about having to be away from home. And trips were long in those days, because the costs of travel were high; those of us in overseas educational publishing would go off regularly for three or four weeks to Africa or Malaya or Hong Kong. It was tight-knit, too. People would have been horrified if you didn't have a very strong commitment to Longman, and to the idea of Longman as a publisher.

Elizabeth Burchfield arrived in England from New Zealand in the early 1950s. She began her publishing career as a secretary in the production department at Penguin Books, which was then based in Harmondsworth, Middlesex.

Elizabeth Burchfield After being at Penguin for three years, I felt it was time to move on. I wrote to various publishing houses, and one of them was OUP – although I really knew nothing about it – which called me for an interview. So I had an imaginary dental appointment and went up to London. I was interviewed by Raymond Goffin, who was Deputy Publisher, which meant second in command in the London office of OUP. This was in a most beautiful brick building called Amen House, at the back of Warwick

Square in the shadow of St Paul's. Raymond Goffin said he hadn't anything at the moment, but he would like to keep my name.

A couple of months later he wrote to say that the Publisher, Geoffrey Cumberlege, needed a secretary. So – another dental appointment – up I went to London to see Mr Goffin again, and very briefly met Mr Cumberlege, the Publisher himself. His room was dazzlingly beautiful. It had a plaster ceiling, with a plaster wreath of leaves and flowers. There was an open fire in winter, and above the fireplace was a plaster over-mantel in which Jock[8] Cumberlege, who collected early English watercolours, had hung one of his paintings from home.[9] He sat behind a handsome desk on which stood a pewter table lamp, and there was a big mahogany dining table where unsolicited manuscripts were laid out for him to glance at and decide whether they were worth taking advice on or whether they should be sent straight back.

Could you describe that first meeting? He was rather shy of me. He gave me the most cursory interview and conveyed the impression that if Ray Goffin thought I would do, then, 'OK. When can you start?' But I do remember trying to describe to him what it was like at Penguin's and saying, 'We publish thirty books a month, every month', and he said, 'We publish every Thursday.' Which was a bit of a slap in the face from him. And of course, at OUP we did have publication day every Thursday. But that first impression was of an eagle-faced, elderly man with beautiful hands, tall and thin, well dressed.

He was, I later discovered, a brilliant mimic with a tremendously amusing line in anecdotes. And he knew everybody – that was what amazed me at the time. It was characteristic of the senior people in OUP that if they needed an opinion from an expert, they knew an expert, and they knew them personally. Of course, Jock was a member of the Athenaeum, and I suppose a lot of these other people were also members, and he had known them from his Oxford days or from when he was in the army in the First World War. He had joined the Press in 1919 and been sent out to India, with no training of any kind, to take over from E.V. Rieu, who subsequently became general editor of the Penguin Classics. Geoffrey Cumberlege had an extraordinary range of friends and many of them were his authors. And they were either friends because they were authors, or authors because they were friends.

Elizabeth Burchfield joined OUP in 1954. Rosemary Goad and Anne Walmsley joined Faber & Faber in 1953 and 1955 respectively.

Rosemary Goad I worked for Ann Faber initially, but subsequently discovered that I had really been taken on because Fabers were about to appoint Charles Monteith as the new whiz editor. He was formidably clever

8 Geoffrey Cumberlege was known to friends as Jock.
9 A landscape by Richard Wilson (1713–82) [Elizabeth Burchfield].

– he had been a barrister and was a fellow of All Souls – and Geoffrey Faber had decided he could understudy T.S. Eliot[10] on the poetry list. Charles arrived shortly after me, and for a while I worked for him and Ann at the same time. Fabers, which was then in 24 Russell Square, was both formal and informal. Everybody was 'Mr' or 'Miss', and all the Misses had been hired as typists. But if you had a good boss, which I think we all did, they let you do a tremendous lot, so we were promoted fairly quickly. As I saw it, the firm was ruled by men but the women had quite an interesting time.

To begin with, I shared a room with Valerie Fletcher – who became Mrs Eliot – and two others. We used to tease Valerie rotten – it's shaming to think of it now – because she had come to Fabers because she had a passion for T.S. Eliot and his works. I always liked her. She was quite funny about the Eliot coterie; she definitely had a sense of humour. So did he, of course; he could be very dry. But if any of us swore, we used to get frightful stick. I don't think we did it much, but one of us – I can't remember who – was looking out of the window one day and said 'bugger', without realising that he had come into the room, and there was a great fuss – T.S. Eliot said we should never use that kind of language. We were all terrified, quaking in our shoes. But he could also be very funny. A newsheet used to arrive once a month – goodness knows where from – called *Bulgaria Today*. Eliot used to take it and annotate it very wittily, then push it back under Charles Monteith's door. We all used to enjoy reading those comments.

When would he come into the secretaries' room? If Miss Fletcher failed to respond to the buzzer, he would be along. He used to come in quite a lot. I was in awe of him when I first went there, and used to think, goodness, I hope he doesn't get in the lift. What am I going to say? I got over that. He was very friendly.

What kind of conversation would you have had with him in the lift? 'Nice day.' It was only a short ride.

Anne Walmsley I only remember Eliot from Fabers as a bowed figure in a dark coat and hat, coming in the front door. One used to make way for him. He would greet Swannie,[11] the lady in reception, then walk into the lift. I had arrived all starry-eyed about contemporary literature from reading English at Durham but, apart from Audrey Mayall, who had read English at Oxford, I think very few of my fellow secretaries were graduates. Somehow it got around the office that I was passionately interested in Eliot's poetry, and I remember being rather laughed at, and realising I must keep it quiet. But Valerie Fletcher, who was T.S. Eliot's secretary, did get to know about it, and she suggested we had lunch together at Carwardine's. I remember she had fish and chips – she was a Leeds lass – and that we talked about Eliot.

10 T.S. Eliot was a director of Faber & Faber.
11 Ethel Swan.

I don't remember what we said, but we talked. I liked her northern accent, I liked her down-to-earth manner – I liked her very much, actually. I think probably I had acquired a bit of a Durham accent, and I had to become the proper London Faber secretary.

What was that? It was rather 'jerseys and pearls' and one went home to the country for the weekend. They were called 'the Faber young ladies'. Audrey has a story about a tailor in Marchmont Street who said, 'I never understand where Sir Geoffrey[12] manages to find all these excellent young ladies to work for him.'

Elizabeth Burchfield Ann Lingard started as a secretary in OUP's children's books department. Apparently, when she told Mr Goffin that she really couldn't manage on her salary, so please could she have a little more money? he said, 'But surely, Miss Lingard, you have private means?' And this was not a joke. He took it for granted that any young woman of her kind in London would have a private income. We wore twin-sets – not jerseys – and a string of pearls. And your shoes had to be comfortable because you were always running for a bus.

Rosemary Goad There may have been the odd twin-set and pearls at Fabers, but not many. We wore blouses and skirts with cardigans or neat sweaters. Fabers was definitely wackier than OUP, which was considered upper-crustily intellectual and possibly a bit stuffy. Fabers would think of itself as left-wing – there were quite a lot of people there who weren't, but a lot were. If you had dressed too 'little Missy' you would have been teased. Clothes coupons had finished, but there still wasn't a terrific choice – you went to the office rather soberly dressed.

Anne Walmsley Fabers was starting to publish not just African but Caribbean works. I remember being on the top of a 73 bus at Knightsbridge and reading a proof copy of *Voices Under the Window* by John Hearne – a novel by a Jamaican, about a pre-independent Caribbean colony. It was published in 1955 and must have been one of the first things I read at Fabers. I went on to read other books by John Hearne, and became hooked on his descriptions of the landscape and society. Eventually I thought, spend the rest of my life walking the London pavements in black court shoes? There must be more to life than this.

In 1959 Anne Walmsley left Fabers to teach at Westwood High School on the north coast of Jamaica.

In February 1961 I read in the *Jamaica Gleaner* that Mr T.S. Eliot and his wife were coming on holiday to Plantation Inn on the north coast. When the

12 Sir Geoffrey Faber.

senior English mistress knew, she said, 'Wouldn't it be wonderful if he could come and talk to the girls?' She had heard that I used to work at Fabers and that I knew the Eliots. Then I had a telegram from Valerie: would I have lunch with them at their hotel? That was extraordinarily generous – I was a junior colleague who had gone to teach in Jamaica, they were on holiday, and they invited me to lunch. So down I drove. I walked through the hotel and onto the beach, where Valerie greeted me, and there was this man in a panama hat, waving at me from the sea.

The contrast with that sombre figure at Fabers, in his grey homburg and overcoat, could not have been more marked. Out he came and dried himself, then we had drinks and lunch. I tentatively said, as directed by the senior English mistress, that we realised they were on holiday and that we shouldn't really ask, but it would be wonderful if he could possibly spare time to make a visit to the school. Valerie said, 'We are refusing all invitations. We have turned down the University of the West Indies and the PEN Club[13] of Jamaica.' I said, 'Of course. I realise I shouldn't have mentioned it.' And Mr Eliot said, 'No, don't apologise. If we decide to come, it will be entirely our concern.' And we left it at that.

A couple of days later I was teaching Form Two when I received another telegram. It was dated 28th February 1961 and came from Ocho Rios, near their hotel. 'From Eliots to Miss Anne Walmsley at Westwood High School. Would it suit Miss Parsons[14] and you if we come for half an hour at five thirty this Thursday informally no speech?' Of course we said yes. They had to hire a car, and it was a drive of about an hour and a half over extremely rough roads – in the early '60s the north coast of Jamaica hadn't been developed at all. The girls were all out on the driveway when the car arrived, and the teachers were up in the staff room – which had a balcony – on the first floor. Tea was served with Jamaican delicacies, and the staff were introduced to the Eliots. Then T.S. went into the library where the sixth-form girls were assembled, and read to them. He read *Song for Simeon*. The old man talking – the most appropriate poem to read. And he signed their copies of his poems, because the sixth-form girls were studying Eliot. Then off the Eliots went.

A few days later a letter to the headmistress arrived: '3rd March 1961: Dear Miss Parsons, I am writing to let you know how highly my wife and I appreciated the welcome you gave us . . .'

The other remarkable thing was that the Eliots took such an interest in what I was doing. As a result of reading magazines from Barbados and British Guiana – *Bim* and *Kyk-over-al* – I had planned to go there in the Easter holidays. When Eliot heard, he said, 'If you're going to British Guiana, you must look up my old friend Arthur Seymour.' So I was able to write to the

13 International Association of Poets, Playwrights, Editors, Essayists and Novelists.
14 Headmistress of Westwood High School.

editor of *Kyk-over-al* and say, 'Mr Eliot says I must get in touch with you.' Arthur Seymour became a leading poet of Guyana.[15] He told me that when he was in London he had looked up at 24 Russell Square and thought to himself, 'That's where T.S. Eliot works. He's a poet, I'm a poet. I shall call on him.' And he did. Eliot had remembered his visit, and told me to get in touch with his friend.

Rosemary Goad When I started to work for Charles Monteith, who was extremely lively in acquiring new work, sometimes I would go to see plays for the firm. The plays were where it was all exciting and new, because Fabers had started publishing play scripts, which they hadn't done before. And we had to move quickly in those days, because Methuen and several other publishers followed us, so there was keen competition for playwrights. *Who started the play scripts at Fabers?* Charles Monteith, quite definitely. And he began well, with *Look Back in Anger* and *Waiting for Godot.* Beckett used to come in to see Charles. He looked exactly like his photographs – very distinguished, very gaunt. I always longed to talk to him, but never got beyond offering him a catalogue or a cup of coffee. Everyone wanted to see Beckett. He didn't come in very often – John Calder published his poetry and prose works, we only published his plays – and a buzz would go round the building when he was there.

Another writer who had that effect was John Osborne, who was madly good looking when he was young. He used to arrive with Mary Ure, a very glamorous blonde who always wore a beret.

When did you first meet Ted Hughes? I don't remember the date; we would have to check the year of his first book.[16] But I do have a vivid memory of T.S. Eliot coming into the room I shared with Valerie Fletcher, as she was then, and saying, 'These poems have got to be typed *now*.' I can see Valerie and myself typing them at high speed – I can't remember why they had to be done in such a rush – and staying late and sorting them out on the floor. Then Ted Hughes and Sylvia Plath were suddenly both there. That was the first time I met them.

In those days nobody at Fabers knew that Sylvia was so talented – it's extraordinary when you look back. But they were a golden couple. Oh yes, they certainly impinged – at a very early stage. Ted Hughes was Eliot's great discovery. Eliot was very, very keen on him. But Seamus Heaney came through Charles Monteith, who was born and brought up in Northern Ireland. Charles used to go to Ireland to look for talent, so he may have heard about Seamus from one of his Irish friends and seen his work published in *The Listener.*

15 British Guiana became Guyana after independence in 1966.
16 *The Hawk in the Rain,* 1957.

Elizabeth McWatters began her bookselling career in Belfast in 1961.

Elizabeth McWatters I started bookselling in Gardner's in Botanic Avenue, just around the corner from Queen's University. That's where I got to know Seamus Heaney, before he had a poem published – he used to come in the mornings to buy a newspaper, usually *The Irish Times*. After a while he began to flick through the pages first: 'Ah no, it's not in. But I'll take it anyway.' I asked him, 'Did you write a letter?' I didn't know who he was – he was just a customer. He said, no, he had submitted a poem. Then suddenly one Thursday morning, his face lit up and he caught my eye: 'Look, there's my poem.' I said, 'Oh, congratulations. I'm delighted for you.'

He was very shy, and so was I, but as time went on we'd stop and chat. He started to be published in *The Listener*, then he told me that some of his poems had been accepted by Faber and the book was due out soon. Would I order some copies? Gardner's had only ever sold paperbacks, but I ordered some and it was great – I was selling his book away merrily. Seamus was new to this and would come in to see how many had sold.

A week after the book was published, he came in on the Saturday night – the shop was open late – and asked if we would change a cheque for him. He was out of cash and he was taking a young lady out. I said, 'No problem. Is it a personal cheque?' 'No, it's one made out to me from Faber & Faber.' I said, 'It must be all right, then' and changed it. This was his first cheque from them. It was for £25.

Has he changed? He hasn't changed at all, but I think his life now is totally different. If you want Seamus to sign books today, you have to bring him in after hours. Ten or fifteen years ago, there would be queues out into the street, but poetry readings today are almost out of the question. He still likes small, intimate readings. How do you pick a hundred people when you have three or four thousand wanting to come?

Did he ever do poetry readings in the shop? He did, yes – if it was a book launch, he would have read a few poems. But it didn't matter what Seamus read; if he read from the telephone directory people would listen to him. He was always very charming. That would embarrass him, wouldn't it, to hear me say that?

Belinda McGill *The Times* arrived on the breakfast table on New Year's Day 1964, and I saw an advertisement in the Personal column: 'Managing director of expanding publishing company requires personal assistant. Write Box number . . .' It didn't say which firm it was. I spent the rest of the day composing a letter and a CV, which I duly sent off.

I didn't hear anything for about ten days, then a letter came asking if I would go for an interview in four days' time. I hadn't actively wanted to go into publishing, but it certainly appealed as an idea. As I walked up Shaftesbury Avenue to Earlham Street, where the Bodley Head was in those days, I passed a hat shop. In the window there was a beautiful fur hat, rather like a Russian hat. It cost four guineas. I thought, if I get this job, I'm going to buy that hat. I went into the building and met Max.[17] It was an interesting interview: we talked mainly about Graham Greene and Ralph Richardson and Anthony Quayle,[18] because I had seen their names as directors on the bottom of the letter. After about twenty-five minutes, he said, 'Right, I've got other people to see, so that's it. I'm going to make a shortlist. I'll be in touch.' I got up and said goodbye and my heart was in my boots. I thought, I've blown it; I'm not going to get this. And I went home and waited.

Perhaps it was only a week later, but it seemed like months, another letter came from Max: would I go for a second interview? On the way up Shaftesbury Avenue I checked that the hat was still in the shop. This time he asked slightly more efficient questions. Then suddenly he threw his pen down on the desk. 'Do you want this job?' I said, 'I do.' 'Well, I'm bored with interviewing people. You've got it.' I literally danced down Shaftesbury Avenue into that hat shop. It was as much money as I had in the world, but I paid my four guineas and got on the train and went home. I then had six of the most wonderful years of my life. It is a parcel of my life that's very special – six years of loving to get up in the morning, and almost hating the weekends because I couldn't go to work. It was that much fun. It is carefully preserved in a special compartment in my memory. I take it out and look at it, then close it up and put it away again.

17 Max Reinhardt, managing director of the Bodley Head.
18 Graham Greene (writer); Ralph Richardson and Anthony Quayle (actors).

3 | THROUGHOUT THE BRITISH EMPIRE AND ELSEWHERE

Diane Spivey joined Hutchinson as an export sales assistant in 1977.

Diane Spivey The old contracts were bound in great folders. Some of them had been Sellotaped in and the Sellotape had become dry and golden-coloured, and the staples had gone rusty and there were stains. They were kept at Hutchinson's Fitzroy Street office, in what had been the coal hole, under the road. You had to go down into this dank cellar to look for them, and bring them up to check whether you could grant people the right to use material from the books. They were remarkable contracts, because the terms were completely different from the ones you get today: they tended to have no advances, and very high royalties of maybe twenty per cent. They were grandly typed and looked extremely official, unlike contracts now, which are all word-processed. And they included a clause that gave the publisher the right to publish the book 'throughout the British Empire and elsewhere'.

Bruno Brown The job I applied for was as number two in the Bombay office of Oxford University Press. Which sometimes meant being in charge, because the general manager, Roy Hawkins, also looked after the offices in Calcutta and Madras. My final interview was with Hawkins in OUP's London headquarters near St Paul's, when I also met Humphrey Milford, who was head of the Press at the time. I was ushered into his room, and there was Sir Humphrey, seated at a tiny table piled high with manuscripts. He asked me to sit down. 'So you want to go to India, do you?' 'Very much, if I get the job.' 'Remember,' he said, 'if you go to India you will never come back.' I later knew what he meant, because people did get quite nice jobs overseas and couldn't be accommodated on coming back to England. But I thought, well, I'll see about that.
What were your first impressions of him? Tall, distinguished, white-haired. And unexpected, as you can tell. He turned up years later, when I was back working in London and Geoffrey Cumberlege had succeeded him as Publisher. Cumberlege introduced us and Milford said, 'Ah, Brown. I took you on, didn't I?' 'Yes.' 'Well, that was a good day's work.'
When did you leave for India? October the 1st 1937. It was a bit difficult to get a passage, but I managed eventually, with the help of a friend of my father, who worked for the P & O.

Was that something you had to organise yourself? Yes, it was. One was plunged into doing things – it's one of the good things about the Press. In a firm like Longmans, I am quite sure that a new recruit was put through a rigid routine and not allowed to do anything on his own hook. I remember making enquiries about our rivals when I got out to India, one of which was Macmillan, and being told not to worry, as the manager there was disaffected because he had to get permission from head office before he coughed. Whereas the Oxford Press always followed a policy of extreme devolution.

What was the journey like? Great fun. Thanks to my father's friend I had a first class cabin on the top deck, which was absolute bliss. I was a bit alarmed by some of my fellow passengers, a number of whom were old and distinguished civil servants who didn't take kindly to young men. Their wives were rather fierce, too. But I met two soul mates. One was an Indian professor from Calcutta, who was very courteous and took me seriously when I started asking asinine questions. The other was a young man called Mallam. I think he had been to Oxford and, like me, was travelling out to his first job. He was a bit easier to talk to than most of them. He was going to Madras, so I never saw him again, and I got the surprise of my life when I read a novel by him in which he described the voyage and his fellow travellers.

Did it accord with your view of it? Yes, it did. Fortunately it was all right, but it's a bit of a shock to find somebody putting you into a book.

Who was the Indian professor? Mukerji. A very nice man. He was interested that I was going to out to join the Oxford Press. He himself was published by Longmans.

What were your first impressions when you disembarked? It was extremely hot and sticky – and dark, because the sun had gone down. Incredibly crowded and noisy. I was met by Hawkins, who said, 'You're going to stay with me for a fortnight until you can get yourself fixed up.' He was living with a friend in a very nice bungalow up in the Malabar Hills. Frightfully romantic – I was thoroughly taken with the whole thing.

How did you travel from the dock to his bungalow? By chauffeur-driven car. That rather impressed me. A big American car – a Nash, I think. The sad thing was that after the war came and India began to alter completely, his cars got smaller and smaller.

What was the last car you saw him with? A baby Fiat. But it was quite adequate. That must have been several years after the end of the war, when I was rather up and coming.

Bruno Brown's job in India included sales, commissioning and editorial work.

The OUP office in Bombay was on Ballard Estate, in a three-storey building owned by the P & O. From the outside it was rather impressive, with one of those porches that are big enough to shelter you from the monsoon rain. You went up a magnificent staircase to the first floor, where Hawkins had his office, and where there were smaller offices for people such as accountants. I quickly organised myself an office on the landing over the porch – all one had to do was to partition off the stairs. It wasn't a proper room, but it was airy and light and everything went on around me.

I seem to remember that the offices were arranged around the warehouse, so the centre of the building was occupied by books. It was very hot and stuffy in there – once a year we had to count the stock, which was difficult. The manager, Nirodi, was a marvellous chap who taught me a hell of a lot about publishing.

What was he like? Short, fat, a loud mouth. His method of organising his work and staff was to sit in the centre of his office and yell. There was one Parsee there, so Nirodi would frequently call for him.

I was fascinated by it all, and very ambitious, so I was ready to learn anything that anyone cared to tell me. And they were very agreeable; they *did* tell me. When I came back to England after the war, full of energy and a desire to get on, I had only to think back to what I had been taught in Bombay to decide that I hadn't got much more to learn. Whenever I couldn't understand something – which was basically, how many do I decide to print and reprint? – Nirodi explained it. It was really a matter of common sense: for a book that was already in print, you checked up on the sales for the last two or three years, and based the number on that. It's the same for any publisher; you keep an eye on stocks and the current rate of sale – straightforward mathematics.

How was your job presented to you when you arrived? It was all very routine: 'This is the time of year when your predecessor went to call on the universities in the Punjab; you should do the same.' And I was told to go away and read the files. Every book had its own file, and if you read that carefully, you could see whether the book was likely to sell well or had come to the end of its natural life. Also, copies of every letter were circulated to various members of staff, and dredged back a month later and re-read. They reminded you of things you hadn't done, such as writing to an author to see how they were getting on with writing their book. And the author, who hadn't forgotten at all, but was falling behind and feeling very guilty, was impressed by the fact that you were still chasing him.

We also had a number of travellers who went round calling on schools. The editors didn't take much notice of sales; once a book had been seen through the press, they forgot about it – although what you really depended on was how many copies you were selling after you had published it.

What was your job title? Assistant manager. Hawkins was in charge, theoretically, of everything in India. There was also an editorial manager, Miranda Heywood. She had been brought up in Birmingham and was ambitious to go into publishing, so she moved to London and got a job with Duckworth –

it was quite easy if you were a secretary. Then she thought she wanted to travel, so she wrote around to all the publishers who had offices in India. The Oxford Press was the only one that wrote back. They said, 'If you get out here, we'll give you a job.'

When I arrived, Miranda was chief editor, and a good one too. But she had met and fallen for a German, so her future became very dicey. She left fairly soon to go back to England where, having married this German, she became an enemy alien. She returned to the Far East, where her husband was a prisoner of war, I think. She never met up with him again, but they had one child, who had been born in 1938. So Miranda set about making her own living – and I'm still in touch with her.

When did you first meet her? On that first day. She was sitting in the small office next door to Hawkins. They were the only Europeans there out of perhaps fifty or more staff; the rest were Indians – that was another good thing about the Bombay office. Furthermore, most were from Madras. The Madrases spoke much better English, so we always recruited from Madras – except for that one Parsee, who was from Bombay.

Were there any women working there apart from Miranda? One or two. There was Mrs Dallah, who was a secretary. Subsequently, when Miranda decided that she would marry this chap, we looked for someone to replace her, and we pinched someone from the Longmans' staff next door. I had been told that there was a very good editor who wanted to work for the Press because we were known to give editors their head instead of telling them what to do. She had been a teacher, which was one of the ways to learn the business.

What was she called? Barbara Smith. She was Anglo-Indian. When India got its independence, a great many Anglo-Indians upped sticks and came back to England. She did – and she married, of course.

How did you persuade her to come and work for OUP? It wasn't difficult, because we do it better than Longmans, believe it or not. The Press has always been more humane than other publishers. We had a reputation for being good employers, and we were.

What distinguished OUP's attitude from Longmans'? It was a matter of temperament, I think. But the way that the average Indian was treated by the average European was distasteful. If an Indian clerk irritated his European boss he could expect to be shouted at. Hawkins amazed me – even he would shout at them. But it certainly wasn't his normal method.

Did they ever show any irritation back? No, they wouldn't dare. That was one of the things I didn't like. If you answered back to the boss, you'd be out of a job.

Can you remember any incidents where Indian staff were dismissed? We didn't dismiss the staff; we just didn't take them on if they weren't good enough. The Bombay office was under the direction of head office in London, where it was looked after by a chap called Ray Goffin – who did so on the basis of not interfering at all. He had been a university professor in Guwahati and was very knowledgeable about India, and very sympathetic too. There was a manager employed by Longmans who wanted to marry an Indian, so Longmans sacked him. Dear old Goffin snapped him up, because he was jolly good – and he remained so until he retired.

Who was that? A chap called Philip Chester.

Were there ever any conflicts between the Indian office and OUP in England? There was one famous occasion, soon after I turned up. We published a book called *Indian Administration* by Palundi, who was an example of the new kind of Indian academic specialising in Indian law and administration. It was a sensible book, but political dynamite. An old-fashioned civil servant type wrote a stinking review in the *TLS,* so some busybody in Oxford – a Delegate, probably – complained to Milford, and a letter arrived from Milford to Hawkins: 'What's this I hear about this subversive book?' Hawkins wrote back and said it was a very good book and Palundi was a distinguished man whom we were glad to have as an author. And Milford was perfectly satisfied.

The post between Bombay and London took at least a fortnight each way, so you could only count on an answer after four weeks. That was rather useful. I'd write and say, 'This is the situation. This is what I recommend.' Then I would go ahead and do it. I knew that nobody in London would take much notice. Towards the end of my time there, air mail came in. That was expensive, but we did use it for business purposes.

What kind of thing would you write about to OUP? Shipments, money, authors passing through. Or you would get a letter from London: 'Such and such an author will be calling on you.' The implication was, look after him well. So you would give them a good meal and tell them how their books were going.

Where would you take them? The Taj Mahal hotel. I went to the Taj quite often on my own hook; it had a nice bar in the basement where one could have a whisky after work.

What if the authors' books weren't doing very well? You tried to keep them off the subject. You were careful not to exaggerate either way. They would get their royalty statements in due course.

It was in India that I became interested in books for teaching English as a foreign language, which was something I specialised in for the rest of my professional life. There was no indigenous publishing, so most of the schools had depended on books published in England, which was pretty stupid because they were unsuitable. I discovered from one of our reps, Rishi – who was a very experienced schoolmaster and knew his stuff – that the schools in Kashmir were teaching English from a series of readers which centred on the sea. No school child in Kashmir had a clue what the sea was. So one went to a suitable teacher and said, 'Write a series of books using local circumstances as the background', and a fairly keen teacher called Kaul wrote a series of English readers which we called the Shalimar Readers. I don't think they lasted very long, but they certainly lasted well enough to make a good profit, both for the Press and for Mr Kaul.

Who chose the title? I think I probably did.

Do you remember why you chose it? Yes. Because I liked the sound of the word.

Why did you consider it important that the English language books were relevant to the locality? It was much the most efficient way of teaching the students to learn English, because then they were familiar with the situations they were reading about.

Was that OUP policy or something that you noticed yourself? That was my policy. I thought that it was inefficient and rather miserable for these children to be expected to learn English from supplementary readers that were totally foreign to them.

Where had the books with the unsuitable vocabulary come from? Various English publishers. Blackie's, many of them.

Martha van der Lem-Mearns I was promoted to being editor of Blackie's books for overseas, which essentially meant modifying books that had already been published for Britain. This was around 1960, and I do remember having to insist that some illustrations – snow scenes with robins, for instance – were taken out because they wouldn't mean anything to readers.

Bruno Brown We produced translations in Indian languages of our successful English books, and I always felt uncomfortable about it because it meant we were publishing books we couldn't read. I was convinced that we published far better books in English than either Macmillan or Longmans, but as we couldn't read our Indian language list, we couldn't decide whether those books were better or not. Our most successful Indian language publishing was carried out in the Madras office, where Philip Chester, who became the manager there, built up marvellous lists in Malayalam, Telugu and Tamil.

When I was in India, of course, the constitution was being changed and independence was around the corner. There was a good market for books by Indian authors, many of whom had been taught from English or American books and thought they were unsatisfactory – and they usually were – so set about writing their own.

Do you think that was a new demand? It wasn't a new demand; it was an old demand.

How do you know? From the schoolmasters one talked with, and also from one's own travellers – we had good ones calling on schools and colleges. And the file was full of letters from university teachers saying, 'Please can you let us have a history of India.' They went back quite a long way.

Why had there not previously been good books written by Indian authors about Indian history? Because the publishers hadn't tried to get hold of them. And English teachers – who prescribed the books – thought that Roberts on the history of India should be good enough. Unfortunately there were not many Indian historians, but they were coming along, and when you got a bright young don in the University of Calcutta writing a book on the history of India, there was a lot of competition for it. Macmillan and Longmans were also looking for Indian authors, so sometimes we'd be chasing the same one.

Gandhi was writing a book for us when he was put in jail. I sent the proofs to the prison governor with a covering note – 'Would you please hand this over to our author, M.K. Gandhi?' – and Gandhi returned them with various comments, which I duly incorporated in the text. They were mostly grammatical points – he could write well. From the sales point of view, it was a bit of a scoop to be publishing a book by Mahatma Gandhi. It was his autobiography, an elementary first shot, which was sold as an English reader to the schools.

Was there ever any difficulty in getting the proofs to him? There was certainly a delay. I think some wretched civil service type got hold of it and started to read it, thinking it was subversive. It would have been a shock when he found that it was the equivalent of an elementary reader.

What kind of financial arrangement would you have had? We would have paid him a standard royalty, which was ten per cent of the published price for every copy sold.

Would he have had a fee to start with? Oh no, he wouldn't have had an advance. It was a post-war phenomenon, this business of paying enormous advances which are never earned.

After three years in Bombay I was due to come back on leave, but France fell and India was cut off completely, so I joined the army out there. There was no call-up in India, but I felt I had to be involved. Looking back, it was a bloody stupid decision. If I had been married, I would have spent the war in Bombay, like Hawkins, earning a living. But in due course I resigned from the Press. Hawkins was very annoyed about that; he didn't believe in the war.

How did he react? He called me into his office and showed me a letter which he had written to Sir Humphrey Milford, reporting that I was leaving the Press and joining up. He got a stinking letter back from Milford saying that I was not to be sacked, but to be kept on the books and paid an honorarium. It was quite a small amount, but it was nevertheless something. This is what happened: you didn't sack the members of the staff who joined up, you just reduced their salary.

And what was Hawkins' reaction to the letter from Milford? I don't know. All he could do was to show me the letter and say, 'Right, off you go.' So I joined the local English battalion, and they put me into the officer stream. Two or three friends of mine were also in the Bombay Light Horse. We all went down to Belgaum and were trained to be soldiers.

Bruno Brown was commissioned into The Royal Artillery. He served with the 5th Field Regiment, which was captured by the Japanese at the fall of Singapore in 1942. After the war he returned to London, where he became OUP's sales manager and, in 1956, succeeded Geoffrey Cumberlege as Publisher.

After joining Longman in 1958, Tim Rix trained as a schools representative in the UK before working as an editor and sales executive for school textbooks for the Caribbean and English Language Teaching (ELT) textbooks for Latin America.

Tim Rix One day I was called in by John Chapple and my immediate boss, Adrian Higham, who had just come back from a trip to Malaya and was recommending that somebody should be sent out to look after Longman's publishing there, which until that point had all been done from London. They said, 'What we had in mind is that you would go for two and half years, come back for six months' leave, then go out for another two and half years.' It was real colonial stuff. We[1] flew out in March 1961, first class in a Comet from London. In those days Longman flew all their reps[2] first class.

The Longman office was in a modern building in Ampang Road, on the outskirts of Kuala Lumpur. My window looked across to Bukit Bintang – Bintang Hill – where there was a convent surrounded by tropical trees. If you were in on a Sunday – which I sometimes was – the air conditioning would be off so you would open the windows, and hear the monkeys chattering in the trees. Inside the office the sounds were muted, apart from the clatter of typewriters. On weekdays I would drive in – a pale-blue Morris Oxford had been exported with me – and start work by nine. The first task each morning would be the correspondence. Ninety per cent of the communication was by post, and when the books in English were sent to London for editing, as they were when I first arrived, there was an enormous amount going back and forth. I also spent a great deal of time travelling around Malaya, visiting authors – we had some Malay, and Chinese, authors by then – and calling on schools with our Chinese rep. There were still various rest houses dotted around from the colonial days, where you could have a shower, then dinner – Brown Windsor soup and shepherd's pie – and spend the night under a mosquito net.

Were any other British publishers there? OUP, Macmillan and Heinemann. Evans Brothers visited, but I don't think they had anybody in residence. Heinemann became represented by Leon Comber, who was briefly married to Han Suyin, who had written a novel called *A Many-Splendoured Thing*. He had previously been in the Malayan police where he became an expert in Chinese secret societies. OUP was represented by Ray Brammah. He had been in Malaysia for years before I arrived and was very pro-Malay – he spoke fluent Malay and lived in a Malay house. He became a great friend. We would sometimes meet up on our travels – I used to go to Brunei and

1 Tim Rix and his first wife.
2 Longman's representatives resident overseas.

Sarawak and what was then North Borneo, but became Sabah. The first time I was going, Ray told me everything I needed to know: who would be there, who the booksellers were, how to treat them, and where to go for dinner.

The great thing was to go by boat – unfortunately, I only did it twice. This was a medium-sized cargo ship, normally carrying about six passengers, which set off from Singapore and sailed round the islands: to Sarawak, Brunei and North Borneo, then to an island whose name I can't remember, to the west of Sarawak. To reach Kuching[3] the ship went down miles of river winding through the jungle. It moved very slowly, because the river was quite narrow and shallow, so the engine would just be a gentle throb and you could hear the cries from the jungle as you cruised along. I wish I could have gone by boat more often. Mostly I flew everywhere

What did you have in your luggage? Books, of course – in the same kind of suitcase I had as a rep, going round schools in Birmingham. The problem with books is the weight. That was another reason for taking the boat: flying was a problem if you wanted to take many books; the excess baggage could get completely out of hand.

There were a lot of mission schools in Sarawak, and I would hire a car and drive inland to visit them. We sold enough books there easily to pay for the visit and still be in profit. I can't remember exactly what the turnover in Malaysia and Singapore would have been then, but at present day prices, it was probably something like a couple of million pounds.

In Brunei there was virtually only one bookshop, so I attempted to sell textbooks there. Unfortunately, that bookseller tried to lead a revolution against the sultan, which was a big mistake. The British had Gurkhas there, who made short work of it. I think the sultan put him in gaol, which saved him from the Gurkhas. This would have been in about 1963. The bookseller had seen what had gone on in Malaysia[4] – although it had failed – and the communists were now fighting in Vietnam – where, indeed, they were going to win. There was revolution in the air.

Part of the reason I had been sent to Kuala Lumpur was to develop the business for Longman's English Language publications in South East Asia, so I also travelled to Thailand and South Vietnam. The first time I went to Saigon – which would have been 1961 – nobody bothered too much about driving out into the countryside to visit a restaurant, but eventually you were warned not to leave the city at all. The Vietnamese war was at its height and Saigon was full of American soldiers, but that didn't make a lot of difference to our business – the demand for English books was growing and there were good bookshops, which were partly a legacy of French colonialism. Many schools in Saigon were still teaching French as the first

3 Principal town of Sarawak.
4 The communist Liberation Army, which had waged a guerrilla war against the British in Malaya from 1948, was not officially defeated until 1960.

foreign language, but that was changing because of the American presence, and the waiters and hotel staff were all learning English.

How keen were the Americans to promote American ELT publications in Vietnam? There wasn't any American ELT publishing then, and there was no American equivalent of the British Council to spread the use of American English throughout the world. Their drive was all anti-communist. American imperialism has never had much to do with language in the way that British commerce has.

How was the role of language seen in those days by the British Council? The thinking behind the British Council was that if you spread the English language, you were not only giving British culture to the world but you were also creating a market. 'Trade follows the book' was Stanley Unwin's famous aphorism, and that was a British Council tenet as well. The more British books you could get into the foreign marketplace, the better you were doing for trade as a whole – and in order to get the books out, you had to get the English language used. In the 1950s, something like forty per cent of the British Council budget went on developing English language teaching; it had three full-time staff in the London office who did nothing but work with publishers, organising book exhibitions all round the world. And in several countries they not only had English language officers, but also book officers, whose job was to work with libraries and bookshops as well as institutions, to promote British books. But that has faded away over the last fifteen years.

Do you know why? Because of changes in publishing, I think. Instead of forty educational publishers, you might have six, who are probably part of conglomerates. Maybe the British Council thought, why should we spend money helping these corporations? Of course, the Council was moving over to information services. Also, one effect of conglomeration is that publishers have less interest in African markets. You can't make serious money in Africa by the standards of Pearson or Reed Elsevier or Thomson.

What are the implications of that? It means there is a book famine in Africa. It's not the publishers' fault: Africa has gone backwards economically in the last ten years, so they haven't got the currency, and they haven't got the money to buy books to any serious extent. That's why Book Aid International struggles so hard to supply books to developing counties, particularly in Africa.

What is Book Aid International? Book Aid International was started as the Ranfurly Library by the redoubtable Hermione, Countess of Ranfurly. She was the wife of the governor of the Bahamas, years ago.

At that time, Karl Lawrence was running the Island Bookshop in Nassau, Bahamas.

Karl Lawrence One day Lady Ranfurly met some children playing on the street who couldn't read or write, so she started the Ranfurly Library as a means of collecting books for schools. She must have announced this on a

Sunday, because one Monday morning the Island Bookshop was besieged by titled ladies coming in to buy books to give. I traded on it and said we would give fifteen per cent discount to anybody buying books to donate. We must have sold several thousand pounds worth to get her started.

Tim Rix When Lady Ranfurly returned to England, the then colonial secretary suggested she expand the project and send books to other colonies and ex-colonies which desperately needed them. So she did. And over the last twenty years it has become more and more professional.

And this is something you're involved with? I'm the chairman of it, yes. It can be tough going. All the right things are said about alleviation of poverty and millennium goals and all the rest of it, but it is surprisingly difficult to persuade people that if those goals are to be achieved, the availability of books and information and libraries is critical.

Karl Lawrence The Island Bookshop was very small when I got there in 1953, and I had been recruited to increase the turnover by a degree of magnitude. Very early on, we had a visit from Ken Jackson Marshall, the Collins representative in the Caribbean. News of my arrival had appeared in *The Bookseller*, and Collins had obviously told him, 'Go to the shop and find out what he's up to.' He took our first order for *Collins Classics*, *Collins Dictionaries* and *Collins Gems*, and we soon carried all the Agatha Christies in print. You couldn't have met a more 'Englishman abroad'. Ken Jackson Marshall referred to people as 'one of us', called me 'old boy' and for a long time addressed me as 'Lawrence'. It was a good five years before we got onto 'Ken and Karl' terms.

What did he mean by 'us'? 'We English.' He was a Scotsman, actually. He saw the British as the natural leaders of the world: they set the standards – standards of morals, standards of manners and standards of dress.

What part do you think that attitude played in the export of British books? A lot. The idea was that British was best, and that British books helped make it the best. A lot of effort was put into book exports, because the British government believed they opened up the markets for British goods: the book followed the flag, and trade followed the book.

Do you think that was true? Yes, I do. Modern novels referred to British products: if you read a British crime novel, it didn't talk about a Chevrolet, it talked about an Austin. That's a simplistic way of putting it, but that's what was thought.

What kind of clothes would Ken Jackson Marshall wear when he came to see you? A lightweight, tropical suit, or light jacket and dark trousers, with a panama hat and always a tie. People in Nassau would recognise him.

Tim Rix Longman did very big business in Egypt, and we sent the same person out to negotiate the order each year. He used to go to Cairo impeccably dressed in a suit and tie, with a bowler hat and a rolled umbrella. He was a man called Robert Coombs, whose father had also worked for Longman, years before, as a general manager. Having the same person go each time was valuable because it built up trust, especially as he was so incredibly English and upright and proper.

Karl Lawrence Ken Jackson Marshall came three times a year, and frequently stayed for ten days at the British Colonial – which was the best hotel in the Bahamas, as befitted the Collins rep – doing his paperwork from visits to other parts of the Caribbean. He carried his typewriter around with him – I think it was an Imperial – and typed up every order and all his own correspondence, which was voluminous because he sent reports back to London. My recollection is that it was Ken who organised the writing of *The Birds of the West Indies* by James Bond, which was where Ian Fleming got the name when he was writing the first of the Bond books.
How would Ken Jackson Marshall travel? I think he came by boat the first time – on the *Reina del Mar*, which would have called at Kingston and then come up to Nassau. The man from Oxford University Press came out on the Royal Mail steamer and used his cabin as a showroom; he had the books laid out on the table, propped up on the bunk and round the walls. He carried books from other publishers as well – I think he came out to see if there was any prospect of becoming a freelance sales rep in the Caribbean. That must have been 1956 or '57. The boat would have stopped in Hamilton, Bermuda for four days, before coming to the Bahamas. Then it would have called at Port au Prince, before going on to Kingston, Jamaica.

Anne Walmsley returned to London from Jamaica in 1963 and initially worked at the BBC.

Anne Walmsley I had a phone call out of the blue: 'Can you possibly come round to Longmans this evening after work?' So I went to the office in Grosvenor Street, where I was taken up to see Bill Kerr, one of the directors, and given a glass of sherry. He said, 'We want to appoint somebody to a new job, to be the publisher for the Caribbean, and we think you'd be suitable. Would you like to do it? You'd have to travel to the Caribbean twice a year and meet all sorts of people you don't know. Would you mind?' So I started in November 1966.

This was the first time that Longmans had appointed a publisher specifically for the Caribbean market, and my brief was to develop the list, which consisted primarily of school books. There was a great expansion in secondary education throughout the Caribbean at the time. In Jamaica there were new Junior Secondary schools, and a completely new curriculum had been devised for them. This was the new market that we were publishing for.

Gloria Bailey began her book trade career at the Publishers Association in 1983. She attended St George's Girls' School, Kingston, Jamaica from 1967 to 1972.

Gloria Bailey I have a feeling that a lot of the books we used at school were from the UK – which is strange, because Jamaica actually does a good deal of business with America. I know we used textbooks by Longmans, because I remember the logo – the little ship with a sail. When I came into publishing, it was something that clicked – that I had actually seen that logo before, as a schoolgirl.

Anne Walmsley In 1970 we set up Longman Caribbean in Jamaica and Longman Caribbean in Trinidad, and appointed local directors and managers. This was also the year when Guyana became a co-operative republic. In 1969 we had received a circular letter at Longman in Harlow – it had obviously gone to several publishers – from an aide to Forbes Burnham, the premier of Guyana, saying that they wanted to bring out a volume of his speeches to coincide with this. My boss, Roger Stacey, was very quick off the mark – he saw a great opportunity for getting our books in with the Guyana government – and accepted this offer. It didn't actually do us any good at all, because in no way was Burnham or his government going to be dictated to by a UK-based publishing firm. But in February 1970 we went to Guyana to launch his book – and to launch the Longman Caribbean companies.

That same February there was also a Caribbean Writers and Artists Convention at the invitation of Forbes Burnham, who hoped to encourage writers and artists to return and work in the Caribbean. The Convention had a particular mission, which was to plan the first Caribbean Festival of the Arts, to be held in Guyana in 1972. So this group of artists and writers was there, and I was there with the Longman team, which included not only Roger Stacey, but Mark and Lady Elizabeth Longman as well – about as colonial as it could look. Mark was the epitome of the aristocratic Englishman. He was a real Longman of Longmans: tall and lean and charming, but a little detached. Amongst the writers and artists there were many of my friends from the Caribbean Artists Movement, so I felt myself pulled in both directions.

I can't remember who the initiative came from – whether Mark Longman heard about the Convention and asked if he could talk to it about publishing possibilities, or whether he was invited to do so. But I was asked to speak to Edward Brathwaite[5] – as he was then – and ask him to come and advise Mark Longman what to say to this rather scary gathering. I distinctly remember Brathwaite coming to the Pegasus Hotel, where we were staying, and talking to Mark Longman, who was actually your good, liberal humanist, well-read, well-educated person. But there was a faction in

5 Poet, historian and co-founder of the Caribbean Artists Movement (later known as Kamau Brathwaite), who had returned to the West Indies in 1968 after studying in Britain.

the Convention which said no way did they want to be addressed by the old imperial publisher, so he never got to talk to them. And I could see their point.

Tim Rix Overseas educational publishing had been made easy by the existence of the colonies. Nevertheless, its entrepreneurial aspects were amazing, especially as British publishing was often thought to be a rather dozy industry. The begetter of Longman's overseas educational publishing was C.S.S. Higham, who travelled endlessly himself and brought up a generation of Longman people who expected to go all over the place. The last thing you did was to sit in an office in Kuala Lumpur or Nairobi. You got out and visited the schools and found out what the teachers liked or disliked, and what the syllabus makers were after. That's what real educational publishing is about.

Robin Hyman joined Evans Brothers in 1955.

Robin Hyman Evans Brothers was an old-established publishing house that had been created in 1906 by Robert, later Sir Robert, Evans. He brought in his brother Edward a year later. They started by publishing educational periodicals – *Teachers World*, *Child Education*, *Pictorial Education*, *Art and Craft*, *La France*, *Music Teacher* et cetera – and gradually added school books, children's books and trade books. In the 1950s we published a run of war books – *The Dam Busters*, *Cheshire VC*, *The Man Who Never Was*, *The White Rabbit* – which did incredibly well. *The Dam Busters* sold over a quarter of a million in our hardback edition. We then sold the paperback rights to Pan, and it was the first Pan book that ever sold over a million copies.

Evans Brothers was never a spectacular name, but it was more substantial than people imagined. When I left in 1977 the world staff was around 250, which in publishing terms is not small. I had been with the company for twenty-two years. During that time I had run the production department, then, as I became more senior – and particularly after becoming a director in 1964 and later managing director – my work widened into editing, selling and general management. It also involved extensive travel.

Evans Brothers was one of the first publishers to get heavily involved in publishing in Africa. Noel Evans had returned to the firm after serving in the navy during the war, and in 1947 he made a pioneering visit to Nigeria to see if it was a place where Evans could build their export business. Like most UK publishers, they first tried to sell exactly the same books they sold in Britain, then they began to adapt them for African countries. That evolved into publishing books specifically for Africa, but still written mainly by English authors. The next stage was the publication of books written by citizens of African countries for their own markets. Joop Berkhout, a dynamic Dutchman, became our manager in Nigeria in 1966 and played an important part in our development.

I was on a visit to Nigeria early in 1970, just as the Biafran war was ending, so Joop Berkhout and I decided that we would attempt to get into Biafra. We drove from our headquarters in Ibadan to Enugu, the capital of East Central State, to try to see whether the schools were still operating and whether anybody had any money to buy textbooks. There were armed guards everywhere and corpses by the roadside; there was no accommodation and we slept on the floor of a schoolroom in Enugu. At the time it didn't feel we were living in danger, but looking back . . . And if somebody at a roadblock pointed a rifle towards you, you did occasionally wonder.

And did they? Yes, of course they did. If you were as destitute as a lot of these people were and thought you could extract some money to buy a loaf of bread, you'd do it. I imagine everybody would.

So how did you manage when you had a gun pointed at you? Well, obviously we could demonstrate pretty quickly that we weren't militants, we were merely book publishers – a fairly harmless profession. If they searched, as they sometimes did, there were no guns to be found. What we had in the boot were books.

Who did you meet on that trip? The surviving booksellers and book buyers, and one or two educationists in the ministries. There had been a great deal of devastation. And those bookshops bore no relation to the western concept of bookshops; in many cases they were sheds in the market. We also tried to find out whether authors of ours had survived or not. We found one man who had been working as our representative there before the Biafran war, who had virtually gone into hiding. We knew what his address had been, so we went to a house outside Enugu where he might or might not have been, and he was there – he had actually got through the war, and was delighted to see old friends. That journey was an experience, because we were trying to see what we could do as publishers to help to get education going again immediately after the strife.

What could you do? Start supplying a few books and hope that one day you might be paid for them. That was always a problem, because we couldn't be a totally philanthropic institution. We had to survive ourselves.

How philanthropic were you in practice? I think we gave various books to the schools. We were hoping that they would soon start to operate virtually normally. And they did, far more quickly than anybody would have anticipated.

We appointed our first Nigerian managing director, Layi Bolodeoku, in 1977. Evans Brothers wanted to put the business into Nigerian hands in order to encourage local development, but it was also something that we were compelled to do following the Nigerian Enterprises Promotions Decree of 1972 by which companies had to be at least forty per cent owned by Nigerians by 1974. Another decree, in 1976, increased that to sixty per cent Nigerian ownership, to be implemented by 1978.

In the meantime, Evans Brothers were developing extremely fast in

Nigeria. The country had a lot of income at the time, particularly from oil, and in 1975 the government had introduced Universal Primary Education, which was a marvellous opportunity for publishers to produce books with potentially very large sales for the primary school syllabuses. But the competition was considerable. In England, a new textbook for primary schools would have faced competition from up to thirty other publishers – this was before numbers were severely reduced by acquisitions and mergers – but in Nigeria the competition tended to be mainly from Longman, Oxford University Press, Macmillan, and Heinemann Education, and – eventually – from local publishers. Even so, it was still pretty cut-throat.

How would schools have decided to use a book by Evans rather than one produced by Longman? The choice was often in the hands of a state purchasing authority which had the power to say, 'We will adopt this particular title for all the schools in this part of Nigeria.'

Tim Rix At one point Macmillan made an attempt to go into partnership with the government of Ghana to take over all textbook publishing. The attempt collapsed in the end, partly because it was so outrageous.

How did you know about it? Because we had an office in Ghana and we knew what was going on; we were trying to fight it off. There's a story which Mark Longman used to tell against himself, about going to see Harold Macmillan to protest at this. Macmillan sat, with hooded eyes, listening to Mark going on and on about what Macmillan were up to and how outrageous it was, and Mark finished by saying, 'I suppose you will be doing this in Sierra Leone next.' There was a pause, then Macmillan said, 'Sierra Leone? What do they call that now?' So many of the other countries had changed their names. Mark didn't know how to reply.

How much interest did Harold Macmillan take in the business in Africa? Quite a bit. He went on visits to Africa, and even when he was prime minister he would tend to have a word with the minister of education in favour of Macmillan.

Robin Hyman We went to Sierra Leone in 1973. Because we were major suppliers of textbooks to that country, we were received by the president himself, Siaka Stevens. Joop Berkhout and I, and our local representative, Victor Richards, had a long discussion with him about textbook supply and the Sierra Leone economy. For two days afterwards, this was the lead story in the newspapers and on the radio and television: 'Publisher's Delegation Sees President' or 'President Sees Evans'. To some extent news was controlled in these countries, so this was a permitted story, that the president had discussed textbook supply with visiting publishers.

I wonder about the combination of altruism and business in British publishing in countries such as Nigeria. That question is one that I and other people would have wrestled with: how can you reconcile the fact that you have to be a profit-making organisation with your wish to help educational development? My colleagues and I were genuinely concerned. We wanted to help educational standards to develop in the countries we operated in, by producing worthwhile books at prices that weren't extortionate. I hope one struck some sort of balance between the two issues. From time to time you can do a bit to alleviate specific problems by giving a collection of books to an individual school or to a charity. You can't really go much further than that in your capacity as an employee of a publishing firm. But if you choose to donate money from your own income to one of the charities that is helping in some way, that's different.

Presumably you could have been in trouble with your competitors if you had been giving books away. You had to be careful about how that would be interpreted. You can make donations to schools and organisations, and various campaigns and events, such as International World Book Day, encourage publishers to give books to particular causes. And indeed, going back to that conversation with Siaka Stevens, we had just given 10,000 copies of assorted books free to Sierra Leone schools, which was obviously appreciated. But you can't do a huge amount of that if you are going to remain in business. You have to make a profit, or your staff don't get paid.

By the end of the 1970s Evans Brothers had about a hundred staff in Nigeria, and a high percentage of the company's profits were coming from Africa. In the light of history, we probably over-expanded in Africa. I was involved in that, because I was a director from 1964 onwards, and managing director in my latter years. We all, corporately, had a responsibility for what went on.

Tim Rix The 1970s were disastrous years for the British economy as a whole: we had to cope with inflation, and with trades unions that were completely out of hand. But while many British publishers were struggling through the 1970s, Longman was very profitable indeed, because of the Nigerian oil boom.

One of my first jobs after becoming a joint managing director in 1972 was to go with Julian Rea[6] to deal with the transfer of forty per cent of the shares to local ownership. Other British companies – Guinness, for example – were going through the same thing, so we consulted each other about it. At the same time, the business of Longman Nigeria was expanding fast, along with frenetic growth in the Nigerian economy. There were enormous construction projects, and power cuts all the time because the electricity supply could not keep up. At one point there were 320 ships full of cement and other products outside Lagos harbour, which made it almost impossible to get our books in because there were no empty berths in the dock, so we

6 Divisional managing director of Longman's Africa division.

had landing craft – as used on the Normandy beaches – taking books onto the shore north-west of Ikeja.

But through all this Longman was getting paid, because the Nigerian government was taking huge royalties from oil exports and pouring money into education. The sales of textbooks boomed. Then the Nigerian economy crashed. In the last good year, there was an inward cash flow of ten million pounds from Nigeria to Longman in the UK, paid almost in advance of the due dates. But the following year – I think it was 1980 – the Nigerian government introduced currency restrictions and the flow of money into Longman Nigeria collapsed. Our turnover fell in one go to about five or six million pounds, which – because of the currency restrictions – we didn't get paid for at all.

The Nigerian crash was a serious watershed for us. It meant that we had to make twenty or thirty people redundant in the Africa division in Harlow. I don't think there had ever been any redundancies in Harlow before, and that made it doubly traumatic.

What was your role at Longman then? I was chief executive.

How did you decide that there were going to be redundancies? Just by looking at the figures. The Africa division employed sixty or seventy people and its revenues – from Nigeria alone – had gone from ten million to nothing, and we had a bad debt of about five or six million. There was no choice but to cut the costs significantly. Luckily we had an agreement with ASTMS,[7] which was the key union, on terms for redundancy – and they were generous, so that people who were made redundant would be well looked after, especially by the standards of the time. But it was unpleasant. Some of the people we were making redundant had been in Longman for years. Nothing like that had ever happened in Longman – neither had it happened much in British publishing. Redundancies became commonplace in the succeeding decade because of all the mergers and acquisitions. But in 1980 they weren't.

What happened to Longman Nigeria? Longman Nigeria had to cut back, but they still had their books, and to some extent they were still getting paid for them – they just couldn't pay us, because of currency restrictions. So Longman Nigeria kept going.

Robin Hyman left Evans Brothers in 1977 and formed his own company, Bell & Hyman, after buying the long-established firm of George Bell.

Robin Hyman When I left Evans Brothers in 1977, our profit that year was over two million pounds, virtually all of which had come from Africa, and mainly from Nigeria. But exchange controls meant that transmissions of cash from Nigeria soon became extremely difficult. The market for books was still there – and we had a Nigerian infrastructure of editors and sales

7 Association of Scientific, Technical and Managerial Staffs.

staff – so the company could still sell large numbers of books within the country. The problem was getting money out. That became an increasing worry for the London company.

Three years after I left, Evans Brothers was sold to Harold Lever, who was a Labour peer, an economist and extremely astute financially. Lord Lever sold the periodicals to the American educational firm, Scholastic, which left the problem of how to deal with its book publishing business. In 1982 I met him at a dinner of the Society of Bookmen, and the next morning – as soon as I had got into the office – he invited me to tea that afternoon. The object was partly to see whether I would buy the company, assuming I could raise the money. But Bell & Hyman was a very small firm, and it would have been impossible to start taking over debts of millions from Nigeria. How much is a debt of three million – or whatever the figure was – worth, if it's being sold? It might be worth a great deal or nothing at all. That wasn't something I could dabble in. But what I did say was, 'If we can separate Africa, I could be interested in buying the other side of the business.' So, in early 1983, Lord Lever sold the educational and general list of Evans Brothers to Bell & Hyman – which meant that I was reunited with many of the books I had been involved with in my early publishing days: *The Dam Busters*, *Cheshire VC*, *The Man Who Never Was*, *The Bull of Minos*, *The Book of a Thousand Poems* and my own *Dictionary of Famous Quotations*, as well as the *First Dictionary*,[8] which we re-designed as *The Bell & Hyman First Colour Dictionary*.

A Nigerian entrepreneur, Otunda Ojora, then bought Evans from Harold Lever, and his company is the owner to this day. Most of the African publishing is now done in Africa, although some educational and children's books are published from the London office. I'm shortening a very long story, but that is essentially what happened to the House of Evans.

8 *The Boys' and Girls' First Dictionary* by Robin Hyman and John Trevaskis was first published by Evans Brothers in 1967.

4 | MY SON WANTS TO BE A BOOKSELLER

Oxford and Cambridge

Nicholas Heffer The generations of Heffers and Blackwells came in between each other. Basil Blackwell was generally known in the trade as 'the Gaffer', but my grandfather, Ernest Heffer, had called him 'the Lad'. My father, Reuben, was older than Richard and Toby Blackwell, and I was younger than them, but older than Miles, Nigel and Philip. But we knew them all quite well, because they were Oxford and we were Cambridge.

Frank Stoakley left school in 1920 at the age of fifteen, and started work at the booksellers Deighton, Bell & Co. in Cambridge.

Frank Stoakley I had only been there a fortnight when Mr Prior called me into his office. 'I was talking to Mr Heffer yesterday,' he said. 'He is looking for two young boys, and proposes to interview candidates next Thursday. There would be more scope for you at Heffer's, because we largely represent Cambridge Press books.' So at Prior's suggestion I went. There were ten of us and eight of them were county schoolboys, so I thought we hadn't a ghost of a chance, the other fellow and I. This was 1920, and my last five years at school had been four years of the Great War and one year of the return to peace, but not the return of teachers, so we had a lean time of it from the learning point of view. Mr Heffer sat us down in his office. He set us sums, and we had to write an essay. Then he asked us a few geographical and general knowledge questions. At the end of the afternoon, he said, 'I'll write to your people and tell them the two who have been selected.' And that was me and a chap named Asher from the county school. We started on the 20th of June. Asher went into publications – Heffer's did publish a few books – and I went into the Oak Room. It adjoined the Lion Hotel's stables where farmers drove up and left their carts while they went in for meals or drinks.

Tommy Joy left school in 1918 at the age of fourteen and went to work in the Bodleian Library, Oxford. Three years later he moved into bookselling.

Tommy Joy There was an advertisement for an apprentice at Thornton's University Bookshop in Oxford. My mother, who was always the one that pushed me in those directions, made enquiries, and I started an indentured apprenticeship, binding me down for five years, to learn the secrets of book-selling. By this indenture I was paid ten shillings a week, with a two shillings rise each year, so I was twenty-one before I was earning eighteen shillings a week. It may sound to people of today like sweated labour, but I did not so regard it, and I don't so regard it now. I had a most wonderful grounding: I became proficient, not only in the Greek and Latin classics, but in almost every subject, including Oriental, Semitic and theology.

The conditions were Dickensian. There was one toilet for about fifteen people, and that was not very salubrious. There was a coke stove in the basement which provided our only washing facility – a bucket of water on that coke stove – for all that staff. But that's how conditions were in those days. I was happy enough, excepting my desk was under a glass roof, which was mighty cold in winter.

Frank Stoakley The Oak Room was a long room with a gallery and a glass roof over the top, so there was hot sun coming straight through onto oak wood and glass. In the middle of the room we had a big wooden case full of rare books. I had to dust the top and sides, and all the books – I used to do a section at a time. The manager of the Oak Room was from Blackwell's of Oxford, and he thought Cambridge was below them, particularly for literature – which in a way we may have been, because we are renowned for science. My little desk and stool were up on the gallery, and he had a lovely leather swivel chair underneath, with a large oak table beside him. He did a lot of betting, and I don't think he went home to dinner – he went to a pub down the road. In the afternoons he would fall asleep if it was warm in the room. He used to say, 'Warn me if you hear the old man[1] coming.' I had to drop a pile of books to make a noise – I used to drop them flat, not end-on. One day I overheard the old man say, 'That boy is a clumsy boy, he's always dropping books. He'll damage them. You must tell him off about it.' And the manager said, 'Yes, I know. I've told him until I'm sick of it, but he never ceases to do it.' I thought, you basket, you.

Within a few months a vacancy came up in the science department because the boy there was leaving. His father was a German called Roth-mann, who had come to England and worked as a journeyman[2] in my father's bindery.[3] He then went to Deighton Bell's foreign department, where he also got his son a job, so I took the place in the science depart-ment. The manager, Mr Anstee, was lame – he lived in the village of Trumpington, where he had been knocked over by a horse. He was a fatherly man, but he had only been to the village school. One day I said, 'There are books here on organic chemistry and inorganic chemistry. What's

1 Ernest Heffer.
2 A qualified worker, paid by the day.
3 Stoakley Bookbinders, Green Street, Cambridge.

the difference?' 'Don't ask me.' 'Well,' I said, 'haven't you got a science dictionary?' 'That's a good idea. See if you can find one.' So I did. The only one was a paperback published at sevenpence. Just the elements of science, but it told me what I wanted to know. I went back and told him. He said, 'Get them to buy one downstairs.' I said, 'Wouldn't it be better if we kept one up here?' 'Oh,' he said, 'better still.'

In those days undergraduates flogged us their school books to help them buy their university books, and we re-sold them thirteen as a dozen – we used to issue a cheap little catalogue and send it out to colleges in India and the colonies. Eventually I said, 'I want to know where those towns and universities are. Can't we get an atlas?' 'You're an enquiring young chap, aren't you? You're quite right, you're quite right.' That's how he was decent. Anstee wasn't stupid. He didn't down you because you wanted to know something; he wanted to help. 'Yes,' he said, 'order one. And while you're at it, get a little globe.'

Tommy Joy You had to buy your books when you came up to the university, and you sold them as soon as you had finished – so we were buying and selling the same books at Thornton's time after time. We also sold books by mail order all over the world. In those days, shops like Thornton's and Blackwell's did enormous business with libraries worldwide. *How did you think of the students in those days?* I regarded them as being very well-off gentlemen, whom you treated with a certain respect and awe. That was the attitude of most of us who lived or worked in Oxford, because all of us depended on the university and the university students for our living.

Nicholas Heffer In my father's and grandfather's day, if you were a student it was enough to give the name of your college when you applied for credit. At the end of every term, Heffer's sent a list to the college tutor of every student who owed more than £20, because, according to a statute of Cambridge University, students had to pay all tradesmen's bills in town before they were allowed to take their degrees.

Bruno Brown I finished Oxford owing quite a lot of money to Blackwell's. *Why?* Because I had been buying a lot of books and not paying for them. *How easy was it for you to get credit?* Frightfully easy. Blackwell's gave enormous credit to all the undergraduates. I think they eventually collected. But they did subsidise an awful lot of undergraduates until they were earning. *How long did it take you to pay them back?* I was rather helped by the war, because I was still trying to pay it back – and I did a certain amount of paying back – when I had to leave my job at the Oxford Press and join the army. When I did so, I wrote to Blackwell's and said, 'Owing to the current state, I'm afraid I won't be able to repay you until after the war.' It never occurred to me, of course, that I might not survive.

How did Blackwell's respond? Perfectly simply: 'My dear boy, pay when you can.' Great business.

Tommy Joy An uncle of mine was the chief accountant at Blackwell's, and I had asked him if he thought I could earn a living in the book trade. He suggested that Thornton's, being a smaller establishment, would be a better place for me than Blackwell's because I would learn the whole business. And that was absolutely true. I had the value of being in the atmosphere of a university bookshop, where, as well as the stock, one gradually learned bibliography. If there were a lot of customers to be served, the manager would say, 'Forward, Joy.' But that didn't happen much. I tended to be in the background, cataloguing and valuing and pricing. In all my years in retail distribution, I've done very little serving indeed.

In the early 1920s, when Tommy Joy was apprenticed to Thornton's, Reggie Last was working in the Oxford branch of W.H. Smith.

Reggie Last The university booksellers – Blackwell's and Thornton's – were in The Broad. W.H. Smith was in The Cornmarket, supplying books to the general public. Mr Asquith[4] used to come in regularly on Friday nights on the way to his country house at Sutton Courtenay. After a few weeks he asked my name, then he would look for me to serve him. I used to be waiting at seven o'clock, when his Rolls Royce drew up outside. 'Well, Last,' he would say, 'what have you got for me today?' I always found him a couple of good thrillers – Agatha Christie, Edgar Wallace or John Buchan.

Frank Stoakley After a time, I said to Anstee, 'Why don't we stock proper university books? We only have a handful.' 'I wouldn't know what to buy.' 'Neither would I,' I said, 'but I can find out.' 'How are you going to find out?' 'Ask the lecturers and professors.' 'You daren't talk to them, do you?' I said, 'They're not God yet, are they? When I was a chorister[5] I mixed with the undergrads and the dons and the fellows and the master. I know them all.' 'Well, if you dare, ask them.'

So I began to ask them: 'How many students have you got this term? What books are you recommending?' When the publishers' travellers came in, I ordered the books so they were ready. The lecturers were pleased, because the other shops in Cambridge would only buy books when the students ordered them, and half a term was gone before they arrived. We collared the university trade, and the business grew and grew.

Tommy Joy When an undergraduate came in to say he wanted to sell his books, we would say, 'Right, our representative will be with you at such and

4 Herbert Asquith, British prime minister (1908–16); leader of the Liberal Party (1923–26).
5 At Queen's College, Cambridge.

such a time.' I would go off on my bicycle and value the books, and probably pay for the books there and then. But I didn't take the books – I was followed by a porter who would collect them and bring them back. Then they would have to be properly valued. You wrote the cost price in code in the back of every book, and when you did the stocktaking you added up the letters to calculate the value of the stock. The word we used was Chrysolite: C is one, H is two, R is three and HO is two shillings and sixpence. I use the same code to the present day – I can add up in those letters as easily as in mathematical figures.

Frank Stoakley I bought Professor Rutherford's[6] library for Heffer's. Two or three of his books went to America, where they tried them on a Geiger counter and it jumped all over the place. The Americans phoned Rutherford's department and spoke to the librarian: 'Who bought Rutherford's library?' 'Mr Stoakley at Heffer's.' 'Is he still alive?' 'Why?' 'Whoever bought them ought to be dead. They're absolutely lousy with the radium.' So I went to see my doctor and told him what had happened. I said, 'I know George Crowe, Rutherford's assistant, because he goes fishing and shooting with my father, and he's lost two fingers from his right hand getting stuff ready for the professor to work on.'

I had handled those books for two weeks when I was valuing them, then when I got them to the shop it took me three days to price them up. The whole lot had gone in a fortnight – people came from all over the place for them, and they were scattered everywhere. The Americans were thunderstruck that I hadn't been affected. But I once produced warts all over my hands and couldn't make out why, except that I had bought a medical library from Egypt. The doctors said they had never seen warts like it – I had to go to hospital for treatment every other day for a month – and they considered I had caught them from these Egyptian books.

What happened to those books? They were sold. People were very keen on second-hand books that were either out of print or rare.

Tommy Joy In Oxford you couldn't move from one bookshop to work in another, because they all had an arrangement between them which stopped it. That was why, ultimately, I had to go to London. But after finishing my apprenticeship at Thornton's, I saw an advertisement for a job in the theological department at Heffer's, the university bookshop in Cambridge. I applied and got the job. I then received a letter from Heffer's, saying that I couldn't take it, because I still had an agreement with Thornton's. That wasn't true. Mr Thornton had said, 'I'd like you to work with us for another year or so.' And I had said, 'On the clear understanding that I have now

6 Ernest Rutherford (1871–1937), pioneer of sub-atomic physics who proposed (with Frederick Soddy) that radioactivity results from disintegration of atoms; director of the Cavendish Laboratory, Cambridge.

served my apprenticeship and will not be bound down.' But Mr Thornton wrote and told Heffer's that I couldn't take their job, that I was bound to him for another six months. He was a good man and I've got much to thank him for, but I'll never forget that. It was wrong.

What stopped you from writing to Heffer's and telling them it wasn't true? I did. And they wrote back and told me off. They wouldn't believe me. But it's curious to think what might have happened. I should have gone to Heffer's of Cambridge, and undoubtedly stayed there – good shop, good people. My whole life would have been different.

Frank Stoakley became the manager of Heffer's science department in 1945.

Frank Stoakley A man who had been a bookseller in Sweden came to Blackwell's of Oxford and was put in charge of their publications.[7] He once came to see Heffer – they knew each other well – and said, 'We want to talk to your man Stoakley and ask if he would come and join us. Have I your permission?' 'Well,' said Heffer, 'that's very tough. He's one of the last people we want to lose, but it's not our right to stop him improving himself. All right, you can do so.' So he came to see me. 'Mr Stoakley, we've heard in all circles how good your department is. In fact, we have a dozen ex-Cambridge lecturers who have come to Oxford as professors. Some of them are not even scientists, but they know of your department.' I said, 'Yes. And the four or five who *are* scientists get in a car and come back to me once a month to buy all their science books.' He said, 'I was afraid of that. I have been put in charge of science as a director at Blackwell's. Will you come and take the job?' I said, 'What's in it?' 'Well, what do you get here?' So I told him. 'I think we could double that, for a start. And if you can raise the turnover by ten per cent in your first year, you are a director.' I said, 'It isn't entirely up to me. I have my wife to consider, and my two boys are at school here.' I went home and put it to them, but my wife was so down about it that I didn't take the job. I have regretted it since, but I thought, well, family comes first.

Tommy Joy I could see that in Oxford there was no prospect of making the kind of advance that I wanted. That is why, in 1935, when a job in Harrods' library was advertised, I decided to have a go. I was lucky there. This was the day of the big circulating libraries, and Harrods' was one of the largest – *The Times'* and Harrods' libraries were rivals for the top class of subscription. People paid about £2 a year to be able to have any book they wanted immediately. We had thousands of subscribers, and my staff was well over a hundred. I was second in command of that until the war came.

---

7 Likely to have been Per Saugman, a Dane. He began his career at Munksgaard's bookshop in Copenhagen and became managing director and chairman of Blackwell Scientific Publications.

Glasgow and London

Willie Kay was born in 1918 at Port William, Wigtownshire.

Willie Kay My father was the senior tenant farmer on the Maxwell estate. One day he was an usher at one of the Maxwell family's weddings, where he met Mr Herbert Maxwell Graham, who was a director of John Menzies. 'What's your youngest boy doing?' he asked my father. 'I think he's maybe going to the university in Glasgow to study for the ministry.' 'Why not send him to our office in Glasgow, and if he's interested in books we can train him up?' The next morning, my father said to me, 'You're to go up to Glasgow a week on Monday to John Menzies, and they'll see if you might make a bookseller.' I said, 'Oh, I see. You'll be coming up with me?' 'Of course I'm not coming with you. You're going to look for a job.' So I had to go the 120 miles on my own.

I had never been in Glasgow in my life. I had been told to go to 90 West Nile Street and ask for Mr Leckie, the director. I walked up West Nile Street and saw numbers 87, 89, 91 and so on. There was a policeman standing at the crossroads. I said, 'Excuse me. I can't see number 90.' 'Young man,' he said, 'do you not know that in a big city like Glasgow, the even numbers are on the right from the general post office, and the odd ones are on the left?'

No 90 was Glasgow House, John Menzies Wholesale. It was a very big building, because it was the headquarters for Menzies in the west of Scotland, not only for books, but for stationery, newspapers and magazines. I went in. 'Reception. Please ring bell if required.' I rang the bell and a window went up: 'Who are you looking for, son?' 'I have an appointment with Mr Leckie.' 'Oh, with Mr Leckie? Take the lift one up. His secretary will be sitting in an office just where you come out – she will take you in to see him.'

So Mr Leckie interviewed me and said, 'We can offer you a job, yes. We expect you to be punctual in the morning – and if you're punctual in the morning, you can be punctual at leaving.' He told me to come the next week, and to ask for Mr Wood, who was the assistant director in Glasgow. Mr Wood was very strict. 'Boy,' he said to me, 'can you roll an umbrella?' 'No, Sir.' 'Well, I'll show you how. Mr Leckie and I go alternate weeks to a board meeting at the head office in Edinburgh, so you roll an umbrella for me and Mr Leckie, week about.' To this day I'm an expert at rolling umbrellas.

On my first day I was told to go out with the collecting boy to pick up odd copies of books from the various publishers. We each had a bag that you put over your shoulder like a mail bag. It got heavier and heavier as you went round, and you worked out the route so you picked up the heaviest last. The first call would be Oxford University Press, round the corner in West George Street. Cambridge University Press was also in West George Street, but on the other side, and away up the hill. McDougall – later known as Holmes McDougall – was in Buchanan Street. Blackie and Collins were in Cathedral Street, a fair walk from West Nile Street. There were never many books to get from Blackie – mostly children's books by authors like Percy Westerman and W.E. Johns. But there would be a big collection from Collins because they had so many departments – classics, fiction, children's, atlases, bibles and diaries – so that was the call you did last.

The boy I went out with that first day was named Brizzell. He eventually became a director of John Menzies. He was on the next rung up to me in the book department, and he taught me how to handle bibles: minion was the smallest type, pearl was next, then diamond – you had to know them all. If there was a Z in the stock number, that meant it was a bible with a soft leather cover and a zip fastener – ladies liked their bibles with a zip. All the stock was coded: N for hymns; NP for hymns and psalms together, and NPZ for hymns and psalms zipped together. When I moved to the showroom Brizzell taught me how to look out stock for customers. There was Stephen & Pollock of Ayr, James Simpson of Largs . . . Booksellers came from all over the west of Scotland and from Ireland. 'What's selling well in fiction?' they'd ask. 'Oh, really? Well, I'll take three of that.' The big Glasgow booksellers came, too. Mr Knox was head of John Smith's at that time. John Smith's is the oldest bookshop in Scotland, older than Thin's. A fine firm. I think it was founded in 1751.

Robert Clow began work at John Smith's in 1961.

Robert Clow Rumour has it that John Smith's started in 1743 but there is documentary evidence to prove that it started in 1751, when the third son of the Laird of Craigend set himself up as a bookseller in King Street, just off the Trongate. He was succeeded by his son, John Smith II, who seems to have modestly expanded the business. He was succeeded by his son, John Smith III, who was friendly with Dr Chalmers, a young divine from Fife who wanted to publish a volume of sermons. John Smith agreed to do this, and published Chalmers' *Discourses*, which sold for ten shillings and sixpence. Quite expensive for the time. But 10,000 copies were sold in Glasgow, so Chalmers wrote another book and asked Smith to publish it. This one was a flop. Chalmers accused Smith of not trying hard enough to sell his books and the two families fell out. Chalmers then published his next volume of sermons himself – he used a small stationer round the corner called William Collins to print it. And that was the first book that William Collins ever produced.

Before John Smith III died, he assumed two people into the company: one called Watson and one called Knox – that was Jack Knox's grandfather. Watson soon died, so Grandfather Knox ran the business, then assumed his son into partnership. The grandson, Jack Knox, was sent to London to train at Bumpus, but his father died suddenly, and Jack Knox was called back to take over John Smith's at the age of twenty-two.

Willie Kay A great bookseller, Mr Knox. He knew his business so well that he could more or less pick up a book and judge it: 'Yes, I'll have fifty of that.' He had that sort of decisive mind. At Christmas, Menzies Wholesale carried publishers' stock on sale or return,[8] and Mr Knox would send his buyer, Mr Alexander, round to pick books, but my boss always said, 'Don't send those books to Smith's. Mr Knox will be in later to go over the order.' Mr Knox nearly always went above his buyers and doubled the numbers. I remember him doing that with a book called *The Adventures of Sajo and Her Beaver People*,[9] published by Peter Davies. It turned out to be a bestseller that Christmas.

What year was that? That would be 1936, when I was in the showroom – I had joined Menzies two years before. Yes, John Knox was a fine bookseller – and a fine, God-fearing man, but not over-religious. Scrupulously fair and always polite to everybody. I remember him coming up one night: 'I hear you're going to work in Edinburgh, Willie. I wish you all the best. Remember, if I can ever help you at any time, get in touch with me.' What a nice man he was. And of course, it was he who trained Ross Higgins.[10] Ross was a great pal of mine when I was Menzies' head buyer in Edinburgh.

How did you first meet him? I'll tell you how I met him. It was a very foggy Christmas Eve in Glasgow and we were open till five o'clock. I was just an assistant in the book department, and I was on my own in the office on the ground floor. The phone rang about half past four when I was getting ready to lock up the building because I was the last person there. 'Good afternoon. This is Mr Higgins speaking. Have you by any chance got a copy of Penguin book number so-and-so?' I have a feeling it was number three, *Poet's Pub*.[11] I said, 'I think so. If you'll just allow me go up to the stockroom, I will confirm it.' I had to go up five flights of stairs – the lifts were off – then I came back and said, 'Yes, we have a copy.' 'I would like it delivered today. Can you do that?' So when five o'clock came, instead of going to get the train down to my sister's at Paisley, I walked up Sauchiehall Street and surprised him with a copy of *Poet's Pub*.

Robert Clow I had a vague idea that I wanted to do some form of executive work. I also had the notion, having spent a lot of my childhood in the Far East, of going abroad. South America sounded interesting and my aunt suggested I apply to J. & P. Coats, Cadbury's and Rowntree's. When I went up to Glasgow to be interviewed by J. & P. Coats, I stayed with a family called Knox – a brother and two sisters – who had been my guardians when I was young.[12] They had been friendly with my parents since their youth,

8 A term of trade permitting booksellers to return unsold stock to publishers.
9 Grey Owl, *The Adventures of Sajo and Her Beaver People*, Peter Davies, 1936.
10 Ross Higgins, later a director of John Smith's.
11 The first ten Penguins, including *Poet's Pub* by Eric Linklater, were published in 1935.
12 John (known as Jack), Elsie and Margaret Knox.

when they had lived in opposite tenements in Glasgow, and the families knew each other well. When I got home, having been interviewed by J. & P. Coats, Jack Knox sent me a letter saying, 'Rather than go into cotton, have you thought of going into books? It's much more interesting. I can't promise you anything, but I am looking for a successor in due course. I would undertake to train you and, if you're suitable, you might follow me.' And I thought, perhaps immaturely, 'Well, you might end up as your own boss in a bookshop – and in John Smith's in Glasgow'. So I decided to become a bookseller.

Michael Seviour When I left school I thought I'd like to work in publishing, so after my national service I had lunch with Peter Hebdon, a director of Michael Joseph, because my father had met his father, travelling up to London on the train from Orpington. Peter wrote back a week later: 'There's an advertisement in *The Bookseller* for a stockroom assistant at Bumpus. It might be worth having a go, because if you do go into publishing later, it will be useful experience.'

So that is what I did. My father came up to London with me to the interview. J.G. Wilson[13] saw us in his office, which was a total mess with papers strewn around. He said, 'The boy could come and do a bit of collecting.' I didn't know what the hell that was, but thought, well, at least it's a job. He said, 'We pay a bit above the odds.' They didn't. Four pounds ten shillings a week, I think it was. That was 1951.

Robert Clow Jack Knox had been sent to Bumpus to learn the trade, so that was what he organised for me. The idea was that you made your mistakes outside John Smith's and returned with some understanding. And it worked quite well – I learned what not to do, in Bumpus. There had always been this connection between the two companies. J.G. Wilson, who was the managing director of Bumpus when I worked there, had trained at John Smith's in Glasgow under Jack Knox's grandfather. He was a wizened, slightly hunched, speckled, bird-like man, with a wonderful Glasgow accent which he had never lost. J.G. was a true Scot. When I went in to ask for my first rise, because my salary in those days was £6 a week and I just couldn't live on it in London, he said, 'Clow, when I was in Glasgow my salary was three shillings and sixpence halfpenny a week. I could live on that, so why are you having difficulty on £6? How much more do you want?' I stupidly said, 'Ten shillings, Sir.' 'Very good, you can have ten shillings.' If I had said fifteen, I might have got fifteen.

Michael Seviour Most bookshops in London had collectors who went round publishers' trade counters to pick up customers' orders that they

13 Managing director of Bumpus.

didn't have in stock. There were three collectors at Bumpus. One was a chap called Bill, who looked like Burglar Bill – he was elderly and didn't shave much. He said, 'Right, mate, I've got to take you out', and off we went. Pretty well every publisher had a trade counter in London. There were three rounds: the Euston Road area; the City round; and the Covent Garden round, which was the one I mostly did. One of the collectors was retiring and I took it over from him.

And how did you actually carry . . . Just stuck it over your shoulder like Father Christmas. Later I noticed collectors going about with grips. I used to laugh at that. You thought, 'Oh, nothing as common as a sack.' In my day, you would see these chaps walking around with sacks over their shoulders. Although the Times Bookshop actually had someone who drove a van round.

Ian Miller became an assistant bookseller at Mowbray's Anglican bookshop, London in 1949.

Ian Miller Most of the time you walked, with a big zip bag. The first call from Mowbray's in Margaret Street would be Novello, the music publishers in Wardour Street, for titles like *Cathedral Psalter* and Stainer's *Crucifixion*. Then you walked down Oxford Street to Soho Square, where Adam & Charles Black had a trade counter – one copy of *ABC of Railway Engines* – then you might go to Watkin's in Cecil Court. George Harrap was at 182 High Holborn; Whitaker's trade counter was at 32 Store Street. You would turn off New Oxford Street into Bloomsbury Square for the Student Christian Movement Press and the Intervarsity Fellowship, then progress through the back streets to Russell Square for Faber & Faber. I have seen T.S. Eliot going in the front door – a rather gaunt, serious looking man – while I crept in through the back. Red Lion Square for Cassell. Sheed & Ward, the religious publishers, were on the left-hand side of the Strand towards Trafalgar Square; William Collins had a London trade counter at 9 Bow Street opposite the magistrates' court; Gollancz was in Maiden Lane; Chatto & Windus were in William IV Street. Then you cut through the market to Long Acre for Odhams, worked back to the junction of Charing Cross Road and Oxford Street, and probably jumped on a bus for the last bit, just off Regent Street, where the Oxford Press had a music showroom – although you might have done that one already, before you went to Novello.

Michael Seviour Cambridge University Press on Euston Road was a bone of contention with collectors. There was a long room with a counter at the end, and an elderly, rather stout gentleman who would disappear into the back when he saw a collector come through the door. Very disobliging.

Ian Miller The men on Novello's trade counter were the most miserable ones. There'd be a long drawn out, 'Oh, it's Mowbray's again. What do you want?' We usually wanted a dozen *Cathedral Psalter*s. The books were kept upstairs and came down on a chute. If you put twelve *Cathedral Psalter*s – which are quite heavy books – into a wooden box and send it down a chute, the box comes roaring down, hits the bump at the bottom, and half of them fly out. We would be waiting as though we were on the slips at cricket, to catch anything that shot over the counter.

Michael Seviour Apart from the Euston Road, it was quite a friendly voyage. At Christmas they used to give the collectors an envelope with five bob inside.

Robert Clow In those days, Bumpus was a relatively small shop on the south side of Oxford Street, near Marble Arch. It was somewhat anachronistic, to be polite. The old man[14] was almost immobile and sat most of his day in the office at the back of the shop, receiving gracious, titled ladies from Mayfair. He would tell them what they ought to be reading, and they would all succumb to his charm. He would charge the books to the ladies, then Mr Bowles – who ran the religious section at the front of the shop – would take the books away to be packed. Three or four days later, the ladies would come in and ask Mr Bowles if he wouldn't mind crediting the books, because they had rather more than they'd bargained for. I suspect that the old man was so persuasive that they couldn't say no.

When I arrived I was put downstairs in the stockroom for a fortnight. The old man's idea was that one just looked at the books to familiarise oneself with them. Firstly, I felt isolated; secondly, sore in the legs; thirdly, it would have been useful to have some guidance. There was a stock man called Mr Bland, who petrified everybody. His assistant was Michael Seviour, a placid, gentle man, who had a knowledge of books and a liking for books. If one wanted information, one tried to get it from Michael Seviour as opposed to Mr Bland.

Michael Seviour In the front of the shop was Miss Cocking, who was in charge of fiction; a rather raddled-looking elderly lady with a stick, who limped about. A customer came in one morning, leaving a taxi waiting outside, and said to Miss Cocking, 'Do you have a book on the Spanish guitar?' 'The Spanish guitar, Sir? How well I remember my father; he played the Spanish guitar. I used to sit there as a girl and listen to him. Wonderful days.' 'Yes,' said the customer, 'but do you have a book on it?' 'Yes,' she said, 'the Spanish guitar was wonderful. Mr Johnston, do we have a book on the Spanish guitar?' 'No, Miss Cocking, I'm afraid we don't.' And she said, 'I'm very sorry, Sir, I'm afraid we don't.' And he said . . . I don't know *what* he said, but he buggered off and got his taxi. That was Miss Cocking.

14 J.G. Wilson.

Robert Clow When Lawrence Durrell was being published – *Justine,* I think – Miss Cocking told me what a filthy book it was, and her advice was not to read it – I'd be about twenty-two at the time. She had broken her leg, or legs, several times, and walked with great difficulty. Because of this infirmity she used to get off early at five o'clock. I was always slightly sorry for her, until one day, when I had been on an errand and was coming back to the shop, there was Miss Cocking at the head of the bus queue outside, taking her stick and actually battering the other members of the queue in order to get on the bus first. I was really quite shocked.

Miss Dworetzki, who had been a bookseller in Gdansk and managed to get out in the late 1930s, ran the foreign department and mothered the youngsters. She had several foreign students: an Italian lad called Enrico Calamandrei and a very sweet Swiss girl from Basel. We three came under her feathers. John Sandoe was also training there. He later ran the best bookshop in London, in my view – the most wonderful selection of books, all personally chosen. He was known as the beautiful John. And there was a beautiful girl called Diana, who worked on the cash desk. I took her out once or twice, but I think her aspirations were greater. Bumpus was a shop full of people who were highly individualistic.

Michael Seviour Miss Hitchcock – or Miss 'Hitchcoe' – lived behind some curtains at the back of the shop. Nobody ever knew what she did other than get the old man his coffee. She would emerge with a mug and go through the back door to fetch it from a café. This would take about half an hour, and by the time she got back you wondered how much coffee there might still be in the cup. But she was inveterate at knowing what was going on, and used to tell stories to J.G. I'm not aware that she ever did anything else other than get this coffee and just walk around very slowly. A cadaverous sort of old lady.

Then there was Mr Garland, who was about eighty-five and had been a buyer in the old shop. He was a dear old man with side-whiskers, and really didn't know what he was doing. As you came up the main stairs there was a bookcase, then there was a small gap where he sat at a little Victorian sloping-topped desk – sometimes he would knock an ink pot over the top and you had to be careful that there wasn't anybody passing underneath. Mr Garland used to feel that he was still a buyer. He wasn't. But the reps who'd been coming for years would say, 'I thought you'd like to see this, Mr Garland' as though he was still buying books. One day a rep came in with a valuable art book, left it with Mr Garland, then came back: 'Can I have the book now?' 'Oh,' said Mr Garland, 'I've just sold that.'

One of the great events downstairs was Miss Harrison, who was in charge of maps. She had a bad leg swathed in bandages – she used to sit with her leg up on the counter – and she had a stick. The customer would say, 'Have you got such and such an *Ordnance Survey* map?' and she would reply,

'On the top shelf in that pillar. No, no, no, there. Not there, further along', and wag this stick. Mr Evans was her assistant. He was fat and bloated and fed on cream buns. Miss Harrison would drum her stick on the counter: 'Mr Evans, Mr Evans, what are you doing now? Will you get that map for me?' Occasionally somebody might say, 'Oh, bugger' and Mr Evans would get red in the face and all upset: 'Such filthy language I will not hear.' Then he would be seen with a cream bun in his mouth, Miss Harrison shouting and waving about the place. It was a carnival down there.

The accounts department, where you went for your pay packet at the end of the week, was run by Miss Harlock, a stout lady who could have a been a sergeant major. When the Wages Council[15] put the pay up, she said, 'There's more money in there this week. You'll have to thank Mr Wilson.' As though he'd had anything to do with it. Mr Cox was the accountant; he wore pince-nez and a shabby blue jacket, and would potter about holding papers and grunting occasionally. They had a typist, and they also had a girl called Celia who was tall and lean and white skinned. Where the room extended beneath Oxford Street, there was a tiled wall with a flat top like a shelf, just below one of those glass pavement-gratings that lets light through to cellars. Nobody knew what the space was for. But once a month Celia would not feel very well, and she would be lifted up and put on a blanket to lie along the top of this wall underneath Oxford Street with all the people walking overhead, until she felt better. So occasionally you would go in the accounts department and say, 'Ah. I see Celia is up on the wall again.'

There were some quite normal people about. Peter Giddy[16] was there at that time. Mr Hopkins, a quiet, kindly man who looked after antiquarian books. And Miss Green, who was a very knowledgeable bookseller but seemed to suffer from sleeping sickness. She would sit there having her afternoon tea and gradually go forward; you would watch the cup, then she'd go 'Ooh!' and the cup of tea would come up again. Miss Green was down on her knees checking stock one day when a customer asked Mrs Bennett – a rather jolly woman who didn't know A from her backside – for a particular religious book. Mrs Bennett said, 'Just ask the lady who's at her prayers, Madam, and she will be able to help you.'

Robert Clow Miss Green was good friends with Miss Williamson, who looked after biographies and was always knitting. For months, she was knitting a sort of green garment. Then one day, in triumph at completing it, she put it on and it turned out to be a totally green dress from neck to hem. We all said, 'Oh, how wonderful. It looks lovely.' But each day, as she came into work wearing the same dress, it got progressively lower because

15 The Bookselling and Stationery Trades Wages Council.
16 Peter Giddy later became general manager of Hatchards.

the weight of the wool was so heavy. By the end of a fortnight it was down to her ankles, then we never saw it again.

Michael Seviour Have I mentioned the old gentleman who used to write letters to people who hadn't paid their bills? He sat on a high stool at an old Victorian desk and used a quill pen. As he wrote, the line went up to the right, so the whole letter was at a forty-five degree angle. I could never believe that these letters were ever sent, and since it seems very few people paid their bills, it didn't seem to make very much difference whether he wrote them or not. He was known as 'Uncle'. 'What's Uncle doing?' 'Uncle's writing letters.'

I often wonder what happened to all these people. When Bumpus went to Baker Street they all just disappeared. I know that a number of older assistants found jobs at other bookshops. And at a higher salary, in most cases.

Robert Clow J.G. Wilson had been *the* London bookseller in the 1930s, and most publishers referred to him reverentially. The 1930s had been a good period for literature, and at the back of the shop, beside his office, was a room full of those books that publishers will give to booksellers – first editions. J.G. had all these signed copies from writers such as Arnold Bennett and J.B. Priestley, and there was a privately printed edition of *The Seven Pillars of Wisdom*, fully bound in black – I presume it was Arabian sheepskin – and inscribed to him from T.E. Lawrence, which, I must say, I envied.

But by the time I went to Bumpus it was the post-war period, and new writers like Lawrence Durrell were only starting to establish themselves. The Sitwells were still writing, and so was Evelyn Waugh, but I don't think he materialised in Bumpus. We had one lad working there called Peter Porter, whom I now hear on Radio Three reading his poetry, with his Australian accent modified considerably by the passing of time. There was another young poet, who would always try to make sure he had the opportunity to speak to Dame Edith Sitwell whenever she came in. Which she did fairly frequently, dripping with semi-precious stones – perhaps that's being unkind; perhaps they were precious stones – looking like a Tudor portrait with her hairline way back from her forehead, and this aristocratic nose down which she looked. But she wouldn't have had anything to do with us, it was just the old man who would see her.

Ian Kiek Heywood Hill was the last literary salon of London, run by the great Handasyde Buchanan. He was – that awful word – a real gentleman. Never in all the years could he manage to say 'Ian' to me. 'Oh, Mr Kiek.' And I would say, 'Oh, Mr Buchanan.'
Where was the shop? Number 10 Curzon Street, next door to where every-body goes to have their hair cut.[17] Bow windows, very small. I remember

17 G. F. Trumper, gentlemen's barber.

the first book I subscribed to Heywood Hill, in November 1949. It was by Joyce Cary, and Mr Buchanan ordered twelve copies. If it had been by one of the Mitford girls, he would have started with 500.

Anybody who was distinguished – or thought they were – would go to Heywood Hill; you never knew who you were going to see there. I've seen one of the Sitwells – Osbert, I think it was – sitting in the chair there. He would suddenly say, 'Handy! When is the hair shop going to be open?' and Handy would say, 'Very shortly.' Everybody who went in there was somebody. You never saw money exchanged. They would wave a book in the air, and at the end of the month a bill would be sent.

What was the difference between Harrods and Heywood Hill in terms of the clientele? The kind of people who went to Heywood Hill probably wouldn't go to Harrods. Noel Coward went to Heywood Hill. All the Sitwells went there. It was a Hamish Hamilton bookshop, and not a Michael Joseph bookshop. That is, in fact, an accurate description of Heywood Hill. Whereas Harrods was more Michael Joseph. There is a subtle difference.

What is it? Heywood Hill was very much a man's shop, whereas at Harrods the customers were mostly ladies. And whoever went into Heywood Hill never took any money out of their pockets. They would say, 'Handy, what's cooking today?' and Handy would say, 'This is just out.' He was a magnificent bookseller. I remember going into Heywood Hill with a book called *Majesty*.[18] Booksellers were taking them by the hundreds. I went into Heywood Hill and this nice young man said, 'Mr Kiek, I think we'll have twelve.' 'Only twelve?' Heywood Hill himself had come down from Suffolk and had just walked in. He roared with laughter. 'He's right, Mr Kiek.' *Majesty* was not their sort of book.

At Bumpus, the man I saw was Mr Wilson. 'Hello, Mr Kiek. Will you have a sherry this morning?' 'No thank you, Mr Wilson.' When Bumpus had to leave Oxford Street and move to Baker Street, it was clear to me that it would be the end. But if by any chance you meet Michael Seviour, he will tell you about the whole business.

Michael Seviour Bumpus was losing money hand over fist. The directors – who included several publishers, Mr Bowles the bible expert and J.G. himself – decided they didn't want it to go down the tubes and brought more publishers onto the board. Among these were Alan White of Methuen and Allen Lane of Penguin. J.G. Wilson was eighty-something. If they were going to save the shop, they had to bring in somebody else as managing director, and they settled on Tony Godwin.[19] I didn't know Godwin personally, but I had read about him and I certainly knew of Better Books,

18 Robert Lacey, *Majesty*, Michael Joseph, 1977.
19 Tony Godwin established Better Books on the Charing Cross Road in the late 1940s. He became managing director of Bumpus in 1958. In 1960 he joined Penguin Books, where he became chief editor.

the avant-garde bookshop he owned on the Charing Cross Road. I remember Mr Bland[20] saying, 'This young chap who's coming in to run things, we'll have to nurse him along. I gather he's not used to running a place like this and he'll have a lot to learn.' Brother, I thought to myself, you don't know what's going to hit you. And nor does anybody else in this place. You haven't got a clue. And they hadn't. Godwin was a bit ruthless, but he had to be. A lot of the staff went. As I said, most of them got jobs in the book trade at better wages, so it worked out all right. But Mr Bland couldn't stand it, because his whole empire had collapsed. He went to work for the Times Bookshop and I took over his job.

Godwin was responsible for moving Bumpus to Baker Street. J.G. Wilson didn't really want to go. Godwin gave me the key to the old shop and said, 'Your job is to shut this place and it mustn't be later than twelve o'clock on Saturday morning because if it's longer we're in big trouble. And you must make jolly sure that J.G. Wilson isn't hanging around on the premises. If he is, you've got to get him out.'

I remember being in there on the last day. J.G. had gone. I stood in the basement and it was like standing in an empty ballroom. Right through, from one end to the other – the stockroom, the town department, the maps, the children's, the accounts department – it was completely gutted. I stood there in this vast space and thought of all the things that had been there, and now it was totally empty – just a concrete floor – and right down the other end you saw the glass pavement-gratings in Oxford Street with the light coming through. I was all alone, and it was five to twelve. I went and locked the back door, and said, 'Right, that's it.'

Bumpus moved from 477 Oxford Street to 6 Baker Street on 6 November 1958. Michael Seviour became manager of the new shop.

Edinburgh, Aberdeen, Oxford

Louie Frost started work in Thin's bookshop, Edinburgh in 1948.

Louie Frost When the men came into work in the morning, they would go through into what we called the 'back shop' where they had old but respectable jackets hanging on a row of pegs. They would take their suit jackets off and put their old jackets on, then go to their departments, where they would tidy up the shelves and dust where needed. They did that for the first half hour in the morning. The shop was open, but it would still be quiet. Then at half past nine, back they would go, wash their hands, take their old jackets off and put their suit jackets back on.

---

20 Mr Bland ordered all the stock and customer orders and supervised his assistants and the collectors.

John Milne took over Bisset's bookshop in Aberdeen from his father in 1954.

John Milne You would have your duster or your brush, and every morning you would start on the shelf where you had stopped the day before. As you worked your way along, you would pick up a book, look at the title and the publisher, and if you were sensible you would open it and read a couple of pages, then say, 'Right, that's it, back on the shelf.' So when someone came in and asked for a book, you could say, 'I saw that yesterday', and you could stretch out your hand and have that book. It's not done nowadays – there isn't the discipline of learning about the inside of books. I don't want to denigrate present book staff, but I don't think there's the depth of knowledge that existed in the great old bookshops like Thin's. Blackwell's and Heffer's were the same – full of people who were wrapped up in books and knew nothing else but books.

Louie Frost I thought the book trade was pretty much a closed shop, simply because I didn't use bookshops when I was a kid. I think a lot of working-class people would have felt that. You might have been given the odd gift voucher, but otherwise you wouldn't have money to go and spend in a bookshop.
What did your brothers and sisters think about you working in a bookshop? I suppose they were happy that I was happy, but they didn't think you really worked very hard. And of course, bookselling was one of those 'clean jobs'. You've got to work in a bookshop to realise, haven't you?
To realise what? That it's not a clean job – that books attract dust and you're always working on them.
Did they tease you? They did tease me about it, yes.
How? They just said, 'Fancies herself because she's got this posh job in a bookshop.' Thin's was really considered quite posh.

John Milne My grandfather was a printer in Aberdeen. He worked for the Rosemount Press, then set up his own business, the Central Press, in Belmont Street. My father joined him in 1919 after war service, and became a master printer. He worked extremely hard all his life and was very successful. He was particularly proud of the medical books that he printed, which were mainly for E. & S. Livingstone, the Edinburgh publishers.

I went to university and intended to be a lawyer, but law and I were not really made for each other. By then my father had bought the bookselling business of James G. Bisset, and I had met a girl in Aberdeen whom I wanted to marry. We both wanted to settle in Aberdeen, which was a strong influence on my decision to go into bookselling. Sheila and I were engaged as soon as I finished my national service. I had known that in time the business would be mine, but when we married in 1953, my father gave me Bisset's as a wedding present. That was something I had never expected. And in the autumn that year, I went to Thin's in Edinburgh, where I spent six months preparing to step into the top position at Bisset's.

How did you know Thin's? The Central Press printed books for Oliver & Boyd, which was run by the Grant family but the Thins were also directors, so my father was able to approach Ainslie senior and say, 'My son wants to learn to be a bookseller. Can you help?' Old Ainslie Thin was a marvellous counsellor to me. I was working in his shop as an assistant, but he would often ring through and say, 'Come on down', and we would have half an hour together when I would hear the outpourings of this experienced old man. He was the uncle of the present Ainslie Thin, the managing director of Thin's.

Wouldn't he have been concerned that you might find out trade secrets? Not Ainslie. He was happy to think that a keen young man was coming into the book trade. Thin's did do business with Aberdeen University library, and he said, perfectly frankly, 'I know this may cost me, but I'm happy to think there's another good bookshop in Scotland coming to add to the others.' I feel very much in his debt. I took my place behind the counter there, and learnt and learnt and learnt.

What did you learn? I learned the book trade. I knew nothing about the discounts, about seeing reps, about building connections with the university, about hiring the right kind of staff. 'Look around the staff here,' Ainslie would say. 'There are a lot of experienced people. Look at them, watch them, listen to them, and see what kind of people you will need in your shop.'

Ainslie Thin My uncle had been a prisoner in the First World War. He had rather an aristocratic appearance – a head of white hair, a slightly bronzed face and a nice smile. He had a strong character and very much ran the business – everyone did exactly what they were told to do. I think he was a person you rather admired, but feared. When I was young, he tended to snap questions at me: 'What have you been reading, boy?' and 'What do you think of Shakespeare?' – questions which weren't necessarily easy for people who weren't soaked in literature to respond to. I wasn't soaked in literature – I was still at school – but Uncle Ainslie had been running a bookshop for decades and was extremely well read, so almost anything one said to him on that subject would doubtless be inadequate.

Louie Frost He could be a bit of a holy terror, but I found him an absolute charmer. He seemed to me like a very old gentleman. He sat at the end of the front shop, at a massive big desk where he interviewed the reps, then called staff up for advice about books from different departments.

Ainslie Thin He certainly tended to dominate the publishers' representatives when they showed him new books: 'My goodness, the paper's not very good.' 'What's André Deutsch doing with his binding now? This is not really well done, is it?' The rep would get more and more discouraged, but he would order a perfectly sensible quantity of the book eventually. He did ask the staff for advice, but a lot of the buying was done just by Uncle Ainslie. He felt very strongly that that was the only way to keep control of the finances of the shop.

Louie Frost Jimmy Thin[21] arrived first, and that was a whirlwind. He raced everywhere – upstairs and downstairs – then you'd find him sitting in a corner with a pile of books, reading. And a while after Jimmy, along came young Ainslie.

Ainslie Thin My main subject at university was chemistry and I had more or less decided to join ICI, but in my second-to-last year someone from ICI came and spoke to us about twenty-five years of unfruitful research in which every soap powder he had nearly discovered wasn't quite good enough to put on the market. He was a miserable old sod and so much discouraged me that I came away knowing this was something I definitely didn't want to do. About that time, my Uncle Ainslie came to my father and said, 'We need another Thin in this business. What about young Ainslie?' And I joined them in September 1957.

I went to train at Blackwell's in Oxford, which was arranged between my uncle and Sir Basil Blackwell. I arrived in October, when the students were coming back, so the place was pretty hectic. When you're new in a bookshop, people keep asking for books you've never heard of, authors you've never heard of, and subjects you've never heard of, so one is slightly frightened that one will be stupidly ignorant in response to customers' queries. Richard Blackwell was the person in charge by that time. First thing in the morning, he would stand at the bottom of the stairs, looking at the new books – but also watching out for members of staff arriving late. As I was often one or two minutes late, I used to scuttle past. His brother, Toby Blackwell, was also there. I once heard Toby say, 'Why on earth do they have this fellow Ainslie Thin here? He'll just find out all about the mailing list and go back and write to the customers?' Which was hardly practical, since they had about 100,000 customers on it. But later on, Toby and I got to know each other quite well.

In the mid-1950s Ian Norrie was working for the London bookseller Hubert Wilson.

Ian Norrie The first time I met Basil Blackwell was when I went with my erstwhile boss, Hubert Wilson[22] – who was going bankrupt – to see how the Blackwell accounting system worked. The top people at the Book-sellers Association were always concerned that bookselling assistants weren't

---

21 Son of Ainslie senior (J. Ainslie Thin) and cousin of young Ainslie (D. Ainslie Thin).
22 Head of Alfred Wilson Ltd, the London bookselling firm established by his father.

trained well enough. Hubert was going on about this to Basil Blackwell, who said, 'Hubert, I want assistants to come here aged sixteen with their heads full of nothing, so I can fill them with the names of authors, the names of books, and the names of publishers.' He knew there was no mystique about bookselling, and that if he could get an intelligent, open-minded young person, he could teach them all he believed they needed to know.

Per Saugman Sir Basil Blackwell said to me, 'It will be difficult for another shop to teach my grandsons something that we can't teach them here.' I said, 'Yes, but they would see that the world isn't as custom-built and rose-red as here, where they have an enormous university backing the shop. They would see people who have to sell books to survive, whereas the sheer volume of books that we stock here is almost a guarantee for our success. No other shop has been able to expand its stock over the years to embrace several hundred thousand titles. It might be useful to see how a small bookseller fights for his living, and what attention he has to give to the librarians of his city.' When librarians came into George's bookshop[23] in Bristol, I won't say the whole staff stood to attention, but it wasn't far off – the librarian moved round the shop as a king, because he was our best ally.

When you have seen bookselling at close quarters, you never quite forget that nothing is automatic in bookselling – you really have to fight for it. For many years at Blackwell's we thought – and we were right – that producing catalogues was the best service we could offer to customers. And customers did appreciate it. Today they say, 'I haven't been in the shop for a long time. I do, of course, get your catalogues.' Then they order the books from the Amazon [sic].[24]

Ainslie Thin Blackwell's also sent me down to George's in Bristol to help over Christmas. They were getting me for nothing, because I was being paid by my own firm, but I was gaining a lot of useful experience. It can be pretty awkward in a family business when staff have been there forever and this guy who has been given a special position comes in and has to earn his keep. It's only when people find you useful to have around that you start getting a bit of respect.

Robert Clow Jack Knox was pitched in at the deep end when he had to come back from Bumpus to start work at John Smith's because his father had died. He was lucky that a lot of the staff had been there all their lives, so they would know their business. When I returned from Bumpus in 1961, I had at least learnt about bibliographical tools, and how to handle customers. *How were staff in Smith's expected to address customers at that time?* Courteously

---

23 George's was then owned by Blackwell's. Per Saugman worked there during his training in 1949, and later became a director of this shop.
24 Online bookseller.

and formally. You would 'Madam' the grandes dames and 'Sir' most of the businessmen. I don't think you would 'Sir' the academics, unless they were professors.

Tommy Joy I never found it was infra dig to say 'Sir'. Of course, I was brought up in Oxford where the 'Sirs' were boys of about seventeen or eighteen. They were only children compared with me, but if they were university people you said 'Sir'.

Ainslie Thin Peter Watson, who became the manager of our front shop, had spent his early days in bookselling – so this is probably going back to the 1930s – at Douglas & Foulis, which was a very upmarket Edinburgh shop. If Lady So-and-so came in to buy a book, she would be driven up in her car, she would get out, and the only person who spoke to her was the manager, while the rest of the staff stood round the shop like fielders on a cricket pitch. The manager would try to find out what Lady So-and-so wanted, and if she wanted a gardening book he would click his fingers at the person beside the gardening section and that person would rush up with two or three of the latest books. If it was a sports book, he would flick another finger, and that person would rush up and show a few books on tennis. But the only person to talk to the customer was the manager, and the others were there – literally – to assist.

Mayfair, Tunbridge Wells and Piccadilly

Eric Norris At Truslove & Hanson in Mayfair, the downstairs staff would say, 'If Lord Louis Mountbatten comes in, ring down and say you have a query for the accounts department. That will indicate to us that he is in the shop, so we can come up, quietly walk around and have a gaze at him.'

Julian Fall Tommy Rayward, who joined Goulden & Curry at Tunbridge Wells in 1908, had to go outside to serve customers who stayed in their carriages in the street. I used to go out to one myself. The chauffeur would come upstairs and say, 'Lady Bennett's in the car. She wants some books for her grandchildren. Would you like to take a few down?' I would gather up perhaps a dozen books and go out and sit in back of the Rolls with her, where she would go through them. 'I like that one, I don't like that one. I think I sent them that one last year – have you anything else by the same writer? He seems to have been a success.' People never write back and say 'What a dreadful book'; they always say 'What a success' – so you're quite safe in that respect. She would decide on the books, then I would get some plain visiting cards and she would write, 'From Granny with love' – I would have the addresses of all her grandchildren upstairs – then I'd send the books off. But certainly until about 1930 it was usual for much more business to be done like that.

Before 1939, and even more before 1914, there were wealthy business people living in large mansions around the outside of Tunbridge Wells. By the time I arrived in 1948, that was much reduced, and most of those big houses were either derelict from the war or had been turned into flats or pulled down, but the clientele still included a fairly substantial back-bone of business people. There were also wealthy women who were either widows or maiden ladies and had a whole house, or perhaps a suite in a hotel. They were often very good customers, but expected to be looked after.

Then there was a third category, which has now completely vanished, of rather faded maiden ladies who had not quite enough to live on comfortably but wouldn't dream of doing any work. They had just enough to live on in a small and rather seedy hotel, and would get up late and have breakfast, then go and have coffee, walk round the town, look at the shops and walk back for lunch. There were quite a lot of those, and they were usually dreadful customers. They would buy a twopenny birthday card and expect to have it put on their account – we ran quarterly accounts when I first went there – or perhaps they didn't like it and would bring it back the next day, so you would have to go through the rigmarole of putting credit notes through and crossing them off again.

A lot of customers only paid their accounts once a year, which was accepted at that time. There was a wine merchant in Tunbridge Wells whose accounts went back unpaid for years and years. But gradually John Goulden and I got rid of that and went back to monthly accounts. I would have done away with accounts altogether, but we felt that customers still regarded them as a convenience. It *was* a convenience for them, but it was an awful expense for us, running the damn things and collecting the money.

Eric Norris Behind the scenes at Truslove & Hanson there was a cabinet containing names and addresses of ladies and gentlemen, with what their credit was worth. When they came in you would say, 'Excuse me, I'll just check something', then go and look in the cabinet. 'Not to be trusted,' the records would say. 'Must have cash.'

Reggie Last managed Truslove & Hanson in Sloane Street from 1946 to 1951.

Reggie Last Truslove & Hanson was the best-stocked bookshop in London. People wrote to us from all over the country for books, and recommended Truslove & Hanson to others who wanted good service. We were friendly with Hatchards, although – if I may say so – they were a little jealous of our success. The Queen bought her books from Hatchards, but when the Queen of Spain visited Buckingham Palace, they sent her to Truslove's. I sold her a set of A.A. Milne's books bound in leather at about ten guineas. We had a lot of customers whom Hatchards felt should be theirs.

Ian Chapman became sales manager of William Collins, Sons & Co. in 1955.

Ian Chapman Hatchards, which had been founded in the 18th century, was a bookshop with the most fantastic history, but it had suffered problems in the early 1950s and was clearly losing money. It was owned by Teddy Cole, who was a huge man – and I remember him coming to one Booksellers Association conference wearing a white tuxedo, which made him look even more gigantic. Cole announced that he was going to sell Hatchards – and sell it to the Kardomah coffee house next door. Billy Collins[25] said, 'We can't allow this to happen. Surely to goodness Smith's could afford it?' We approached W.H. Smith, but they wouldn't buy it – and nobody else in the book trade was prepared to bail out Hatchards.

In the end, Billy said, 'We're going to buy it. I'll ring up Cole and see if we can go and meet him. Will you come with me?' So we walked up to Hatchards – Billy used to wear a Sherlock Holmes cloak swept round his shoulders, and he looked very dashing – and went to the side entrance where there were stairs leading to a suite of offices. Halfway up there was a wrought-iron gate with a buzzer, which we pressed. A voice said, 'Hello?' Billy said, 'This is Billy Collins and Ian Chapman to see Mr Cole.' We stood there for what seemed a long time, until two very large gentlemen with bulges in their jacket pockets came down and opened the gate, then ushered us into a large office where Teddy Cole was sitting behind a partner's desk. Because he was slightly lame he had a walking stick, which was lying on the right-hand side of the desk. He didn't get up when we walked in.

There was some brief general chat. Then Billy said, 'Now, Mr Cole, you really are not going to sell this business to the Kardomah?' Cole said, 'And what makes you think that?' 'Because you can't.' 'What do you mean? I can do what I like. It's my business.' Billy said, 'Yes, it is. It's also your decision. Do you want to go down in history as the man who sold this great bookshop where prime ministers and royalty have been coming for generations? To go down in history as the man who killed it? Is that what you want?'

There was silence. Then Cole picked up this walking stick and thumped the desk. 'No,' he said, 'I certainly do not.' Billy said, 'Right, let's talk. We would like to buy this business, and I think we can come to an arrangement which will be good for you because you want rid of it, and good for us because we have all kinds of plans to develop Hatchards in keeping with its traditions.'

It took about three months to bring the deal to a conclusion. Billy said we were fortunate to get it, because it had a very favourable lease which at that time was pegged until 2016 – I was interested to hear recently that the

25 Sir William (Billy) Collins, publisher-salesman and chairman of William Collins, Sons & Co.

lease has been re-negotiated. Eventually we started to develop a chain of franchised Hatchards shops. That was a mistake. You can replicate a brand, but Hatchards was more than that – it was a living entity, with an atmosphere of its own.

Collins bought Hatchards in 1956. Peter Giddy became its general manager in 1964. Tommy Joy joined him as managing director in 1965. Brigitte Bunnell went to work there in 1977.

Brigitte Bunnell You didn't get a job in Hatchards unless you had connections – they never advertised any vacancies. I heard from a friend who worked there that she was leaving to return to university, and she said, 'Shall I put a word in?' So she had a word with Mr Giddy, who said, 'Send your friend along.' That was probably the shortest interview I ever had. As soon as I said, 'I'm a qualified German bookseller', he said, 'When can you start?'

The shop was at 187 Piccadilly, next door to Fortnum & Mason. It was everything one could dream of in a bookshop, but I had never dreamt that I might work there. All the European royal families had accounts and would come whenever they were in town – otherwise we supplied them through mail order. At that time we had the four royal warrants, which made Hatchards the sole suppliers for books to various palaces. The customers included politicians, actors, writers, artists, musicians, but lots of ordinary people and tourists also came through the door.

Hatchards wasn't the stuffy, dusty place I had expected. It had a warm, intimate atmosphere – the dark wood, the staircase with the old handrail, the tables of books, and long tablecloths to the floor so that you wouldn't see if any overstock was underneath. The books were displayed on the tables in a loving way that made you want to touch them – as you walked round, you would gently run your hand across. We had daylight on all the floors. Sash windows, so when it was hot you had to climb over a book display to push them up and get fresh air. Old ledges where you could deal with paperwork, or, when you wanted to recommend books to a customer, you could open out two books side by side for them to compare. The luxury of space. The shop was packed with books, but it was like a welcoming drawing room, where you wanted to spend time.

At the front of the shop was the famous old wooden desk, where every author wanted their book displayed. There was another table in the centre of the shop. You needed a good sales history to have your book on there, but it had a glass stand in the middle, where we promoted unknown fiction authors – maybe a foreign writer who had just been translated. Then the reps could say to other bookshops, 'Hatchards has taken twenty copies. Hatchards believes in this book.' A number of famous names started on that table, including William Boyd, Jilly Cooper and Jeffrey Archer, who dedicated his first book to some of the booksellers in Hatchards. When it was time to take the books off and shake the tablecloth out, we went outside into the bus lane and really shook it hard, because it was heavy, heavy, heavy. And to move the table to hoover underneath, my goodness, you needed some of the strongest men we had in Hatchards.

Keith, our packer and porter, had been there for years. At five o'clock he would open up, and he was the last one to lock up. Keith's packing was immaculate, and if you phoned up from your department and said, 'I have two art books to be sent to Brazil' and described them, that was enough for him to work out the postage. Orders came in from all over the world. There were no online booksellers like Amazon then. Hatchards was a lifeline for a lot of people abroad.

Michael Seviour When we unpacked books at Bumpus we saved all the paper and smoothed it out, and every bit went down to the packing room where there were three men working all the time, packing mail orders for this country and overseas. They would pick up a bundle of books together with the invoice and work out the shape, then they would select pieces of paper and corrugated cardboard and make a parcel. It was all done by eye. And they used string in those days. Their packages were beautiful to look at.

Brigitte Bunnell In some cases we didn't just sell books: I remember a long questionnaire for a school quiz that came from a royal household – we sorted that out and found the answers for them. Nothing was too much. A customer once came into the poetry department and quoted one line of a poem they were desperate to find – no other detail, just one line. Jenny Green, who worked in the poetry section at that time, found the poem. Another lady came into the paperback fiction department one lunchtime. She had read one page in the book of someone sitting next to her on the tube. She hadn't seen the title, she hadn't seen the author; she just described what happened on that page. An assistant found the book. That was what was special about Hatchards.

Take Joy Parker, the legend in bookselling. Dirk Bogarde was a big fan of hers. She would walk round that table in the front shop with the customer, and important people would be like school kids in her presence. 'What do you think, Joy?' 'No, not for you. But here, I've got the book for you.' They would finish up with a big pile of books that Joy had chosen for them. Later they'd be back: 'Joy, you were right. Have you got another one like that?' For years after she retired, we had to listen to, 'Joy always used to know what suited me.'

What did she look like? She was a big woman with thick, white hair cut short. Glasses on the tip of her nose. Sometimes we said she was like a matron in a public school, and all those public schoolboys came back for more. Stephen Simpson is another legend. He really *is* Hatchards now, at that front desk. When I started, Stephen worked in the literature department – you could quote half a word and he would go to the shelf and get the book. He had a lot of loyal customers. Lauren Bacall would sweep through the front door and just stand there: 'Get me Stephen.' He's another one who is part of the atmosphere, part of the caring. Looking things up, doing the summer reading list for Balmoral. Nothing's too much trouble.

Tommy Joy Generally speaking, the royal family did not come into the shop. Their orders were made by telephone, and sometimes in writing.
Are you able to tell me the kind of books they were buying at that time? No, for two reasons: firstly, I couldn't divulge what they were reading; and secondly, what they were reading is nothing to do with what they were buying. Time after time they would be buying for a present. Then there are reference books. You have to have dozens of up-to-date copies of *Who's Who* in the palaces, because they need to know the right honours for each individual they are writing to. *Whitaker's Almanack*, if I remember rightly, listed all the MPs, so they also needed a lot of those.
How would you send the books to them? Just ordinary delivery. I often took them myself. I used to like it when I went through the gates of Buckingham Palace.
What kind of car would you go in? Nearly always by taxi. But if I was on my way home, I'd be in my own little Morris.

Trevor Moore worked as a rep for many publishing companies, including Hutchinson, Cape, Deutsch and Random House.

Trevor Moore Peter Giddy of Hatchards has to be the greatest bookselling enthusiast of all time. Peter would pick a book that he liked – sometimes it was a book that was being hyped up, but sometimes it was just one he had picked up from the bookseller's equivalent of a publisher's slush pile – and say, 'Gosh, this is special. We'll do something with this.' And he did.

Brigitte Bunnell As a bookseller, Peter Giddy reminded me very much of my dad:[26] rushing around getting books off the shelf for a customer, or walking round the table saying 'Where's such and such?' because he had just read a particular book and wanted to find them a copy. And they had the same passion for reading – Peter Giddy has been known to bump into a lamppost, walking between Hatchards and Piccadilly Circus with his nose in a book.

Some of our customers couldn't afford to buy books. They would read one, put it back on the shelf with a bookmark in, then come the next day to carry on reading. Peter would watch that, and he would give them the book, or go into his office and get a proof copy for them. A handful of regular customers used to come in to talk to the staff – pensioners, who didn't have money for books. Peter would make sure they had something to read. We

26 Franz Determann, bookseller.

had several shoplifters who, it turned out, couldn't afford books. Because we were still independent and didn't have to follow a head office policy of prosecuting, Peter always let them off. 'Don't pinch them. You only have to ask.' By the time he had finished, they would be part of the club that waited for proof copies to come out of the office. That was Peter Giddy.

Then there was Julian Toland, one of the booksellers who left Hatchards to help Tim Waterstone start Waterstone's, and who now owns Village Books in Dulwich. One of the most brilliant booksellers.

What made him a brilliant bookseller? Knowing his books and knowing his customers, then selling his books to his customers so they then became the customers' books. I can't put it more precisely. Ian Chapman was the chairman of Hatchards when I was there, and he came regularly to talk to us. Again, he had the right passion for books, mixed with shrewd business sense. He made us feel proud to work in Hatchards, and proud that Hatchards was part of Collins. He wouldn't interfere – Peter Giddy and Tommy Joy were running the shop. But Ian was very much a part of it.

Karl Lawrence returned from the Bahamas to join Collins' expanding bookselling business in 1964. He was initially based at Hatchards.

Karl Lawrence *The Sunday Times* worked out their bestseller lists by phoning round particular bookshops to find out what had best sold. The first time I took the call at Hatchards, I asked someone what to report and they said, 'Wait a minute, we'll just find out what we have to say this week.' It turned out that Billy Collins would always indicate several Collins titles to be included in Hatchards' bestseller report, whether they had best sold or not. I was somewhat disconcerted when I came across this. The one that went in the report that week was *The Penkovsky Papers*.[27] It sold quite a lot, but it certainly wasn't a bestseller.

How influential was that bestseller list? I think all bestseller lists are influential, unfortunately. There will always be people who say, 'Gosh, everybody's reading that, I'd better get it', even if they only read the dust jacket. Whereas word of mouth is more influential for people who actually read.

Ian Miller When publishers claim to have sold thousands of an important novel, booksellers often say, 'You may have sold them to the bookshops, but we haven't sold them to the customer.'

David Whitaker When Whitaker created BookTrack,[28] that was the first time that there were really reliable bestseller lists. Not just in Britain, but anywhere in the world. And not just lists of the top ten, but lists that could tell you what was the 4,772nd bestselling children's book in the country.

27 Oleg Vladimirovitch, *The Penkovsky Papers*, Collins, 1965.
28 In development from 1995; fully operational from 1998.

How did they do it? Louis Baum[29] must get a lot of the credit for the original concept. He said, 'The TeleOrdering system looks at booksellers' order files, right? And it does that on a nightly basis. Why can't it look at booksellers' sales files on a nightly basis?' And BookTrack grew from that.

Weren't booksellers nervous about a computer having access to their sales? It was completely anonymous: it just took details about sales from a bookshop of a certain size, and within a certain catchment area. It's useful for booksellers to be able to check their stock against the BookTrack sales lists. Are they stocking the hundred bestselling children's books? Have they got the hundred bestselling gardening books? But publishers also find it useful: they know how many books they have sold to bookshops, but they don't know how many copies the bookshops have sold on. It was Benett Cerf, the great American publisher, who walked into his empty warehouse and said, 'Gone today, here tomorrow.' A publisher may have sold 20,000 copies of a title, but next week those copies might start to come back because the book isn't selling. Also, if the publisher knows what is actually selling from the bookshop, he might not order a reprint that turns out to be unnecessary.

So that was the basic concept. But technically it turned out to be very much more difficult than anybody had envisaged. It cost far more than anybody thought, and took far longer to establish. Publishers said it was frightfully useful, but they wouldn't agree to pay. David Young[30] deserves quite a lot of credit, I think, because Collins was one of the first companies to sign up – which it ought to have been, because of the numbers of bestselling books that it publishes.

I got the first outside customer myself. Brian MacArthur of *The Times* said, 'David, I've heard about this bestseller list of yours, and I've been wondering about it.' So we had breakfast at Simpson's – finnan haddock, I expect – and I told him all about it. He said, 'Is it really as good as you say?' 'Yes, it is, Brian. It's the first and the only factually-based bestseller list there has ever been. If you take it for *The Times* newspapers, this is what we will charge you, and if its validity is ever challenged successfully, you can have all your money back.' He said, 'OK.' So then we had *The Times* on board, which helped. But I did none of the work involved in setting up BookTrack. I had retired as executive chairman in 1992. It was Sally and Martin[31] who drove it through.

How had the bestseller lists been compiled previously? By taking half a dozen bookshops and asking them to fill in forms. It wasn't a satisfactory way of doing it. And I have never heard of anybody doubting the validity of BookTrack.

29 Editor of *The Bookseller* from 1980 to 1999. *The Bookseller* is the book trade's weekly business magazine. At that time it was published by Whitaker.
30 David Young was then managing director of HarperCollins trade division.
31 Sally Whitaker (David's sister) and Martin Whitaker (his son) were respectively managing director and deputy managing director of Whitaker at that time.

Charing Cross Road

Tommy Joy It's a very peculiar place, Charing Cross Road, for books. You get highbrow literary shops – or you used to; you get shops selling mass-produced books; and you get a place like Foyle's, where at one time they would have books on every subject under the sun and which specialised in second-hand – what you may call 'the ordinary business'.

In the early 1960s Michael Seviour became manager of Better Books, which was still owned by Tony Godwin.

Michael Seviour One day Tony Godwin said, 'You probably don't know this, but we own a basement further up the road in Charing Cross Road, under the flats. There's a great load of stuff in there – old magazines and books and what have you – and I've had a notice to say we have to clear out. I'm thinking of putting an advert in the paper to say that anybody can come and take whatever they like free of charge, because that's our best way of clearing it.' I went and had a look. It was a really big basement, full of stuff going back years, but none of it particularly useful. So Godwin said, 'Get the staff up there and take anything you want, then we'll put the advert in.' I think he advertised it in the *Evening Standard* and the *New Statesman*.

On the morning in question I went and opened the place, then went back to Better Books. A couple of hours later, a uniformed caretaker appeared. 'Are you responsible for what's happening up at the flats?' he asked. I said, 'Not personally, but I am the manager here, so I know about it.' 'Well, you've got to get up there and clear them out. If there's an accident, there'll be hell to pay. You've never seen anything like it. The stairs are jammed. There's a swarming mass down there. If there was a fire, who knows what would happen?'

So I went up, and it was absolutely true: there were people on their hands and knees, and people climbing over each other. Absolutely amazing. We hadn't got a megaphone, but we gradually managed to persuade people to go. We said, 'Look, you can take what you can now, but you must not be more than ten minutes; you have to get out.' Eventually we got the place cleared. Then short pieces appeared in the *Evening Standard* and other news-papers saying, 'The streets of London may not be paved with gold, but in the Charing Cross Road people were able to take books for nothing for the first time, until the authorities sadly stopped it.' So it was quite exciting. And it got rid of a lot of the stuff.

In the mid-1960s Michael Seviour moved from Better Books to Dillon's, where he became ground floor manager and literature buyer. In 1965 Better Books was bought by Collins and Karl Lawrence became the manager.

Karl Lawrence I was told, 'You can manage Better Books and do what's necessary to put it to rights.' I took it over on the 1st of January 1966. Better

Books was an avant-garde bookshop with an excellent reputation, on a prime corner site on the Charing Cross Road, and Tony Godwin had also taken over the lease of a large shop next door. That part of the business was run by Bob Cobbing, who was a poet – a very good guy and a good salesman, but not very good at managing the finances. It was stuffed full of avant-garde poetry and avant-garde poets who came in to get books on credit, and to chat and smoke pot. Performances were held in the basement – the People's Theatre used to perform there – and we used to hold lectures. One of these, soon after I arrived, was given by Timothy Leary, who evangelised about taking LSD. That didn't fit very well with the Collins image.

Of course, the staff were appalled when they heard that Collins had bought it. Collins was an establishment publisher that produced and sold popular literature, a publisher for nerds. It was alien to anything that they believed in. The Age of Aquarius was getting underway, and Collins had no place in the Age of Aquarius. I was not greeted with enthusiasm. In fact, I think they distrusted me the day I walked in. They all wanted to walk out. One of my roles was to keep them there so that we didn't have to pay for redundancies, and also because without them the business would have had to close. None of us knew anything about it. I don't know why Collins bought Better Books. It didn't really make sense to me. The story I heard is that Billy Collins met Tony Godwin, who was at Penguin by then but still owned Better Books, and Billy bought the bookshop over dinner.

Ian Chapman Tony Godwin was a good friend of mine. He phoned me up from Penguin and said, 'Can we have a drink this evening? I'm anxious to speak to you tonight, because tomorrow I have to fly to New York.' I said, 'Sure. But would you mind coming to St James's Place?' 'OK. Where shall we meet? I'd rather it was outside the office.' 'The bar in the Stafford Hotel?' So we met there at seven o'clock. We chatted for a bit, about Penguin and how he was getting on with Allen Lane, then I said, 'Come on, what's the urgency about this?' He said, 'As you know, I own Better Books. I've got more than enough to do, and I just can't go on with it. I hoped Collins might consider taking it on under Hatchards.' I said, 'I don't think it's us, Tony. I really don't think Better Books fits with Hatchards.' But Tony insisted: 'I've got to get this settled, Ian. I really am in a hole. I'll tell you what I'll do. You can have the stock valued, and just give me the cost of the stock. Anything that you write off is fine by me. I just want it off my hands.' And like an idiot, I said, 'OK, that's a deal.'

I'll never forget phoning Tommy Joy the next day. 'Tommy, I hope you will forgive me one day, but I'm afraid I'm going to ask you to come round with me to Better Books.' 'Why?' 'Because I've just bought it.' He said, 'Does Billy know about it?' I said, 'Not yet. It's a surprise he's got coming to him.'

We went the next morning and had a look around, then went away and had a cup of coffee. I said, 'What we're going to do is clean this thing up and see where it takes us. But whatever else we've got, we've got the freehold of a couple of shops, so we can't go too far wrong, Tommy.' Then I had to tell Billy. 'Ian, what did you do that for?' I said, 'You're quite right. There's no logical reason. Tommy's horrified. And if I've learned one lesson, it is never to go out for a drink with Tony Godwin. But it's OK because we've got the freehold.' He said, 'It's surprising, I must say. See what you can do with it.' It wasn't one of the best deals I've ever done in my life. But it helped Tony – and I was very fond of him.

Michael Seviour Tony Godwin used to say, 'Eighty-five per cent of book-selling is really just routine, and what matters is the other fifteen. But that eighty-five per cent is no different from selling cornflakes – it's nothing to do with bookselling, but just what you have to do to run a business.' I don't think that a lot of people in publishing always realise that. I was surprised at the number of publishers who said they knew somebody who was keen to do some bookselling before they went into publishing and 'They'd be very good, you know.' Most of them were totally useless. To be quite honest, some of them just wafted about. But they probably went on into publishing and did a very good job.

Mostly children

Maureen Condon and John Prime ran bookshops in King's Lynn in partnership from 1968 to 1982.

Maureen Condon One day a man came into the shop wanting books for his children and asked if he should buy them an encyclopaedia. I knew he wouldn't be able to afford that, so I said, 'I wouldn't buy a whole encyclopaedia. I would just buy a good book on the subject they're inter-ested in – fishing or building or birds – otherwise you might overwhelm them.' He became a really good customer. He had been coming in for a long time before he told me that he couldn't read, and was asking me to choose books for his children because he didn't want them to feel as deprived as he felt.

We had one or two other customers who were non-readers, who would ask us to choose books for their grandchildren. That's something you might not get in a large bookshop – they trusted us enough to do that. Bookselling is time-consuming, if it's done with care. You can't say, 'It's uneconomic to spend so much time with one customer who will only buy one book.' You know that if you encourage those particular customers, their children or their grandchildren will eventually come in by themselves. But at the stage where those people were coming in, it was a question of making them feel comfortable.

Ian Miller I used to tell publishers that it would be good for them to go into bookshops and see how the public reacted to their products. One took up the challenge and I arranged for him to spend some time working in the children's department at Hudson's. He couldn't believe that it could take half an hour to sell a Ladybird book for half a crown.

Louie Frost Thin's had the biggest school department in Scotland, and teachers came from all over the country to browse. My staff there were women, because it was mostly women – mothers and grandmothers – we dealt with as customers. We always had a former teacher on the staff, because it's hard to choose for a child who is having difficulty in school, and you have to be careful that you're not selling something for the sake of selling it, otherwise it could do damage to the child.

You had to be very welcoming to parents who came in. When I was in charge of the school department at first, some of them had never really shopped in bookshops, but somebody had told them, 'Wee Davey's having trouble? Go up to Thin's; they'll give you a hand up there.' We had quite a good reputation for being helpful. You had to be very careful, because a lot of those customers were nervous. A lot of them felt as I felt about bookshops when I was a child: they thought that if they went into a bookshop, people would look down on them. But that attitude has changed. Nowadays people say, if I can afford it, I can go there.

Margaret and Dan Hughes ran Sam Read's bookshop in Grasmere from 1969 until 2000.

Margaret Hughes It is mostly children I remember. A little boy who wanted a natural history book which cost twelve and six. I put it aside for him and he came in every day to look at it. I think he bought it for ten shillings in the end. He said, 'You see, I come from St Helens. There's not a lot of wildlife in St Helens, so you have to make do with books.' I could have wept.

A little girl who wanted a poetry book. I think it was *I Like This Poem*, one of Kaye Webb's Puffins.[32] She was longing for it and her mother wouldn't buy it for her. Poetry is one of my obsessions. I put the book in a Sam Read bag and I ran down the road after them and gave it to the child: 'Here you are, that's from me as a present.' Her mother was not best pleased, but she at least let her keep it.

There was another little boy, who wanted *Bears in the Night*. He was about three. He had his parents, a sister and a grandmother with him. I looked for it and I looked for it, and eventually I said, 'We haven't got it.' He looked round this room that was jammed full of books and he thought, this is very silly, they must have it. So he wouldn't go. First of all his mother stayed with him and the others went round the village, then his father stayed

32 Kaye Webb was children's editor at Puffin Books from 1961 to 1979.

with him and the others went round the village. Then his grandmother stayed with him and the others went round the village. And he found it. I had searched for it and I couldn't find it. *He* found it. Then he knew that Sam Read's shop had every book in the world, and I can still hear him running down the street, waving it – he wouldn't have it in a bag; he held it in his hand – and calling out, '*Bears in the Night, Bears in the Night.*' I didn't think we had it. But he had totally believed it.

Maureen Condon We said that children were always welcome in the bookshop if they were not accompanied by an adult. They would come in after school, and we would have droves of teenagers leaning against the wall, reading poetry, or asking, 'Is there another Tolkien coming out?'

Margaret Hughes We used to open in an evening, and it got terrifically busy. One night Dan was queued out with people waiting to be served, when this little thing came up – he had those round, pink National Health glasses on – and he said, 'Mister, have you got any *Dr Seuss* books?' Dan said, 'Let's have a look.' He left the queue waiting, went along with this kid, crouched down and had a look. 'Yes, there they are – *Dr Seuss* books.' The kid said, 'Have you got *The Cat in the Hat Comes Back*?' 'Well, we'll just have a look, lad, we'll just have a look. There it is: *The Cat in the Hat Comes Back.*' 'Oh,' he said, 'I'm glad you've got it. I've got it at home.'

Maureen Condon Occasionally children would rush in, all wet from the rain, and start putting books on the floor. I would say to the mother, 'Your child is welcome to browse, but would you mind taking off his wet Mackintosh?'

John Prime On one occasion a lady came into the shop with two or three children. One of them put a book down on the floor and knelt down beside it, then started pressing the spine flat. The mother did absolutely nothing, and Maureen went up to the child and said, very gently, 'Look, dear, I'd love you to look at the books, but don't press it flat against the floor like that.' And the child let out a tremendous scream, ran to her mother and said, 'That woman's being nasty to me.' And her mother said, 'It's all right, dear, you've still got Mummy.'

Ian Norrie ran the High Hill Bookshop, Hampstead from 1956 to 1988.

Ian Norrie After being angered by the behaviour of a child one day, I put a notice on the door: 'Children of progressive parents admitted only on leads.' There was an article about it in the *Daily Mirror*, it was mentioned in various gossip columns and on the radio, and it went into many editions of the Collins *Companion Guide to London*. It also drew an angry letter from a lady who wrote to the *Hampstead & Highgate Express* to say how outrageous of this Mr Norrie to announce that parents of progressive children would only be admitted on leads. She had it the wrong way round, so I was able to write another letter, putting her right. This got me enormous publicity.

Maureen Condon Some parents didn't wish to leave their babies outside, and in those days prams were much larger than the buggies that are used today. One day I came back from lunch and said to John, 'Oh, you've sold the encyclopaedia. That's a miracle – I only put it out an hour ago.' He said, 'I beg your pardon?' And it had actually been stolen. There were twelve volumes, and it cost about £150. We suspect that John had been distracted – he used to get very involved talking to customers sometimes – while someone piled the encyclopaedia into the pram and waltzed off with it.

Tony Pocock One day, out of the blue, someone who had been in the navy with me and was working for the Oxford University Press, rang and said, 'There's a job going on the *Oxford Junior Encyclopaedia*. I think you ought to apply.' So I did, to the Secretary to the Delegates, A.L.P. Norrington. I went to Oxford one Saturday – there was nobody else in the Clarendon Press building except for him – and in not more than half an hour I'd got the job. That was the great moment of my life. I started on the 1st of January 1951.

The *Oxford Junior Encyclopaedia* was divided into twelve volumes, each with a different subject. I was landed with *Law and Order* first, which was a difficult way to begin. My second was *Great Lives*. Articles of 500 words or under, plus certain subjects which I particularly wanted to write, were entrusted to me. So I did Nelson and Wellington because I had asked for them and because the two general editors, Laura Salt and Robert Sinclair, decided that the boy needed something to get his teeth into.

Laura Salt headed the educational division at OUP in Oxford, and I think everybody would agree that the school book era under her was something special. She had been a headmistress and an inspector of schools, and neither at Oxford nor in the marines had I met anybody quite as formidable. She hadn't much time for my so-called humour. Actually, I did make her laugh quite often, which was a good thing.

How? By telling silly jokes about her colleagues, I think. She had a big white poodle, very well behaved, which slept at her feet until it was time for lunch, when she took it for a walk in the parks. I would go with them sometimes, and exchange views on how things were going. I learnt a lot from Laura by talking about publishing generally: how to put a book together, and how to balance the cost of printing and paper and royalties against the price you felt you could charge. I got to know her quite well, and she was no longer frightening – although I knew the boundaries and would never dare overstep them. She was an important moral influence on the whole department. We all wanted to behave. 'What would Laura say if I did this? What would Laura do?'

What might she have done? She might have sacked one, of course. Or she might have just given one a rocket. That would have been formidable enough.

How old was she? About sixty, perhaps.

What did she look like? Small, tough, grey-haired, stern mouth, hurrying along in the park with the dog.

What of her is in that encyclopaedia? The whole book is hers, because she insisted on rewriting and re-editing every single article that came in. She had a marvellous eye for simplification. Everything had to be crystal clear to the twelve-year-old reader.

Who bought it? School libraries. And at the general sales conferences which London reps attended, I spoke for the *Encyclopaedia*. I used to ask the reps little questions to see if they could answer them. 'Tell me roughly what Nelson's main attributes were.' 'Oh, I don't know,' they would say. 'Turn your attention to Wellington. Come along, I need to know everything you can tell me about Wellington. You rep there – that one – what do you know about Wellington?' 'Oh, I don't know.'

Why did you do that? Why not? Better than just meandering on about the next volume, I thought – ask them questions about it. They soon sat up.

Did they have any questions for you? Of course. 'What's the price? Will the price go up? What promotion are you doing?' That kind of thing.

Stan Remington Around 1955 Odhams decided to go into door-to-door bookselling, so they launched a new imprint called the New Educational Press. This door-to-door business was very un-Odhams: there were teams of representatives who called at the door and tried to get an order for an encyclopaedia. If they did, they got a nice commission; if not, they didn't earn anything. So you can imagine that this would be a business with some pretty dodgy operators. The man they brought in to run it was known as Commander Roberts – as he insisted we called him – because he had been in the navy.

The New Educational Library was a set of books on French, geography, history, English, aimed at students studying for School Certificate exams. Odhams had previously been selling it through direct mail, but when we sold it under the door-to-door imprint, we had to double the price in order to cover the cost of commissions. But we didn't live on that for long, because we soon negotiated a deal with OUP to produce the *Oxford Junior Encyclopaedia* in our own special binding. I think we sold more on the doorsteps in Britain than Oxford sold across the world.

That was a very fraught business. We had a complaint from one educational authority because one of these reps had stood outside a junior school asking children their addresses. The mothers decided that he was up to no good, chased him down the road and nearly lynched him. The reps were told that they mustn't say they were from Oxford, but they could say that it was the *Oxford Junior Encyclopaedia*. Those kinds of reps? Forget it. When they got to the doorstep it would be, 'I'm here from Oxford and I've got this wonderful *Oxford Encyclopaedia*.' Then they'd go into their spiel. That was designed so that at no point would anyone ever say no, and you would never discuss the total payment with the customer, it was always 'So much a month for so many months.'

When it got back to the Oxford Delegates that people on doorsteps were claiming to be selling their book, my boss had to go down to Oxford to make a personal apology to the Delegates and say that one particular man was being fired. Six months later we were opening a new sub-office in Newcastle. My boss went up with Commander Roberts to meet the manager. Just as he's walking in, he sees a man sitting there and thinks, I remember that guy. He says, 'Isn't that So-and-so?' 'Well, he's not called that now,' says the manager. 'He's changed his name. He is behaving himself.'

It was a terrible business – there were so many stunts. The rep would be getting about twenty per cent of the total selling price and people only had to put down a deposit of about five per cent. Some of the reps were paying the deposit because they were getting four times as much back in commission. Most of those sales didn't stick too well, as you can guess. We occasionally sent out collectors where we had something really dodgy, such as when a rep had invented the names and addresses then disappeared with £1,000 worth of commission. But in some cases the characters were the type who would say to the old man who went to check, 'You'll get your books if you come here again – you'll be found in the ditch with them.' It wasn't the nice world of books.

You said it was a very un-Odhams thing to do. Well, you think about it. You were forcing things onto pretty poor people – it was very much the lower end of the market. And you were using sales people on a no-salary basis. We're talking about a union company here. When I joined Odhams, one of the first things I had to do was join a union, even though I was an executive. The door-to-door business was full of pitfalls from the point of view of complaints and opprobrium.

Why do you think Odhams did it? They were doing anything in books that they could think of. Their women's magazines were selling like there was no tomorrow; they were in expansionist mood. The *Encyclopaedia Britannica* and the *Arthur Mee Encyclopaedia* were sold that way by other companies – there was major door-to-door business going on. One good thing about it was that it got books into homes that probably wouldn't have had any at all. People were used to paying the tally man five shillings a week, so paying like that for a set of books was just part of life.

Do you know how Commander Roberts went about recruiting? There were ads in the press: 'Make easy pocket money. Earn up to £100 a week' – which in those days would have been big money. But mainly – and this is where Roberts shone – he would chat up another publisher's area sales manager and suddenly you had another thirty reps in the north west of England, with the manager earning an over-rider of three per cent, rather than the two and half per cent he'd been on with Grolier or Britannica. Then a few months later you would suddenly lose them all because one of the other publishers had offered the manager four per cent.

The key audience for all these books, including the *Encyclopaedia Britannica*, was parents of children under eleven. Each area had its own sales techniques. One was to try and find out where children lived – watch them go home at night – and look out for Mum going in, then try to sell to her before Dad got home, because Mum was easier to sell to than Dad. But in the end we had to insist that Dad signed the form, because there were a lot of cases where Mum signed, we sent the books, but Dad wasn't having any. At that time, the idea that the woman would be committed on things was really not on. It was largely hit or miss, and the fact that we had vast numbers of reps out. As long as a proportion of them got orders, we were selling plenty of books. But some of those reps were earning virtually nothing.

Given what you've said about their working conditions, were there no protests from the union at Odhams? It's funny, isn't it? There was hardly any awareness. Somehow these people weren't seen as part of Odhams. They were odd people, not very reputable, doing this funny business. The mother of chapel would have thought, they're not part of my team, they're not like the people in the office.

How would the people in the office have regarded those reps? It's not so much 'regarding' as being unaware. Ignoring, almost, how we got the business. They were just amused by some of these stories that used to get circulated. The business went on until Odhams merged with Hamlyn.[33] Paul Hamlyn didn't like door-to-door selling and he didn't like the books – they hadn't enough colour in them, they were very much work books – and the business faded out at that time.

---

33 Odhams had been bought by the International Publishing Corporation (IPC) in 1963. In 1964 Paul Hamlyn sold Paul Hamlyn Books to IPC and became head of its book publishing division.

5 | FRIENDS FOR LIFE

Per Saugman When I came to England in 1949 English publishers wanted to know what the feeling was in Denmark about English books. I told them that English design didn't make the blood flow faster in Danish veins. Kate Greenaway or *Winnie the Pooh* are one thing, but Danish publishers couldn't understand how the English could go on producing pictures of children who looked like morons – they think Noddy is a nut case. But of course, one was tactful. England had been at war and all their energy had gone into that; they couldn't modernise quickly. Nowadays English children's books are among the finest in the world.

What were you comparing them with at the time? Dutch books, Swedish books, Danish books. Even some German books were coming through by then.

Klaus Flugge When people ask, 'Why are you a children's book publisher?' I sometimes say I didn't have enough children's books as a child. There wasn't much publishing during the war. And in East Germany after 1945 much less took place than before.

I was born in 1934 in Hamburg, where I lived until 1943 when it was devastated by bombing. My mother escaped with her three children the night before our house burned down, and we went to Grabow, a little town in Mecklenburg, halfway between Hamburg and Berlin, where a distant relative lived. In 1945, the eastern part of Germany was being occupied, and a lot of refugees came west, trying to escape the advancing Russians. The English and the Russians met in Mecklenburg – right in front of our apartment, in fact, where they embraced and danced. Unfortunately the English then withdrew because the border had been agreed some time before, and that produced a stream of refugees going over to the West. We stayed, of course. My mother had nowhere to go; she had three small children; she felt unable to move. And she hoped that our father would return, which did not happen. He had refused to join the Nazi Party or become an officer. He left with the army in 1940 and eventually went to Kiev and beyond – then back again, in the retreat. Hundreds of thousands of prisoners of war died in Russian prison camps; my father was one of them.

Most of the Russian soldiers we saw in Grabow were from Mongolia or Siberia. They arrived in horse-drawn carriages, and the looting was extensive. We were lucky that nothing drastic happened to us, although they took over our little apartment and my mother had to cook for them. As far as I know, she was fairly well treated. Maybe we were fortunate enough to have the right soldiers in our apartment – I like to think that's what happened.

I left school in 1949, when I was fifteen. There were a few of us there who didn't want to accept the doctrine we were supposed to swallow. We knew that the communist system was a dictatorship; we knew that people were put into prison for having different opinions; we knew that the Russians took what they could and transported it to Russia. I stood out as a rebel. I couldn't go on to *Gymnasium*,[1] because there was no money. If I had been a good communist perhaps they would have given me a scholarship. I would have loved to go to university. During my last year at school I packed and delivered books for the only decent bookshop in town, and when I had to leave school I applied to become an apprentice in that bookshop.

What was it called? Volksbuchhandlung Theodore Körner. Bookshops were state owned. A bookshop was considered to be a political instrument; booksellers were part of the intelligentsia, and the intelligentsia had to be communist. The owner of this bookshop had left for the West. The guy in charge was a refugee from Breslau – he had gone as far west as he could, then got stuck in Grabow – and as he was a qualified bookseller he was put in charge of this bookshop. Bookselling was taken seriously in Germany. Many booksellers had a university degree and a diploma from the book trade academy in Leipzig. Another academy was created in Frankfurt after 1945, but Leipzig was the original centre of the book trade – even Sir Stanley Unwin went there. I was fortunate to be accepted into the bookshop with my lack of education, and considered myself lucky, stuck in that town as I was, to be surrounded by books and interesting people.

Why were books attractive to you? I loved reading. Why, I don't know, especially since there were not many books in our home or at school. But I was able to get some books through an aunt in Berlin and from neighbours. I was fascinated by geography and history. I read books by Stefan Zweig and Emil Ludwig – wonderful writers who wrote before Hitler came to power. Also, when the Russians started to pillage they chucked things out, so I was able to collect a lot of books from the street, which they had just thrown out of the windows. I was lucky to be apprenticed, as I said. I wanted some intellectual occupation and the only one possible was to be apprenticed to a bookseller. What else could I be, apart from a street sweeper?

Marni Hodgkin I was born in 1917 in New York. Grew up, went to school, went off to college – Swarthmore in Pennsylvania – and thought I would spend the rest of my days in New York, a city to which I was deeply

---

1 A secondary school providing a classical education.

addicted. But fate was to take a different turn: I married an Englishman[2] and came to England in the spring of 1944. Alan was in radar research under the RAF, which had flown him over to see people in the States. We were married in New York and he put in to return 'with wife'. They struck out 'with wife', sent Alan back on a troop ship, and sent me to England on an eight-knot convoy – tiny ships in every direction as far as you could see – which took eighteen days. After landing in Liverpool, I made my way to Malvern and the TRE – Telecommunications Research Establishment – where I was eventually put into the film unit. Then I had a baby and had to leave. Alan was released from the RAF at the end of the German war and came straight back to Cambridge. Trinity College was his employer, so to speak. And I have lived here in Cambridge ever since.

Could we go back to New York? Where did you say you were born? Nineteenth Street in Manhattan; I lived all my younger life in Manhattan. The very first home I remember was on 24th Street, where we had a key to Gramercy Park, so that was where I learned to ride a bicycle.

My first school was the Lincoln School, which was miles away, all the way up Fifth Avenue, through Harlem, to the upper West Side near Columbia University – the Lincoln was the grade school associated with Columbia. A wonderful trip. I used to do it by bus. I knew which side to ricochet to as we went up or down Fifth Avenue: here was Best's and there was Bergdoff; there was Tiffany's and here was Saks. The art of window dressing was just beginning; there were beautiful mannequins with strange, exotic backgrounds, and now it was hats, and now it was furs. Those windows were fabulous, and I loved them.

Who actually lived in that apartment? My mother and father, me and Ellen, and eventually Phoebe. As a gesture of emancipation we each had our mother's maiden name as our middle name, and I was Marion de Kay Rous. She came from an old but impoverished New York family, so we were all in the social register, but we did not move in debutante circles. My grandfather was a gentleman scholar; he was art critic on the *Times* for a while and he was consul general in Berlin. His wife – my grandmamma – was a southerner, and they had eight children. The boys went to university, but the girls just went to the New York public school. My mother then went to work at the Century Company – one of the big New York publishing companies – but only as a file clerk.

How did she get that job? Through friends of the family, I think. 'What will we do with Marion?' She was Marion, so I became Little Marion and got heartily sick of the name. On the train going to college, I realised that nobody there knew my name and I could get off the train and call myself anything I wanted. So I got off the train and said my name was Marni Rous.

In fact, my mother was formidably well educated, because hers had

2 Alan Hodgkin, physiologist, later Master of Trinity College, Cambridge.

been a house full of books. She taught me to read when I was about five. Did she teach me on the equivalent of John and Jane? No, she did not. She taught me on a book of poems by Walter de la Mare, called *A Child's Day*, and I can remember tantrums and tears. But first she taught me the alphabet off a tin plate. I can see it now; it had the alphabet round the edge.

Do you remember where you were when you were learning? Mostly on Long Island. Everybody had long summer holidays in America, and we spent them in Southold, right on the bay, with dredgers going 'Katonka katonka katonka.' There are now tremendous houses with manicured lawns, but then it was wilderness. It was very remote; you drove up a long track and there were two houses in a clearing. There was no electricity and only a pump for water. In front of our ramshackle house was a cedar tree – when I went back some years later it had fallen into the sea.

Where would you have been when you were learning to read in that house? On the porch – there was a screened porch looking out over the sea. I can remember it vividly. You could hear the katy-dids calling: 'Katy-did. Katy-didn't.' I think they are a kind of cricket – they rub their legs together to make 'Katy-did', but in the night-time, unlike cicadas, which cry during the day.

What other sounds do you remember from there? Owls. And I remember the smell of kerosene, because we had kerosene lamps to read by. It's an enormously evocative smell.

Which books were particularly important to you as a child? I couldn't say at this distance. We had the classic picture books: the Caldecott books, Walter Crane, Kate Greenaway, Howard Pyle. *The Secret Garden*, *The Back of the North Wind*, *The Water Babies*, E. Nesbit. All of Andrew Lang's fairy tales. Mummy read aloud to us a great deal; she read right through all the plays of Shakespeare and a great deal of the *Old Testament*, because she felt that it was important for us to know what the *Old Testament* said, for which I'm deeply grateful. I greatly deplore that, in this country, children are brought up not knowing the basic stories of European art.

As a child, Mummy herself had been read *The Secret Garden* by Frances Hodgson Burnett, who was a dear friend of Edwalyn de Kay, my grand-mamma – Mrs Burnett came and read it to the little de Kays as it was being written. Her son Vivian, the model for Lord Fauntleroy, was married to a cousin of Mummy's and they had two children, Verity and Dorinda. I can remember being taken with them to see Mrs Burnett. She was sitting up in bed – she was very old – wearing a sort of tiara of what I took to be emeralds. She had in her bedroom an enormous doll's house and she told us that when the doors were shut the dolls came alive. I knew that they didn't – I was a very stodgy child – but she said it with such conviction that my reason tottered. Suddenly you felt, maybe?

How did she come to be reading to the de Kay children? She wanted to see how it worked on children. Mummy said she could do a Yorkshire accent to perfection. A not very good book of hers called *Rackety Packety House* is based on the de Kay family. She also wrote adult novels – unreadable now, but very successful in their day. One of Mrs Burnett's sisters said, 'Whenever I see Fluffy reading a book' – she was called Fluffy by her family – 'and she's either roaring with laughter or weeping desolately, I know she's reading one of her own.'

Do you know how she'd come to be friends with your grandmother? I don't know what the connection was. I can see Vivian's face so well. People think of Little Lord Fauntleroy as being so pewey, but the whole point of the book is that he is American, with true values about people, and the Earl of Dorincourt and the rest are horrible snobs until he teaches them to be more egalitarian. Vivian was a terribly nice man. He died by plunging into a canal to save a drowning man: saved the man, but drowned himself. He was not a bit 'lace collar and curls'.

By the time Marni Hodgkin was in her last year at Swarthmore College, she had decided that she wanted either to write or to edit children's books. She was awarded a Henry Fellowship for postgraduate study at Cambridge University, England, where she proposed to write a children's book based on the Popish plot. The start of the Second World War prevented her from taking up the fellowship – she had been due to sail to England in October 1939 – so she began to look for work in New York instead.

I think I wrote nineteen letters to houses that had children's lists. I also submitted to Viking a manuscript called *Mushroom Hat*, about a little boy who always had to wear a big sun hat because he got badly sunburned. So I was summoned to Viking by Miss Massee, then the leading children's editor in New York. I always called her 'the Queen'. She came from the Midwest and was very upright, with white hair, bright blue eyes and pink cheeks. She had a tremor, so she always had to hold her wrist when signing her name. At that interview I thought, this lady's going to be dead within a month. Not a bit of it. She was wonderful.

May Massee had made a tremendous killing some years beforehand with a book about a bull called Ferdinand who refused to fight; he lay down in the ring and preferred to smell flowers.[3] It hit the anti-war ethos – this was in the 1930s – and was a runaway success, in honour of which she had her inner office panelled and an emblematic bull put on the ceiling.

May didn't really have a job for me at all. However, when I revealed that I was crazy about children's books and had read a great many, she gave me a book by an author called Peggy Bacon to take home and review as though it was a manuscript coming in. When I read it, I realised that the theme was exactly that of the manuscript I had submitted to her; it was about a boy who burned easily and was derided by his peers. I wrote a précis and critique of this book – it was a very good book – and when I handed it in, I said, 'Miss Massee, I had not read this book before.' She said, 'Don't worry. It's not plagiarism; this happens all the time. Books for young

---

3 Munro Leaf & Robert Lawson, *The Story of Ferdinand*, Viking, 1936.

children are about simple subjects, therefore they recur.' And she took me on.

In those days a children's editor had to be a jack of all trades: you had to be able to lay out an advertisement or a title page, to deal with both the artists and the writers, to edit and proof read. Later, at Macmillan, I insisted that I had my finger on all these things: I chose the jackets, I chose the type, I chose whatever. That was also true of the Bodley Head's children's book editors, and it was certainly true of Grace Allen Hogarth.[4] It wouldn't be true now. It's traditional for old people to say, 'It was much better in my day.' I don't say it was much better, because I think the books overall are better than they ever were – although there have always been too many, and there are certainly too many now. And nobody's list is ever composed of entirely good things; everybody has their dross. May used to say, 'Take the English . . .' We had a hearty contempt for English books, I may say. She said, 'The thing is, the English produce the classics – the real stars – and perhaps we don't really reach that level in America. But the rest in Britain is absolutely abysmal, and the standard of our run-of-the-mill in America is much higher.'

What was it about English children's books? They were feebly written, they were written to a pattern, they were just not very interesting or challenging. These days I tend to feel that American books have become obsessed with not frightening children, that they have gone overboard in that sense. But in English children's books of the 1930s, there was never anything that opposed the established order. American books were in essence more questioning, more exciting.

Do you remember any English books that May admired? She admired Ardizzone, for instance. That was what she was saying: that when they're good, they're very good. I don't think she was interested in foreign books – though we published *Pippi Longstocking* in translation from the Swedish. She had very perceptive and strong opinions about children's books, and she ran her department with a rod of iron.

On one terrible occasion May was abroad and I had designed a splendid double-page spread for *Publishers Weekly*, the American equivalent of *The Bookseller*. It was to be printed in red and navy blue, and when it arrived, the red bits had come out as pink. It looked like hell. I flew into a boiling rage and wrote a furious letter to the editor, which I took to the head of the firm, Harold Guinzberg, and said, 'May's away. Will you OK this letter?' He smiled slightly and said, 'Yes, Marni, you are quite right.' Then May came back. She called me in and she gave me the dressing down of my entire life. She reduced me to a pulp. Quivering with rage, as well as with her tremor, she said, 'Marni, if I were in Timbuktu, you would apply to *me*, to *me*, to *me*.' I said weakly, 'But Harold is the head of the . . .' 'I am the head of this

---

4 Influential children's book editor.

department,' she said, wiping the floor with me. That was how she ran her department. But we routinely won either the Newbury or the Caldecott medal. And May always said, 'We ought to have had both.'

It was at one of those prize-givings that I met Grace Allen Hogarth. She was a children's editor working for Houghton Mifflin in Boston, but married to an Englishman, Billy Hogarth. After the war she became children's editor of Constable, in London. She trained Julia MacRae,[5] for instance, and Patrick Hardy.[6] When I was a young wife with small children in Cambridge, she used to come regularly and exhort me to get back into children's books. 'English children's books need you, Marni. You've been trained. May has imparted to you all the secret lore that you need. For heaven's sakes look around you. You can see that children's books are in a terrible state in England. Get back in.' I would say feebly, 'But Grace, I have four little children.' I didn't go to work for Hart-Davis until 1960, but in the meantime I did manuscript reading for her, and a couple of editing jobs. Twelve shillings and sixpence, Grace paid me, for reading a manuscript. But I would have done it for nothing.

Klaus Flugge I left East Germany on the 19th of June 1953. I was still relatively young – only eighteen. And I left my family behind.

Did you tell them you were going? Yes. My mother approved. In fact, my mother came with me to Berlin and we had a sad parting at a metro station: one stop was East Berlin and the next stop was West Berlin; she stayed on the platform, then went back to Grabow, and I went to the refugee camp. From then on I was entirely on my own. I knew that my experience as a bookseller wouldn't count for anything; West Germany was overrun with East German refugees. Indeed, when I got to Hamburg, I finally got a job with Lingenbrink, a big book wholesaler and distributor, but I was paid less than anyone who had West German qualifications. And it was tough to get that job in the first place.

What did you take with you? Two or three books of poetry: Tucholsky, Ringelnatz. I couldn't take a suitcase because they might have stopped me at the border, so I just had a little bag. They were already trying to stop people from leaving East Germany, so you would just be strolling, pretending that you would be coming back.

What was in your heart when you left? Apprehension. A certain sadness to leave my family. And there was a girlfriend I had at that time. Yes, apprehension. But also the excitement of getting to the promised land.

---

5 Leading children's publisher who worked at Hamish Hamilton and Walker Books, then established Julia MacRae Books in 1979.

6 He succeeded Grace Hogarth as editor of Constable Young Books, took his list to Penguin, and ran his own company from 1982 to 1985. An annual lecture is given in his name.

Klaus Flugge emigrated to New York in 1957. While working in a bookshop owned by Doubleday in Grand Central Station, he was offered a job by Lew Schwartz, owner of the publishers Abelard-Schuman. In 1961 Schwartz sent him to develop the business in London, where the company already had an office.

Lew Schwartz must have been out of his mind to send me over to Britain to run a publishing company after twenty months of working for him. I came here in 1961, so I was twenty-six. The London office published some British books, mainly on the adult side, and imported books from Abelard-Schuman New York. By publishing more books here, he could expand his market in Britain and the Commonwealth,[7] which would allow him to publish certain books that might not otherwise be financially viable.

Lew's idea was also that we publish transatlantic editions – for instance, that he would send me manuscripts to be illustrated. He was aware that great children's book illustrators lived in England and that we could use them for books to be published in America – people like Quentin Blake, Charles Keeping, Victor Ambrus, Edward Ardizzone. The great children's book illustrators of the 20th century. And I did, indeed, commission books by them.

How easy was it to decide to accept his offer? To go back to Europe was, I felt, somewhat retrograde. But the opportunity to run a publishing company in London – to have a proper production department, a proper sales department and an editorial department, as I eventually did at 8 King Street, Covent Garden – was an opportunity I didn't want to miss.

Klaus Flugge ran Abelard-Schuman's London business from 1961 to 1975. In addition to building its general publishing, he created a strong children's list.

The problems of transatlantic publishing meant that there was a constant shortage of cash, and sometimes I had sleepless nights because there was pay day on Friday and I didn't have enough funds.

What would you do? Sometimes I drew it out of my own pocket; sometimes I made a phone call on Wednesday – 'Lew, I'm sorry, I haven't got the cash' – and he would wire me money. Sometimes I went begging to the bank manager. I'm sure it happened once or twice that I couldn't pay the bills and printers knocked on my door. There were some uncomfortable moments. But when it came to the crunch, Lew Schwartz coughed up. He was always sympathetic; he had cash problems as well. There were also times when I had sufficient money in the bank. But eventually I couldn't justify my own rep force so I advertised and got Blackie to come in. We then had a combined sales force. And when Lew Schwartz sold his company, Blackie was there to buy the British end, so Blackie became the owner of Abelard-

---

7 The British Publishers' Market Agreement gave British publishers exclusive sales rights throughout Britain and the Commonwealth, prohibiting the sale of American editions in these territories. The Canadian market was open to both British and American publishers.

Schuman. The combination was a good one. Blackie was an old, established publishing house.

Martha van der Lem-Mearns It was December 1955 when I started at Blackie's. It was at 17 Stanhope Street, near the Glasgow Royal Infirmary. Upstairs there was a long corridor with a library at the end, where the editors worked. The room was divided by bookcases, so we each had our own private corner. A girl called Katherine Rudd, whom I recognised from university, sat in the left-hand corner, and in the middle of the room was the scientific editor, Mr Thomson. On the side of the room where I worked, newspapers and journals were piled along the wide windowsill: *The Herald, The Times*, the *Times Literary Supplement, The Illustrated London News, The Times Educational Supplement*, and various other publications for teachers. Part of my job was to read them to make sure I knew what was going on in the world of books. It was a lovely atmosphere, although it seems Dickensian now. We did the editing by hand. There was one portable typewriter between us, which we used if there was a very messy manuscript to tidy up before it went to the printer.

By the time I arrived, the children's department had moved to London, but a file copy had been kept of every book that Blackie's published. Their authors included G.A. Henty, R.M. Ballantyne and Angela Brazil, who was tremendously popular from the 1920s to the 1940s. I had read a few of her books as a teenager: *The Madcap of the School* and *The Most Popular Girl in the Sixth*. She wrote one about every six months. The children's book editor in Stanhope Street had been W. Kersley Holmes, who used to write for *Punch* and was also a poet. He had retired by my time, but still came in on Friday afternoons for tea in the library. Angela Brazil must have been a millstone round his neck, because she had just kept on and on writing these books. He said, 'After she died I was waiting for *The School at the Pearly Gates*.' He could never quite believe that it was over.

I had been interviewed by Mr W.G. Blackie and a man called George Ogg, who was the managing editor. They asked about my background and education, and checked which school I went to, because the Blackies were a Protestant family and didn't employ Catholics. Mr Blackie had grey hair and a walrus moustache; he was a bit like an Airedale terrier. A nice man, but he wasn't really interested in the day-to-day running of the book publishing.

The Glasgow office mainly published educational books, for infant schools through to sixth forms. Simple things, such as cards with multiplication tables or spelling lists that had first been published in 1900, sold in vast quantities overseas, because we had agencies in Calcutta, Bombay and Nairobi. Blackie's also published what they called Rewards, which were editions of classics, such as *Treasure Island*, for school prize-givings. They were meant to have some sort of educational or improving quality to them, and were sold directly to schools.

I edited the books for very young children and English textbooks up to sixth-form level. When I arrived, there were manuscripts waiting to be edited, piled up in a safe in Mr Ogg's room. I was more or less just told to get on with it – they must have started me off with nice clean manuscripts that just needed checking and proof reading. I remember working later on a geography course for primary schools which used to arrive as a heap of photographs and scrap paper – almost on the backs of old envelopes. Unbelievable now.

Where did they come from? Mostly from schoolteachers. It was quite different from publishing children's books, where manuscripts come in unsolicited. There was a team of sales representatives who not only sold Blackie's books but also tried to solicit material for school books: 'We need an O-level cookery course. Can anybody do one?' Just occasionally someone would send something in. A course for O-level needlework, by a woman called Neal,[8] came like that and was given to me to look at. It was hand written, almost two inches thick, and beautifully presented, all in ink – and she had drawn the illustrations herself. We published that, and it was tremendously successful.

Mr Bennett did the scientific diagrams and illustrations for Mr Thomson, and the underwear sections of that needlework course were considered part of his empire. He would appear every so often and say, 'Good morning, Miss Mearns. I'm having trouble with my gussets. Could you come upstairs and explain where my seams should go?' and I would trot upstairs with this elderly gentleman. He was thin as a rake, very tall, and ate nothing but something called slippery elm, which he brought each day in a flask.

Every morning the library door would open and I would hear, 'Good morning, Mr Thomson.' 'Good morning, Mr Bennett.' 'What about a walk round the Necropolis today, Mr Thomson?' Blackie's was situated near a Victorian cemetery on a hill. On fine days, one of the lunchtime pastimes for some of the staff was to walk round the Necropolis and look at the tombs, but Mr Thomson and Mr Bennett went invariably unless it was pouring with rain, so Mr Bennett didn't have to come down every day and repeat this question. Before he went out, he would say, 'All right, Mr Thomson, see you later. DVWP.' Meaning, 'deo volente, weather permitting'. He said this every day without fail.

When the travellers came up we all used to go for dinner in the Ivanhoe Hotel. Twelve assorted men in their forties. All English, as far as I remember – most of Blackie's business must have been done in England. We had to explain what books we were going to be publishing and where we hoped they would sell them. It was quite an intimidating experience for a young editor to face a roomful of hard-bitten sales representatives. But they were

8 Melita M. Neal, *Needlework for Schools*, Blackie, 1961.

always very civil. They seemed to have been at Blackie's for a long time. They were well dug in.

Judy Taylor On the 1st of January 1951 I started at the Bodley Head,[9] which was then above Bryce's bookshop on the corner of Museum Street. The entrance was in Little Russell Street; you took an old iron lift to the second floor, where the whole firm occupied about eight rooms. The offices of Allen & Unwin were below, but quite separate from us. I was given a desk in the middle of a big room divided by bookshelves which held countless file copies of Bodley Head books. At another desk was a young man called Tony Brown. Tony was the office boy and I was the office girl. Our job was to stick the stamps on the post, work the copy machine, and deal with requests for catalogues. Before long I was being asked to read the manuscripts of children's books that came in, because I was the youngest in the firm and therefore thought to be 'closest to the child'.

By 1956 we knew that the firm was for sale, and every now and then Sir Stanley would arrive with somebody in tow. One person he brought round was a good-looking youngish man, and we later heard that this was Max Reinhardt, who was already a publisher in a small way. After buying the company, Max interviewed us all individually and I explained that my particular interest was children's books. Our children's book editor, Barbara Wilson, was offered a job somewhere else. I had been her assistant, but Max thought I was too young to become the children's editor. He was quite right – I was about twenty-six. So, being Max, he made enquiries about who would be the best person to advise on children's books and was recommended to talk to Kathleen Lines. She had been a librarian in Toronto, where she was trained by Lillian Smith, the queen bee and guru of children's books.[10] Kathleen Lines – or K, as we called her – came to this country before the war and worked in the children's department of Oxford University Press. Max engaged her as a children's book adviser to the Bodley Head, and she taught me everything that I knew about children's books.

If you are in charge of a publishing list, it could be tempting to publish something you know is going to make a lot of money. But K taught me that we must publish books that may last for ever, where there is value to the text; and that you must never talk down to a child, therefore you must never let anyone write down to a child – you must respect the child's understanding and give them a challenge. And you must make the books beautiful. This is where John Ryder came in. Max's attitude to everything was, 'Always get the best.' So he employed a designer and production director

9 John Lane The Bodley Head had been bought from the Receiver in 1936 by a consortium of publishers that included W.G. Taylor of Dent and Stanley Unwin (later Sir Stanley), who became chairman of the Bodley Head.
10 Pioneer children's librarian, who founded the Boys' and Girls' House (children's library) in Toronto.

called John Ryder, who had been at Phoenix House and was a very fine typographer, and gave him the job of defining a Bodley Head style. You can tell a book designed by John Ryder; it is beautifully laid out, impeccably designed.

Surely a publisher would be interested in publishing something that would be as profitable as possible. We were building up the reputation of our imprint. We never advertised our children's books by title; we advertised them as 'Bodley Head Books are Best'. We wanted to convince the adult, who is after all buying the book for the child, that they were going to get good value from a Bodley Head book; that it wouldn't insult the child and it wouldn't offend the child. It might frighten the child, but then, certain fairy tales do. But only the best is good enough.

K also attracted certain authors to the Bodley Head: Lucy Boston was one, Rosemary Sutcliff was another. Gradually the children's list came together and I needed help. K had worked for Abelard-Schuman at one time, where she had met Jill Black, whom she recommended as another children's book editor. And when Jill was having her first child, Margaret Clark came on a temporary basis and stayed ever after. The three of us – Jill, Margaret and I – worked together for many years.

Marni Hodgkin In those days the children's editors – I think – were much nicer to each other than they are now. We all felt that we were rather despised, therefore we were a band of fighters.

Who was in that band? The Bodley Head, for instance. Mabel George of Oxford University Press was not. She was the May Massee of England at that time, and Oxford books were in a slightly different format from the usual range. Looking along a shelf of books, you could tell the Oxford books. Eileen Colwell, who was then the top librarian of children's books, told me that children realised this. Some children would say, 'I don't like that book because' – in essence – 'it's too intellectual', and others would say, 'I like those books because they're really, really interesting.' So Mabel George was a world unto herself. She was formidable, and her list was wonderful.

Did you know her personally? Not well. But sometimes I would go up behind her and give her a pinch. 'Oh, Marni, don't do that!' I never knew whether she was cross or not. I admired her deeply. And Margaret and Judy at the Bodley Head were terrific.

What did Grace Hogarth say when she encouraged you to get back into working with children's books? 'They still think we're not real editors, we're second-class citizens. We need you. You've worked in America where children's books are books in their own right, and very proud they are to be.'

Judy Taylor Grace Hogarth brought from America the idea that children's book editors should meet regularly. We were all in our own little offices and never knew what other publishers were doing until the books were published and reviewed. In New York there is the Children's Book Council; they meet regularly to discuss mutual problems and swap books and so on. Grace Hogarth was horrified that none of us knew each other, so she invited me and several others to her club. She was older than we were, and she belonged to the University Women's Club – we were all frightfully impressed. She propounded this idea that we should meet regularly, so we did; we met for lunch. I think it started with about six of us, and it's now grown into the Children's Book Circle, open to anyone – booksellers, publishers, authors, artists, you name it – who works in children's books.

Martha van der Lem-Mearns left Blackie's to work for Nelson in London in 1962.

Martha van der Lem-Mearns The Children's Book Circle held meetings – I took Gwyneth Mamlok,[11] who was one of our artists, to their annual dinner – and there were occasions such as the Carnegie awards. When I was working at Nelson's, it was expected that I would go to all these events.
How would you say children's publishing was regarded? It was very much the youngest child in the publishing family. Children's books was its own world: everybody knew everybody else, and moved from one firm to another in a musical chairs sort of way. All the time I was in London, the same people seemed to turn up at these meetings for years. I remember Gwen Marsh at Dent, Robin Murdoch at Blackie's, Roger Benedictus at Hamish Hamilton and Julia MacRae, who became a publisher in her own right. The women were quite strong minded and knew what they were talking about. Professional people. Many of them were colourful, with distinct personalities: Julia MacRae wore a floating chiffon scarf, and Gwen Marsh had brilliant red hair swept up on top of her head. There were no mice among them. These editors were quite powerful in their own way. They could influence authors' and illustrators' lives a lot, just by commissioning their work.

Marni Hodgkin I laboured long and hard in both Hart-Davis and Macmillan to try to get them to realise that children's books were real books and their authors were real authors, and I failed in both. They remained to the end thinking, 'Children's books? Well, this old biddy can get on with them.'

Klaus Flugge There were a few men in children's book publishing, such as Antony Kamm at Brockhampton Press and David Gadsby of A. & C. Black. But I grew up in a household of women and was happy with them – I wouldn't have dreamt of joining one of those British clubs that didn't have women members. Julia MacRae, for instance – we became friends a little later on. Judy Taylor, who ran the children's book department at the Bodley Head, I admired very much. Margaret Clark, whom I once tried to hire as a children's book editor but who preferred to stay with the distinguished

11 Author/illustrator of Nelson's *Candy and Peppermint* series.

house of the Bodley Head – these were all important women who published the cream of British children's books.

Judy Taylor Children's book editors were not paid very much, they were nearly all women, and they really had to fight in many firms for the money that they needed to expand their lists. It took a long time to get recognition for children's books, and that was mainly won through publishers realising the contribution they made to their profits, when children's book editors began to be recognised as important in the publishing house. Max Reinhardt was in the forefront – when he made me a director of the Bodley Head, it was the first time that a children's book editor had become a director of a publishing company. And when I was elected to the council of the Publishers Association, they had never had a woman there before.[12] It's changed since then, I'm glad to say, although I still don't think that children's book people get quite the recognition they deserve.

Do you know why that change happened? Partly, I would suspect, because there was some marvellous publishing going on in the children's book world which was recognised as such, and we were on the crest of a wave. We were selling lots of books, we had a high profile, we had space afforded to us every week in all the national papers, and children's books were taken seriously. Today they are again not taken seriously, except for the odd title like *Harry Potter*.[13] But historians of children's literature are talking about that time[14] as the second golden age – the first was in the 1920s – so I suppose it was a recognition of that. And I just happened to be lucky enough to be working for a publisher that was doing well, with a high profile.

What was it about the Bodley Head that allowed that to happen? It was Max Reinhardt allowing us to do what we believed to be best, and giving us our heads. He always said that if we made a mistake he would come down heavily on us, but I don't remember him ever doing so. Which doesn't mean to say we never made any mistakes, but he was very tolerant and understanding. We had a very good team there – that was the great thing we had. They did happen all to be women, except when Antony Kamm was there. His experience had been in teaching, and this was helpful because it got a lot of our books into schools, which we had thought of as being only receptive to school books. In the 1960s and early '70s, the amount of government money going into schools and libraries for the purchase of children's books was phenomenal. You knew when you were printing a book that you could be assured of 2,000 copies immediately going to public libraries, which doesn't happen nowadays.

12 Judy Taylor became a director of the Bodley Head in 1963 and a member of the PA council in 1972.
13 J.K. Rowling's bestselling children's series, published by Bloomsbury from 1997.
14 The 1960s and 1970s.

Klaus Flugge By the 1960s, the market for children's books had opened up a lot. Libraries bought the bulk of the print run – maybe the government spent more money on libraries in those days. Also, there had been an expansion in the library service in America as a result of the National Defence Education Act,[15] and suddenly more American publishers came over to buy picture books and fiction. The old story: they looked to England because they could speak the language. And the British Commonwealth still bought most of their books from Britain. When I arrived at Abelard-Schuman, export sales were about forty-one per cent of our turnover in London.

Judy Taylor Bodley Head children's books were sold in Australia by William Collins, and the relationship was a close one. It must have been the very early '70s when I first went to Australia. The representatives there were keen not only to work you hard, but also to play hard. With one of them – Stephen Dearnley – I drove from Sydney to Melbourne. Steve knew how to live in the bush in Australia: he would make the fire and produce the billycan, and we cooked on that, and watched kangaroos and flocks of galahs and white cockatoos. That was magical.

When we were in Adelaide I took a few days off and travelled by train to Alice Springs because I wanted to see the School of the Air, which teaches the children on outback stations – thousands of miles away sometimes. It's all done by radio: each child has their call sign, and the teachers in the studio would call them up, 'Hello Whisky Echo, are you hearing me?' then a little voice would come back, 'Hello, Whisky Echo here.' Then they'd say, 'OK. We're going to have music today. Turn to page three of your song book.' Then they would play the piano in the studio, and you'd hear these little voices all coming in. It moved me to tears.

One day I was there and they were doing their reading: 'Turn to page so-and-so of your reading book', and there was a picture of a boy and a girl in a garden. The girl was wearing a dress and a cardigan and sandals, and the little boy was in shorts – a typically English picture. They all relied entirely on English books. One little boy was asked to describe the picture, and he said, 'It's obviously winter, because the boy's got his sweater on and the girl's got her cardigan on.' But it was a picture of two English children at the height of summer here. That drove home to me that we were publishing for people on the other side of the world whose seasons were completely different, and led me to publish a book about Christmas on the beach in the blazing sun. It was fun to do that, so that children in this country had pause for thought about what it was like down there at the same time as here. The book was called *A Seaside Christmas Tree*. It was by Sarah Garland, who later became my stepdaughter, funnily enough. So I became aware that we were

15 The 1958 National Defence Education Act, which gave funds to educational institutions including libraries, was designed to ensure that highly-trained individuals would be available to help America compete with Soviet advances in science and technology.

doing books for children in completely different settings from us, and that when we, in those days, talked about having tea with nanny – or even having tea – one realised that they didn't. It didn't necessarily mean we didn't publish books like that, but we were aware that there were other things we ought to be publishing as well.

Klaus Flugge My dream was always to start a publishing company. I picked out several publishing houses with their own distribution and a small children's list, which might be able to provide the sales and distribution that I needed. One was Dent, one was Macdonald's, and the third was Hutchinson. I met Charles Clark, the managing director of Hutchinson, who introduced me to the chairman, Bimby Holt, and they both were keen to have me on board. They offered to buy twenty per cent of the shares, so we made an agreement, and I started my own list in the autumn of 1976. I still remember the invitation that we sent out for the first reception, which took place at 3 Fitzroy Square, a building with huge chandeliers and a wonderful staircase: 'Hutchinson is proud to announce the formation of a new publishing company called Andersen Press, specialising in high quality children's books at reasonable prices.'

Klaus, do you enjoy stories? Yes, indeed. This is another reason why I love being in children's books: I like telling them and I like reading them. What I'm trying to do at Andersen is not to publish formulaic books. The great art is to find a story that makes children want to read, and also gets adults to read to children. Most great stories can be enjoyed by both.

Why do you think reading to children is important? Because it extends their horizon, it develops their imagination, it makes them see things in their mind's eye that they wouldn't otherwise see. You can't start early enough.

Do you remember being frightened by anything you read as a child? I remember being frightened of the dark. Susan Varley did a wonderful book called *Monster Bed*, about a monster that worries about a human being under the bed. Monsters – the most popular subject you can think of, for children. Monsters or dinosaurs.

Judy Taylor The most famous book of all that I bought was *Where the Wild Things Are*. It was a book that had been to eight other publishers first, and it was sent to me by Harper & Row's agent in London. The letter that came with it said: 'I am sure you won't want to publish this, but I've got to try eight publishers before I'm allowed to return it to my American bosses, and you're the eighth.' And I absolutely adored this book. I don't know whether you know it? A wonderful, poetic book – with monsters – written and illustrated by Maurice Sendak. It just struck a chord with me. I had difficulty – and they would be the first to admit it – with my colleagues at the Bodley Head. Jill Black, who was a young mother at the time, said that she certainly wouldn't give it to her child, because it would give the child nightmares.

And neither Margaret Clark nor Kathleen Lines wanted to publish it. But I was determined to do it, and so eventually I was allowed to. And thank goodness I did, because it has turned out to be one of the most famous picture books ever published, I think.

Klaus Flugge David McKee did a book called *Not Now Bernard*. It's about a nice little boy who wants his parents' attention, but every time he says something the standard phrase is 'Not now Bernard.' Eventually he says, 'Dad, in the garden there's a monster that wants to eat me', and again, 'Not now Bernard.' What happens? The monster actually eats Bernard. I was worried when I got the book. I said, 'David, my God, this is going to be difficult for anyone to swallow, especially our dear teachers.' But he said it should stay that way, and in the end I agreed; I realised it would be much diluted if we changed the ending.

When it came out, we had lots of complaints. I remember a Scottish librarian writing in: 'How dare you publish a book with an ending like that? I shall never buy another Andersen Press book.' This was twenty years ago, and the year before last[16] it was put on the National Curriculum. That is a book which very few other countries would dare to publish. But the British are sophisticated enough to accept it.

Marni Hodgkin As the world has got nastier, people are more and more apprehensive about frightening children. Particularly the Americans, I may say. I don't know what it is. A sort of self-protective guilt, if you will, on the part of adults. I think children are very tough. The thing that's so fascinating about children's books is that you have to balance the child's enjoyment, the parents' feelings about what the child should or should not read, and the bookseller's view of what the parents are going to feel about the book. Not to mention the critics. Between the child and the book there are a number of adults – parents, teachers, librarians, booksellers – all of whom have their own view of what is proper for the child or not.

Do you remember deciding not to publish any books because you thought they were unsuitable for children? Indeed I did. I turned down two Roald Dahls: *Charlie and the Chocolate Factory* and *James and the Giant Peach* – not once, but twice: once at Hart-Davis and again at Macmillan.

You may be amazed to hear they were at liberty for publishers to snap them up. But I thought there was a latent nastiness in both that I didn't care for. A kind of malicious quality. People say, 'It's the subversiveness that children love', and *Charlie and the Chocolate Factory* is frequently cited as the most popular English children's book on earth. But there was something about them that I did not want to publish. It was as simple as that. I did not

16 This was recorded in 2004.

want to put my name to them. In that, I showed my very deficient business sense, but I have never regretted it.

Klaus Flugge David McKee originally came to Abelard-Schuman with two books. I loved both of them, but thought that I couldn't spend on more than one advance, and I took *Two Can Toucan*. That was the first children's book I published at Abelard, and David McKee's first book.[17] He became one of the leading creators of picture books in this country. I should have been more courageous and taken both books – advances were very small in those days. *How much did you pay for the first one?* Very little. One or two hundred pounds? I forget. Against royalties, of course. Most artists who did illustrations for an existing text were paid a flat fee, and some of them were pretty upset when a book became a classic and they didn't get a royalty. But we did pay a royalty. Artists were always important to me. Britain had – still has – some of the best, which is why the British are the most successful publishers of picture books in the world. Not necessarily thanks to sales in this country, but thanks to the international co-productions,[18] or the international rights, they sell. And even though *Two Can Toucan* was based on a pun in English, I managed to sell a German edition, a Danish edition, a Swedish edition and – in the end – I also sold a French edition: *Toucan Tout Blanc*.

Judy Taylor Young children's picture books often feature animals rather than people, because animals don't date, so the books will last forever. But even with animals you get problems. Chatto & Windus published a picture book which originated in America, about a monkey called George. When the book came over here they decided that because of the King – George VI – they couldn't call the monkey George, so they changed his name to Zozo.

Marni Hodgkin I have always regretted not keeping a copy of the first book that William Pène du Bois – a wonderful illustrator – did for May Massee,[19] which was called *Elizabeth the Cow Ghost*. It was about the ghost of a cow, and I can see the cover now – navy blue, with the cow floating in the air. Oh, what a funny man. But that, I think, had gone out of print before I got to Viking. It must have been a small printing.

Martha van der Lem-Mearns At Nelson's we were presented with a series of children's books to publish as co-editions. They were by Hatier, the French publishers, and we had to make up new titles. I remember going to the reps' meeting and announcing this series. There was *Galahad the Guinea Pig* and *Hannibal the Hamster*, and when I said, 'The third one will be called

---

17 David McKee, *Two Can Toucan*, Abelard-Schuman, 1964.
18 An economy whereby two or more publishers who publish in different markets, or in different languages, share the production costs of a book to be issued under their respective imprints.
19 At Viking, USA.

Teresa the Tit', I could see that Neil MacFarlane, the sales manager, was having great trouble keeping his face straight. But not one of them said, 'We can't sell a book called *Teresa the Tit.*' I still don't know why somebody didn't ask, was it a coal tit or a blue-tit? We could have called it *Brenda the Blue-tit*. I'm afraid it went out as *Teresa the Tit.*

Klaus Flugge In those days, hardly any artists made enough money to live on; having a publisher who published one of their books a year simply wasn't enough, so they needed other work. I used to send people to Longmans when they needed additional money, because educational publishing is different from children's book publishing.

Judy Taylor Shirley Hughes illustrated picture books for Gollancz – the first I remember of hers are the Lucy and Tom books – but she used to draw for the Bodley Head as well, in black and white. One day I said, 'I know you're bound to Gollancz with your picture books, but is there a book you have always wanted to do, and for some reason haven't been allowed to?' She immediately said 'Yes', and I asked her to show it to me. She brought into the office a picture book called *Dogger*, which I am delighted to say went on to win the Kate Greenaway Award. And after all these years that book is still going strong.
Do you know why she hadn't been able to do it elsewhere? For Gollancz she was only doing very short picture books for little children. *Dogger* is one stage up – quite a long story – and a different kind of picture book. If you found that an author or an artist could do a book for you that their regular publisher didn't want, it was sometimes the beginning of a relationship. They would then do another book for you, and the relationship would continue, probably with them working for two publishers at once.
    One way round an option agreement[20] was to get a series going. Hamish Hamilton did the *Antelope* series and the *Reindeer* series, and would approach authors to do a book for those because that would be seen as a one-off, therefore not to be breaking an option. But it would be a way of getting to know the author or artist, then possibly persuading them that you were a better publisher for them than the one they were working for. That was how many people managed to switch publishers.
I've heard people say it just wasn't done to do that. Yes, well, it *wasn't* done to do that. I was absolutely furious. It was particularly Hamish Hamilton, and I remember talking to other people, 'It's outrageous. Noel Streatfeild's done a book for them, and Rosemary Sutcliff, and . . .' All breaking away from their regular publishers and doing these books. But then we all began to do it. And when Sebastian Walker started Walker Books, he quite openly approached all the best people and paid them enormous sums of money so they couldn't

20 By which an author is bound to one publisher.

afford not to. He got John Burningham and Helen Oxenbury and Shirley Hughes – everyone was doing a book for Walker Books. That was really the beginning of the breaking down of what we thought of as a loyalty agreement. We were furious with Sebastian Walker for luring away our best people. He would usually get artists to start with a series of four books, and pay them the unbelievable advance of maybe £1,000 for each book. We were probably paying £100 or £150. They were all terribly badly paid, when you look back on it.

Why were you so cross about it? Because it was the way we had been brought up, to believe that our authors and artists were loyal to us. It was just a publishing convention.

How did it affect your personal relationship with Shirley Hughes when she went to Walker Books? Not at all. We were good friends. One would never have said anything to the artists involved. We probably just moaned amongst ourselves and when we met other editors. But only because it was unconventional. It did break down the barriers. Sebastian Walker changed the face of publishing and, I think, for the better. But we were outraged at the time.

Why was it important for a publishing house to have exclusive publication of a particular artist? It was a convention. It happened in all publishing, not just children's books. If you were an author, people would ask, 'Who is your publisher?' Nowadays they ask, 'Who are your publishers?' unless they know you've only written one book. Or if they are talking about a particular book, they say, 'Who published it?' or 'Who are you taking it to?' But previously, you were identified with your publisher and your publisher was identified with you, and that was, in a way, a strength. Nowadays it doesn't seem to matter any more. It did seem awfully important then. You would always ensure that there was an option clause in the contract, which said that the author undertook to submit his or her next book to you. But it was difficult for an author who had a disagreement with their publisher to get out of an option on the next book. There were various ways it was done. One person I know deliberately submitted a very bad book and the publisher turned it down, therefore the option was broken.

Were you aware of anybody doing that at the Bodley Head? My lips are sealed. I only know of it happening once. But not in the children's book department.

Klaus Flugge At Andersen Press the first picture book I published was by Tony Ross – *Goldilocks and the Three Bears*. Not a very original title, but his pictures were new. Startling images. I immediately saw he had great talent as an illustrator. We sold that to Germany, France, Denmark, and even to Greenland – it is rare that Greenland buys books. Tony had come to see me when I was running Abelard, and decided to come with me when I left, even though I didn't have a name for my new company. He is now one of

Britain's most loved creators of children's books. He is amazingly fast – he can do a book in a week – and he has done over a hundred for Andersen. *What made him decide to come with you?* That's a good question. I always thought it was quite courageous to go with this little publisher who didn't have a name. I found out not long ago that he asked Ralph Steadman – whom I had published at Abelard – and Ralph said, 'Go with him.' David McKee came too – I published his first book in 1964, at Abelard, and we have published at least one a year ever since. He came to the Bologna Children's Book Fair this year to celebrate forty years of publishing with me, and I gave a party for him and Tony Ross in the 14th-century Palazzo di Re Renzo, where Andersen held its very first exhibition.

Judy Taylor At the Bologna Children's Book Fair we would all have dinner together in the evenings round an enormous table in a restaurant – children's book editors from all over the world, who all knew each other's books, talking about what children were interested in. The last time I went must have been about 1980, and by then the scene was different. It's so big now, and everybody rushes about from appointment to appointment so there's no time for this relaxed evening discussion. But that was when we made good friends of editors from different parts of the world. You knew which editors you liked particularly and, when you had a very special book to sell, you would go to them first, and they would come to you first with their favourite books. That was one of the values of that kind of occasion. It wasn't just a business relationship. You made friends for life.

Diane Spivey first went to the Bologna Children's Book Fair in the early 1980s as rights director at Methuen.

Diane Spivey As you came down by train from Milan to Bologna you would see the first almond blossom, and the fair felt warm and hospitable – unlike the Frankfurt Book Fair, which is in the autumn and often cold and wet. It is sometimes cold and rainy in Bologna, but you never remember it that way. It's held at Easter, so it always feels like the beginning of a new year. Bologna is much smaller and generally much friendlier than Frankfurt – partly, I think, because the children's book world is friendlier. It is competitive – very competitive – but it is acknowledged that it's not quite so cut-throat as adult publishing.

Our main aim at those book fairs was to sell Methuen's picture books to the Americans – we were trying to get co-edition deals. Our key customers included Dial Books, Dutton and Random House in the States. There was a wonderful editor called Phyllis Fogelman, who was at Dial for years and years, and her production director was Christopher Franceschelli, who later went over to Dutton, I think. He was slightly older than us, but certainly on our wavelength.

That was a key time for the growth of European children's books. The

British market was more in tune with – and becoming influenced by – the German and Scandinavian markets for picture books. There was a great flowering of talent in children's book publishing, with artists like Tomi Ungerer. Suddenly the British were open to the idea of Scandinavian styles. That brought picture books up a notch and made them stylish things to own.

In the 1960s and 1970s, as joint managing director of A. & C. Black, David Gadsby developed a children's list aimed at primary schools.

David Gadsby There was a much more adventurous approach to children's book publishing in the Scandinavian countries. Of course, I'm generalising – England, America and Japan were doing some marvellous children's fiction and very attractive picture books. But the Scandinavian countries were producing books that discussed topics which are commonplace now but weren't then. They dealt with issues of unhappiness – divorce, bad language, violence – with much greater consideration of the world that children actually lived in, rather than the story-book world which was common in a lot of children's fiction at the time.

A. & C. Black published a Scandinavian book called *I Was So Mad I Could Have Spit*, which was fairly extreme for those days. It enraged some teachers – I still have the furious letters – that we would publish a book about a child going crazy with anger and rage and kicking and cursing and so on, which they felt was wholly inappropriate in a children's book. In fact, it provided a good point for discussion with children.

Klaus Flugge The most recent book I published by David McKee is called *The Conquerors*, which he created because he was shocked by the Iraq war. I have been able to sell it to thirteen different countries – even to America, only a couple of weeks ago, after twenty other publishers there turned it down.[21] I had no problems selling it anywhere except in America, where I suppose people felt it was the wrong book at the wrong time.
Who is publishing it in America now? Christopher Franceschelli, who started his own company, Handprint Press. The book is about a general who conquers one country after another until his army occupies the last one left. The soldiers don't feel like fighting any more and befriend the population, so the general becomes furious and replaces those soldiers with others who, in turn, are no longer interested in fighting and befriend the population and take on their customs and their songs and their stories. In the end, the general realises that he himself has taken on some of the customs – in fact, he starts telling his child the stories. It is a perfect example of how a conquered country educates the powerful country which, in the end, absorbs the culture of another. This is badly told – I should read it to you. But that would take a little time.

21 This was recorded in 2004.

6 | HAS ANYONE MENTIONED ELIZABETH WEILER?

Michael Geare began his career in the book trade in the late 1950s as sales director of Four Square Books.

Michael Geare When I first came into the business many a man had to pluck up his courage to go into a bookshop. There were these daunting lady booksellers in ravelled cardigans; intellectual, clever women. You thought, I'm going to go in there and they will instantly interrogate me as to what I want to buy. It was the absolute reverse of what now happens, when nobody comes up and tries to help you too much, unless you ask for help. A bookshop is now a welcoming, relaxing place; you can read a whole novel there over a few weeks without ever being addressed by a member of the staff.

Do you remember feeling daunted in a particular bookshop? Yes, there were one or two in London. Has anyone mentioned the name Elizabeth Weiler? She and another lady ran a bookshop in South Ken. They were frightening women – they really were intellectuals – and I feared that I might be involved in some conversation in which I would be out of my depth. Will you be talking to Gerry Davies[1] again? Well, try to pump him on the subject of lady booksellers in the 1950s and early '60s who made their shops not attractive, but daunting, and see if he doesn't back me up.

Ian Norrie Elizabeth Weiler had a little bookshop in Chelsea in the King's Road. It was a fairly untidy shop. She had no money so hadn't spent anything on making it smart, but she knew an enormous amount about books. An intelligent, intellectual woman. She understood the Chelsea public and was an excellent bookseller. She was also a musician – she played in the Chelsea Symphony Orchestra.

What instrument did she play? Violin, I think. She was a sweet person with a lovely smile. Died last year.[2]

Trevor Moore When I was working for Cape I covered some interesting bookshops, including the Chelsea Bookshop with the indomitable Miss

---

1 Secretary to the Booksellers Association (1955–63); director (1964–65; 1970–80). *See* Chapter 10.
2 This was recorded in April 2000.

Weiler. She was a formidable figure – a large lady with a deep voice and grey hair tied back in a bun. But great fun to deal with – always interested and positive and chatty. She used to do very nicely with the books that I sold her, or that *she* ordered from me. Miss Weiler wasn't the sort of bookseller you sold things to; she bought them from you, if she decided to.

And how did she respond to Cape books? To some, very well. But she wasn't avant garde in any sense. She would have bought *Spaniard in the Works*;[3] she would have treated that as a commercial proposition, but I don't think she would have felt any great empathy with it.

Maureen Condon Elizabeth Weiler studied at Cambridge University for a degree, but because women were not awarded degrees at the time she didn't get hers until a year or two ago. That woman had real cause to be 'formidable'. But you never heard people say that about their male equivalents in the trade. You heard, 'He's a remarkably intelligent person; he knows the trade backwards and he's a fantastic bookseller.' One thinks of Una Dillon, who ran the University Bookshop in Malet Street; Christina Foyle in the Charing Cross Road; Margaret Mynatt, who ran Central Books. Those women were never part of the boys' club, but they obviously ran bookshops which were excellent in every way. Think of Gerti Kvergic – I imagine running The Economist Bookshop would be a difficult task, and intellectually demanding. But the men used to say, 'That woman scares me stiff.' I don't think they thought they were being slightly unjust. But I think they *were* being unjust to people such as Una Dillon.

How? In not crediting her with her huge achievement. I thought Dillon's University Bookshop in Malet Street was brilliant.

When I talk to people now, they are very quick to say what an enormous achievement it was. Yes, they say it now. But how many female presidents of the Booksellers Association were there in the past?

John Prime I don't think there has ever been a lady president of the Booksellers Association. I've looked back in the records to 1949 – a period covering twenty-eight presidents – and there is no woman there. And this was a period when there were so many outstanding women in the trade. Una Dillon, for example, who founded Dillon's bookshop. Christina Foyle. Gerti Kvergic, who was the manager of The Economist Bookshop which, in her day, was very successful. Then there were women who kept certain firms going during the Second World War when the men went off to the front, such as Pat Hudson and her mother. At one time Hudson's was the outstanding bookshop in Birmingham. The brothers came back after the war, and if you'd asked most people, 'Who's running Hudson's bookshop?' you would have been told, 'John and Barry.' The same thing happened with

3 John Lennon, *A Spaniard in the Works*, Jonathan Cape, 1965.

Austick's of Leeds: when the Austick brothers – David and Paul – went away, it was their mother who kept the firm running. It was in a very shaky condition and she pulled it round during the war, which was a fantastic undertaking. But afterwards, she disappeared. True, she was getting quite elderly, but it was David and Paul who were remembered. But I'll be quite honest with you – and this is an awful admission – I had never really thought about this question of there being no lady president until we started these interviews. I really wasn't very aware of it at the time.

Michael Seviour I think these women were formidable in the sense that they would always be on their feet at meetings.[4] They had something to say, and they would say it in a very determined way. They were forceful. Perhaps they had to be, to run their shops and be accepted in the book trade. Although, as I say, the book trade was largely run by women.
What do you mean? There weren't many women managing directors of bookshops, but lots of departments were run by women. Unlike in many other businesses, young men going into bookselling would often find they had a woman boss.

Ian Norrie I went up from Seaford for my interview, and I remember a dear friend, who wasn't in the book trade but who liked books, saying, 'You'll never get a job at Foyle's. It's a *very* big bookshop.' But it was dead easy to get a job at Foyle's; what was difficult was to get *re*-employed there. I was interviewed by this lady – I didn't know who she was – with a funny little voice. 'What department do you want to work in?' I said, 'I'd like to work in Music and Drama.' 'Music and Drama. Yes.' 'How much would I earn?' 'Six pounds a week.' 'Couldn't it be a bit more?' 'Yes. Six ten. Start Monday week, nine o'clock.'

I arrived on the Monday morning and I wasn't shown to the Music and Drama department, I was shown to the post table – to which all incoming people to Foyle's every Monday morning were shown – a long trestle table, where I sat with about thirty other people and opened the enormous amount of post from all over the world for Foyle's book clubs and mail order business. I felt very resentful about this. There was a woman with a great shock of hair and a tweedy suit, tall and aggressive: 'Stop talking, stop talking, you two.' Every now and again the woman who had interviewed me came out, and I glared at her. Then somebody said, 'That's Miss Foyle,' so I stopped glaring at her and said to this dreadful overseer, 'I was supposed to be selling . . .' 'You get on with what you're doing.' At twelve o'clock we were told we could stop for lunch. I was boiling with fury by then, but thought, what can I do? They're going to pay me at the end of the week and I need the money. Just after lunch, Christina Foyle called me in. 'There's no

4 Of the London branch of the Booksellers Association.

vacancy in Music and Drama. You can go into Philosophy and Religion.' So I said, 'Yes, OK. Thank you.' Anything to get into books.

I came to like Christina Foyle. She was fun, she was gossipy, she liked talking about the trade, and whenever I went to a Foyle's literary lunch[5] she would always come over in the bar beforehand and have a chat with me. Once she even sat me next to her and we chatted throughout. I was organising an outing for the retired booksellers' Retreat[6] and she wrote to me afterwards and said, 'I'd like you to bring your outing down to the abbey.'[7] So we drove all our friends down to her abbey in Maldon. We had the most lavish lunch on the lawn and were shown over the library and the grounds. She gave a bungalow to The Retreat. She liked the book trade. The last time I saw her, when I interviewed her for the National Life Story Collection,[8] I wished we'd had the tape on over lunch because we gossiped much more then.

What was it like, doing that interview with her? First of all, it was extremely embarrassing to have to pin the microphone into her cleavage – I didn't like doing that. Then she began by saying, 'Would you like a glass of champagne?' and I said, 'No, not yet, thank you.' This was about eleven o'clock. So we were brought tea or coffee, and had champagne later with our lunch. She didn't talk quite as fluently as she used to; there were long gaps while I sorted out what I was going to say next, although I had on my knee – illicitly – a piece of paper with questions, which Cathy[9] had told me *not* to have: 'Just say what comes and remember what you want to ask her. It's off-putting if you have a list.' I'm afraid I ignored that. Christina was getting old and was repeating herself. There was one story about Bernard Shaw coming to a literary lunch, which I had heard several times. It was one of her party pieces.

Christina Foyle One of the best luncheons we ever had was for George Bernard Shaw. But he wrote to me afterwards and said, 'If you ever want me again, you must remember I'm a vegetarian.' Is that all right?
Ian Norrie Yes, I'm hoping so. I'm just testing my microphone.

Ian Norrie I couldn't concentrate properly on the interview because I was always looking at the dials on the machine. I really didn't know whether anything was getting recorded, and this I found very off-putting. Whenever I'd interviewed anybody before, I just took along my tape-recorder and switched it on and assumed it was working – I wasn't thinking about the technology. But I was thinking about it when I was doing Christina. The

5 Foyle's Literary Luncheons were started by Christina Foyle in 1930 and continue to this day.
6 Housing association in Kings Langley, Hertfordshire run by the Book Trade Benevolent Society.
7 Beeleigh Abbey in Essex, then Christina Foyle's home.
8 Now National Life Stories.
9 Cathy Courtney of National Life Stories.

recording wasn't long enough; I eventually ran out of questions, then she was wanting lunch – although she hardly ate anything, of course. When I was talking to Ronald Whiting[10] we just went on and on. Cathy says I talked too much, but I think Ronald had at least eighty per cent of the time. He should have had ninety-five per cent, I know that now. But we just talked and talked, whereas with Christina there were gaps where she dried up and I dried up. It couldn't have possibly done justice to her, but I'm glad we at least have that.

Where were you when you did the interview? We were down at the abbey, sitting in a little room that was full of books. That's when she made the famous remark: I asked, 'Are you going to sell Foyle's?' and she replied, 'No. Where would I get my books?'

Christina was a great reader; she was genuinely literary in that sense. She read biographies mainly, a bit of history, some fiction. She read all night, she told me, because she didn't sleep.

Ian Norrie *You don't seem to have taken very much part in book trade affairs. But you were a member of the Booksellers Association, of course?*
Christina Foyle Oh, yes.
But you never played much part in that? Not really, no. I suppose because I've always had so much to do. It was all I could do to cope with . . .
You didn't fancy it? Have another cup? Do.

SB *How was Christina Foyle regarded in the trade?*
Ian Norrie As a terrible employer. It was taken for granted that everybody knew this.
Did she know that? Oh, yes. She wasn't stupid in any way at all. She did have a strike there.[11] I went and contributed to the fund, to the pickets outside. Alan Hill[12] did, too. Several people of our political persuasion in the trade contributed to that. Many publishers liked her company; she sold a lot of books and she paid her bills, too. But I would think Foyle's was a ripe case for unionisation so employees could have some protection. She rationalised it in that interview; she said she wanted people to have the freedom to come and go as they liked. But it's very hard for somebody to work for such low wages that they don't have any opportunity to save.
What was the outcome of the strike? Tommy Joy must have told you about it, because he solved it, I think. He was called in as mediator and he drove down to the abbey and back, like de Gaulle going to and from Colombey les Deux Eglises when he was made president. Tommy sorted it out for her. He told me he did.

10 Ian Norrie interviewed Ronald Whiting for National Life Stories' *Book Trade Lives* collection in 1997.
11 In 1965 (and again in 1982).
12 Of Heinemann Educational Books.

Tommy Joy Christina came to me in tears when there was the first Foyle's strike, and I settled it for them. She said to somebody, 'If I had one penny in the world, my last penny, Tommy could have it.' But she's forgotten that. I had been at Hatchards less than a year, and I went to Billy Collins, who was my boss, and said, 'This is a very tricky business I'm going to get mixed up in. If you get pickets outside Hatchards, I will resign instantly.' 'Oh, no,' he said. 'We've got every confidence in you.'

Can you tell me what happened? I think that they were not very well paid. And Christina is a bit of a martinet. All I know is that suddenly there was a strike. At that time I was on the Bookselling and Stationery Trades Wages Council where we, as employers, met the top people in those bookselling unions. So I knew these people, and I talked to their head: 'Look, this is silly. It's only harming people. Let's settle the strike. Tell me exactly what you want, then I'll tell you how far we can meet you.' That's the only ruddy way to do it. If someone digs their toes in, you're done. But one of the things they wanted was to have an office with the trade union leader there, in perpetuity. That would have meant trouble, so I wouldn't give way on that. Any rate, after about a week I'd solved that strike. There was subsequently another one, but they didn't call me in for that; they thought they could manage it, which I think they did.

And there was an issue about pay? Yes. Certain places have a reputation for not being very good payers, but how far that's true . . . You'd have to have the whole picture in front of you to be able to judge that.

Do you remember having an impression of whether they were being paid a fair rate? At Foyle's? I thought it was a little bit less, perhaps, than it should have been. Yes, I think it shouldn't have been brought to a head.

Why do you think Christina came to you? Why didn't she sort it out herself? I don't know. She was out of her depth, I suppose, and at that time I was a sort of leading boy, particularly of the wages councils.

Had you dealt with unions before? Yes, on this Trades Wages Council, where you would have about ten trade union people and ten managers. Things come round in circles: the Bookselling and Stationery Trades Wages Council always wanted something which is right to the fore now – a minimum wage. I firmly believed – and I'm being proved wrong – that if the minimum wage was too high, there would be a lot of sackings and a lot of unemployment.

Ian Norrie Tommy recommended, I suppose, that she made better conditions. I bet she didn't. I think the strike petered out eventually. That may have been when she started employing a lot of foreign labour, because the joke at one time was, 'Have you tried to get it at Foyle's?' 'No, I don't speak any of the languages they do.' They did speak some English but a lot of it couldn't be understood.

Ian Norrie *Did you ever have a pay structure for assistants?*

Christina Foyle Not really. We start them at £170 a week and they get commission. Some of them get £300 commission a week.

But they work on contracts now, don't they? They just come, you know. We just take them on.

They just come and go as they always did? That's right.

Wasn't there a time when, if you employed a person for six months, you had to go on employing them unless . . . Well, now it's two years. So it's really such a long time that it doesn't matter.

I see. And do you find people stay longer than they used to, or . . . No. We've got very few who've been there longer than two years. Very few.

And there was a time when you employed a lot of foreign labour? Well, you couldn't get staff. In the '60s there was full employment, so I started advertising abroad: Austria, Belgium . . . I had a directory and I went all through it. I got up to Finland. We had ever so many applications and I offered them jobs straightaway. But I was asked to call at the Foreign Office, where there was a table with six very serious-looking men. They said, 'Sit down, Miss Foyle.' This was at the time of the big spy drama. They said, 'We'd like you to explain how it is that you're bringing over numbers of people from Eastern Europe. They have been leaving from the port of Leningrad. What is behind all this?' I said, 'Well, you can't get people here. There's full employment and we need a lot of staff so I've been advertising. I've got up to Finland.' One of them burst out laughing. He said, 'Take my advice: don't advertise in France.'

Ian Norrie She was a remarkable person. As a young woman she started these literary lunches. She had very little formal education – she must have been hell to teach, I should think, because she knew her own mind so much. She was ill when she was very young, and came into the business when she was about eighteen or nineteen. The slump was on. She said to her father that she wanted to start these literary lunches; that was her contribution to try to give a boost to the business, and it was immensely successful. She ran them with the help of Ben Perrick,[13] and they have gone on being successful for nearly seventy years. The ladies of Mayfair, Belgravia and Kensington went to them in their dozens; Lady Diana Cooper was a regular. They all thought Christina was wonderful. She was very charming to them and knew them all by name.

I think she tended to model herself on the Queen in her appearance. When I was working at Foyle's in 1948 she used to wear terribly tight little skirts and seemed to have difficulty walking about because of them. Later she became very smart with her hair always beautifully done, and looked a bit regal. That would go down well with these ladies. And she got together a fabulous list of speakers. Practically everybody who was anybody over the

13 Foyle's publicity manager.

last half century has spoken at a Foyle's Literary Luncheon: prime ministers, presidents, all the leading writers, actors. Who's that dreadful author – the pink lady? Barbara Cartland. She seemed to speak there every two years. They all adored *her*, too. The meal used to be atrocious; really poor food and indifferent white wine. But at the last one I went to, Christopher Foyle – who is now the head of the business – had taken over, and we had a very good lunch indeed.

Christopher Foyle I have very pleasant memories of my aunt when I was young; going down with my parents to her country house and enjoying her company. She was always a bit distant – a bit like the Queen; you slightly had to keep your distance – but there was less of that when she was younger. I think that was just her way, as she got older, of dealing with her interpretation of people's motives towards her. And very often people did want things from her, because she became a very wealthy woman.

Do you remember her being good fun at all, when you were young? Oh, yes. She was a great raconteur. She said that she never boiled a kettle, but I don't remember that as being true. I vaguely remember her doing things like cooking bacon and eggs – and certainly making tea – in her house in the country. And I remember having an enjoyable time with her and my uncle; going sailing with them, for instance – they had a dinghy on the Crouch. And my cousins, particularly my two older female cousins, have very warm memories of Christina when she was younger, and of her being very generous to them.[14]

What did she look like when you were young? I remember her as being a good-looking, dark-haired woman. Pretty. Blue eyes. An attractive woman.

What about her husband? He was called Ronald Batty. In a way he was in her shadow, and wished to be. His family were in the property and estate agency world, and he complemented her very much in the business because he used to monitor the financial results and make investments – mostly in property – with the profits that Foyle's made in the 1940s, '50s and '60s.

As Christina became more autocratic in the business and this bad staff-management atmosphere developed under her leadership, nobody but him could encourage her to do things differently to ameliorate that. He didn't do it often, because it was an effort even for him, but he was the only person she would pay attention to. He was shy. She was known as Christina Foyle – not by her married name – and he was like her prince consort in the background. But I think he enjoyed that role, in a way. And I think they shared similar views of people and of the world: they didn't like committees, they didn't like bureaucracy. In some ways they were quite right wing; in others, quite anarchic. She really liked eccentrics, such as some of these raffish characters in Soho. When I worked in Foyle's in the 1960s there was a

14 Christina Foyle did not have children, but her older brother and younger sister did.

chap called Sir Francis Rose whom she took up with, a baronet who took snuff and had no money – he was always popping in and asking me to lend him a fiver.

Ian Kiek I remember walking into Foyle's on one occasion, and the man who arranged all the literary luncheons at the Dorchester said to me, 'Ian, got your car handy?' I said, 'Yes, Ben. Where do you want to go?' He said, 'It's not me, it's Christina.' I said, 'What? Christina in my Cortina?' He said, 'She wants to take a wealthy Italian antiquarian bookseller down to her home in Essex.' So I drew my car up and in got Christina with this Italian bookseller. On our way down to her abbey we stopped and had lunch. It must have been June, because there were strawberries. And when we got to her fabulous place – it was so beautiful – she said, 'I'm sorry I haven't got time to show you around, but just look round yourself.' I remember so well that occasion. Then I drove back to Foyle's and saw Mr Rush, who was the cashier and goodness knows what else. I said, 'Mr Rush, I want ten quid, please, from you.' He said 'What's that for?' I said, 'Petrol, for taking your Christina back to her abbey.' So out came the £10 for the petrol.

Christopher Foyle One thing about Christina: she was always very loyal to people who had done her a good turn and who didn't expect anything in return. Before the war, Foyle's was often nearly broke because my grand-father was continually expanding. He was always borrowing money from the bank. He owed money to the Inland Revenue, and a lot of money to publishers. He used to send Christina, who was an attractive young lady, round to beg people for more time to pay.

Christina Foyle My father used to send me all over the world to collect bad debts. He sent me to the Soviet Union.
Ian Norrie And did you succeed? No, because the people who owed us money had either been executed or sent to Siberia. But when I came back I was asked to write for the *Daily Express*: 'No Communism for Me'. And I was asked to speak all over the place about my experiences in Russia.
When was that? 1932.
And you didn't collect a rouble? No. My father was always sending me to see his creditors, and he always made me see the Inland Revenue. I got rather friendly with the head, Mr Greenwood. He was very kind. I invited him to a luncheon. And on that occasion Sir Alfred Munnings was there. Have you heard of him? I was having a drink with him, and he said, 'Who have you put me next to?' I said, 'Our Inspector of Taxes.' 'Goodbye,' he said and disappeared.

Christopher Foyle When I knew my grandfather – years later, after he had retired – he used to be driven up to Foyle's every Friday in his Rolls Royce.

He would potter about the shop, where he'd hand out tips – £5 notes – to members of staff. Then he would go to the Trocadero Restaurant on Shaftesbury Avenue. He always had lunch in the room where the orchestra played, and he would invite any member of the family or friends or business associates who were in London that day to join him, so there could be anything from four to fifteen people there. He would often have John Dettmer and his wife, and a chap called Sydney Goldsack. Later, my aunt told me this was because two publishers who had been kind when Foyle's was almost broke before the war were Heinemann, where the man who gave them credit was John Dettmer, and Collins, where it was Sydney Goldsack. After that, they were guests for lunch whenever they wanted, and they were invited to every single Literary Luncheon by my aunt for the rest of their lives. In the same way, when Foyle's had a strike in 1965, the person who helped out as an intermediary between her and USDAW[15] was Tommy Joy, the managing director of Hatchards, so he and his wife were guests at every Foyle's Literary Luncheon from 1965 until they were too old to come.

Ian Norrie I spent about ten days in Philosophy and Religion, then the woman from the post room appeared and beckoned me. We got into the lift and she poked me with a pencil as we went up, saying, 'You're going to work in Music and Drama. You mustn't call the manager "Charles". He's Mr Saunders. And you've got to sell a lot.' Then she left me, and Mr Saunders said, 'Hello, I'm Charles. You're Ian, aren't you?'

At that time Christopher Fry was at the height of his vogue as a playwright. *The Lady's Not for Burning* had been an enormous success, and the book of the play, which Oxford published, had sold tremendously. Then *Venus Observed* came out, in which Laurence Olivier was appearing at St James's Theatre. Richard Foyle[16] subscribed ten copies, I think. I had one, and other staff wanted them, so Foyle's made no profit on those. Better Books across the road ordered 1,000, which was a tenth of the edition, and the book was reprinting within a very short time. Those plays of Fry's were tremendously popular, and people were buying the play script of *Venus Observed* for six shillings. But because it was reprinting we didn't have any copies, so we had to tell people, 'Go to Better Books. They've got it over there.'

Michael Seviour One of the more exciting things that happened at Better Books from time to time was to see somebody running down the road clutching a book and the Foyle's detective haring after them.

Ian Norrie The detectives were with us, really. They were anti-Foyle in a way, because one of them was actually nicking books and was alleged to

15 Union of Shop, Distributive and Allied Workers.
16 Christina Foyle's brother, then in the business.

have had a second-hand bookshop in south London. My friend George Depotex, who was in charge of the ground floor, had a consignment of *Concise Oxford* dictionaries – which were in short supply at the time – to sell. At the end of the first day Christina came down and asked, 'How are you doing with the *Concise Oxford*, Depotex?' He said, 'It's going very well, but I'm a bit worried. We haven't got as many as we should have.' She said, 'Let's go out and look at the cars in Manette Street', and they rushed out. They looked in the detective's car which was parked there and found a great supply of the *Concise Oxford Dictionary*. So he was sacked on the spot.

You said you came to like Christina Foyle? I only came to like her later; I hated her when I worked there. Later I found she was good company and intelligent. Amused and amusing. To have gone on bearing a grudge against her because she was an awful employer when that was in the past would have been silly.

Diane Spivey At one point Christina Foyle joined Women in Publishing.[17] We were all completely nonplussed and not quite sure what to do. I don't think she ever came to a meeting, but she had obviously decided that she wanted to join this group. She wasn't really who we were intending to lure along, but we thought it was interesting that she felt she should join.

How did people join? You just came along to meetings and paid on the door if you weren't a member. You didn't have to be referred; there was no restricted membership.

So how would Christina Foyle have joined? I think she would just have sent a cheque to the membership secretary. I really don't know what triggered it; I'd love to know whether she felt she was giving it her patronage, or whether she felt she had something to gain from receiving its newsletter and getting a feel for what was going on with younger women in publishing. *Are you sure it was her?* Yes. I don't recall us having any doubt that it was definitely her who had paid her subscription and joined.

Ian Norrie If you want to compare and contrast, Christina Foyle and Una Dillon would make an interesting essay. They were quite unlike each other. Una was an academic with a degree from London University. She had been doing social work, then decided to open a bookshop, which she eventually managed for the university. It became Dillon's University Bookshop, London's best academic bookshop. A dedicated woman, who treated her staff extremely well. She was short of money a lot of the time, so she couldn't pay them all that well, but she had a devoted staff which eventually became larger than Foyle's in number.

17 Women in Publishing was set up in 1979 by a number of women in the book business, to promote the status of women throughout the industry.

Michael Seviour Gillian Shears, who became the manager of Dillon's African department, was the twelfth member of the original Dillon's staff. She told me that when she got married, Miss Dillon called her in and said, 'In this company, when men have got married we have always thought that we should give them a rise. I don't see why we shouldn't do it for girls when they get married, too. I think that's fair.'

Ian Norrie Una also had three remarkable sisters: Carmen was an art director who worked on Laurence Olivier's Shakespeare films, among others;[18] Tessa was a physicist, and the other sister became a nun. They were all spinsters, and devout Roman Catholics. Una was a charming person, ethereal. She knew what was happening in her bookshop and cared about it, too.

John Prime The first thing always that would strike you about Miss Dillon was her charm. She would listen to what you said, and she would ask you questions about it. She was very interested in people. Perhaps that's why she was so successful as a bookseller.

Michael Seviour Una Dillon is a great loss to this oral history because she could have told you all about her first little shop in Store Street. I remember reps telling me that when they went in they would say, 'Miss Dillon, the accounts manager has been on to me about your payments.' She would go to her box file: 'Well, let me pay this invoice, then we'll see if we can pay some more next time.' She did run on a bit of a shoe-string.

Ian Kiek I first met Miss Dillon when she ran this little bookshop in Store Street for the academics, in the heart of London University. My friend Peter Hebdon[19] said to me one day, 'Ian, it's no good you having a love affair with Miss Dillon; we want her money.' So I said to her, 'Look, Miss Dillon, Michael Joseph's wants some of your money.' 'Well, dear,' she replied, 'there's the cheque book. Write it out and I'll sign it.' It couldn't have been much, perhaps £50. She signed it and I took it back. 'There you are, Peter. From Miss Dillon, with her love.'

Michael Seviour And she would have been able to tell you how many times the university came to her and tried to persuade her to open a university bookshop.
Did they do that more than once? Yes. She really was very concerned about taking it on. She said, 'What do I know? I've run a tiddly-piddly shop and that's fun, but we're talking about big expansion.'

18 Henry V (1945); Hamlet (1948); Richard III (1955). Her other films include *Accident* (1967) and *The Go-Between (1971)*, both directed by Joseph Losey.
19 Sales director of Michael Joseph.

Ian Norrie Una Dillon came onto the committee of the London branch of the Booksellers Association at my instigation and remained on a lot longer than I did.

Michael Seviour She was very much into book trade affairs. She would say, 'Do you belong to the London branch? Do you go to conference? Do you get involved in committees? Are you actively looking to do things for the trade?' So, from having taken nil interest, I began to get involved in it.

Why do you think it was important to her? I suppose she could see that there was going to be a big expansion in university bookselling. And, even then, there were mutterings about the Net Book Agreement. She was keen for smaller booksellers to get involved, but they often don't have the time. If they take a day off, who mans the shop? Whereas if you're in a larger shop you can do these things. I think she felt that people who had the time ought to give some of it.

John Prime Una Dillon took her own decisions on what to stock and what not to stock. She wouldn't have controlled everything, but she gave her staff the main lines she wanted them to follow, and she didn't have to contend with an accountant breathing down her neck and saying, 'Books in Middle English just sell one a year so you have to get rid of them.' She would have felt that, if the shop was going to be respectable, certain sections would have to stock particular books.

Michael Seviour One day Ann Higgins, who was Dillon's paperback buyer, came to me and said that Penguin had subscribed a book of cartoons by Siné,[20] and there was a particular cartoon which she found distressing and blasphemous. She said, 'I won't order it and I won't sell it. I don't mind what happens; I will resign if necessary.' I said, 'Before you do anything excitable, I will go and talk to Miss Dillon.' I took the offending item with me and told her what Ann had said. 'I feel that she has a very good point,' I told her. 'I don't believe it's intentional, but I do think that it would be objectionable to a lot of people.' Miss Dillon got on the phone to Allen Lane and told him about it, and there was a big stink at Penguin's. The story is that Allen Lane got hold of Bill Rapley, who I think had been the first Penguin rep. They got a van, went to the Penguin warehouse, got all the copies of this book, put them in the van, took them to Allen Lane's farm and burnt them all.[21]

Tony Pocock Una Dillon was friendly with the leading publishers. She

20 *Massacre*, Penguin, 1966.
21 There are various published accounts of Allen Lane destroying this stock. The most recent is in *Penguin Special* by Jeremy Lewis (Viking, 2005).

demanded the terms[22] she wanted, and got them, because publishers trusted her. Most booksellers used to say, 'We must have forty per cent.' 'Why?' one asked. 'We want forty per cent. Don't you argue.' But Una used to back up her requests with good arguments related to the cost of the building and the cost of stocking the books we wanted her to stock; the cost of the staff that we wanted her to have and the training she ought to give them. These things cost money. We all trusted her enough to know that she wouldn't make these requests unless she really needed to. It wasn't a try-on, as in so many cases it was. Other booksellers probably wouldn't have thought it through, or bothered to enlarge their stock. Dillon's certainly stocked the right books from OUP, and they kept them re-stocked, so you knew that their stock control was good.

You mentioned trust, and I'm interested in how important that was in the relationship between a salesperson and a bookseller. Trust is very important indeed, I think. If a bookseller says, 'I must have this discount in order to do that', one has to trust that they have produced the right argument so far as their shop is concerned.

How would a bookseller abuse that trust? By saying they would improve their sales by ten per cent or twenty per cent or whatever, when really there was no hope of their doing it.

What would have been wrong with booksellers using the discount just to improve their profit margins? It would depend how they used their extra profit – to build a better shop, for example. Most of them would just stuff it in their pockets and run.

Why shouldn't they? Because we wanted a better book trade. It's better now,[23] but in the 1950s and '60s it was amateurish. There were very few good stock-holding bookshops.[24]

Trevor Moore One of my favourite calls in Chelsea was John Sandoe, which was, and remains, a unique shop. When you looked into the window you saw nothing but books, face out, looking at you. When you entered the shop there were books everywhere: shelves to your right, shelves in front of you, shelves to your left. An archway led into another room, with books to the left of that archway, and an old-fashioned display unit with books piled up on the top of it. Through the archway, books. And a rickety, winding staircase with books displayed at various points, leading to another room which was full of paperbacks shelved behind other paperbacks, so there would be six or seven Iris Murdochs facing out and another collection of Iris

22 The price at which the publisher supplied stock to the bookseller, calculated as a percentage of the cover price.
23 This was recorded in 1999.
24 Those qualifying for membership of the Charter Group. This scheme, set up by the BA in 1964 on the initiative of Tony Pocock, Ian Chapman and other publishers, sought to raise standards in the trade by offering higher discounts to booksellers who met specific criteria which included levels of stock and staff training.

Murdochs behind. But Felicité Gwynne could instantly find any book she was asked to supply, and to watch her dealing with customers was an education.

Sandoe's at that time was the sort of shop where most of the people who went in were known to John and Felicité. They knew exactly who wanted to be sold books, and who just wanted to browse. I remember Felicité approaching one customer who was looking around: she slid a book towards her and said, 'I think this might be rather your cup.' That was how Felicité sold books. And I will never forget the occasion when a woman came in and asked for a book that Sandoe's clearly didn't have in stock, and Felicité just looked at her and said, 'Why are you asking? Are you the author's mother?' The poor woman almost collapsed, because of course she *was* the author's mother. Don't ask me how Felicité knew that.

After I had been the Cape rep for a while and had got to know Felicité, she would recommend authors I hadn't read, such as Elizabeth Bowen and William Trevor. One day she asked me if I ever wanted to go to the theatre. I said, 'Well, yes, I like the theatre, but . . .' 'I'm rather looking for someone to take me to the theatre sometimes,' she said. So I went off to the Royal Court now and again. She also introduced me to the opera. Although I'm a besotted music lover, opera has never quite been 'my cup'. But I was introduced to Mozart's *Don Giovanni*, and I remember Felicité talking about what Mozart meant to her. She had wonderful enthusiasm for the things that she loved, and it was a delight to be treated in this way by a woman who had so much to impart. And she paid me the compliment – which wasn't a particularly well-paid compliment, as it turned out – of saying: 'We're looking for someone to help us out on Saturdays. I think you might fit the bill. Would you like to give it a try?' So for a period of about eighteen months I worked on alternate Saturdays with Felicité. It was fun. But bloody hard work.

What did she look like when you knew her? She was in her mid-fifties, I suppose. Iron-grey hair done up in a bun, with strands that fell down either side. Glasses – which she used to peer over – half-way down her nose. She was rather beautiful, I thought. She looked not unlike her older sister, who was Elizabeth David. And she lived in Elizabeth David's house, a few streets away from John Sandoe's bookshop.

What kind of clothes would she have worn? She certainly didn't dress in the height of fashion, but she had a natural elegance about her. She had worked as a civil servant during the war, in the War Office or the Foreign Office, something of that sort. She never really talked about it, but I suspect that, like many other women of her generation, she had had an unfortunate love affair with someone who was killed in the war. I don't recall her ever explaining how she came to be working with John, or how she got into bookselling. But she was one of the most natural-born booksellers I've ever come across.

Ian Kiek I used to call on Felicité Gwynne when I was working for Michael Joseph. She was the sister of Elizabeth David, and she said to me one day, 'Ian, would your firm like to publish Elizabeth's next book?' I said, 'Would they not! Lovaduck! Would they not!' So I went back and told Charles Pick and Peter Hebdon.[25] They said, 'Who is this Elizabeth David?' I said, 'Just publish her.'

At that time, Victor Morrison was Michael Joseph's production director.

Victor Morrison We published Elizabeth David's *French Provincial Cooking* early in the 1960s. I think it was one of the best books we ever did in my time. It was very much an Elizabeth David production in that she didn't really approve of big, colourful cookery books, and she told me that she wanted to do the jacket. All the reps thought it was going to be nice and glossy, with delicious food – everybody was expecting something fairly conventional. Elizabeth was in France with a photographer friend from *Vogue* and they took a photograph of a half-drunk glass of wine, a plate and a half-finished piece of paté on toast. That summed up her view of food as something you enjoy. She used to say, 'It's much better to take photographs of the crumbs after the meal.' So we made this jacket and presented it at the sales conference. The reps said, 'You don't expect us to sell a cookery book with a jacket like that, do you? It will never sell.'

Ian Kiek *French Provincial Cooking* was a terrific seller from the word go. I remember going into Harrods one afternoon, and their buyer said, 'Well, do you think 350 would be about right, Ian?' I said, 'That's about right.' So that was the first order: 350 copies from Harrods. When I went back and saw Charles Pick – and this was typical Charles – he said, 'What, only 350?' Then quietly smiled. Of course, it was a terrific success. Bit early to say 'classic', but anyone who knows anything about cooking thinks of Elizabeth David as being more than a writer of cookery books.

SB Which other women stick in your mind from the trade?
John Prime Gerti Kvergic of The Economist Bookshop. I'm not quite sure how you pronounce her name, but 'charming' would not be the word you would use about Gerti. She was abrupt and sharp, dogmatic and impatient, and not only did she not suffer fools gladly, but they weren't all fools whom she thought to be fools. She could be quite a difficult person at a branch meeting,[26] where she would stand up and make an unwarranted attack, it seemed to me, at some proposal.

But I have to say that she was an extremely successful bookseller. Economists visited that bookshop from all over the world; it was a model

25 Directors of Michael Joseph.
26 Of the Booksellers Association.

of an academic shop. I'm not sure if she had a financial interest in it. She left a considerable amount of money to various causes in the trade when she died, including to this estate:[27] there is a stone set into the wall of the main building here, saying that she made a bequest. And she had no trouble with the bookshop staff while she was in charge. Unfortunately, as soon as she retired, trouble started – and it started in the form of a strike, which was very unusual in the book trade. So there must have been a different side to her from the one I saw.

Cherry Lewis The Economist Bookshop was then in Clement's Inn Passage. It was owned fifty per cent by *The Economist* magazine and fifty per cent by the London School of Economics, where my father was a professor.[28] I suspect the reason I got a job there was because he said something to Lionel Robbins,[29] who was on the board of governors of the bookshop, and Robbins said something to Mrs Kvergic. This was most uncharacteristic of my father, who was not a string-puller at all. But Mrs Kvergic wasn't averse to grand people. Every time Lionel Robbins came into the bookshop it was like a royal visit: the whole place stood to attention and she came out from the back *without* a cigarette hanging from her mouth.

The shop wasn't grand or smart – it was really quite small, quite dark, quite narrow – but we spent a lot of time keeping it tidy. Sometimes Mrs K. said, would we dust it? Would we re-arrange the window? During a busy term-time day, especially at the beginning of term, the books would all get pushed back on the shelves hugger-mugger, so Iris[30] and I had to straighten them. You would gently pull them all forward so they were hanging slightly over the shelf, then, with the ball of the palm of your hand, you would push them in very carefully so they all lined up with the edge of the bookshelf. Mrs K. taught me how to do that and I've done it all my life – it's a marvellous way of getting books to look straight.

I think we called her Mrs K. because we were nervous about pronouncing 'Kvergic'. She had come to England from Vienna before the war – although I certainly didn't know that at the time[31] – and spoke English very well, but with a thick accent. She had been married, but wasn't married at the time when I met her. I'd say she was then about forty-five or fifty, and obviously very cultivated. Quite a tall lady, and she always wore shoes with a good two inches of heel. Dark hair, and dark eyes that were made very big by thick glasses. She wore orangey-red lipstick and nice clothes – brown or grey and rather classy. I think she was very handsome. She certainly had a presence: I can see her now, standing at the top of the step in the back office

27 The housing association at Kings Langley run by the Book Trade Benevolent Society.
28 James Meade (b. 1907).
29 Lionel (Lord) Robbins, professor at LSE from 1929 to 1961.
30 Iris Leech, a fellow assistant.
31 Cherry Lewis drew this detail from the obituary of Gerti Kvergic in *The Times* (14 November 1986).

with a cigarette hanging out of her mouth and some papers in her hand. She had very long, slim fingers, and always wore a ring with a great big semi-precious stone. And she had no inhibitions. If she didn't like the way you'd done something, she'd tell you.

When the travellers called – in those days publishers' reps came round with enormous, bulging briefcases – they would whisper, 'Is Mrs K. in?' They preferred to see Tony Comerford, who was second in command. There was one rep who would always say, 'I am allergic to Mrs Kvergic.' He always said it, and we always laughed. The travellers treated her as a joke. Mrs Kvergic *wasn't* a joke; she was a very remarkable woman. She was running a successful business – The Economist Bookshop made a profit for the LSE and *The Economist* – and she was extremely intelligent and knowledgeable about her subject. And she was generous. I got two pay rises when I worked there, and I wasn't even there for a whole year.

When I went back to work at the shop in the winter holidays of 1956, there was a man in the packing department – Mr Hansluck – who was a Hungarian refugee. He was around forty or fifty years old and couldn't speak English, so all one could do was to take in a pile of books and hope he would wrap them. Somehow he'd come to Mrs K.'s notice and she'd taken him on. She was a caring person, although she didn't show it very much. And of course, she was running a business; she wasn't there to be motherly. *What would you say her attitude was to books?* Primarily it was commercial; she had to decide if a book was going to make money. But, as The Economist Bookshop was a university bookshop, she had to balance that assessment against whether the book would be needed by someone in the university: 'I know none of the students will be able to buy it, but I'd better have a copy in stock and risk having to write off £10 at the end of the year if it's not sold.'

Efric Wotherspoon I make it my business to know what my customers like to read. Some people like detective stories, others like love stories . . . And we have a lot of yachtsmen coming in for maps of the Mull of Kintyre and charts of the west coast up to Oban and beyond.

Willie Kay I remember going to Campbeltown to meet Mrs Wotherspoon. I went with Graham Fraser, the Collins traveller. He said, 'We'll have dinner with her tonight at the local hotel. You'll find she is a great character.' And so she was. She was really a very good bookseller, and charming company. She's a real Gael, you know; she speaks the language, which I don't. And for a small town like Campbeltown she sells a fair number of books. At least, she did in those days.

Efric Wotherspoon My grandfather, Duncan Martin, was the captain of the *Medea*.[32] There's a photo of him here: a tall, broad-shouldered man with a brown moustache and beard. I was only two years old when he died in 1915 – his name is on the war memorial. He thought a bookshop would be nice to have for his daughters – my mother, Katherine, and a sister called Janet. You'll see 'K. & J. Martin' still above the door. In the 19th century it was a grocer's shop. My grandfather took it over about 1901.

When did you first think you would work in the shop? I never thought I would work in the shop. But I never thought I'd be widowed, either. My husband was killed near the end of the war, in April 1945, and I came back from Glasgow in 1950.

You had three children when you came back. Was the shop profitable enough to support you? Yes, it was at that time. I had my war widow's pension. And the shop used to be busy – the whole street was busier than it is today. We opened at nine – on a dark morning we lit the gas at nine o'clock – and stayed open until ten o'clock at night. I send for a taxi at five o'clock now to go home. It's been exceptionally quiet for the last year or so. But every shop in the place feels that. It gets very busy at Christmas and in the summer, but in between there are long periods when nobody comes into the shop. You look up the main street and there's nobody to be seen there at all. Quite a lot of shops in Campbeltown are closing down. I'm very surprised by that. If it wasn't that I have money of my own, I would find it very quiet. This wee while I've had to use my own money sometimes to pay the girls' wages.

Tommy Joy I was very much a feminist – always have been. I always thought that women could do the job. I used to say, 'The trouble is, they do it better.' Having said that, it's always seemed to me you couldn't possibly beat a woman as your second in command, but – and this is something you probably won't agree with – I did sometimes wonder how far they were the best at the top, because they can act emotionally, which would cloud their judgement. If they didn't like a person, they wouldn't promote that person. To like or not like a person is nothing to do with it. The question is: 'Can they do the job?'

Did you know any women who were managers? Several. But mostly because they owned their own bookshops. I've got an article here about Elsie Bertram – I think I may have talked to you about her. She started in a little chicken house at the bottom of the garden, and she's just sold the business for £30 million.[33] But she was brilliant. She had the necessary things that are required: she was charming, she was tough, she looked good, and she had very many qualities. And you need all that. She did what most men failed to do.

---

32 A steam yacht built in 1904 for local landowner Macalister Hall, used (as *Corneille*) by the French navy in the First World War; now in San Diego.
33 One obituary (*Independent*, 8 November 2003) gives this as c. £50 million.

What? She built up this huge wholesale business in books. And even Maxwell couldn't do that.

Ian Norrie Wholesaling virtually died when Simpkin Marshall crashed in 1955. It started again in 1968, when Elsie and Kip[34] set up Bertrams because the Odhams and Hamlyn warehouses had been flooded and there was a dreadful backlog of orders not being fulfilled. All the time I was dealing with them their service never faltered. We ordered Hamlyn books from them to start with, then began to use them for day-to-day orders, because publishers would refuse to supply books below a particular value, which meant you had to wait until you had a sufficient quantity to make up the order. Bertrams made the same stipulation, but they supplied books from a range of publishers, so it was not the slightest bit difficult to make up a £50 order. Bertrams were a blessing to any bookseller who used them.

Elsie Bertram When I had my seventieth birthday,[35] one of the people from Pan gave a speech about me and said it was only their inefficiency that allowed me to reach the position I had in the book world. Before Bertrams began, a bookseller would give an order to a publisher and it would be three or four weeks before they received their books. We said 'Next day delivery.'

I was at a Booksellers Association conference in Harrogate, when Ainslie Thin was chairman.[36] They gave an award for people who had made a difference, and Ainslie announced that Bertrams had won it. He said, 'I think Elsie's there, if she'd like to come up', and gave me a great big banner with a picture of Concorde on it. When I sat down again there were three men sitting behind, and I heard one of them say, 'They only cover Norfolk.' And I took great delight in saying, 'I'm sorry, gentlemen, but if you speak to Ainslie he will tell you a very different story.'

I'm interested in why there were so few other wholesalers at that time. I suppose nobody had thought about doing it. For us to do anything like that was a big surprise to people, because no one had ever done it.

What about Simpkin Marshall? Oh, gosh, yes. They went bust. I was at a booksellers' conference at Coventry where we divided into groups for discussions, then the chairmen of each group took it in turns to go on the platform to report. When it was my turn, Robert Maxwell stood up. There had been a ruction in the morning, when Barry Hudson from Birmingham stood up and said, 'How some people have the effrontery to speak like they have done, I really don't know. He was useless as a bookseller, he was useless with a newspaper . . .' He had slammed Robert Maxwell into the

---

34 Elsie Bertram's elder son, Christopher.
35 Elsie Bertram was born in 1912.
36 Ainslie Thin of Thin's Bookshop, Edinburgh, President of the Booksellers Association from 1976 to 1977.

back of beyond, and the whole conference was in an uproar because nobody had ever dared talk like that.

But it did me a load of good, because the thing that had worried me until then was that I had on a rather tight-fitting dress and I was wondering how I'd get up that big step onto the platform without going head over heels. However, when friend Maxwell stood up, I had him to cope with instead. He said, 'You are doing a very good job in a very limited way.' I said, 'Thank you.' 'But,' he said, 'what we want is a single copy order house.[37] What we want is something like Simpkin Marshall.' I said, 'Can you envisage the size of a wholesaler which could carry a copy of every book published? How could anyone afford to have a warehouse that size on the chance of getting an order for a very rare book?' He said, 'Touché' and sat down.[38] Gerry Davies[39] was in the row behind. I can see him now: he leaned out from his row because Maxwell was in front of him, and he was clapping like this, very quietly. Everybody was thrilled that I answered like that.

If you were aware of Simpkin Marshall and what had happened to it, didn't that concern you? No, because it was more or less history to us. We knew what they'd done and we could see it just wasn't feasible.

What had they done? Stocked as many titles as ever they could. And you just could not do that. Our policy was to stock the bestsellers and only buy the books that we knew we could sell, so the turnover would be quick. Because it had to be quick. You had to be clever in not carrying too much stock.

What was the advantage for booksellers in coming to you? If they sent the order to the publisher, it took three weeks. If they sent it to us, they could have it the following day. Did I tell you about the bookseller in Cornwall who rang us up at about four o'clock in the afternoon? A German customer wanted a dictionary but was flying home at midday the next day. The bookseller said to me, 'It's ridiculous to expect you to get this to us.' I said, 'Well, we'll have a bash.' And at quarter to nine the next morning there was a knock on his door and Securicor arrived with that dictionary. I think that is outstandingly our finest hour. And bless him, he told the story in *The Bookseller*. Those letters in *The Bookseller* – we always used to love to find one. I still carry on getting *The Bookseller*. I'd feel lost without it.

How do you think people see you in the book trade? With affection, I hope. I wouldn't like them to think I am a dragon.

Did you get fierce? Only if people didn't pay their account. There were several times when I went and took their stock away. You have to be a bit brave to do that. On one occasion I went in the van with one of the boys. This sounds horrible, doesn't it? The grapevine had warned, 'Things are imminent', and we'd had one cheque bounce a day or two before that, which was quite an

37 A wholesaler that would supply single copies to booksellers.
38 Simpkin Marshall had gone into liquidation in 1955 under Maxwell's ownership.
39 Secretary to the Booksellers Association.

indication. I said, 'It's not too far away; we'll go down and get the stock.' I didn't mind – jack of all trades.

When I went into the shop, the bookseller wasn't there. They said, 'He'll be along soon.' The van was parked in the marketplace opposite; it had 'Bertram Books' on the side. I said, 'Quick! If he comes along and sees our van, he'll disappear again.' We shot across, pulled the signs off the van and put them inside. When he arrived, I said, 'You know what I've come for.' We had the calculator, and the boy who had driven the van took the books off the shelves, and we rattled them up until we got to the amount that the bookseller owed us, then put them all in the van. I said, 'What about the cheque that bounced?' He rang his solicitor and his solicitor told him to go and see the bank. So I went with him. Then I asked him, 'Is there a pub nearby, where I can get this boy a drink?' The bookseller said, 'I would buy him one, but I haven't got a penny on me.' I thought, no, I really don't think you have. He said, 'There's a café here.' 'Well,' I said, 'you'd better come as well.' And what did he have? Sausage and chips, then apple tart and custard. I got home about twenty to six and said to Kip, 'I've got every penny.' He said, 'Jolly good. Good day's work.' End of story.

Was there anything difficult for you in going and doing that? What, going to get the money? It was matter of pride. If I'd not been able to get it, I would have thought I'd let the side down.

7 | BRING BACK THE ORDERS, HARRY

Trevor Moore The major difference between the trade then and the trade now is the sheer number of reps on the road.

Ian Norrie At the side of William Jackson Books on Southampton Row was a passage leading to the export department. This was where publishers' travellers came to subscribe their books to my boss, Frederick Joiner. Once through the door, they were presented with a counter, where they waited until Joiner deigned to leave the bench where he would be working with the packers. He was violently rude to many of them, but they all began by being polite. 'Good morning, Mr Joiner, how are you?' 'What the fuck have you got this morning, then? Hold on, hold on.' He would take their books back to his bench and look up his records to see which overseas customers had ordered this or that book, and how many copies, then come back and tell the reps what he wanted. If he was in a very bad mood, he would throw the books back: 'I'll have four of that bleeder, and four of that bleeder. Don't want that effing thing.' One day, one of the reps threw a book back at him. That was good; he respected that man more.

Joiner was an ignorant and ill-educated person, who had gone to work at about the age of twelve with a book exporter in the City, and realised that he could run a business in this strange way. And every Monday, Tuesday and Wednesday morning, these chaps came in and stood at the trade counter, waiting to be blasphemed at by him. I became friends with many of them.

Charles Pick, from Michael Joseph's, was an ebullient gentleman and a thorough salesman, who had previously been with Victor Gollancz. It was no use Charles practising his salesmanship on Joiner, because Joiner didn't know what he was talking about. But books to be sold in William Jackson's shop, rather than through the export department, were bought by myself and John Ford. There, Charles' salesmanship did come into it. Michael Joseph brought out a series called Mermaids, which were laminated books, halfway between paperbacks and hardbacks. Charles was telling John Ford and myself about these one day, and we were looking at him sceptically because we knew about his salesmanship. Then he suddenly said, 'And they're washable', and John Ford and I collapsed. So did Charles, to do him justice – he saw the funny side, too.

Charles Pick I had said to Victor Gollancz, 'I'd like to go out and sell books.' He said, 'What do you know about selling?' I said, 'I can learn.' 'No,' he said, and dismissed it. I persevered. 'Look, there are all these new lending libraries starting, and we don't cover them at all. I'm sure if I went out I could get new business.' In the end he gave way. And I made a success of it – I brought in a lot of completely new business just by finding these places.

I went into a shop in Hampstead – it was a second-hand bookshop, but they had some new books in the window – and said, 'I know you don't stock a lot of new books, but there's a marvellous one coming next month called *Burmese Days*, by George Orwell.' And it turned out that I was talking to George Orwell, under his real name, Blair. He was the chief man in this little bookshop and I was trying to sell him his own book. He wasn't the star that he is now, this was long before *Animal Farm* or *1984*. He talked about how difficult it was to sell books, even second-hand ones. We had quite a discussion on that subject, because he was wondering how his book was going to sell.

Ian Norrie Tommy Lamb was from Macdonald's. He used to repeat his patter and you could tell it was the patter he'd been given in the office. 'Our people think' was Tommy's great thing. He was an amiable person but got a bit belligerent if you didn't buy, so we used to say 'OK, Mr Lamb, we'll take three. But if they don't sell, will you take them back?' 'Our people don't take things back.' Then there was my lifelong friend, Ronald Whiting, who at that time was the junior rep for Allen & Unwin – tall and thin, with sleeked-back hair. He already had a wife and two children, and was earning about £6 a week, plus ten shillings expenses.

Ronald Whiting The expenses were expected to cover bus and tube fares, and to enable me to buy myself a cup of tea. If I wished to take a buyer out for a cup of coffee, that came out of the ten bob, too. Over a period of three years, my salary increased by fifty per cent. Or you could put it another way and say that by 1950, after doing a highly successful job for three years, I was being paid nine quid a week.
Ian Norrie And were your expenses increased? No. My expenses remained constant at ten shillings a week. I don't think there was anybody else repping in London at less than £1,000 a year, and most reps were probably earning considerably more. The Hutchinson representatives, for instance, got £20 a week in expenses. That was beer money – if you wanted to sell books round the stations you had to buy beer for the bookstall managers.

Ian Norrie Gilbert Hart was the Chatto & Windus rep. A handsome, youngish man who had apparently never read a book in his life, working for this strong literary list, bringing Virginia Woolf, William Faulkner, Aldous Huxley and, later on, Iris Murdoch. He was the one who chucked the book back at Joiner. He was a most friendly man, and totally unliterary – God knows why Chatto & Windus decided to employ Gilbert Hart as a rep.

Ron Cortie was a different cup of tea; a working-class boy from south London with a great love of literature and music, who had left school at fourteen. His mother ran a corner shop that sold books and magazines. Ron loved reading. When he was in France with the army in 1940, he was laughed at by his fellow soldiers because he had a copy of *War and Peace*. It was there that he became friends with Gilbert Hart. When they came back after the war, Gilbert said, 'I'll introduce you to Chatto & Windus', and Ron got a job there, where he eventually succeeded Gilbert on the export territory. Ron used a special brand of blarney that sensitive people who have to be salesmen adopt to get through their day. 'Hello, Mr Joiner. How are you today, Mr Joiner? I've got this book here. Chatto & Windus are absolutely mad about this. It's the wonderful new Huxley, Mr Joiner. Have you read Huxley, Mr Joiner?' Joiner hadn't read anything.

One of Ron's great friends was Reg Dignum who represented Victor Gollancz. Reg also had this extra skin – he was even more deeply into music than Ron, and he cared for left-wing causes. You heard him coming up the passage: 'Hello, Mr Joiner. How are you doing this morning? I've got some wonderful books here. Oh, goodness me, isn't it cold outside?' Reg would never stop talking, and you wondered how he ever took anything in – yet now and again there was evidence he had heard something you said. He was a very good rep for Gollancz. He didn't really believe all the rubbish he was talking on their behalf. And you didn't really listen.

Then there was Alfred Boon, from the Boon side of the Mills & Boon family, and upper crust among reps. He had been a rep for Methuen since 1905, and earned £5 a week before the First World War, which was good. I can see Alfred Boon now, standing at the counter with Joiner raging, and Boon being absolutely impervious. Some of these older reps had a certain dignity about them. Roger Hutchinson of Heinemann had a Guards tie and a pipe; he would walk up to the counter very smartly dressed. He had to subscribe a book by Aneurin Bevan which he certainly didn't agree with, because he was a dyed-in-the-wool Tory, but he did his job. The moment Joiner saw Aneurin Bevan, the language was dreadful. I remember Roger taking his pipe out of his mouth and saying, 'There's a lot of good sense in this book, Mr Joiner.' Roger was succeeded by David Harrison, who was much younger and very left wing, and we became friends. He just thought calling on Joiner was like going to Madame Tussaud's.

Frank Stoakley At my desk in the science department of Heffer's I had two seats: one for travellers and one for professors. One day Lord Rothschild came in and said, 'Can I just interrupt before you carry on talking to this rep? I'm trying to trace a Professor Partington. Do you know him?' I said, 'I know him very well. He is Professor of Chemistry, and he's sitting right beside me.' Partington laughed his head off at that. He said to Lord Rothschild, 'What made you think I was a rep?' I said, 'I can answer that.' He was carrying a little case and wearing a trilby. Lots of my travellers looked exactly like that.

Ian Norrie Even the ones who couldn't afford it wore suits, ties, waistcoats, raincoats. Freddy London of Oxford University Press was quite a dandy. He had to show us all these terribly abstruse books that OUP published every week. Most of them we didn't buy, because it was a very academic list. But Freddy London was a gent. As was John Muggleston of Evans Brothers, who carried popular books, including *The White Rabbit* and *The Dam Busters*. He wore a bowler. Griff of Duckworth had a bowler and a black coat.

Elizabeth McWatters Pat Seyd used to travel for Harrap; he carried all their language books. He had a bowler hat, black umbrella and briefcase. I remember him coming in once when he had just been stopped by the police, and they assumed he was an undertaker. I never knew anybody who wore bowler hats other than undertakers.

Ian Norrie Harry Smith came every Monday morning from Hutchinson, which had acquired about forty different lists by then.[1] He was a great big chap who looked like a horse, but he was basically an office boy who was sent out round the exporters two mornings a week: 'Bring back the orders, Harry.' The only orders he got from Joiner were the ones that our customers had sent in – there was no speculative buying. If the South African libraries wanted forty-eight copies of the new Dennis Wheatley, and nobody else wanted one, Harry got an order for forty-eight. 'But Mr Joiner, they're not going to like this. I was told to get a hundred for this.' Poor old Harry would moan and carry on.

Ian Miller In my early days at Hudson's there was a rep called Lynch-Blosse who carried Allen & Unwin. He used to learn the advance information sheet and recite it parrot-wise – he would sit down with you and say, 'Now, I want to show you this, Mr Miller. This is a book about so-and-so.' I would have the same advance information sheet and I would say, 'This is the book about . . .' You could actually do a duet with him.

Trevor Moore In 1959, when I was a clerk in Hutchinson's sales department, the London reps came into the office at lunchtime to write out orders and collect samples. They were important people as far as I was concerned. Harry Smith carried the Arrow paperback list, as did 'Baron' Wilder. Harry Smith was large and ebullient. 'Awright, mate? How you going? I've had a

---

1 Early 1950s.

great morning down up Waterloo station. Boy, oh boy!' The Baron was never to be seen without his bowler hat. He was quite an elderly gent in rep terms, but well preserved, with a military moustache, and relatively posh in the way that he spoke.

Then there was Roy Beddingham, who carried Hutchinson and all its associated imprints. He always wore a trilby. He read the *Daily Mail* and had predictable views on everything. He used to look at the books he was carrying and ask – over and over again – 'When are we going to have something for Mr Everyman?' I remember the sales director, Geoffrey Howard, walking into the office one day, saying, 'My dear Roy, when are you going to realise that Mr Everyman, Mr *bloody* Everyman, does not buy books?' Which seemed to answer Roy Beddingham's frequent complaint better than any other response could have done.

Willie Kay Hutchinson had two travellers who used to call on John Menzies Wholesale in Glasgow. Mr Campbell[2] always called them 'Wheeler and Wolsey'. 'They're like two funny actors,' he said, 'because they know nothing about their business. They should be selling shoes.' I'm trying to remember the names. Was it Beddingham and Butler? No, Butler was Heinemann. I think the name of one was Beddingham – I can't remember the name of the other. But they always travelled together: one carried Hutchinson's fiction list and the other would maybe have the non-fiction or the children's books. They came about every three months to Glasgow and we had to see them, because Hutchinson was a big publisher at the time. *What did you learn from Mr Campbell about how to deal with publishers?* 'Listen carefully to what they say. Let them talk as long as they like. But believe half of what they tell you and you'll go quite far.'

Trevor Moore Vic Jones[3] used to say, 'People tell me I'm a great salesman, but I never sell anybody anything. I just talk to them about what books I've got, and they buy 'em from me.' I remember Peter Giddy[4] laughing: 'Oh, come on, Vic. The old flannel all over again.' 'No, Peter. I'm telling you it's a winner. Just believe me.' And Vic was always right. Well, generally right. *Where would you see him?* On that particular occasion we were having coffee round the corner from Hatchards, in Jermyn Street. Otherwise, we'd meet in Foyle's, or in the Book Café, which was a haven for reps' gossip. A grotty little greasy spoon, really, opposite the side entrance of Foyle's in Manette Street. Vic did central London for Bodley Head and various other lists, and he always had stories about Max Reinhardt.[5] I used to love listening to him – he would repeat conversations pretty much verbatim, from the sound of it.

2 Head buyer.
3 Publisher's representative.
4 When general manager of Hatchards.
5 Owner and managing director of the Bodley Head.

How did he talk about Max Reinhardt? With enormous affection and admiration, and a certain amount of frustration as well – I think he could be maddening, but was clearly a great publisher. He obviously understood what Vic's job was about and got the same pleasure out of Harrods taking 500 copies as Vic got from telling him about it. As a young man, Vic had worked for the old Simpkin's in Paternoster Row when deliveries were still made by horse and cart. One particular packer grew roses at home. If he saw a horse he would watch it closely, then, at the right moment, he would race out with his little shovel to collect the fresh manure, bring it back, wrap it up in a parcel with all the expertise of a Simpkin Marshall packer, and take it home on the train for his roses in Purley.

Diana Murray Murray's always had a lot of representatives who went round the country, promoting and selling our books to bookshops and to schools. Twice a year they had representatives' luncheons or suppers. Often we would have those in our house, or in our garden if it was fine. My husband[6] felt strongly that people who had been living in hotels and eating out all the time, would enjoy having a meeting in a family house. But he always insisted that it ended at half past nine, because he thought it was important they should all be able to go to the local pub on their own to talk about Murray's and to air any complaints about us among themselves.

Julian Fall John Murray was a very patrician house indeed. In fact, the John Murray rep who came to us[7] didn't even bring a catalogue – he just used to have a piece of paper in his pocket, and he would say, 'We're doing a new book by So-and-so. You'll want ten, won't you?' And he was always right. That was Gerald Harris. He had been in the trade all his life; he knew exactly how many we could sell of anything. But he didn't exercise any salesmanship at all; it was a social occasion more than anything else.

Trevor Moore I learnt a lot from John Oliver, who covered Oxford and Cambridge for Hamish Hamilton. 'Trevor, the first rule of the publisher's representative' – he would look over the top of his glasses as he said this – 'the first rule of the publisher's representative is: never pass a public convenience.' Which wasn't bad advice. Nowadays you're hard put to find one.

Bert Taylor worked as a rep for Simpkin Marshall, Odhams Press and Evans Brothers.

Bert Taylor We had a wonderful organisation called the Book Publishers' Representatives Association. Every rep who was on the road, if he had any sense, joined that organisation. Every year we had a pre-Christmas dinner at

6 John (Jock) Murray, publisher.
7 Goulden & Curry, Tunbridge Wells.

the Connaught Rooms in London. Sometimes there were 350 reps there, and you would invite friends and wives. They used to pipe the pudding in and set it alight with brandy. I don't think they've got more than thirty members today.

Ian Norrie I used to go with Ron Cortie and Gilbert Hart of Chatto to the Book Publishers' Representatives Association guest night at the Connaught Rooms in Great Queen Street. A big, boozy meal with a guest speaker – famous author, bookseller or publisher – where the reps could bring their chosen bookseller customers. Even Allen & Unwin allowed their reps to take customers there. We all had a great evening and the firms paid the bill. What Chatto & Windus spent was nobody's business, because Ron and Gilbert used to bring people from outside the trade – once it was the manager of the Salisbury pub in St Martin's Lane, and once, for some reason, the manager of Strand Electric.[8] The wine flowed, Gilbert bought bottles of whisky and gin, and Chatto expenses paid for it all. The Chatto table was always put near the door because we made so much noise; every now and again, officials came and said, 'Shut up, you chaps.' They were all relaxed that evening; they weren't like they were at the trade counter. They could be themselves.

Bert Taylor I remember going to lunch with the buyer and the directors of Kendal Milne & Co.[9] of Manchester. There were lots of reps there, all of whom were working in Manchester at that time. One of the directors said to me, 'I can't understand how you reps are all so friendly with one another. In the stationery trade, they detest one another.' 'Well,' I said, 'the answer to that, Sir, is that we're all selling different wares. Every publisher has different books, whereas the stationer is selling the same type of stuff.' And that is the answer, really: every publisher's books are different.
What would you say made a good rep in those days? First of all, honesty and integrity. Don't over-sell. Because if you do, two journeys ahead those books are still going to be on the shelves, and the bookseller will say, 'You sold me those. What are you going to do about it?' In those days, if you were on friendly terms with the booksellers, you'd say, 'Don't worry about it. We'll take them back,' and give them a credit note. And they would get to trust you. Lots of booksellers I called on would say, 'You know where the stock is, Mr Taylor. I'll leave you to check it', and base their order on that.

Trevor Moore W.H. Smith had a huge London head office at Strand House in Holborn. But the export side of their operation was run from an equally enormous building called Bridge House, on the other side of Lambeth

8 Lighting specialists.
9 Department store.

Bridge. There was a café nearby, which was one of the meeting points of the London reps, where one was struck by the enormous number of middle-aged men who congregated there and were clearly part of a somewhat exclusive club. I wasn't made particularly welcome by many of those gentlemen at the time, young as I was. Quite a few knew each other in the context of Masonry – a lot of the London reps at that time were Masons.

I first became aware of this through Bob Waite, who was the senior Heinemann rep when I was working for Jonathan Cape. Bob was not a Mason, and took great pleasure in filling me in on the reps who were, and how closely connected Masonry was with the business. I was at the afore-mentioned café with Norman Askew, the Cape sales director, who clearly wasn't a member of whatever club they were members of, when Bob Waite enlightened me: 'You realise they're all Masons, and Norman isn't, and I'm not.' His attitude towards them was one of resigned amusement.

Did you ever feel when you were meeting buyers that you might have been able to do better business if you'd also been a Mason? I often wonder, looking back. But no, at the time I don't think I ever did. Almost without exception, those men had worked their way up, doing long stints in various parts of 'the country', as it used to be called – you were either a country rep or you were a town rep, and you served your apprenticeship as a country rep. I'd been fast-tracked into this position, and clearly some of them didn't approve.

How old were you? Twenty-seven or twenty-eight. So I was old enough – but not in their terms – to take over the West End.

Ian Kiek I found outlets for Michael Joseph and Hamish Hamilton which they hadn't dealt with before. The mayor of Lewes was in charge of W.H. Smith Waterloo main. If you went to him with a book like a Monica Dickens or an H.E. Bates, he would say, 'We'll start with 500.' That is a lot of copies. If you had a book that he knew would sell, even when he understood that you weren't going to go to the boozer with him – which I made it very clear I wasn't – it made not the slightest difference. And I called at Victoria main. If you went in there with a C.S. Forester they almost put the red carpet down for you.

Would you have phoned before you went? No.

Did anybody refuse to see you? What, with a list like Michael Joseph's? They didn't dare, because books were scarce.[10] If I tell you I never sold a book in my life, it's true. I didn't have to.

Trevor Moore Sure, you were employed by Michael Joseph, by Heine-mann, by Hutchinson, by Jonathan Cape. But you were a rep. Other people at Michael Joseph or Jonathan Cape may have been your colleagues, but

10 Ian Kiek became a rep for Michael Joseph Ltd in 1949.

they didn't belong to this world that you were now fortunate enough to be a member of.

Why did you want to be a rep? It may seem an odd thing to say, but it was glamorous. There was something about the freedom, about the idea that you were there on your own, making your own decisions. Reps do see themselves as different from people who work in the office. It's to do with the fact that, up to a point – though not as much as we used to be – we are our own bosses: we decide where we're going to go, how we're going to organise our areas, and who we call on. Also, when reps get together we speak a common language. We've had experiences that people in the office haven't had, and we know a world that they don't know.

How do you think the reps were regarded by other departments within the publishing company? With a certain amount of resentment by some, for their imagined life of no responsibilities, complete freedom, driving off in a company car. So there could be jealousy from some of the people who perhaps worked in the trade departments.

At the more senior level, there was a rather patronising view of reps, I think. I remember feeling outraged at one particular company, when a rather drunk director draped an arm round my shoulders and told me, 'I love reps. There's nothing I enjoy more than the company of reps. Salt of the bloody earth.' I just thought, 'You patronising bastard.' And I would say that view was fairly common among the senior echelons of the publishing world. One thinks of publishing – in the 1960s, when I first got to know it – as an occupation for gentlemen. And the kind of gentlemen that one encountered certainly looked down on us from a very different world.

Michael Geare When Paul Hamlyn was starting Spring Books just after the war and hadn't much money, he owned one silk shirt, which he washed and ironed daily. He went one summer's day to see the buyer at W.H. Smith, Mr Foat. It was a blindingly hot day. Smith's was still in Portugal Street. Foat was wearing a dark suit with a waistcoat, and Paul came in wearing his beautiful silk shirt with a nice tie. Foat looked at him, then went and peered out of the window. Paul Hamlyn said, 'Are you looking for something, Mr Foat?' And Mr Foat of Smith's – looking at Hamlyn in this elegant shirt and tie and no jacket – said, 'I was wondering where you had left your barrow.' Very soon Paul Hamlyn got Spring Books going and built it up. He sold out around 1963, after only about ten years, to the Mirror Group for well over two million pounds, which today would be worth twelve or fifteen million. *How do you know the story about W.H. Smith?* Practically anybody of my generation had heard it. It was a story that went round W.H. Smith after Paul had become so quickly successful.

Willie Kay I'll tell you a story about Paul Hamlyn. He first came to my notice when I was an assistant at John Menzies Wholesale in Glasgow. He had made an appointment with Mr Campbell, who had never heard of him. 'I'll see him anyway,' he said. 'I wonder what he wants?' Paul Hamlyn had a book – the first one he ever published – that he wanted to show Mr Campbell. He came in the morning, straight off the train. He wouldn't have slept much, and his appointment was 'Whenever you want to come in, first thing.' He got to the office around half eight. It was a very cold winter's morning, and he was chittering with the cold – he was just wearing a light raincoat. He came in, introduced himself to Mr Campbell, and I was introduced to him. Mr Campbell says, 'Come here, son. You and I are taking a walk.' Paul Hamlyn looked at him. Mr Campbell took him down to a tailor at the foot of the street and bought him a coat. He said, 'You'll be dying of cold if you come to Scotland in the winter dressed like that.' That was Mr Campbell. And what was the name of the book? *I Know Where I'm Going*. It was a little paperback, a poorly-produced thing by today's standards. I think it sold at two shillings, and we sold 50,000 copies.

That was Paul Hamlyn. I dealt with him on and on, when he became really big, and he never referred to his early days at all. But I know he kept in touch with Mr Campbell as long as he was alive. I think he's a millionaire now, isn't he?

8 | BELOW THE SALT

Michael Geare They had been doing it on the Continent for years, but paperback publishing was a new concept to the British. Allen Lane wrote to the publishers asking to buy rights,[1] and some of them said, 'Yes, you can try it' and some said, 'Absolutely not. It simply means that the public will leave our hardback copies alone and wait until you bring them out in a cheap form.' Allen Lane had considerable difficulty setting up Penguin until he went to Woolworth's, where there was a sympathetic buyer, and the first great hump was over. But I think the old hardback trade would have strangled this child at birth if they could.

Tommy Joy It is argued that the book trade didn't support Allen Lane when he came round with the first Penguins.[2] That isn't true. We only bought what we could sell, and we had no market in those days for paperbacks. Harrods' clientele were too toffee-nosed to buy paperbacks. They wouldn't dream of buying a sixpenny book. They wanted a proper book – with covers.

Willie Kay When they were sold in the book trade in Glasgow, the man who came to sell them was Allen Lane himself, who started the company and became the famous chairman. I think it was ten numbers they published, and the books were sixpence each. Mr Campbell said, 'I'll order fifty copies of each.' 'Oh, Mr Campbell, do you not think that's very small? After all, you're a wholesaler, a big wholesaler.' 'Well,' he said, 'let's start with seventy-two copies of each.' So that was John Menzies' first order. Of course, John Menzies had no retail shops of its own at the time. Eventually we were ordering hundreds and hundreds of books from Penguin, but that's what we ordered at first. And Mr Campbell said to him, 'Tell me, how many copies did Woolworth order?' 'Twenty-four copies.' 'And what did John Smith's order?' 'Six.' Mr Campbell said, 'My order's quite good then.'

---

1 A licence to publish a title in another form. In this case, to publish hardback titles in paperback.
2 Allen Lane published the first six Penguins in 1935.

Ronald Eames joined Allen & Unwin in 1932 as an office boy and later became design manager.

Ronald Eames Stanley Unwin fought the idea of paperbacks to the end. 'It won't last five minutes. The French tried to do this. It won't last. It won't last.'

Charles Pick I shall never forget the first day they appeared on all the W.H. Smith's bookstalls, one Monday morning. The telegrams rolled in from their branches to their head office off the Strand: 'Can we have some more of those books? They've sold out on sight.' I was there, trying to sell Michael Joseph books to Smith's, so I could hear what was happening.

It made such an impact, this sudden arrival of the first ten Penguins. But the traditional bookshops said, 'We're not going to sell sixpenny books, they'll kill us.' When I went to Australia – as late as 1959 – the big bookshops there said, 'What's happening in England with these paperbacks? People are asking for them all the time, but we keep them in the back of the shop in the dark. We don't want to sell books at that price.' But in England everything had moved forward by then, and all the publishers wanted to get on the bandwagon and sell rights to Penguin.

Elizabeth Burchfield A friend of mine who worked on *The Bookseller* once said, 'There are only two publishers whose books are bought on their imprint; one is Oxford University Press and the other is Mills & Boon.' Which is one of the great truths of life. But in the 1940s and '50s, Penguins were bought because they were Penguins, and people referred to paperbacks as Penguins whoever they were published by. More and more paperback firms were coming into the market, but people would talk about 'Penguins' in the way that we talk about doing the 'Hoovering'.

Michael Geare There was an advertisement in one of the newspapers – *The Telegraph*, I think: 'Wanted: sales director for paperback publisher.' I thought, well, I do know about paper.[3] It was Four Square Books, then owned by Godfrey Phillips, which was a tobacco company – they had De Reszke cigarettes, Abdullah cigarettes, and a number of pipe tobaccos, of which Four Square was one. They – imbecilically – had started a paperback book company because they had a small printing firm which produced items for the tobacco business. It was totally unsuited to the printing of paperback books, and no single Four Square paperback book was ever printed in a Godfrey Phillips printing works. The whole thing was a total misconception.

The Godfrey Phillips works were in Commercial Street, in the heart of the East End. A vast, irregular-shaped building. The road at the rear was the

---

3 Michael Geare had previously worked for C.H. Johnson, which manufactured Foudrinier wires for the paper industry. He joined Four Square in the late 1950s.

scene of one of Jack the Ripper's more horrible murders, and the front faced Spitalfields market. I was interviewed by the two directors of Four Square Books, one a man called Gordon Landsborough. He was a gifted, clever, likeable chap and really knew everything about book publishing. On one occasion when we were a book short in the list, he took five days off and wrote the book himself – *Return Via Benghazi* or something. It wasn't half a bad paperback either.

The problem was that the really good authors had already gone. Penguin, of course, had nabbed a lot of them. Pan had resumed operations in about 1949; they were getting paperbacks printed in France and Switzerland, I think – they ran a launch and brought them rapidly across the Channel. Corgi had arrived. Four Square was a little late in the day. We got Dorothy Sayers, but only her short stories – and Brits don't really care for short stories. We got John Masters' autobiography – *Bugles and a Tiger* – but we didn't get any of his novels. We did some good books: we had Salinger's *For Esmé – With Love and Squalor*. But there again, somebody else had *The Catcher in the Rye*. After two or three years we absorbed another small paperback publishing house called Ace. They were a bit more downmarket than Four Square, but also more arty – they were doing translations from Continental authors. Ace were a bit riskier than we were.

Our bestseller by a mile was *The Second Sex* by Simone de Beauvoir. We put a rather sexy jacket on, and people bought it by the tens of thousands. I'm sure they never read it. Paperback publishers then were making the jackets imply that the book was saucier than it really was. There was a feeling that you were bringing in a new group of readers: part of the philosophy of the time was that if you could catch people with a really tatty Western – people who otherwise never read anything except the *Daily Mirror* – you might get them to say, 'Gosh, I've read a book and I enjoyed it. Very convenient. I'll go through this experience again.' And in that way you got people hooked.

How successful was that? Speaking for the trade as a whole, very successful. On tube trains people had tended to be reading the morning or the evening paper, then increasingly one began to see them reading a book. And – unless it was a borrowed library book – it tended to be a paperback. They *were* convenient. I think that the range of people who read books increased considerably. But I can't claim that Four Square was ever a leader in the paperback business in the '50s. The trailblazers were Penguin and Pan, undoubtedly.

How did you consider paperback publishing? As marketing. In hardback publishing you actually met real authors, and if you managed to get a good relationship between the publisher and the author, you would be playing some part in the shaping of a book. But in paperback publishing you never saw an author; you simply reprinted books that you had read and thought, 'If I can get the rights, this will sell.' I was snobbishly aware that, although I was in publishing, I wasn't in proper publishing. So when I was able to escape to what I thought was proper publishing, I was glad to do so.

Michael Geare became sales director of J.M. Dent in 1962.

Karl Lawrence When I went to the Bahamas in 1953 to run the Island Bookshop, the company refused to carry paperbacks. The only other shop that sold books there was Mosley's Bookstore, and they just stocked a small selection of paperbacks from a wholesaler in Miami. Paperbacks were so cheap that there wasn't enough profit. But I insisted that the Island Bookshop wasn't a proper bookshop if it didn't sell Penguin books. And later we began to sell Fontana.

Why were you so keen to stock Penguins? Probably because I wanted to read them myself. Penguins were very big in England. Pocket Books had a similar role in America, but after I got to the Bahamas the competition to Pocket Books from imprints like Ace, Ballantine and Gold Medal took off.

When we bought Mosley's Bookstore, our company was the only bookselling outfit in the Bahamas. We then put paperbacks all over the place – in the airport, into supermarkets, grocery stores and gift shops – and started to make huge sales. We also had a shop on Paradise Beach, where we sold paperbacks and magazines. The bestsellers there were American thrillers – the biggest sellers of all were the Fawcett Gold Medal series with lurid covers – and we also sold Westerns and science fiction from Ballantine.

Mark Barty-King founded Transworld's Bantam Press imprint in 1984.

Mark Barty-King Ian Ballantine had played a part in the start-up of innumerable paperback publishers, including Bantam and, of course, Ballantine itself. He had also been involved in helping Penguin get started in the USA. He was a man with clear ideas about paperback publishing. At the annual Bantam sales conference at Quay Biscayne in early December, we all had the habit of going for a morning swim. But you would only go in if you had seen Ian Ballantine in the water first, because Ian knew the habits of jelly fish and could tell when it was safe to go swimming and when it was not. That made him a man worth knowing.

Karl Lawrence Back in the mid-1950s Penguin covers were still in plain colours – green, blue or orange – with the title in a white panel across the middle. American paperbacks all had graphic covers; I still have one that was given to me by New American Library which has a woman in a slinky evening dress smoking a cigarette. It looks terrific – good American '50s art. The covers sold the books, and they didn't necessarily relate to the content.

Somehow the English paperback looked inferior – although that's probably unfair, because they were publishing for their market. Collins' White Circle crime novels had elegant covers in black, white and green. Pan covers had good art, but it was cerebral art, not popular art, and they weren't laminated, whereas American paperbacks always had shiny covers. Lurid is a word that was used a great deal about paperbacks; they were seen to be questionable literature, on a par with things like *Inside Detective* magazine – not quite proper, a bit below the salt. Penguin never had that sort of literature; it was always quality content.

Peter Mayer became chief executive of the Penguin Group in 1978.

Peter Mayer The growth of Pan Books had much to do with the toffee-nosedness of Penguin with respect to books written about the war – on the theory that if you publish books about the war that happen to be thrilling, you must be publishing war-loving books. Penguin had turned down a whole slew of books – such as *The Dam Busters* – and Pan, which was built by the marvellous Ralph Vernon-Hunt, had enormous success with them.

Willie Kay The chairman of Pan Books was a well read man called Aubrey Forshaw, and he had a highly efficient sales director, Ralph Vernon-Hunt. They seemed to pick up the right authors for paperbacks, but they were always careful to consult with the wholesaler: 'Did you sell that book well in bound copy?[4] Do you think it will sell in paperback?'

The biggest order I ever gave from Menzies was 12,000 copies of Paul Brickhill's first book, *The Great Escape*. I learnt later that I had ordered several thousand more than W.H. Smith. I had read it in bound copy – I think that was published by Faber. Aubrey Forshaw came to Edinburgh one day, and said, 'We're thinking of publishing Brickhill.' I said, 'I'm sure that will sell well.' It was fairly soon after the war and people were still reading war stories, particularly about people who had escaped from German hands. I didn't just order it from the top of my head – I had to think how many customers would buy from us, and how many copies they would buy. I knew this was a book that all the Menzies wholesale branches in the country could sell, not just the ones in Edinburgh and Glasgow. I built up the order by thinking, Inverness will want three or four hundred, and phoning the manager up to check: 'Do you think you could sell 400?' 'Well, if you recommend it. I've certainly heard of the book.' I built up an order of nearly 8,000 copies like that, then I thought, 'It's sure to sell.' And it did. I got a complimentary copy bound in leather of *The Great Escape* from Pan Books, with a note from the chairman. That tells you something about the buying power of the wholesaler.

Robert Clow Every year Pan used to give a party in Glasgow for the booksellers. In the early days Ralph Vernon-Hunt[5] used to come; in latter

4 Hardback.
5 Sales director of Pan Books.

days it was perhaps organised by the representative. Publishers were incredibly generous. I suspect this went on throughout the United Kingdom; they probably went on a royal progress over a fortnight, touring the dining resorts and all the bookshops in a clockwise direction.

But the party to end all parties was given by New English Library in the Brighton Pavilion, when they invited every bookseller and publisher attending the BA conference,[6] so there were about 600 guests. Rumour had it that they'd been given £50,000 to establish New English Library in Britain. The dinner started with champagne in copious quantities, then we all sat down to tables. On ours we had Ralph Vernon-Hunt and his missus, Eliza and Christopher Shaw,[7] my wife Katrina and me, Ross Higgins[8] and a few others. We dined on quail's eggs and asparagus, and Ralph Vernon-Hunt had fourteen plates of asparagus. I was appalled, but he obviously enjoyed them. When we ran out of champagne, Eliza Shaw said to the waiter, 'Could we have more champagne?' and he said, 'I'm sorry, Madam. We've been told not to serve any more.' And Ross drew him aside and said, 'Excuse me, but that is our hostess, so I think perhaps you ought to find some more.' And more champagne came. This went on until the cabaret started at midnight.

During the course of the evening all the publishers were totting up how much it would have cost New English Library to host this party. It must have been one of the most extravagant ones ever given – and in the splendour of the Brighton Pavilion. An extraordinary chapter in the history of the book trade. Both Ross and I marvelled at it, and rather regretted that it was never repeated.

How did it affect your trade dealings with New English Library? Not at all. Some of their titles were good and we could sell them, others we couldn't. You just stocked what you could sell. But certainly everybody knew about New English Library.

New English Library resulted from the acquisition and renaming of Four Square by Times Mirror of Los Angeles. It was a sister company to New American Library.

Karl Lawrence I went to work for André Deutsch in 1966, a year after returning to England. As soon as I joined the company he began to take me out to lunch with the managing directors of the paperback publishers. The firm's biggest income came from selling paperback rights, and André was an absolute genius at it – he had recognised immediately that the sale of paperback rights was going to bring him in a lot of money. So we would lunch with Clarence Paget and Ralph Vernon-Hunt from Pan, with Tony Godwin and Oliver Caldecott of Penguin, and with John Watson and John Boothe from Mayflower. We would come back from lunch at two thirty,

6 This conference was in 1965.
7 Chief executive of New English Library.
8 A director of John Smith's, Glasgow.

and by four o'clock I would have a summary letter of what we decided we had agreed, with the prices we had agreed. André would vet it – and always change it in some way – and it would be in the post that night, clinching the deal – because we always wrote the letters as if they had been done deals.

We sold Clarence Paget at Pan the paperback rights to a book called *Games People Play*, which we had bought from Barney Rosset at Grove Press in New York. It was an incredible bestseller in America, and we sold it, I think, for a £4,000 advance, which was quite big in those days for paperback rights. I'd written a letter to Clarence, confirming it, then – after we'd posted the letter – André called Barney, and Barney said, no way. He wasn't going to sell it to anybody except Penguin, and it had to have the cover that had been on the hardback in America. So we went through the trauma of André having to call Clarence and tell him he had to call it off, and me speaking to Oliver Caldecott at Penguin to work out what was going to be paid for it. I think we doubled the advance and agreed the book jacket illustration – and that Penguin would pay for the artwork – and that they would give us money towards the promotion of the hardback, which was not supposed to be done, but André did that a lot. I think other people did it as well.

Going vertical: hardbacks and paperbacks from the same publishing house

Charles Clark became an editor at Penguin in 1960.

Charles Clark One day[9] when Allen Lane was passing along Vigo Street he noticed that the former office of John Lane The Bodley Head was for sale. He thought it would be a good idea to buy the lease and go back to where he had started out in hardback publishing.[10] That was the impulse – but it was Tony Godwin[11] who worked out the rationale, which was that Penguin ought to do 'vertical publishing',[12] instead of having to pay the big hardback publishers high advances for paperback rights. He asked me to write an article about it, which appeared in the *Times Literary Supplement*. Arthur Crook, the editor, called it *Paperback to Front*, and it caused quite a fuss. Martin Secker of Secker & Warburg spent a lot of time trying to find out who had written this article – at that time the articles were all anonymous in the *TLS*. I don't think Arthur ever told him.

Vertical publishing is now commonplace in the trade, but at that time, Penguin was the only mass paperback publisher to set up its own hardback imprint, which was called Allen Lane, The Penguin Press. The aim was to be able to buy a hard-soft package from an American publisher, for example,

9 In 1965.
10 Allen Lane had begun his publishing career at John Lane The Bodley Head in 1919.
11 At that time, chief editor at Penguin.
12 Publishing in both hardback and paperback.

and to enlarge our ability to commission leading authors by saying, 'Now we can publish you in hardback first, then we will publish you in paperback', which pleased a lot of them.

One of The Penguin Press's most famous publications was *Akenfield* by Ronald Blythe. Tony Godwin commissioned it, and I saw it through after he left – it was one in a series of books that we commissioned jointly with André Schiffren[13] for both UK and US publication. André provided us with books by the American oral historian, Studs Terkel. I got to know Studs quite well. He used to come over to Britain – he was very good about promoting the books – and he came to my house and we sat chatting for some time. It was one of his early books we were publishing – it may have been *Hard Times*.

What were your impressions of him? Amiably crumpled, with an anecdotal manner. The kind of person you could see doing what he did for a living. You felt that you were part of a life-long interviewing process, because he was always asking you questions that you had to think about before answering.

Carole Blake Michael Joseph was a hardback company and sold its paper-back rights to paperback publishers, but it was slow to realise how important rights were becoming. I arrived in 1970 to run the rights department and contracts department, and discovered that they didn't have a list of titles, they didn't have a list of current contracts, they didn't have a list of contracts that had reverted, they didn't have a list of rights that they had licensed. But they *did* – thank God – have a really good file copy room, and they had cabinets of contracts. I said 'I can't sell any rights until I know what you own.'

It took me about six months, down in the damp basement, making handwritten lists which I typed out. I then sent out pages and pages with lists of authors and titles, to the paperback imprints in London, saying, 'Michael Joseph owns the paperback rights to these books, which have either never been licensed, or the paperback edition has gone out of print, so the rights have reverted to us.'[14] And suddenly offers started coming in. The very first was from Patrick Janson-Smith at Corgi, who rang up and said, 'One of my favourite books is on that list. I can't believe it's not in paperback. I'll give you £1,000 for it.' I thought, 'Gosh, this is good.'

Do you remember what the book was? I wish to God I did, because it was such a ground-breaking moment. One of the last deals I did there was over lunch with someone else from Corgi, which had been publishing the *Hornblower* books on a licence from Michael Joseph for ever. The licences ran for a limited period which was usually eight years. I spotted that a number of

13 Studs Terkel's longstanding publisher and editor, then at Random House in America.
14 Rights revert automatically when a book has been out of print for a period usually specified in the contract.

them had run out – nobody had noticed – and suggested to Corgi that they might negotiate new contracts. In other words, pay us another advance. We got at least six figures, I think, over that lunch.

Mark Barty-King Before going to Granada, I asked the opinion of various people in the trade as to what it would mean to move there. Everybody said, 'Don't go near it. It's absolute murder.' But I thought it was a great opportunity to learn the paperback business. Granada had the hardback imprints of Rupert Hart-Davis and MacGibbon & Kee – which it brought together as Hart-Davis MacGibbon – and its paperback imprints were Panther, Mayflower and Paladin, which had just started and was run by Sonny Mehta.

Paladin was a great success. Its first list – which included *The Female Eunuch*[15] – was an extraordinary collection of beautifully designed books. And it has to be said that Granada had a classic right at the start, which was *Papillon*[16] – the greatest escape story ever. You'll find it everywhere, to this day, and I don't think the cover's ever been changed. Steve Abis, who was a brilliant art director, came up with the image of a rusty padlock with a butterfly on it. Very simple. That must be one of the greatest covers ever.

It was obvious by then that paperbacks would soon be ruling the roost. Some hardback publishers were already printing their own paperbacks, and the deals they were doing began to make a huge difference to the amount of money paid to big authors, because it included the full paperback royalty. That was a sea change in the way that paperback royalty percentages were calculated and earned. At Granada, we had the freedom to buy a book for both hardback and paperback, so we could offer the author a much better deal. Granada was ready to be built, and a key building block was our ability to offer a vertical deal relatively easily – that kind of contract made it much easier to bring authors in.

The first thing I did at Granada was to go on a trip to America and buy volume rights in one of the early Ludlum novels, *The Rhinemann Exchange*. That was the first vertical deal we did with him. Granada had published Robert Ludlum before, but he hadn't been getting the full benefit of the paperback royalty, which he now was. *The Scarlatti Inheritance*, which was Ludlum's first book, had been a big success here; Ludlum was an author that one very much wanted to retain. That also happened with Muhammad Ali – his autobiography back in 1974 was bought on a vertical deal by Granada. *Where did the idea of vertical publishing come from in Granada?* I think it came from Jim Reynolds.[17] It came from agents, too – especially American agents.

15 Germaine Greer's *The Female Eunuch* was published in hardback by MacGibbon & Kee in 1970 and in paperback by Paladin in 1971.
16 By Henri Charrière. Published by Granada in 1970 under the Hart-Davis MacGibbon imprint.
17 Managing director of Granada's hardback division.

The way that the author benefited from the paperback earnings made it attractive for the agent as well.

How did more traditional publishers regard it? I don't think they liked it. But it was so popular with authors and agents that once it began most publishers had to follow pretty quickly.

Carole Blake Michael Joseph was vulnerable to losing an author when they sold paperback rights, because if that paperback house made a great success with the book, they might want to woo the author away and publish the author in hardback themselves. And if – as is usually the case now – the same publisher publishes a book in hard and soft, they will pay the author full royalties on both. But when an author stayed with Michael Joseph, Michael Joseph got half the paperback royalties. That's something that agents aren't keen on, because it means that the author only gets half as well.

Michael Joseph had published Dick Francis for years before he was successful. It was the bricks-in-the-wall approach: each book did just a little bit better, and Michael Joseph didn't pull out. These days authors are expected to become very successful very quickly – with rare exceptions, publishers don't hang on in there and build an author. Dick had several books that just sold a few hundred more than the last one, and by the time one of them really broke out there was a lovely backlist that Michael Joseph and his paperback publisher could benefit from. He was always published in paperback by Pan. And when Pan became part of a hard-soft group and tried to woo him away, he said no, he would never leave Michael Joseph. And when Michael Joseph eventually had a paperback house of their own – which was Sphere – Dick Francis didn't want them to publish him in paperback there. He was extraordinarily loyal to both Michael Joseph and Pan, and still is.

Victor Morrison became managing director of Michael Joseph in 1975.

Victor Morrison When Edmund Fisher left Michael Joseph's to go and run Sphere Books, I succeeded him as managing director. Sphere was the paperback arm of Thomson, and Edmund had a vision of Thomson as a big force in publishing – like HarperCollins today – and he wanted to use the books from the Thomson hardback firms to build up a large paperback arm. In some ways this was a good idea, but it didn't always take into account the wishes of authors. In theory, the hardback publisher could sell the paperback rights to any paperback publisher they wanted. But as authors began to get more powerful, they sometimes said, 'I want to go to this paperback company and not that one.'

The classic instance was Dick Francis. Edmund felt that Dick was a particular friend of his, and I think Dick was very fond of him. But Dick was even fonder of his paperback company, Pan Books. Edmund was always trying to persuade me, as the hardback publisher of Dick Francis, to say to Dick, 'You are going to get the same money – maybe even more money – and you're going to go to Sphere Books.' Dick Francis said, 'No, I'm not.' So every now and again there would be rather fierce exchanges between Edmund and myself. Edmund would say, 'You are legally entitled to say he must move to Sphere.' I'd say, 'I know very well. But Dick Francis is immensely valuable to us. He's a very good friend of the entire company and I'm not going to do anything which will offend him.' As far as I know he is still at Pan Books. I'm sure that Penguin, who now have Sphere, would love Dick to go to Penguin. But I don't think he ever will.

Carole Blake There isn't as much loyalty from authors to publishers these days because – I think – there's very little loyalty from publishers to authors. Publishing is so much more finance oriented; shareholders want profits today, not tomorrow. Publishers will probably say that the advent of the power of agents contributes to that; that agents just want to move an author around to get a bigger advance. In some cases that is true; in most cases, it isn't. Most of us want a steady upward progression for our authors – hopefully, a career. All things being equal, I would caution my authors to stay in one place, because you seldom get the same sales if you have books with different publishers.

Peter Mayer When I arrived at Penguin[18] it was vaunted – correctly – for having the greatest backlist in British publishing. But there were waves already moving towards the beach – big, nasty waves – to do with hardback publishers retrieving the titles they had licensed. Happily, part of Penguin's backlist was on full-term licences, which had been agreed with maybe five or six companies in the days when there had been no other paperback publisher around, so those rights could not be reverted from Penguin. But the other books – probably the majority – were on term licences.

Diane Spivey Methuen was mainly a hardback publisher, but we were trying to get a paperback list off the ground – Magnum Paperbacks was launched about 1981 – so we were beginning to think about holding back paperback rights for ourselves. Every time a licence renewal came up with Penguin, for example – when they had come to the end of their eight-year licence to publish a title in paperback – we were having to look very care-fully at whether we wanted to re-license it or take it back. You could use that to push the terms up with the paperback houses, which meant there was a certain amount of haggling. Sometimes you could actually end up in an auction, where you had two companies bidding against each other. Other times it would be a tiny deal worth a couple of thousand pounds for

18 In 1978, as chief executive.

somebody's biography. That could be fun – it was the most sociable type of rights selling, because you were selling to your friends down the road rather than to a foreign publisher or a newspaper.

But on one occasion I had done a deal with Penguin for the paperback rights to a book – I think it was a first novel[19] by the playwright John Arden – which was then shortlisted for the Booker Prize. I went along to an editorial meeting the day after the shortlist had been announced, and was told to take it off the table with Penguin, because Methuen now wanted to publish it themselves. Which I was furious about, because it made me feel I was letting my contact down. It was the first time I really had to fight my corner in a boardroom – and I lost. I remember getting up and saying in a very choked manner, 'In that case I'd better go and let them know as soon as possible' and storming out of the room, when all I really wanted to do was burst into tears. I had to ring up Penguin and say that we weren't going through with this deal. I think I was dealing with Geraldine Cooke at Penguin, and remember her being very good about it. Obviously quite annoyed, but understanding what was beginning to happen – publishers wanting to take books back for themselves.

Peter Mayer There were three ways to deal with that problem: start to originate more books in hardcover yourself and later publish those books in paperback; do more paperback originals; or buy companies with long back-lists. During my nearly twenty years at Penguin I think we bought about nineteen companies. Penguin's purchase of the Thomson companies[20] marked a great change in British publishing. There were four: Michael Joseph, Hamish Hamilton, a packager called Rainbird, and Sphere, a paperback publishing company. I think they were losing money and Thomson wanted to bail out. We explained to Pearson that a lot of books on these companies' backlists were already by Penguin authors, but I'm sure we didn't say publicly that it was because we were scared of losing them. In other words, if the Thomson companies had been sold to anybody else, we would have been at risk of more depredations from our backlist. We were already losing books to lots of publishers. So then, in addition to Allen Lane originating hardcover titles we had Michael Joseph and Hamish Hamilton – three companies publishing new books. It was a difficult integration, but we started to originate books right away. That was another move to produce a backlist for the future.

Trevor Moore A lot of booksellers never understood what rights reversions were, and I did find myself explaining to young buyers in Waterstone's or Ottakar's that once upon a time Jonathan Cape didn't have a paperback list.

19 *Silence Among the Weapons*, Methuen, 1982.
20 In 1985.

They published the works of Len Deighton, for example, and sold the paperback rights to the highest bidder – or the one the publisher regarded as the most suitable – so a deal would be done with Pan or Arrow or Corgi. In the fullness of time the contract would expire and the rights would revert to the original hardback publisher. That's when – to use another phrase which became familiar – the rights would be 'clawed back', and the books would be published by whichever paperback house the original hardback publisher was now in partnership with.

In the world of general publishing, if you didn't have a partnership with a paperback house, or if you didn't own a paperback house – or the paperback house didn't own you – you were in trouble, because you couldn't compete in the same way.

Mark Barty-King I left Granada in March 1984. There were various other jobs that I looked at. I was offered a job by New American Library – I don't know how seriously. But there had been whisperings that Transworld would start a hardback operation and that I would be the person who would run it. They had to get into hardback publishing, and get in pretty quickly, in order to attract the authors they wanted. Transworld – which was mainly Corgi – wasn't one of the paperback imprints that you included in the top three. I had no reason to believe that I particularly wanted to go there. But a lot of people said I should, including Ed Victor,[21] and others I really trusted.

I met Paul Scherer,[22] and we spent the best part of four months doing projections on what sort of a list it would be, and the figures. Paul and I had endless meetings at the Stafford Hotel – it was all kept under wraps and was very exciting. We prepared the ground: how we would set up a general hardback list that fitted what Transworld was doing on the paperback side, starting with six titles which we would put out in the market using our own sales force, which we would have to train – bringing in Trevor Moore to give us some authority in that area – and take it from there.

'We didn't mix with the paperback boys'

Trevor Moore I joined Transworld in 1985 as the first Bantam Press hardback sales manager. It was unheard of to have the same representative selling both a hardback list and a paperback list. This is precisely what Transworld proposed to do in setting up the Bantam Press imprint, they were going to sell it through their existing paperback sales force. To the best of my knowledge, in big publishing terms this was unique at that time.

The majority of Transworld reps regarded themselves as Corgi reps;

21 Publisher and literary agent.
22 Managing director and chief executive of Transworld Publishers Ltd (1982–95).

their job was to sell paperbacks, and they were very good at it. Now they had to sell hardbacks. I remember one rep who operated in the north west, whose biggest account was Manchester Airport, and to her, everything was geared up to what Manchester Airport bookstall could sell or not. After one of the sales meetings she took me to one side and said, 'Trev, do you mind if I say something to you? We all like you, we think you're a very nice bloke. But stop going on about what's inside the books all the time. Just tell me how many to sell and I'll go out and bloody sell 'em.' I think that summed up the attitude that a few of them had. But some of them took to it as a duck to water – another rep in the north west loved the idea of getting more immersed in the world of books, as he saw it.

I hadn't realised that there might be a distinction between reps who sell paperbacks and reps who sold hardbacks. Historically there has always been such a distinction. That's the way everybody in the trade saw it: there were paperback reps and hardback reps, and in a large house such as Collins there was a definite feeling of one sales force being superior to the other. And boy, did the paperback reps resent it. The Penguin reps were the exceptions; it was almost as if they were hardback reps – they were a bit special because they were Penguin. But generally speaking, the Corgi rep, the Panther rep and the Arrow rep were looked down on by many of the hardback fraternity. There was always this division. I can't say why, but it was just part of the world that I grew up in. Books after all had always been hardbacks, hadn't they? Until Allen Lane came along with this paperback revolution.

Sylvia May joined William Collins as a trainee rep in 1977.

Sylvia May At Collins we didn't mix with the paperback boys – we didn't know them. Different breed of people. Yet the men I later got to know on the paperback side were all public school boys, so the division is probably historical. There was always the joke among the hardback sales force: 'We've done all the hard work, we've got the books into the stores. All they have to do is recoup on the cheaper edition. Anybody can sell paperbacks.' Which, of course, is nonsense.

Stan Remington Odhams ran its own paperback imprint, Beacon Books, in the late 1950s. It only lasted about eighteen months, but in that period four of our books were chosen by *Smith's Trade News* as Paperback of the Month – one of them was *Leopard in My Lap* by Michaela Denis – so we got it all right on the product range. But we made a bad mistake. We thought that our existing rep force, which was used to selling our illustrated and reference books into bookshops, could do adequate sales on paperbacks. We totally overlooked the fact that paperbacks needed an entirely different approach and had a much wider market than through traditional bookshops. Within two years we decided to wind it up, and that was the end of paperbacks for Odhams.

Michael Geare Four Square were amongst the first to advertise paperback books on the telly, in about 1958. I think it was on Tyne Tees Television, and we managed to saturate bookshops in Newcastle and Gateshead with Four Square books because we were going to be on television. Otherwise we used the staple advertising of paperback publishers in those days: you tried to get your own spinners into the shops, or you tried to get book-shelves ring-fenced for your books. Many a bookshop got itself shop-fitted by three or four paperback publishers, who said, 'We'll pay for these expensive and beautiful wooden fitments, but we expect that bit to be for Four Square and that bit for Corgi.'

We did a great many showcards,[23] which was easy for us, because they were much in use in the tobacco trade and Godfrey Phillips had a work area where they produced them. And you always hoped you could get some mug of a bookshop to say, 'We'll take 500 of your paperbacks every month, and leave it to you to supply them.'

Did it happen? No. By the sophisticated standards of today, it was terribly amateur, but it was less amateur than the advertising done by the hardback publishers. I don't think hardback publishers were really putting out posters and placards, I don't think they were attempting to buy shelf space to be sure that their books would all be shown. These were all paperback inventions, I think.

John Prime In the 1930s, Allen Lane had this great idea that he was going to have slot machines everywhere dispensing Penguins. He wanted to try it out, so he persuaded Eva Reckitt[24] to have one outside the 'bomb shop'.[25] It had to be wheeled out and locked at the front of the shop every night, then brought in every morning. And every morning, apparently, there were letters of complaint shoved through the door: 'We put a shilling in this machine and no book came out of it.' It was a complete failure.

Philippa Harrison was editorial director of Michael Joseph from 1980 to 1985.

Philippa Harrison From the early 1980s the majority of books were bought by a hardback and a paperback company from the same group. It then became necessary to market your hardback more energetically, because your own group would stand to benefit when it came to the paperback publication. Also, you tended to get a small percentage of the paperback's published price as a contribution to the hardback, so how many copies the paperback sold was extremely important to you. Whereas previously, I would suggest, paperbacks were really marketed as 'product' and hardbacks were sold rather than marketed.

23 Advertising display cards.
24 Owner of Collet's bookshop.
25 So called because of the socialist-anarchist inclination of its previous owner, Mr Henderson.

Trevor Moore The big turning point for Bantam was *A Brief History of Time*[26] by Professor Stephen Hawking. The publication of that book, and its enormous success, made people aware that Bantam Press was a serious publishing force. I'm sure that impressed a lot of agents and authors, and it established the imprint's credentials in bookshops.

Carmen Callil was managing director of Chatto & Windus when the CVBC group (Chatto & Windus, Virago, Bodley Head and Cape) was sold to Random House in 1987.

Carmen Callil Paperbacks had really turned the corner and were financing hardback publications. We – Chatto, Cape and the Bodley Head – were just three literary hardback imprints without a paperback imprint, which meant that we couldn't compete with other publishers. Also, our overheads were enormous. Each company in the group was editorially separate, but the services – sales, warehouse, royalty accounting – were joint. They cost far too much for the turnover of the group. The group was too small. That's why it had to be sold.[27]

We then moved on to a completely new saga under Random House. That was invigorating but also incredibly tiring. Flotillas of Americans came and investigated every single part of the company. They changed everything, but it was still pretty intractable, so from 1987 it was a question of sacking people or not replacing them. At Chatto I'd originally had a staff of about twenty-six. I think Chatto now consists of five people. That process took place over the next ten years under the different managements. They were right, but it was extremely painful. You didn't really have time for the sort of publishing I like to do; you were constantly agonising about getting the overheads down. It took about ten years for publishing to change like that, I think.

How did you feel about that different management? It felt as if a lot of fresh air had come in – I very much liked that. You could talk about things; you talked about sales and you talked about money and you talked about paperbacks. We talked a lot about starting our own paperback imprint – which of course we did. Frances Coady was the editor who got it off the ground – brilliantly; Simon Master was in charge at the time.[28] Vintage is now massively important. That was the beginning of the success of Random House in Britain.

Trevor Moore The Vintage list in its early stages was very much strengthened by rights reversions. The paperback contract for Joseph Heller's *Catch-22* had been with Pan Books, then the rights had reverted to Cape and we published it at Random House as a Vintage paperback. That happened with

---

26 Published in 1988.
27 The group, known as CVBC (it included Virago) was sold to Random House in 1987.
28 As chief executive of CVBC.

countless other authors, such as Graham Greene – a Bodley Head author who had previously been published in paperback by Penguin.

Sylvia May There are still people in the trade who call paperbacks 'reprints'. For them, the real publication of a book is in hardback. But today a book can be published first in either hardback or paperback – then later you might bring out a mass-market edition.

Klaus Flugge Many illustrators feel that a proper book should be in hardcover – a picture book especially – because it is shared between parent and child and stocked in the library. But the trend nowadays is that libraries buy less, and people are more used to going to bookshops. As parents now buy more books for children, they buy paperbacks, which are half the price of hardbacks. And the idea of giving a hardback as a present isn't as prevalent in Britain as in most other countries.

What do children themselves think? Several librarians have told me that, in the case of older-age fiction, paperbacks are more user-friendly – they are easier to put in the pocket; they feel more comfortable. I understand that, and have now accepted the fact that fiction has to be in paperback if it is to sell. But if a child wants to share a book with its parents, the bigger the book, the easier it is. I think that if you ask five-year-olds, they will probably prefer a book in hardcover. The first illustrated book by Michael Foreman I published at Andersen was *Teeny-Tiny and the Witch Woman* – a wonderfully gruesome story. In my local library I recently saw an edition from 1989, so it has been in the library for over twelve years. That book has lasted a long time.

But now almost all picture books are also published in paperback. Sometimes they go straight into paperback – if the sales department fears that there isn't a sufficient market or, more importantly, when the foreign rights manger finds it impossible to sell co-productions of a certain book. But if you find foreign publishers to buy your book, you usually do a hardcover. Most publishers on the Continent are not interested in a paperback. They feel – as I do – that a picture book should certainly be published in hardcover first. In ninety per cent of cases on the Continent, a picture book is only published in hardcover – paperbacks don't sell. Also, the artists think their work is cheapened by being published in a paperback edition. I wouldn't dream of publishing a book by Ralph Steadman – and I have published several – as a paperback original. No doubt he wouldn't allow it. And others would be very sad if – as might happen eventually – hardbacks disappear altogether.

Michael Geare People said, 'Let's have lunch.' The publisher's lunch. I suspect it may not be quite so cheerful now, but in those days it tended to be quite a memorable thing.
What would it be like? It went on.

Diana Murray Authors, printers, or friends of the John Murray family would ring up in the morning and ask whether they could come to lunch in Albemarle Street. The butler, who had a blacklist as well as a list of people who would be welcomed, would say, 'Yes, there are two places for lunch today. Yes, you would be very welcome' or 'I'm very sorry, Sir, the tables are full today.' And the family would sit down to lunch with perhaps five or six authors, or whoever would happen to be coming through London at the time. That was over by the time I was involved with the firm,[1] because the family had moved from Albemarle Street in 1929. In my day, lunch consisted of excellent sandwiches, with perhaps a bottle of wine, in the drawing room, and authors, publishers and friends would arrive informally.

Charles Pick began his career in 1933 at Victor Gollancz.

Charles Pick At Gollancz we started work around half past eight in the morning and went on till six. If there was a big push on to write a lot of letters to booksellers, I might stay till eight or nine o'clock at night.
Did you have any breaks? An hour at lunch time. I'd go and get a sandwich somewhere round Leicester Square. Underneath the Criterion there was a brasserie where they had a *plat du jour* which was one-and-a-penny with a roll, or elevenpence without. Or I'd go to J. Lyons and have a roll and cheese with a cup of coffee. Victor Gollancz himself would eat at the Savoy every day unless it was raining, when he would get them to send up a hamper of cold ham or cold tongue for his lunch in the office. That put him in a quite different class from the rest of us, who went and had our shilling lunch in Lyons.

Rosemary Goad Fabers had a 'travellers' lunch' every year at the Savoy, where the directors and the sales department took out the reps – who were

1 Diana (née James) married John (Jock) Murray in 1938.

called travellers in those days. It was Christmas week when this took place. They used to come back absolutely trolleyed – completely rolling, the whole lot. They would bring us back bottles, I remember that. Then we would encourage them to go quickly home.

When you say 'we'? The secretaries, I'm talking about.

Elizabeth Burchfield In 1954 I went to work at the London office of Oxford University Press. It was then in a beautiful row of little brick houses in Warwick Square, very near St Paul's cathedral. We heard the bells of the cathedral all the time, so much so that we didn't notice them, they were just part of life. The square had Hodder & Stoughton on one side, and us at the back, and in the winter, as the afternoon drew in, a man on a bicycle would come round with a pole and light the gas lamp in the centre of the square. Jock Cumberlege, who was Publisher to the University,[2] had a dining room where lunch was served in considerable splendour by the butler – and there were sounds of terrible crashes from the pantry when Geoghan, who was a clumsy man, would drop the tray. One day when Jock had visitors, he had said to Geoghan that it would be nice to have potted shrimps as a first course for lunch. He thought that even Geoghan couldn't make a mess of potted shrimps. But he hadn't spelled out to him that just thin brown bread and butter would be nice, and just cold in the pot would be OK. So Geoghan had cooked them, which was not quite what Jock had in mind. The melted potted shrimps were disgusting.

David Whitaker Father used to lunch three days a week on his own, in the dining room at 13 Bedford Square. On Monday and Friday Edmond Segrave[3] lunched with him. The rest of the week, Segrave was lunching out, probably at the Garrick Club or the Savile. When I joined Whitaker's in 1953 I used to have lunch in the dining room with Father. We both read a book over lunch. Father was basically very shy; he was a private person and he expected other people to be private as well. He didn't want to go out to publishers' lunches. He had a few friends in the trade – a few acquaintances – and they used to come to lunch at Christmas time. Most of them came because Edmond Segrave asked them, but Father knew them as well. Apart from that, he hardly met anybody.

When was the first time you went to one of those Christmas lunches? Oh Lord! Michael Turner, if you interview him, may remember.

Michael Turner David Whitaker is probably my oldest friend in publishing. His father gave the most important Christmas event in the trade: that was Haddon Whitaker's lunch, which took place at 13 Bedford Square. To be

2 Geoffrey ('Jock') Cumberlege, London publisher of OUP, from 1945 to 1956.
3 Editor of *The Bookseller* from 1933 to 1971.

invited to this was a considerable honour – those around the table were all heads of companies. I was rising in Associated Book Publishers at the time,[4] and I had a summons from Haddon Whitaker. 'Michael,' he said, 'you must treat this as confidential. I'd like you to join our Christmas lunch.' I said, 'That's absolutely marvellous, thank you very much indeed.' Then he said, 'Just a moment. I'm not inviting you because of your position in the trade. I need somebody roughly of the same age to keep young David company.' And that illustrates a certain attitude in the business right up until about twenty-five years ago – that if you were head of a publishing house you were something special. The guests at Haddon's Christmas lunches would all be part of the Garrick freemasonry – people from Cassell's, Cambridge University Press, Oxford University Press, Collins, Macmillan, Cape. This was a long tradition, from the beginning of the century, when publishing houses were almost entirely family companies.

Gerry Davies There would be Robert Code-Holland of Pitmans, Geoffrey Faber, Ian Parsons of Chatto & Windus, Jack Newth of A. & C. Black, Dick David of Cambridge University Press, Bruno Brown – later Sir John – of the Oxford University Press. John Boon of Mills & Boon. Names that made you really feel you belonged to British publishing.

Michael Turner Some publishers weren't invited, largely because they were not totally socially acceptable – certainly the more colourful ones sometimes weren't accepted.
Who were the more colourful ones who wouldn't have been invited? Paul Hamlyn is the obvious one, who was regarded as something of a barrow boy. And I don't think André Deutsch was ever there. But don't let me make too much of that. It may have been lack of tables in the dining room at Whitaker's. It was a marvellous occasion, full of laughter and anecdotes. It was just like the kind of conversation at the long table in the Garrick. It was a boys' party.
Were there any women there? No. And that's a fair indication. There was, I think, one publishing accountant – from an audit house. And there were no agents there. Agents were a bit beyond the pale; they were doing their best to extract money from publishers. I remember a certain amount of muttering around that time about publishers who became agents. Now, of course, a lot of them do.

Klaus Flugge When I was finding my feet in Britain, Charles Pick was particularly kind to me. He invited me to lunch, and he didn't hesitate to give advice – about meeting certain agents, for instance; or perhaps we talked about print runs and prices, or the problems of the British book trade. Should I talk to W.H. Smith? Or take out a man called Eric Hiscock? He

4 Late 1950s.

was a famous columnist at *Smith's Trade News*, which was a well-established trade paper in competition with *The Bookseller*. That was the first time I took somebody to a really fancy restaurant and bought champagne for lunch, because I had been told by Charles Pick that Hiscock was very fond of champagne.

Where did you go? I think it was called L'Opéra, opposite the Masonic League, north of Long Acre. That was his favourite restaurant; that's where he had his table. He had lunch there almost every day, then wrote about interesting books in advance of publication.

It was his table? It was his table.

Who invited whom? The publishers invited him, of course.

You started to smile as soon as you mentioned Charles Pick. Because I was pleased to meet someone who had so much experience and talent as a publisher, treating me as an equal. As I keep saying, it wasn't easy: I was a very young man, I ran a company that wasn't well established,[5] and other publishers had no real reason to be nice to me.

Where had you met him? At a Booksellers Association conference – my first one, and a daunting experience – at Gleneagles. In those days they were much grander occasions. I was adopted by the chief buyer of Menzies, which was then the obvious competitor to W.H. Smith. He and his wife invited me to their table, which was marvellous because I hardly knew anybody else. Willie Kay was his name. They were a friendly bunch, all the Scots people I met.

Willie Kay We were always taught in Menzies that if a publisher asked you to lunch or dinner, the next time he asked you, you insisted you would pay. You never accepted anything for nothing, and I certainly never did. You could have the dinner, pay for it, and claim it on your expenses, which were never queried. That was a cardinal rule of Menzies, that you did not accept hospitality *ad lib*. But there was no objection to you having a meal with publishers, none at all. Some publishers you didn't want to lunch with – you felt you'd had enough of them. And I never liked to go and have lunch with any publisher if I thought we weren't going to be doing some business with them, because that would be a loss to the publisher, wouldn't it?

Michael Geare In the 1950s, '60s and '70s, W.H. Smith were wonderful, because they had enormous strength and could have really leaned on paperback publishers. When I was at Four Square Books, I used to give Smith's forty-six per cent discount; if they'd really leaned on me they could have got fifty-five per cent discount – they could have screwed me. They possibly couldn't have done that with Penguin, because Penguin had authors and titles that they had to have – we had not many of those. But they didn't lean

---

5 Abelard-Schuman.

on me. Smith's, being decent people, reckoned that we were entitled to make a living. So they didn't screw us as hard as they could have done. I think that Smith's were still technically a partnership at that time. The partners had lunch every day, and they used occasionally to lunch one in, if one was reckoned to have established oneself reasonably in the trade. I was lunched in by the Honourable David, and by a man called Dick Troughton – Sir Charles Troughton. You went and carved your own meat – there was generally a choice of hot beef or ham, with vegetables. And in conversation over the table with the partners you could say what you liked; you knew they wouldn't take advantage of you. They were an immensely powerful, decent, honourable firm.

Peter Mayer Penguin was regarded as an institution of such cultural importance that many who worked there did not understand that it would fail unless it was run as a business, despite the fact that it was the largest – and best – paperback publishing company in Britain. André Deutsch, I believe, had said to Jim Rose[6] that they should look outside England for someone to run Penguin who would view it objectively, which I think André felt nobody who was British could do. André told Jim, 'You should meet Peter Mayer.' And Jim Rose made me an offer, which I said I would seriously consider.

Ron Blass[7] was then sent to New York to advance the project. Ron said to me on the telephone, 'Peter, we have to meet in a very discreet place. You're famous in New York.' I said, 'No, I'm not.' 'Oh. But I'm certainly very well known in New York, and if they see us together, people will guess.' I said, 'Ron, why can't two people have dinner together? Would it always be conspiratorial? Why don't we just have dinner together?' 'No, we mustn't be seen together. The rumours will get back to London that there's going to be a big change at Penguin.' So I said, 'Well, where do you want to eat?' He said, 'You choose the place.'

When I went to collect him, he said, 'Where are we going for dinner?' I said, 'You wanted to go somewhere very discreet where nobody would know you. We're going to Harlem.' 'We're going *where*?' And we went to a place in Harlem where they served barbequed chicken. There was a take-out counter and a very large yard, and all the people of Harlem were there. They didn't look anything like Ron Blass, who had on some nice trousers with a blazer and white shirt and tie. It was night-time and all these people were eating barbequed chicken in the yard and throwing the bones over the side. Ron said, 'What is this?' I said, 'The chicken is very good. I've been here many times, Ron. And I don't think you know anybody here.' He was furious. 'I guess you think this is a practical joke?' I said, 'No. You were so insistent. I don't think anybody's going to comment on the two of us here.'

6 At this time (1976) Jim Rose was chairman of Penguin Books.
7 Executive vice-chairman of Penguin Books.

And that was the first meeting where we tried to tack down the terms of my coming to Penguin.

Belinda McGill became secretary to Max Reinhardt, owner and managing director of the Bodley Head, in 1964.

Belinda McGill The first week I started work at the Bodley Head, Ralph Richardson came to lunch. Max Reinhardt had brought some smoked salmon and a loaf of brown bread and said, 'Can you make smoked salmon sandwiches?' So I set them out with napkins and a couple of plates, then Ralph arrived. First time I'd met him, and a hero of mine – fabulous actor. He went into the office, sat down. Max came out with a chilled bottle of wine and handed me one of these bottle openers which in those days were new, that have arms; you screw it down, the arms go up, then you press down. Five minutes went by and I still hadn't opened the bottle. The door opened and Max came out and said, 'Haven't you got that bottle open yet?' I said, 'I'm terribly sorry, I can't work out how it works.' And Ralph in the background piped up, 'Maxie darling, next time you interview a secretary, don't bother with the shorthand and typing speeds. Just give her a bottle opener, and if she can't do it, don't employ her.'

Karl Lawrence We had an editorial meeting every Wednesday and André's secretary would go out and get fresh bread and cheese and fruit. The sales reps, the production director and all the editors would be there – and there was never enough bread, so we would fight over the last bit. We'd say to André, 'You've got to buy more.' He'd say, 'We'll buy more next time', then he'd get upset because he didn't get the last piece.

There were fierce arguments over the editorial lunches, and anything that was published was discussed in great detail. André was very forceful about putting his point of view forward, and he expected everybody else to. Even a Mikes book or an Updike or a Naipaul, we would talk about at some length, even though it was a foregone conclusion that we would publish those. We discussed the way it would be promoted, we discussed whether it was a big book or not a big book. For instance, we published *The Mimic Men* when I was there and we recognised then that this was an important book and that we could probably get a book club edition. What we could do for serial rights, what we ought to do for the jacket – all that sort of stuff was covered in that editorial meeting. It went on often until the end of the afternoon.

Michael Geare The lunch I most enjoyed was when Dent's brought out the fourth edition of *Everyman's Encyclopaedia*. It was 1965, I think. Tom Hodges was the principal buyer of W.H. Smith and at that stage he was buying about one quarter of all the books, outside educational ones, that were published – I don't mean in titles, I mean in actual volume. There was a boat moored by Charing Cross Bridge which was a very good restaurant, and I took Tom there. We had an extremely good lunch, and it wasn't until the second brandy – I was judging it, for once, correctly – that I broached the question of how many sets. I finally got him, and he said, 'Don't think, Michael, that I haven't made a bigger purchase before while I've been chief buyer. Randolph Churchill's book about his father – I bought just a few more of that.' But £65,000 in 1965 – that's getting on for half a million quid's worth today. And – it was rather sweet – he bought too many. I knew he had. He came back six months later and said, 'Michael, I've over-bought.' I said, 'Yes, Tom?' He said, 'I suppose you couldn't help me?' And we had just run out of stock and wanted some more copies to fulfil orders, without having to reprint the whole thing. I said, 'Tom, I wouldn't do it for anybody else.'

Sylvia May We had a sales target for every shop. On one occasion I knew I had to get Foyle's to order 200 copies of a book called *Proteus*.[8] I thought, Oh God, this is going be impossible. I went up to see the buyer and said 'I'd really like to take you to lunch.' And we made a date. As we were walking out of Foyle's – he was putting on his coat – he said, 'So what do you want?' I said, 'Two hundred copies of *Proteus*.' He said, 'OK, you've got them. Now we can enjoy lunch.' So off we went and had a really nice lunch. And he was as good as his word; we came back to the department, he wrote out an order for 200 copies and gave it to me.
Where did you have lunch? I think it was a Greek restaurant that he liked. Ghastly. It was a three-hour lunch. And in those days we drank at lunchtime. Two bottles of wine at lunchtime – between two – was nothing in those days. How on earth did I manage that?

Andrew Franklin worked for various publishers including Penguin before starting Profile Books in 1996.

Andrew Franklin People are shocked when one tells them how much one eats and drinks in publishing. It seems indolent and extravagant and wasteful, and people who are content with sandwiches at lunchtime – people like my kids, in fact – get a bit cross.
So why was lunch so important? Still is. I find it rather hard to defend, but I would be terribly upset to see it go.
What's the difference between having a meeting with an author or an agent over lunch, or having a meeting with them elsewhere? It's an exercise in hospitality and generosity to take somebody else for a nice lunch and a bottle of wine, and it's convivial. Why that makes a difference, I don't know. Normally, if you were meeting an author for the first time you would not take them to lunch unless you were really thoroughly intent on persuading them of

8 Morris West, *Proteus*, Collins, 1979.

something. But with agents you would, because you have to develop this long-term relationship. Agents, on the whole, never pay for lunch – except for Abner Stein. He's very generous. Although when I was fired from Penguin and I was out of a job for nine months before setting up Profile, a lot of agents did invite me for lunch to give me advice and tell me not to give up. I was very touched by that.

Earlier on, when I took over the Hamish Hamilton imprint at Penguin, I had lunch with Giles Gordon, probably at the Garrick. He said, 'We'll never do a lot of business together, because you'll need to find agents who are your age and who will bring to you authors of your age. I'm a generation older, and my authors are fifteen years older than you and work with publishers fifteen years older than you.' It turned out to be completely untrue, actually, and we did a great deal of business together. But I knew what he meant, and there was an element of truth in it.

Has the way that you would do business over lunch changed since your days at Penguin? I'm ten years older, so I tend not to have a pudding. You used to wait to do business over pudding, but if you don't have pudding you can't do that, so it's switched to the main course. I think when the history of publishing comes to be written, that ought to be recorded, don't you?

Carole Blake I remember being at a lunch at Christopher Sinclair-Stevenson's publishing company with Giles Gordon. Christopher used to have literary lunches, which were tremendous fun – with a fabulous standard of wine, I have to say. Peter Ackroyd's *Dickens* had just come out, one of the longest books imaginable. I congratulated Giles on it – 'It's the most wonderful book' – and he said, 'Must get around to reading it one day.' I thought he was kidding. 'Don't be daft. You must have read it.' He said, 'No, I haven't. Do you know how long it is?' He'd sold many books by Ackroyd, and sold them very well. At the time I believed him. I wonder if it was true? Giles always did things differently from other people.

Elizabeth Burchfield There was a very nice Greek Cypriot restaurant in St Martin's Lane called Beoty's, where I used to take journalists to lunch. We used to have terrific gossips – I loved having a real heart to heart over a meal – because they're tremendously indiscreet. That was very enjoyable.

What would you have? Taramasalata. And there was the most glorious thing that came in a creamy brandy sauce. Sometimes there were politicians in Beoty's; I remember seeing Richard Crossman once. But it wasn't a grand restaurant like The Ivy where you would expect to see great stars of politics or stage and screen.

Would you have any alcohol if you were there at lunchtime? Certainly. Just wine, I think. I never have been a wine buff, so if my guest was a man, I would let him choose. We never had just a glass of wine; we would always have a bottle, and we would never leave any over. I wouldn't be able to do it now, but it didn't ever seem to be a problem. I went there several times with David Holloway, who was a distinguished literary editor of *The Daily Telegraph*, and I remember going there with Michael Geare from *The Bookseller*. It was a place that he knew independently of me. He greeted the maître d'hôtel by name, which I would never have done – in fact, I always thought that he got his name slightly wrong. It was useful to have good contacts at *The Bookseller*.

David Whitaker Michael Geare's expenses were outrageous. They had been when he was at Dent; he used to run up huge bills at Beoty's – entertaining booksellers in those days. Now, as deputy editor of *The Bookseller*, he was entertaining publishers. I used to have a rule that if we went out to lunch with a publisher, the publisher paid, because they were always trying to sell us something. But if we went out to lunch with a bookseller, we paid, because booksellers couldn't afford to.

Margaret Hughes Booksellers never took publishers out, it was always the other way round. There was a rep called Archie Chown, from Allen & Unwin. Mr Chown seemed a very old rep – a lovely, gentlemanly man. He came round when I was leaving Haigh & Hochland,[9] and I said, 'Let me take you out for lunch.' He said, 'I've been a rep for forty years, and you're the first bookseller who's ever asked me out for lunch. And not only that: you're the first *woman* who's ever asked me out for lunch.'

Trevor Moore There's a great quote from André Simon that the best restaurant in the world is the one that knows you the best, and I used to feel that about The Philadelphia, which was a Greek Cypriot restaurant at the top of Shaftesbury Avenue at the junction with New Oxford Street.

The Philadelphia was a family-run restaurant: there was Nick at the front of the house; there was his brother Victor – a brilliant waiter – and there was their brother-in-law, Paul. The restaurant carried on until they got too old, and the last time I saw Nick he was sitting on a stool in the street, close to the site of his erstwhile emporium. He shook my hand warmly and said, 'Mr Hojas, how are you?' Which goes back to my Jonathan Cape days, when I had a proof copy of a book that Tom Maschler[10] waxed lyrical about in his inimitable way, *The Exploits of the Incomparable Mulla Nasrudin*. I think it was one of Idries Shah's first compilations. I loved it; I felt for those stories all the things that Tom Maschler had felt about them when he 'sold' the book to us. Tom had this wonderful ability to talk about a book as if it was the only book that he cared about. Six months later, when you had started to sell it, you could talk to him about that same book, and he'd look at you

9 Independent bookselling business in Manchester owned and run by Ernest Hochland.
10 Managing director of Jonathan Cape.

blankly. But I do think his enthusiasm for that book was genuine. Certainly mine was.

Cape produced proof copies, and I was reading one in The Philadelphia one day, when Victor came up. He was always interested in what I was reading – they were used to seeing people from different publishing houses – so I showed him the book. 'Ah, Mulla Nasrudin. We call him Mr Hojas. Nick, Nick!' Nick came rushing up, and they both started telling me Mr Hojas stories. Growing up in Greek-speaking Cyprus, they had been told all about this character, who was their version of Mulla Nasrudin. After that, I became 'Mr Hojas' every time I went there. 'Hello, Mr Hojas.'

That would have been around 1961, and I went on knowing them all the way through my publishing life. I would meet up with other reps there from time to time, and I used to like going there on my own. I'd see people like Margaret Clark and Judy Taylor, both distinguished Bodley Head children's book publishers. They would often be deep in conversation. I would also see Michael Joseph's sales director, Dick Douglas-Boyd, who always had his nose in a proof. Every now and again I'd be on his table, because it was always very busy at lunchtime so you just slotted in wherever there was a seat. And sometimes one would sit near Margaret Clark and Judy Taylor and try hard not to listen to whatever they were talking about, which was jolly difficult. They usually cottoned on to the fact that you worked in the same business; it was pretty obvious if you were carrying a proof copy or two.

Judy Taylor Maybe once a month I would go to Rules for lunch with Max and Graham, or Max and Hugh.[11] It was their favourite place. Max would ring down and say, 'Judy, do you want to come and join us for lunch?' and off we would go. They always had the same table upstairs by the window, and there were always three bottles of Beaujolais Villages opened and waiting. We used to have a really good lunch – a proper lunch. Steak and kidney pie was one of Rules' best dishes; I think Hugh liked that particularly.
When you say a 'proper' lunch? I mean a main course and a pudding. I think Max used to have cheese, too. None of your sandwich lunches or salads.

Klaus Flugge L'Etoile was another publishers' lunch place, in Charlotte Street. That's where I first had lunch with Charles Pick. I now go a lot to the restaurant at Tate Britain, and there is always a sprinkling of editors and agents there.

Martha van der Lem-Mearns We used agents quite a lot in Nelson's – or agents maybe used us. There were perhaps half a dozen who would ring up and say, 'Can we take you out to lunch?'

11 Max Reinhardt, Graham Greene and Hugh Carlton Greene (respectively managing director and board members of the Bodley Head).

Carole Blake You're having lunch, and an editor will say, 'So what's new?' 'Barbara Erskine's going to deliver a new novel. Of course, she's very happy with HarperCollins. But there *is* something coming – it's not quite ready yet – that might be your cup of tea.' 'Oh, really?' The point at which you, as an agent, feel that you can stop selling because the editor is trying to start buying, is a very sweet moment – you can feel the power walking across the table. But if the editor's trying to catch the eye of the waiter, then you know you just haven't caught their imagination.

I always have a notebook with me when I'm at lunch, and I've usually got a client list, too. And I do notes before I go to lunch with somebody: I look at what they've bought from me in the past; I look at what they and their colleagues currently have on submission from us at the moment – the 'us' being me and Isobel Dixon, the other book agent at the agency.[12] I also look at my client list to see if there are any authors who are not as happy as they might be with their current publisher, or any authors being published by a publisher I have financial worries about or where I think the editor might be about to leave. If you think there may be a change of circumstances for that author in the next few months, you try to sow the seeds of interest.

Philippa Harrison At the end of a lunch, just as I was moving my chair back, Jonathan Clowes, who was Kingsley Amis's agent, suddenly said very lightly, 'I'm going to move Kingsley from Cape to Christopher Sinclair-Stevenson.'[13] I said, 'Why ever would you do that?' and put my chair back in. 'If you will let me – at Hutchinson – push some of Kingsley's books hard and not push others, I can double their sales.' The book being sold was *Jake's Thing*, which was one of the saleable ones, no question. And he said 'OK.' I jolly well did, too: Hutchinson doubled the sales of Cape, which was quite something.

Martha van der Lem-Mearns When we took out authors I was really quite thrilled. Jocelyn Baines[14] suggested that we did another title in the *In Their Time* series, and said, 'Why don't you take Antonia Byatt to lunch?' There was an Angus Steak House or something similar in South Audley Street, where I took this very nice, shy, slim girl. She was about my age, I suppose – in her early thirties. I can even remember we each had half an avocado – which was quite new in these days – and, I think, a fillet steak. She was so nice, and so modest. We were wanting her to do *The Lake Poets in Their Time*, and she regretfully declined. But she was absolutely charming. And the attitude at Nelson's was, 'Are you sure you've got enough money with you

---

12 Blake Friedmann Literary Agency.
13 Then an editor at Hamish Hamilton.
14 Managing director of Thomas Nelson & Sons.

to pay for this lunch?' There was always an advance of cash before you went out to lunch with people.

Anne Walmsley Once I became a publisher at Longmans, one was taking people out to lunch all the time, both in London and when I did my Caribbean travels. It was the thing to do. It took me a long time to realise that all authors didn't actually like it. They would rather have had the money.

Gerry Davies When I joined the Booksellers Association as secretary in 1955, Ivan Chambers was a member of the council. After I had been there for about three months he invited me to his shop to have lunch. He said, 'I hope you're not a great eater. I shall get some sandwiches and we shall have them at the back of the shop. I don't think I really can afford to be away for a long business lunch.'

The shop was in Museum Street, next door to the publishers Allen & Unwin. Inside there was a slight air, not of mustiness, but of paper and dust. The shelves were a little closer together than would be thought wise today, and you went through a curtained doorway into a crowded back room which was Ivan Chambers' office. He just pushed aside various papers and files which were littering the table, and one of his staff made us a pot of tea.

Ivan Chambers' brain was like a working catalogue. He knew about the books he sold, and was always anxious to get a book that a customer wanted if it wasn't in stock. He was small in stature and had hidden his growing baldness behind thin hair swept back. He had a prominent nose and wore glasses. When you were addressing him he would look at you as I imagine a magistrate would if you were in the dock – an inquisitive man, who wouldn't let answers go by without pursuing another question if he wasn't satisfied. At that lunch we spoke about bookselling, but we talked particularly about our joint love of English literature.

At the Booksellers Association in 1955 we were already beginning to work out the defence of the Net Book Agreement, and I asked Ivan Chambers the questions I asked many senior members of the association, such as, did they remember incidences of people breaking the Net Book Agreement? Particularly I asked him about terms; that is, the wholesale discounts which booksellers receive from publishers. At that time there was general pressure from the association to upgrade discounts to booksellers from twenty-five to thirty-three and a third per cent off the published price. Being next door to Allen & Unwin and – although I didn't know it at the time – with a certain amount of the capital of his business held by Stanley Unwin, Ivan Chambers was well versed in the workings of publishers' minds, which we, as booksellers, regarded as being highly restrictive in that they always kept down the remuneration to booksellers as strictly as possible.

What was he able to tell you about the workings of publishers' minds? That while they wanted the co-operation of booksellers, they were not prepared to make bookselling an economic occupation which would attract people other than those vitally interested in books. As producers, they wanted good quality outlets, but run by people who were knowledgeable about books and would therefore be more dedicated than somebody who came in purely as a retailer seeking profits. Therefore, if the discounts were not too high, this would ensure that you didn't get profit-seeking people running book-shops, but people who were genuinely interested in the trade in books. One has to remember that, historically, publishers once had their own bookshops and sold their own books, so the cleavage between producer and retailer was not as marked as in other trades.

Can you remember what Ivan Chambers thought about that attitude? He believed that publishers should give a larger slice of the cake to retailers than they were in the habit of doing, therefore he joined in all the discussions we had in the Booksellers Association about what methods we should adopt to persuade publishers to give us bigger discounts. But he was a careful man and a tolerant man and, being what I might call a quality bookseller, he was well aware of the argument that if you make bookselling too easy you might attract the wrong people into it.

Elizabeth Burchfield When I went first to OUP the war had been over for nearly nine years. Yet all around there were still buildings where you could see that a whole room, up several floors, had been demolished, and the wallpaper was still showing. There were Wren churches of which just the steeple stood, and the church was either a shell or it had gone. And in the churchyards there were wild flowers, and wild cats which people used to feed. It was interesting to walk around the City in your lunch hour, and eat your sandwich in an old churchyard. It was a beautiful place, in many ways. Now it's a desert with these great, ugly modern blocks, and the wind whistles around them in a way that it didn't on the small scale of old St Paul's churchyard and down to the river and round about.

10 | ELEMENTS OF TRUTH: NET BOOK AGREEMENT 1962

David Whitaker Publishers and booksellers only split and became different trades in the early 19th century. But the publishers then made more money than the booksellers.

Gerry Davies The Net Book Agreement was a voluntary agreement among publishers that they would use what legal methods were available to them to maintain prices.

Tommy Joy In the old days, if you sold books below the published price the publisher wouldn't let you have any more. And it wouldn't be just that one publisher; they'd all get together and stop your supplies.
Can you remember that happening to anyone? Oh, yes. It is curious: although it's a big trade, it's a small trade. We all knew what was happening everywhere, so if the supplies had been cut off, you would know the reason for it. Obviously, because of my position with the book trade associations and my presidency,[1] I toed the line very strictly and showed an example.
Do you remember who they were? Yes, but I couldn't tell you. It wouldn't do. And in any case, the situation was so different then. You couldn't condemn somebody for something which they did forty years ago, when the situation was entirely different.

Ian Miller With the Net Book Agreement, the publisher controlled the bookseller's destiny, because the publisher fixed the price of a book and the publisher fixed the discount.[2] If the publisher said, 'You can only have thirty per cent discount' and you wanted to sell the book, there was nothing you could do about it. Technically, under the Net Book Agreement you could always price a book up, but nobody ever did. So the profit margins of bookshops, which had always been poor, were seen as being dictated by the publishers' discount structure.

---

1 Tommy Joy served as president of the Booksellers Association in 1957.
2 Terms on which the publisher supplied books to the bookseller, traditionally between twenty-five and thirty-three and a third per cent off the retail price.

Gerry Davies Many senior publishers were degreed men and tended to look on booksellers as pre-war graduates looked on grammar school boys who didn't go on to university: 'Decent chaps, but not quite as decent as we are.' Obviously they couldn't do it with the Blackwells. But towards smaller-town booksellers there was this feeling that booksellers were shop-keepers – they were tradesmen. Whereas publishers looked upon themselves as professionals.

I worked very closely with my opposite number at the Publishers Association,[3] and we arranged not only that our presidents might meet each other for discussion of higher matters in the trade, but that the officers of each association would meet every two months. We would bring to-gether five a side, and book a private room at a hotel. I managed to establish parity by saying that the Booksellers Association would collect the tab alternately for the dinner. All the time I was there, I tried to create the impression that while they may not have been as rich, booksellers were as good as publishers. But among publishers there was an attitude, which permeated all their dealings, that they were the producers – the superior party. Even though we had one or two booksellers who would not respond easily to the description of tradesmen – Alan Ward, a man with a private income; Harold Sweeten, who played the stock market successfully – there was still a tendency for publishers to look down to booksellers. But at these meetings together where we drank the same wine – sometimes we may have drunk a little more than the publishers – we gradually got a sense that the younger publishers, like Tony Pocock and Ian Chapman, were more ready to meet us on equal ground. But the older publishers, no. The Geoffrey Fabers – no, they weren't.

David Whitaker Almost every head of house was a member of the Society of Bookmen[4] and the after-dinner speakers would be important people from the trade. Everything was off the record so that members could say exactly what they thought. Few subjects were outlawed, except – unbelievably – terms, because there were bookseller members and publisher members. So they never talked about the most important thing in the trade. It may have been an obscure hangover from the days when it was vulgar to talk about money. Or that may have been an excuse, when what they really meant was, 'For God's sake don't ask for any more of *our* money please; we want it for ourselves.'

That's unfair of me, because nobody before Paul Hamlyn and Robert Maxwell grew rich in publishing. But I have to take that back too, because the Longmans were wealthy, and the Macmillans were *very* wealthy. I remember walking into Birch Grove, Harold Macmillan's house. Alex Macmillan met

---

3 Ronald Barker, secretary of the Publishers Association from 1958 to 1976.
4 A book trade dining club, founded in 1921.

me at the door. I looked around and raised an eyebrow. He said, 'Yes. Built on Hall and Knight's *Algebra* and furnished on *Gone with the Wind*. Those were the days when publishers could make money, and they could keep it.'

Tommy Joy Walter Hutchinson was a very big and important publisher. Not a very popular publisher. I can't remember what the problem was, but one of his representatives came to see me and said, 'We're not going to supply you with any more books.' I was a comparatively new boy in London, so it was rather a blow. But I just smiled and said, 'Well, isn't that nice? I've already over-spent my allowance on books, so that helps me very much.'

When the day came to publish these particular books – there was a Philip Gibbs, a Gilbert Frankau and a Dennis Wheatley – I had great mountains of them, five or six hundred copies of each, when I was supposed not to be able to get these books. I tell you, there were ever so many ways of getting books. We had friends in the trade.

David Whitaker I always talked about 'the trade' long after publishers had managed to convince themselves that they belonged to the publishing profession – I mean, really! Along with lawyers and prostitutes? They're tradesmen. But they didn't think that way; they condescended to booksellers. Mind you, they found condescending to Basil Blackwell rather difficult.

How did booksellers regard publishers? With a certain hostility. The structure of the trade was dictated by the Net Book Agreement. Publishers controlled the retailers' margin; the publisher held the whip hand, and the publisher's view was that the lower the price and the wider the distribution, the more books would be sold. Which is fair. But if you have prices and margins held down and rigidly adhered to by law, the bookseller has limited scope for self-improvement. Ian Norrie in the High Hill Bookshop in Hampstead had a rich, well-read clientele, and he could sell books by the barrow load. Not many other people were in that situation. The great bookshops in the university towns had huge academic lists. W.H. Smith shifted more books than anybody else, and had over twenty per cent of the market; they could, to an extent, demand, and get, better terms because of their size. But most other bookshops were small.

Given what you've just described, why did you support the Net Book Agreement? I thought that it kept the price of books down, and probably increased their availability. Certainly with the abolition of the previous Net Book Agreement in the 1840s, the retail book trade had fallen on exceptionally hard times because every store in the country piled high the bestsellers. Eric Bailey[5] – a bookseller – was the first person to teach publishers what terms

---

5 Eric Bailey of Lear's Bookshop, Cardiff, was both a bookseller and an accountant. He was president of the Booksellers Association from 1970 to 1971.

really meant to the bottom line and what might result from a rigid approach. I mentioned him in a brief history of bookselling that I wrote,[6] and this bit I'm going to read: 'It was Eric Bailey who taught publishers to understand that they shared the responsibility with booksellers of whether or not there should be a bookselling presence on the high streets of England. Not all publishers have yet made up their minds if this is a responsibility they are ready to shoulder.' And as we know, they didn't. Commercial responsibility and publishers have never really gone together.

Gerry Davies When I joined the BA it was already known that there would be legislation against resale price maintenance. And since both publishers and booksellers thought the Net Book Agreement had kept the trade on an even keel, they were aware that it would have to be defended in due course. It became clear that we would have to justify it on the grounds that it was in the public interest that bookshops should be able to stock a great range of books and buy in special orders for customers – and that only by maintaining prices would booksellers have the settled economy they needed to do so without fear of being under-cut. So I started to visit booksellers, enquiring how they did.

Were you surprised by anything you found? No. I always held the belief that people would tell elements of truth which were favourable to themselves and conceal other parts. I'm sure that booksellers were doing that. Therefore I wasn't surprised that some booksellers were very much worse off than they said, because their pride would stop them revealing the fact.

I also talked a lot with publishers, who, although they wouldn't reveal any secrets, were prepared to tell me if I asked, 'Is So-and-so a prompt payer?' I had to be careful, because I'm sure the BA council would not have liked to think that I was getting that kind of information from publishers. I found that many shops – including quite well-known names – were regarded by publishers as being late payers and were almost being put on the credit stop list. The bookselling trade was really in a much worse condition than it thought it was. There were a few exceptions: the bigger booksellers, such as Blackwell's and Heffer's. But even some of those – I can say this safely now – were not totally efficiently run. Many of them weren't aware of their stock turn figures; they weren't aware of the importance of cash flow; they were deferring payment of accounts. And they were certainly underpaying their staff, in many cases.

In one instance, the man who was about to become the president of the Booksellers Association was operating from a very shaky base in his own shop. But he realised it, and was able to give me clues about what to ask other booksellers. He was very good from the intellectual point of view and in the quality of his stock, but he didn't turn it over quickly enough and his

6 *One Hundred Years of Bookselling 1895–1995*, Whitaker's, 1995.

finances were not in good shape. In those days there weren't so many paperbacks of classics, and stocking hardcover editions could be a risky business for a bookseller. And sometimes he bought too heavily; he might have bought a dozen copies of a new book before the reviews appeared, yet he didn't seem able to sense whether it was a bestseller, a moderate seller, or a book that would stick.

Who was that? That was Basil Donne-Smith in Hitchin. He's retired from bookselling now, and indeed is retired from the planet altogether. There was another shop, in Harrogate, a family business where the owner had not realised how much it relied on selling stationery. Up and down the country I found bookshops like that, many of them inherited. They'd had a lovely time during the war when books were in short supply, but in the 1950s they hadn't enough facts about their own business to know which part was holding it together.

I also visited two lady booksellers. Miss Seawright at Bath was a doughty feminist in some ways. She was fairly old when I knew her, and she always had a good shelf of feminist books. Not by any means an extremist; a woman with whose views I sympathised tremendously. And there was the firm of Jardine's in Manchester – Grace Jardine herself had been close to Harriet Weaver and the Pankhursts. These old ladies had lost none of their mettle and fire for the cause which had taken them into bookselling. Most booksellers in those days went into bookselling not for the money, but because they wanted to make their contribution to society and, sometimes, to a particular aspect of politics – but their economics were bad. I found that the bookselling trade was in worse shape than anybody thought, but this gave me vital information to defend the net price. I felt I was fighting a sort of crusade.

If these shopkeepers' profits weren't good, they were tempted to cut down on books and to stock more profitable items – Basildon Bond stationery and pens – for which there was steady demand. Booksellers needed to be certain they could sell books without being undercut, and there were plenty of newsagents prepared to sell books at discount if they weren't prevented from doing so. We also wanted to argue that booksellers needed a guaranteed income in order to train staff, so they could provide a better service. And it was generally accepted in those days that bookshops were rather stuffy, dusty places – so the bookseller needed to afford to take a dynamic interest in making his shop attractive, in order to bring in people who may not have thought of buying books before.

The case against the Net Book Agreement came to court in the summer of 1962 and went on for twenty-four days. We had a panel of booksellers who were willing to appear as witnesses. We graded them into big booksellers, middle booksellers, academic booksellers and small town booksellers. Blackwell's of Oxford clearly were not only big booksellers, but were also academic booksellers. The same with Heffer's of Cambridge. We also had

Sisson & Parker of Nottingham and John Smith & Son of Glasgow. Then we had smaller ones, like the lady bookseller of Havant,[7] who ran the quintessential small town bookshop which was patronised because she was providing a good stock and a marvellous service, getting books almost overnight – even driving to London to pick them up so she wouldn't have to wait for the post.

The QC who eventually appeared for the Crown against us, Harry Fisher,[8] wanted very much to have got the brief to defend us. He was the son of the then Archbishop of Canterbury and no mean intellectual himself. He thought we had a strong case. But one or two publishers who were good university men knew a few barristers, and we picked Arthur Bagnall QC, who specialised in restrictive practices. So Harry Fisher, wanting to be in the case just as much, was finally briefed for the prosecution. It's no reflection on him that he didn't manage to prove us wrong. He was a very astute questioner and cross-examiner and put our book trade witnesses through severe examination.

It was in October that we got the verdict. We all appeared in court at ten thirty in the morning, and the judge delivered the judgement that we had satisfied the court that the Net Book Agreement was not against the public interest. The court judged that if the net book system was not maintained, more booksellers would either go out of business or deal less in books, and – as our lawyer had argued – *ipso facto*, the public would be less well served.

How aware were the public of the issue? Except for a few librarians and regular book buyers, I would think the vast majority of the public were unaware of it – or thought of the Net Book Agreement as it was reported in the press, as being a price ring. The press had been all out to say, 'Here are all these profiteers and they're going to lose.' So the success wasn't reported as much as the failure would have been.

How much opposition to the Net Book Agreement was there within the trade? Nobody who was struggling to run a stockholding bookshop had any reservations at all. They regarded it as the cornerstone of the trade and thought that if we hadn't won the case, the next day everybody would be discounting books. There weren't many people against it: one or two American operators wanting to get into the country, and one or two library suppliers who were already geared up to offering discounts to libraries if we'd lost the case. Paul Hamlyn, of course, with his *Books for Pleasure*, had always said the Net Book Agreement was an encumbrance. But he saw the solution quite easily and took it: he wasn't bound by the Net Book Agreement, because he didn't sign it – so he didn't worry if anybody discounted a Paul Hamlyn book. But I said to him at the time, 'If all booksellers were discounting, you would have to give even more to stay on top.'

7 Irene Babbidge.
8 Henry (known as Harry) Fisher.

Tommy Joy To me it was like the Bible. All my life the Net Book Agreement was the eleventh commandment. It never occurred to me that we would lose it. We believed that if you did away with the Net Book Agreement, you would do away with the book trade more or less as a whole. It had come into being – largely as a result of the Macmillan family – because bookshops all over the country were closing rapidly since they couldn't afford to keep open. And because they were going out of business, and therefore the retail outlets were closing, the publishers got alarmed and brought about this agreement.

Gerry Davies When I was a librarian I wrote several articles for *The Bookseller* where I was being provocative and trying to goad booksellers into becoming more lively. I continued to do this when I was working for the Booksellers Association, where it would not have been politic to have done so under my own name. The pseudonym I used was Peter Littleton. When we were preparing for the examination of the Net Book Agreement by the Restrictive Practices Court, I was very disappointed that some booksellers weren't giving the service which we said was one of the good reasons for not discounting books. So I wrote this challenging article in *The Bookseller*, as Peter Littleton, adopting the guise of a bookseller talking of fellow booksellers, saying: 'I wonder if we chaps are doing as well as we ought to, and backing up the obviously great efforts the Booksellers Association is making to defend our way of life?' This was around 1960, two years before the case came before the court.

When the case came up, the Treasury solicitor representing the Registrar of Restrictive Trading Agreements entered many documents for the court's examination, including several articles by Peter Littleton which had shown that booksellers weren't as good as we had made out them to be. And nobody knew who Peter Littleton was. The Treasury solicitor wrote to the editor of *The Bookseller* and said, 'We can't find this man. What company does he come from? We wish to get in touch with him to be interrogated on his opinions.'

This presented us with a problem. Edmund Segrave, as a good editor, said, 'I never reveal sources.' The Treasury solicitor said, 'It's important to us. We could *sub poena* this gentleman to appear in the witness box.' It would have been rather disastrous for my career if there I was, the chief executive of the defending booksellers, appearing against my own side on behalf of the Treasury solicitor. So without revealing my identity, I conferred with our legal counsel, Arthur Bagnall QC. I told him: 'A strange situation has arisen whereby somebody with a pseudonym has written these articles and apparently we can't trace him. They are very good, but taken at face value they could damage the case we're trying to make.' He said, 'Why don't you, as secretary of the Booksellers Association, write me a paper picking them to bits and saying that they bear no relation to reality?' So I did that. When it came to court, our counsel rose and submitted a devastating destruction of Peter Littleton's articles. And the Treasury counsel accepted it, saying, 'I think we may regard those as just a piece of provocative journalism; we won't call him as a witness.'

David Whitaker Gerry Davies wrote for us for years when he was secretary of the Booksellers Association, always under pseudonyms.

Do you remember what they were? Magliabechi – the great 17th-century librarian – was one. And he dealt with publicity material as Henry Puffmore. There was another column, Critics' Crowner, by somebody else, who was quite famous in the literary world.

Do you remember who? I do, but I wouldn't say.

I'm wondering how long it has to be before it's OK to say. This chap has been dead a good few years now, but we used to have a rule that anybody at Whitaker's who revealed the identity of somebody writing for us under a pseudonym would be fired at once. Not only fired, but with no recompense whatsoever.

Why were pseudonyms guarded so fiercely? If you're going to have a pseudonym, you guard it. If you're going to be sloppy about it, don't have a pseudonym. And one or two people could have lost their jobs. When Gerry Davies was writing for *The Bookseller* – certainly in the very early days – he might have been writing something which was not at that time BA policy. But it might have become BA policy after he'd written it.

11 | THE OPENING OF THE SLUICE

Carole Blake At Michael Joseph I attended acquisition and editorial meetings because I was selling subsidiary rights. William Luscombe, who was running Michael Joseph's Pelham imprint, published a series of *Beginner's Guides*, and he put up a proposal for a *Beginner's Guide to Sex*. I said, 'Surely no one will go into a bookshop and ask for that. No one's going to admit they're a beginner.' I was completely disregarded, and they published it and it sold about three copies. I'm sure you could publish a *Beginner's Guide to Sex* now, because you could sell a lot of copies through Amazon. But I still don't think anybody would take it to a till and admit they needed it.
What would you have called it? I wouldn't have done it. Or else I would have changed the perspective and called it *An Expert's Guide to Better Sex* – of which there are many on the market as we speak.

Karl Lawrence Charing Cross Road had about four or five 'chemist's' shops, that sold sexy books and contraceptives. They would have one small window with a drab display that never changed, of a few curled-up books and purple boxes of condoms, and the door was usually open, although you never saw anybody go in or come out. Those shops were a feature of English life at the time. I once went into one in Leicester when I was seventeen, because I wanted to buy a copy of *The Red Light* by Rennie Macandrew, which was thought to be a reasonably acceptable sex book, and a man came from behind the curtain at the back of the shop to serve me. In the early 1950s, after I was married, my then wife and I decided to read it again. That time my wife went to buy it – from a shop in Birmingham – and she was served by a woman. They must have had a man and a woman waiting behind the curtain, so an assistant of the right sex could go out and serve whoever came in.

David Young Rennie Macandrew, whose real name was Andrew George Elliot, was a real Harley Street gynaecologist. He saw that Thorsons[1] were

---

1 Family-run publisher of health and alternative titles, founded in 1930 and sold to Harper-Collins in 1989.

publishing books and selling them mostly through direct mail, recognised the opportunity and wrote to my grandfather: 'Do you want to publish this?' and Grandfather went ahead. *The Red Light* was censored – a lot of booksellers wouldn't stock it and comments were made in the press. It dealt with homosexuality and stuff which hadn't been published before.

He was an amazing bloke, my granddad. I've never worked out why he did it. He wasn't at all licentious. Obviously he could see the business opportunity. Remember that he started by selling vitamins and women's corsetry by mail order – he was a mail order man in many ways. And to this day, in my view, Amazon will still sell more sex books than any other retailer in the UK.

Per Saugman Somebody came into Blackwell's and said, had we got a book called *The Ideal Marriage*? I knew it from Denmark. I said, 'I'll just ask.' I went to the manager. 'Have we got Van der Velde's *Ideal Marriage*?' 'Yes. Could you ask the young lady to take a seat?' So she sat in this chair – poor girl, she must have been so embarrassed – and this manager of the medical department went to his desk, pulled a drawer out, got a bunch of keys, then disappeared into the basement. He came up again with a paper bag with this book in it, his keys went back in his drawer, and he said, 'I'll serve the lady.' He took her money and that was that. He said to me, 'You understand, Per, we keep books like that in The Box.' He had been down to the big safe, and taken it out of there. That, in many ways, describes what Blackwell's was.

When *Last Exit to Brooklyn* was published, Basil Blackwell was invited to give testimony at court about the book. He said he thought it was pornographic, 'because I feel it has damaged my soul'. They were a very funny lot.

Robert Clow During my training I worked in the Librairie Payot in Geneva. Mr Belowski, who ran their technical and medical section and had a smattering of English, bought their English language books, including lots of lurid Bantam paperbacks. Knowing the Penguin list fairly well, I thought I could buy the English paperbacks more successfully, but Mr Belowski would not let go. I think the real reason was that he enjoyed the old Olympia Press editions. They weren't available in Britain because they were considered to be too salacious, and they were also banned in Switzerland. But the bookshop was full of them, and every one, as it was published, appeared on the shelves, duly thumbed and read from cover to cover by Mr Belowski.

One day when I was working in the stockroom, the assistant said, 'Here's a very good *Teach Yourself* [2] book', and handed me *Teach Yourself Spanish*. I said, 'What on earth are you giving me this for?' He said, 'Look under its jacket' – as you should, as a bookseller. I took off the cover and

2 A series published by Hodder & Stoughton.

there was a volume of whatever the Olympia Press had just published in Paris, but because of Swiss censorship they had wrapped it in a *Teach Yourself* jacket.

Ainslie Thin Sometime in the early 1950s Uncle Ainslie[3] was actually taken to court because someone had come into the shop and asked for a book called something like *Blue Moon*, which happened to be published in Paris. It was ordered for the customer, and seized by the authorities when it came into the country. Poor Uncle Ainslie was taken to court and hauled over the coals for importing pornography, which I thought was rather unfair because he had no idea what the book was. He was such an upright fellow that it must have been particularly uncomfortable for him.

Elsie Bertram began her career in the book trade supplying paperbacks to retailers in Norfolk.

Elsie Bertram Pan had a certain standard. But in Yarmouth, the hotter the book, the more they wanted it. I went into one shop there, in Regent Road, where the bookseller said, 'Don't bother to call any more. Pan books won't sell here.' I said, 'Look, I've left my card and if you do get people wanting books that aren't animal antics, give me a ring and I'll come and see you again.' It was interesting, the type of books that sold in one place and not another. Yarmouth wanted all the spicy ones; Sheringham and Cromer liked the lavender and old lace.

Robert Clow John Smith's got caught up in the *Lady Chatterley*[4] debate, as other booksellers did. I was working up at our university bookshop at the time. Jack Knox[5] decided that he wasn't going to have *Lady Chatterley* in stock. Hadn't read it, and probably wouldn't have liked it, had he. But he decided that he wouldn't ban it in the university bookshop, because academics ought to know better, and if they were studying literature they might want to read it. So we sold it up at the university but not in St Vincent Street. Unfortunately the press got wind of this and John Smith's hit the front page headlines of the *Glasgow Herald* for not stocking *Lady Chatterley*. The article exposed this double standard and the reasons for it, and gave Jack no credit for that. It started off, 'Dapper Mr Knox'. And what infuriated Jack was not the fact that he was written up in a slightly snide manner, but that they called him 'dapper'. He said, 'Dapper, I am not.'

Ian Miller *Lady Chatterley* was banned in Mowbray's; we had a directive from the chairman to say that on no account were we to stock it. I had a

---

3 Ainslie Thin senior, managing director of Thin's Bookshop, Edinburgh.
4 Reference to the controversy which led to the prosecution and acquittal of Penguin Books in 1961 for publishing *Lady Chatterley's Lover* by D.H. Lawrence.
5 John Knox, managing director of John Smith's.

request from the secretary to Canon Bryan Green, Rector of St Martin's in the Bull Ring in Birmingham, who was a well-known writer and broadcaster: 'Bryan wants a copy of *Lady Chatterley* because it's of topical interest, but he clearly can't be seen to be buying it. Can you get it for him?' I said, 'I'm terribly sorry, but Mowbray's chairman has said, "Under no circumstances do you stock it."'

But Canon Green was our landlord, because Mowbray's bookshop in Birmingham was on St Martin's land. So in the end I had to creep up to Hudson's and buy one. Hudson's, which sold thousands within hours, had publishers' reps in, putting the books into envelopes and sealing them up with Sellotape. You couldn't look at a copy – you just paid your three and six and got an envelope. I bought one of these, then crept round to the rector's secretary and said, 'You owe the money to me, not Mowbray's. And tell the rector that if he ever says anything to my chairman, I will lose my job.'
Your job was really at risk? It really was, yes. No way could I have sent an order to Penguin and received an invoice made out to Mowbray's: 'One copy: *Lady Chatterley*, three and six, at two and four.'[6] It wasn't worth your job.

Gerry Davies As soon as *Lady Chatterley* was cleared by the court, the Penguin edition – which had been stored in the warehouse – was being sold everywhere. I was with Barry Hudson in Hudson's Bookshop in Birmingham, when a customer came in and said, 'We can all buy *Lady Chatterley's Lover* now – and there's a butcher down in Solihull who has managed to get a whole stack from the wholesaler.' Barry despatched me straightaway: 'Go through Solihull on the way home, buy yourself half a pound of sausages, and ask him what he's doing, selling *Lady Chatterley's Lover.*'[7] By the time I got there the books had gone, just like pork chops. I said, 'I'm from the book trade', and the butcher laughed. I think he was making half a crown on each copy.

There was such public demand that the reps had been putting them into any shop they could get them into. I had a row with Penguin about that. I said, 'Why don't booksellers get the benefit?' Ron Blass, the sales manager, just said, 'Well, we've creamed off the sales now, so we won't supply any more to outside the trade.' But at least I was able to report to the BA council that we had 'entered a very strong protest'.

Anthony Blond started his first publishing company in 1957.

Anthony Blond There was a very important case in publishing: *Last Exit to Brooklyn* by Hubert Selby, published eventually by John Calder.[8] Which I

6 The booksellers' discounted price of two shillings and four pence.
7 As secretary to the Booksellers Association, Gerry Davies represented booksellers' interests.
8 *Last Exit to Brooklyn* was published by Calder & Boyars in 1966.

was offered. I took an option on it, in fact, but I hadn't the courage to publish it. There was a tremendous trial, which didn't get as much publicity as *Lady Chatterley* but was far more significant because the judgement – Mr Justice Salmon, I remember, led the appeal court – said, 'This book should be published.' After that, anything went. That was the opening of the sluice.

Willie Kay My appointment was at four o'clock with Mr Victor Gollancz. I was shown upstairs into a Dickensian office where, around his desk, there were about six wastepaper baskets full of rejected manuscripts.

Michael Turner I first joined Methuen[1] as a publisher's reader, which meant I had to go through the slush pile[2] and recommend manuscripts that looked possible with a bit of gentle editing. You can't imagine how boring it was in that little room. Everything was looked at, everything was reported on, if only to scribble on the report sheet 'NBG'. I did get enthusiastic about one or two manuscripts – I remember an early one called *Private's Progress* – but I was told by the general editor, 'Look, you have to learn that you don't recommend the first, second or even the third manuscript you read. I'm sorry, but that's pushing it.' So a letter would have been written to the author: 'I'm so sorry, but at the moment this doesn't fit our publishing programme. I hope you have better luck with somebody a little more perceptive.'

That sounds a bit facetious. It was a lot more carefully worded, but that was effectively what it was. One has to grasp here that the level of incompetence was so awful that anything of real promise shouted out. Some books that I recommended – and there were quite a number – were turned down at editorial meetings, and rightly so. I cannot recollect anything I threw out that was successfully published elsewhere. The view from the window into Fountain Court, where people in gowns moved to and fro, played quite a large part in one's life. And I must confess that there were occasions when I fell asleep.

Anthony Blond One of my definitions of heaven is, 'A place where there are no rejection slips, so everything gets published.' And this is not heaven, is it, this world? So most of the books that you get sent are an awful nuisance. I remember some publishers refusing to even open the parcels. Too expensive to handle. I think it's probably now quite common, that

1 In 1953.
2 Unsolicited manuscripts.

unsolicited manuscripts are simply returned unread. The cost of opening them and logging them and acknowledging them is too high. It's very sad, isn't it?

How did you respond to people who sent unsolicited manuscripts? We tried to write a little letter saying something comforting. For years I didn't use a rejection slip. But then I capitulated and did.

What did a rejection slip look like? Horrible. Nastiest little thing you've ever seen in your life.

Philippa Harrison joined Jonathan Cape in 1967.

Philippa Harrison I was at a party given by a Longman editor, and Tom Maschler[3] was there. I had a really good conversation with him about books and the theatre and he said, would I come and be a reader at Cape? I thought, life is looking up. This is actually going to be a job I want to do. He said, 'Start on Monday.' Being me, I said, 'You can't possibly do that. How do you know I'll be any good? You've got to give me a test.' So he did. He gave me a book by Buckminster Fuller about the geodesic dome, 700 pages of interminable boringness, so I read and wrote a report on that. After which he said, 'I'd still like to offer you a job.' And I accepted.

What did Cape mean to you? There was simply no question – it was the best list in London at that time, by miles. Philip Roth, Marquez, Doris Lessing, Wesker, Heller, John Fowles. Almost anybody who mattered.

Why do you think he offered you the job? I think he thought I was bright, *au courant* and read a lot, and he instinctively felt he would be interested in what I had to say about books. That's very unprofessional by modern standards, but I was a good reader so it worked well for both of us.

What did you feel instinctively about him? What I instinctively felt when I worked with him, was that I trusted his judgement about a book, and I'm not a truster by nature. I thought he was a brilliant – not good, *brilliant* – chooser of books. Which is the fundamental job of a publisher.

Rosemary Goad When I first went to Fabers, a part-time reader used to come in weekly and undertake a high-speed preliminary reading of the slush pile. She was the one who wrote on the letter submitting *Lord of the Flies* – then titled *Strangers from Within* – 'Absurd and uninteresting fantasy about a group of children in jungle country. Rubbish and dull.' When Charles Monteith arrived,[4] full of bounce and hope, he thought the slush pile was important, so he ran it with me and other younger editors. After a while, I ran it myself, and I also tried to bring in younger editors.

You always thought it might be marvellous, but it was a real chore, actually. Every manuscript had already been logged into a huge ledger

3 Managing director of Jonathan Cape.
4 Charles Monteith joined Faber & Faber as an editor on 30 September 1953.

bound in dark red leather with *Manuscript Book* in gold letters on the front. Poetry, plays and children's would have gone to the various editors to read, but the general manuscripts were all piled on the octagonal table in the boardroom and we had a huge number to get through. Four or five of us would do them on a Tuesday, the day before the 'book committee', as the weekly editorial meeting was known. We would look at each one and write a brief summary of the plot, with comments – whether you thought it was a possible and should be read by an outside reader, or whether it was obviously out. I would have two pieces of A4 stuck together, with the titles and authors typed on the left and the comments on the right. The list came up at every book committee, so everyone could scan through to make sure their brother-in-law wasn't there, so to speak, and recommend suitable readers where appropriate. The system worked very well. You didn't, on the whole, lose manuscripts, and every single one was looked at. And if you turned something down which later appeared as a bestseller, you could trace back what had happened.

How did 'Lord of the Flies' get past that first reader? Because after she had made her comments, there would be a meeting with the editors. I remember Charles Monteith taking the manuscript and asking me, 'Do you think it's any good?' It was the most amazing manuscript, *Lord of the Flies*, because something had gone wrong with William Golding's typewriter and there was a comma between almost every word, and it had been to thirteen other publishers, so 'dog-eared' hardly describes it. It was terribly untasty looking. I remember Charles being very excited, and Ann Faber, who was a shrewd reader, thought it was very good. So it was taken on.[5] It slept for a bit; it didn't immediately rush away. Very little else arrived in the slush pile, that I remember.

Philippa Harrison I worked right at the back of 30 Bedford Square, in a small, narrow room up some stairs. Cape's other reader at the time was Catherine Storr.[6] We read every manuscript that came in – whether it was contracted or came from an agent – before it was read by anyone else, and wrote a report on it. It was a pretty amazing job for someone of twenty-five – I was the first person to read the manuscript of *The French Lieutenant's Woman*,[7] for instance.

One day a week Catherine and I would go through the slush pile together. We would give ourselves five minutes each on a book and if we both thought no, that was that. But if either of us thought it was OK, we would put it back and one of us would give it more time later. I made mistakes, because I knew how much it mattered to people, so if books were three quarters there, I often tried to help them. But it never worked, and it

---

5 William Golding, *Lord of the Flies*, Faber & Faber, 1954.
6 We were unable to verify the spelling of this name.
7 John Fowles, *The French Lieutenant's Woman*, Jonathan Cape, 1969.

didn't add to the sum of human happiness, because in the end the books weren't published, so it would have been better just to have rejected them. That was an important lesson to learn.

You said that you read 'The French Lieutenant's Woman'? And just gaped. I learned a lesson from that, too, because that was the earliest 'great manuscript' that I had read, and I simply assumed that when it came out, every reviewer would fall on their knees and go 'Aah!' Did they hell. The English reviews were frightful. There had been a film of *The Collector*, and the reviewers basically wrote, 'Nice film script, dear. OK, so you've made loads of money.' I was very young, and I just couldn't believe it. And, for what it's worth, it didn't shake my sense of the book for a second. I thought, who are all these mad people? But then, in America – which doesn't dislike fame – the reviews were ecstatic: 'This book is a masterpiece.' And by the time the book came out in paperback, that view had crossed back over the Atlantic and *The French Lieutenant's Woman* became the phenomenon it is.

I was lucky to have been inoculated by that early on. That job was perfect training if you were going to be somebody who ended up choosing books to publish: you saw almost everything that could possibly happen, without being responsible for it. You never had to think about money, and you never had to think about negotiating, because the decision about whether or not to publish a book would be made by Tom Maschler, Ed Victor and Graham C. Greene[8] after reading the report. The job of reader – which I did for six years – was purely about choice and editing, and you learned from watching which books sold and which books didn't.

Do publishers read their slush piles today? Some do, some don't. It has to be said, we very seldom found anything in the slush pile. I wouldn't say that it's very productive, but I do think it's proper that it should be read.

Rosemary Goad Fabers always thought they were going to find something in what we called 'the manuscripts' and everyone was always optimistic – always, against all the odds. I fought a furious battle to retain the slush pile in the '80s, when other publishers were giving up theirs, and I won. But an enormous number of publishers have closed them down because they say that nobody has time to do the reading, the number of successes you find are not worth the effort, and all good things nowadays come in through agents. That's the argument. I don't agree with a word of it.

How did you argue for keeping it? I argued that to close your doors goes against all the criteria of running a publishing company, and that if you weren't looking for authors and keeping your door open for submissions, there was no point in being there.

Even though a remarkably small percentage of work would turn out to be publishable? Yes, I think so. It's so dispiriting for anybody who's writing to think

8 Directors of Jonathan Cape.

that they can't send work in. And many agents now won't take on anybody new, so it is very hard. I know there's a lot of rubbish – of course there is. But I always thought it was good, particularly for new editors, to look at what was coming in. You have to, really, if that's going to be your profession. What kind of books are appealing to people? What kind of books are they copying? And you need to see a wide variety of submissions to get some idea of standards.

Philippa Harrison When I went to Hutchinson it became my responsibility to decide whether a book was bought or not. You would get into boring conversations with people who weren't in publishing, always asking the same question, which was basically: 'Why, just because *you* say, should a book be published?' It was a very common first reaction from people at parties, for instance: 'What training did you have? How do you know?' To which the answer is actually, 'Experience. And you've either got it or you haven't got it; and if you haven't got it, you get fired.'

Andrew Franklin Early in my career I was at Faber & Faber – a chaotically run company – where, probably because I was the most junior person in the building in Queen's Square,[9] I had to deal with the slush pile. A letter came in that was written on blue Basildon Bond, saying that this person wanted to do a book on Militant Tendency. It is probably largely forgotten now, but Militant Tendency was a rabid part of the hard left, particularly strong in Liverpool. The idea was quite interesting. Not specially interesting, but quite interesting. Then I noticed that the name at the bottom was Michael Crick. He had been president of the Oxford Union and I had known him vaguely when I was at Oxford. It was a really scrappy letter and there was no agent involved, and if you hadn't known who he was, you would have turned it down. But I did know who he was, and I knew he had been formidably clever, so I got him to write a proposal. He then wrote a really brilliant exposé of Militant, fair-minded and measured, which was very successful.

Rosemary Goad A lot of unsolicited manuscripts at Fabers came from people who had thought, everybody's got a book in them, and copied their favourite author. You also found people with a real story to tell, but the manuscript just wasn't put together well enough. In the old days in Fabers, editors would work on books with authors and produce something publishable that probably wasn't going to sell more than 2,500. They were usually reminiscences – books about farming in Wales or living in a croft in Scotland. They would give some quiet enjoyment but they weren't going to make people's pulses race. We did quite a lot of them. But after 1980 or so,

9 Faber & Faber moved from Russell Square to Queen's Square on 1 March 1971.

that kind of book was no longer being published. They were the victims, I think, of everybody becoming more commercially minded.

Carole Blake As a literary agent, I come back from the Frankfurt Book Fair completely exhausted and usually with flu, after the most intensive period of the year, with a lot of follow-up work to do. When I walk into my room there will be nine days' worth of unsolicited manuscripts piled up – hundreds and hundreds and hundreds of sample chapters and outlines – and we won't have a chance to look at them for at least ten days after the fair. I know that I'm eventually going to have to spend a Sunday in the office, going through them, by which point there will be chasing letters from some of those writers, indignant that they haven't had a response within the four weeks I stipulate in my book.[10] I think, if only they could see these piles.

What happens if writers send manuscripts straight to publishers? Most publishers just send them back with a printed compliments slip saying, 'We don't look at unsolicited manuscripts. Try to get an agent.'

Do you know why they won't look at them? It costs a fortune. It's very expensive to have a trained member of staff – there's no point having somebody untrained – assess unsolicited manuscripts. By the law of averages you have to look at hundreds, possibly thousands, before finding one you want to publish – and that one might still lose money. So publishers will say, quite logically, that it doesn't pay. They would rather look through what agents send in, because agents have done the initial sifting.

It would be very easy for us not to look at the slush pile – that's a horrible term, but it's the shorthand – and employ somebody to come in one day a week and just go through it all. But Isobel Dixon[11] and I know that we can only take on a tiny proportion of what comes in, so there's no point paying somebody to read it all. So we take it in turns to look at these piles every couple of days, knowing that we have to be very, very harsh. If we haven't got time to read the material, we haven't got time to represent it. I want to look through those piles and dislike everything, unless something grabs me by the throat – and by the heart. The only way I want to increase my client base is by taking on books that make your fingers tingle with excitement when you pick them up. I think that the moment you stop looking at the unsolicited pile, or you expect it all to be rubbish, you should stop being an agent. The idea of discovering new talent is tremendously exciting.

Anthony Blond A publisher is offered so many things that it's quite a relief to find a reason for saying no. When you turn them down you're never alone. A lot of people turned down *The Exorcist*, for instance. I turned it down once, then bought it later. Do you remember that book? Whoops!

10 Carole Blake, *From Pitch to Publication*, Pan Macmillan, first published 1999.
11 Book agent and director of Blake Friedmann Literary Agency.

I went over to America . . . Are you sure I haven't told you this story? I saw an editor called Mark Jaffe,[12] who is a charming, elegant gentleman. He said, 'Anthony, I owe you a favour.' 'Why?' 'You published a book that I wanted you to do and it didn't do at all well.' And I *had* published a book that he wanted me to do and it *didn't* do at all well. He said, 'But I've got a present for you. It's called *The Exorcist*'. I said, 'Can I read it?' 'No, you don't read it, you just buy it.' So I cabled my partner, Desmond Briggs: 'Please buy *The Exorcist.*' He rang me up and said, 'Do you realise we turned it down when it was at 3,000?'[13] By this time we were having to pay eight. We bought it and published it and nothing much happened. Then I read in the *Evening Standard* that the film had been shown in New York and ambulances had taken away members of the audience because they passed out, and I realised we had something. The paperback sold something like fourteen million copies in America. Fourteen *million*. And it sold all over the world.

Philippa Harrison I read *The Exorcist,* and wrote a report saying, 'I think this is the most enormously commercial book but completely unsuitable for Cape.' I don't know that it would be unsuitable for Cape now, but it certainly would have been then. Although they did publish Jeffrey Archer, so perhaps I was wrong.
Do you remember who did publish 'The Exorcist'? No. But I remember it being fantastically successful.[14]

Diane Spivey What impressed me when I first arrived at Hutchinson was the sheer breadth of publishing and that the books did not always have to be of enormous literary merit – there could be other criteria for publishing them, such as commercial potential, or quality within a particular genre. At university I had been reading books that already had a stamp of approval – set texts, or Picadors, or ones that friends had recommended. Then suddenly I was faced with proofs without covers or blurbs, so there were no clues to tell me whether they were meant to be great literature or pot boilers. Hutchinson published Barbara Cartland's books and other romances, and I realised that I had no yardstick for judging one romance against another – I wouldn't know whether it was good of its type, or just trash. That made me realise that I was not cut out to be an editor, so I decided I would be better off selling books that other people told me were good – and I developed a new respect for editors.

Philippa Harrison That instinctive 'I just know' when you first read a manuscript is completely informed by everything else you have read, and by having seen what succeeds and what fails. By the time I went to work at

12 Veteran US publisher (at New American Library, Bantam Books and elsewhere).
13 It is unclear from the recording whether this refers to dollars or sterling.
14 William Peter Blatty, *The Exorcist*, Blond & Briggs, 1971.

Michael Joseph, I'd had seven years at Cape. I don't think that, *tabula rasa* out of university, you could know about commercial fiction. Possibly, you could know about 'good'. I think they are different forms of judgement. And what does 'just know' mean? It means that you don't find what happens in the book predictable – you find it compulsive.

Do you mean in terms of 'good' or in terms of a bestseller? Bestseller. I can't put words nearly so easily to 'good'. It's to do with an ear for writing, and with the writer's capacity for perception and thought. I was going to say, 'But the most important thing is the quality of the writing.' I'm not sure if that's true, actually. But it's certainly incredibly important.

Andrew Franklin I learned a great lesson later from Peter Carson, who was editorial director at Penguin when I was an editor there. When we discussed the pros and cons of a book that came in – it might have been an 800-page book that was going to be auctioned within two weeks – Peter would always say, 'What we must do is read it.' So the decision would always be made on the basis of reading the manuscript. Bizarrely, that is quite rare in publishing today. A lot of people say, 'Is the author promotable? Is she good looking? What would he be like on television? How have her previous books done?' But actually to go back to the text and ask, 'Is it a good book?' meant that at the core of Penguin what mattered was the book and the author.

Then how do you decide? You have to be able to engage with it yourself personally. You have to look for a spark of originality, particularly with fiction. You don't want to think, the characters have different names and it's set in Chiswick rather than Clapham but I have read this book before. It has to be new and fresh and – this is the hard part – you also have to feel that you know *how* to publish it; which means that you know what you will tell the world about it: how you will package it and how you will persuade other people to read it. If you can't do that, you can't publish it successfully.

Where did you learn all that? You don't learn it in any formal way and you certainly can't teach it. Some people have it and some people don't. I do not think you could possibly teach it on a university publishing degree course. You watch other people doing it and see what informs their judgements. And, of course, you learn from your mistakes.

Bruno Brown By the time I was sixteen I was determined that I wanted to be a publisher.

What did you envisage? Reading a lot of books and meeting a lot of authors and being paid for it.

Michael Turner Publishing was regarded as a bit of a glamorous job. But there was a difference between the popular conception and the job itself. Very few people know how publishers actually spend their day, unless they are dealing with 'famous authors'. And there is a touch of the raffish about that, because the reputation of authors is a bit that way inclined. You get people saying, 'What is x really like? He must have a marvellous life – all those women' or 'all those men.' If you work in banking, it is regarded as safe, but not particularly exciting, whereas people think that a relationship with a famous author may well be.

Charles Pick The first author I met was Dorothy Sayers, soon after I went to work at Gollancz. I had just read a proof copy of *The Nine Tailors*, and I was told to take her upstairs to the production lady. As we went up the rickety staircase at the back of the building, I said, 'Miss Sayers, I've just read your new book. I must congratulate you on your knowledge of campano-logy.' She turned round. 'Young man,' she said, 'Twenty minutes with the *Encyclopaedia Britannica*.' That was a moment of great disillusion. I had thought she must have a lifetime's knowledge of the subject.
What was she like? Very unattractive – stout, with pince-nez, and a rather florid face. But her books were very popular.

Per Saugman In 1953 Blackwell Scientific Publishing was the twenty-third largest out of the twenty-three members of the Publishers Association Medical Group. I looked at these elderly gentlemen – their average age was between fifty-five and sixty-five – all heads of well-respected, long-established publishing firms, and thought, 'Hmm. Nobody is ever going to send us a manuscript. I have to go out and find them.' So I began to speak to people: 'Is there a need for a book on thoracic surgery?' 'I don't think so. But there is a need for a book on the pathology of the kidney.' 'Oh, really? Who should write that?' 'Professor Cameron.' You would check with somebody else: 'I was thinking of asking Professor Cameron to write a book on the pathology of the kidney. Do you think that's a good idea?' 'He is the only man that can write a really authoritative book.' Then you wrote to Professor Cameron – you always wrote, you never rang them up – 'May I come and see you?' and he would reply, 'I'm afraid that I am already writing a book for Livingstone's.' Then you swallowed your pride and replied, 'I'm so glad to hear it. The main thing, of course, is that the book is being written.'

I can say one thing in honesty: I don't think I am much of a genius, but I have been very, very energetic.

Stan Remington Most people think that publishers exist by sitting down at their desks and sorting through a mass of unsolicited manuscripts from which they will pick out the plums and make their fortune. But the big numbers have not generally been in fiction, and certainly not fiction by unknown authors. Vaster numbers have been sold of publications like cookery books – I think *Odham's Practical Cookery* sold nearly half a million copies, long before Delia Smith. And when they are authored books, it is often because a publisher has thought, *that* person has an interesting story, or a particularly in-depth understanding of their subject. I must see if I can get them to write a book.

Per Saugman I had a breakthrough in 1955 after a haematologist in London told me, 'That woman over there is the world's expert on the liver. You'll be all right if you can get a book from her.' So I visited her at home. 'Yes,' she said, 'I am writing a book on diseases of the liver.' She showed me a windowsill full of documents: 'How many pages do you think it will make?' I said, 'Four hundred and sixty-four.' 'What will it cost?' 'Forty-seven shillings and sixpence.' She said, 'That's what others have said. Well, you will hear from me.'

I went back to the office and wrote, as I always did, 'It was a great pleasure to meet you . . .' and told her about the contract. I didn't hear a word from her. Three months later, somebody said, 'Professor Sherlock has just signed up with another publisher. You missed a good book there.' So I wrote again: 'Dear Professor Sherlock, May I remind you of our conversation? I am still interested in your book and would very much like to publish it.' And she replied: 'Dear Saugman, I haven't yet signed with anybody. Go and see my husband at the Middlesex Hospital. He is my business manager.' I said to myself, I will flatter him. So I invited him to lunch – nobody else had done that – and I got the book.[15]

Having agreed to sign with me, Sheila Sherlock invited me to receptions and introduced me to people and recommended other authors to come to Blackwell's. I owe her a tremendous amount – publishing is about connections and connections and connections. Sheila Sherlock herself became one of Blackwell's most important authors. My wife said to her one day, 'Why did you sign up with Per?' She said, 'He was quite good looking, he was keen, and he was my age, so I thought he would last several editions.'

Charles Pick I couldn't imagine any other job that I would have liked more than publishing. It was the thrill of finding new authors, the excitement of launching a new one, then seeing talent develop and mature. I was always interested in finding new authors, rather than taking on those who were already established.

Monica Dickens was an author I discovered. I met her at a dance, and she told me about the jobs she had taken below stairs. While we were dancing, I said, 'If you could write a book in the same way you are telling me these stories, it would do very well.' She was only twenty, but books by people who wrote humorously about their jobs were very fashionable at the time. She said, 'That's my secret ambition. Nobody in my family has written since Charles Dickens.' I said, 'Well, you had better come and see my boss, Michael Joseph.' Which she did the next day. He was intrigued by the idea of

15 Sheila Sherlock, *Diseases of the Liver and Biliary System*, Blackwell Scientific Publications, 1955.

a book about life below stairs written by the great-granddaughter of Charles Dickens. He signed her up and gave her a contract for something nominal like £100, and she took six weeks to write *One Pair of Hands*. We became lifelong friends as a result.

Where was the dance? In Paddington. It was to raise money for the ARP,[16] because the war was coming. That was in December 1937. She followed that one up with *One Pair of Feet*, about working in hospital during the war, and those books have sold and sold ever since.[17]

Mark Barty-King Charles Pick could take a book and make it into a bestseller – I've never seen anything quite like it. Take *Coronet Among the Weeds* by Charlotte Bingham: all London was talking about that book when I first went to Heinemann. He did it by planting the name, and the idea that the book was really special, with all the right people – it was as simple as that. There would be no real marketing campaign in those days; it was all word of mouth.

Bruno Brown When I arrived in India one of my first jobs was to sell the *Concise Oxford Dictionary*. All the teachers were recommending it, but Indian pupils found it hard to use. They would look up a word, and if they couldn't understand the definition they would look up a word in the definition, and eventually came back to the one they'd looked up in the first place. And it had very little about grammar. So I decided that we wanted a dictionary especially for Indian undergraduate types and tucked this idea away in my mind.

One day I read an advertisement by a Japanese publisher for what was, in effect, this book – an advanced dictionary of current English – which was being compiled by three teachers of English in Japan: A.S. Hornby, Gatenby and Wakefield. So I wrote to the Japanese publisher and said, could we apply for the English Indian market rights? Back came a letter: 'Yes, make us an offer.' So I did. They seemed enthusiastic, and Hornby – who was the leading author – was pleased, so we made a definite agreement. At that point the war broke out, so the whole thing went into the melting pot. But after the war we persuaded the senior people in the OUP that this was a promising idea, and we published the *Advanced Learner's Dictionary* in 1948. It sold incredibly well, and continues to sell to this day.

How important was that book to Oxford University Press? Very important. It became the leading book in English language teaching.

Do Longmans have anything similar? They tried, but only recently. We didn't worry about it. It's difficult to catch up.

16 Air Raid Precautions.
17 *One Pair of Hands*, Michael Joseph, 1939; *One Pair of Feet*, Michael Joseph, 1942.

Tim Rix If you were talking to the head of an English department in a school, you were also listening to see whether you thought they would be able to write or not.

How would you tell? Usually because they started talking about ideas for books that they believed were needed, and if they did that well, you thought they might be able to write the ones in question. The famous L.G. Alexander – Louis Alexander – was teaching at the Eton of Greece when he was found by our European sales rep, Dennis Walker.

Louis had been brought up in England – he was half Greek and half English – so he spoke perfect English and perfect Greek. Dennis thought this man was terrific, so he wrote a report back to London saying, 'I am sure this is one of the best ELT authors around.' Louis already had an idea for a book, which in fact became his first. That was *First Steps to Précis*. It doesn't sound wildly exciting, but it became a bestseller.

As a result of that, Louis came back to London in the mid-1960s to become a full-time ELT author financed by Longman. His particular abilities and knowledge – and his use of applied linguistics – meshed perfectly with developments in ELT at that time, so from a publisher's point of view the whole thing was magic. Louis Alexander eventually got into the *Guinness Book of Records* as one of the bestselling authors of all time.

Trevor Moore There was one particular American author who was very important to Hodder, and he was looked after by Michael Attenborough.[18] As West End rep, I was charged with the responsibility of making sure that his new novel was well promoted in all the obvious places American tourists stayed. I used to call on the Smith's outlets at the Hilton, the Dorchester, Grosvenor House and the Cumberland – you just went to the relevant bookstall and said, 'Will you take?' and they always did, because it was good business. No problem at all.

But this author was staying at the Savoy, and you weren't allowed to call there because its bookstall was run by Selfridges – by remote control, as far as we reps were concerned. Michael Attenborough said, 'You must get it into the Savoy Hotel.' I said, 'I'll organise it, I promise.' So I talked to my friend in Selfridges' book department: 'Pat – big favour coming up. So-and-so is going to be staying at the Savoy Hotel from Friday. I want you to ensure that there are at least ten copies on show the whole time he is there. It's very important. Can you please do that for me?' 'Of course, Trevor. No problem at all.' And I kept reminding him about it. 'No problem, Trevor. Stop worrying.'

In the event, of course, Pat forgot, so the author arrived, there were no books, and he exploded – because there weren't any of his books at the Savoy Hotel bookstall, and the minion working in the bookstall had never heard of him. Michael Attenborough told me what had taken place, and it

---

18 A director (and an owner) of Hodder & Stoughton.

was something on the lines of, 'What kind of goddam fuckin' publisher do you fuckin' think you are? Your biggest fuckin' author staying in town; you can't even get his fuckin' book into the fuckin' shop in the place he's staying.' Poor Michael Attenborough had had to take the full force of this diatribe, and I wasn't very popular at Hodder for a while after that.

Mark Barty-King There were some authors that you didn't necessarily get on with particularly well. I think there were some that you probably didn't understand. But they were still authors – they were still people one took one's hat off to.
Not all publishers are as appreciative about authors as you sound. Maybe not, but I've never had to change my view in forty years of publishing: the author is the most important person on the block. You're nothing without an author – you might as well not exist.

Tim Rix When I first went into Longman, authors were bottom of the heap of mankind. It was extraordinary.
How did you notice that? By the way people talked. Authors were a nuisance. Not for everybody, of course. But it was in the culture: authors were a nuisance who somehow had to be coped with because you had to get books out. Pretty incredible when you think about it. I tried hard to change that later. We used to give a huge party in Stationers' Hall every summer for all the authors in overseas and UK schools education. The entertaining was important: it cemented the relationship and meant that authors would take a lot of trouble to get their books right, so we had dedicated people trying to produce the best books on whatever their subject was. And once they had become a friend, the likelihood of them going off to another publisher diminished virtually to vanishing point.

Longman had very few defections in those days. There was one in Malaysia, but it wasn't so much that the author defected as that he was a kind of 'girl who can't say no'. And he admitted it: 'If publisher x asks, "Will you do this?" I do it.' But otherwise I can hardly remember any serious defection of any Longman schools author to another publisher. We assumed that if we treated our authors right and looked after them and entertained them, they would stay with us.

Carmen Callil I think publishers were grossly unfair to authors when I entered the business. At Virago I had known that everybody was contributing to the establishment of the company; our authors took very low advances, and I only paid royalties once a year – I couldn't do them twice yearly, because I didn't have the energy and time. But when I went from Virago to Chatto,[19] I discovered that people like Iris Murdoch were paid

19 Carmen Callil became joint managing director of Chatto with Hugo Brunner in 1982.

chicken feed – £500, £800 in advance. No advance at all, really. I remember coming across one book where they had offered the author descending royalties: as the book sold, they were paid less. I think that was a very old-fashioned attitude – an Edwardian attitude – towards the author. And when I entered publishing that's what it was like. Publishers were grand and had posh lunches and spent lots of money on themselves and had houses in the country. And authors were quite often broke.

Trevor Moore Laurie Lee's book, *I Can't Stay Long*, was published when I was at Deutsch, during the period when he wasn't producing the further volume of memoirs that André was desperate for, to follow *When I Walked Out One Midsummer Morning*, which Deutsch had already published. But Chatto had published his first book. Many years later, not long before he died, I saw this old man in Broad Street, Oxford, peering myopically into Blackwell's window. I approached him carefully and said, 'Excuse me. It's Laurie Lee, isn't it?' He turned round suspiciously and said, 'Yes.' I said, 'Laurie, I don't expect you'll remember me, but my name's Trevor Moore and I knew you back in the days when I worked at Deutsch.' He said, 'Of course I remember you. What are you doing now?' I told him I was working for Random House. 'Random House?' he said. 'That's Chatto, isn't it?' I said, 'Yes, I do actually handle the Chatto list.' 'Chatto,' he said. 'Do you know, they still owe me royalties on *Cider with Rosie*.'

Andrew Franklin When I first went to Penguin, I thought that what mattered to authors was that you sold the greatest number of copies possible, because that's what matters to the publishing company. I changed my mind when I started publishing first-time novelists at Hamish Hamilton, and thought what mattered most was good reviews, because you can't really make a living from publishing first novels, so you're probably working as something else and what you care about is the sense that you have a future as a writer. But I now realise that actually authors care about the whole thing, and they also mind about their relationship with their publishers. Of course, they care about the money, too. Publishing is a business, and if we don't stay in business, then – as Stanley Unwin[20] said – we have failed in our principal duty to our authors.

Carol Unwin married Rayner Unwin, son of Sir Stanley, in 1952.

Carol Unwin We used to get fed up at home with hearing Rayner say, 'I've got to go to Oxford again; I must try to get another chapter out of Tolkien.' Obviously it was in Allen & Unwin's interests to get *The Lord of the Rings* into print, but I think Tolkien enjoyed working on this tremendous project more

20 Sir Stanley Unwin, founder of George Allen & Unwin Ltd. His publications include *The Truth About Publishing*, Allen & Unwin, 1926.

than he bothered about it becoming a publication. I don't think he was frantic to earn money – he was working as a professor in Oxford – so he needed prodding. Rayner had read the manuscript of *The Hobbit* as a child – it had been sent to one or two publishers – and told his father to please go ahead with it because he was sure that children would think it was wonderful. It wasn't a book in the Allen & Unwin mould – mostly they published educational, scientific and philosophical books – but Rayner had seen great potential in it. And later he felt that *The Lord of the Rings* was a very worthwhile project.

From the way you have described Rayner, I wouldn't have thought he would have been interested in fantasy writing. That puzzles me, too. But he had great faith in Tolkien as being hugely imaginative and clever to have thought the book out in such amazing depth – the more he learned about the background, the more staggered he was. I never heard him saying, 'This book could make us rich.' But I do remember him saying later, once *The Lord of the Rings* was published, 'We can't seem to stop it now. I just envisage it going on and on. All the hard work is over.'

When was the first time you met Tolkien? I don't remember. Certainly not until I was married to Rayner, when we must have gone once or twice to Oxford together, just to have a coffee and talk about the book. But I have vivid recollections of Tolkien himself: he would have a secretive little smile and his pipe would be dangling out of his mouth, and he would be telling some amusing story. At least, amusing to himself, because he mumbled, so you usually couldn't quite hear what he was saying. Then he would start laughing hilariously about the story, and puff away some more at his pipe. He was absolutely charming, but he was living in a world of his own. A very likeable man. Rayner and he got on very easily together.

What did he look like? I'm not as good at describing people as he was at describing hobbits, but he was rather hobbit-like really. A very pleasant, smiling face. Not very tall. Mousey-coloured hair.

How did he dress? In rather shapeless suits, well elbowed-out and kneed-out – the same as Rayner would be wearing. I think he always wore a tie.

Somebody listening to this tape can't see how much you're smiling as you're talking about Tolkien. Did you like him? Yes. I liked him very much. It was extremely comfortable being in his company. He was very friendly, and incredibly appreciative – if one had given him a nice lunch, for instance, and we were sitting in the garden with the sun shining and butterflies around, and the buddleia smelling sweet, and he was smoking his pipe.

Where would that have been? At the end of the garden, where our son, Merlin, built a semi-circular sitting-out place with old bricks and paving stones and white pillars with stone balls on top. It was called either the 'demi-lune' or 'the gin and tonic area'. We planted it with climbing roses and a vine. I remember sitting out there with Tolkien, and the afternoon sun slanting across it. It's now become terribly overgrown: the white pillars are completely covered in ivy and have rotted at the bottom. The paving stones are still there, but are covered with moss and little creeping plants. I'm afraid my garden is showing its fifty-two years of our being here.

I'm interested in the relationship between Rayner and Tolkien, as publisher and author. I'm told that they got on very well, and I've heard Christopher Tolkien say that his father entirely trusted Rayner.

What would he have needed to trust him with? That he wouldn't tamper with his writing, I think, and try to change it. Rayner respected him enormously as a scholar, and certainly as a writer. I think there was complete respect on each side. Sir Stanley used to make sure that Rayner dealt with Tolkien, because Rayner had an awful lot of patience, which his father hadn't. I can still hear Sir Stanley shaking his head and saying, 'Are we never going to get this manuscript together? We really have to get on with it before *this* Christmas comes around.' So Rayner would go and have a nice cup of tea and a gentle chat and see whether perhaps a little bit of progress could be made during the next few months. Rayner could be impatient over some things in life, but not when he was dealing with an author of the calibre of Tolkien.

Ronald Whiting *The Fellowship of the Ring*[21] was not the easiest book to get into the bookshops. It was greeted by Tommy Joy, then at the Army & Navy Stores and later famous as the Queen's bookseller at Hatchards, saying, 'I do not sell books on fairies.' That was a fairly common reaction.

Belinda McGill When I first went to work at the Bodley Head,[22] Max Reinhardt was going through the production stage of Charlie Chaplin's autobiography, which had been seven years in the writing. That book put Max onto the international market in a big way. He had been trying for years to get Chaplin to finish writing it, and to get a contract out of him. The contract was actually signed that spring, I think. Max had paid out the advance with no contract; he had just trusted in luck that it would eventually happen. It was a huge undertaking – hundreds of thousands of pounds were involved, which nowadays is commonplace for an advance, but in those days was not. It was quite a gamble that Max took, although he could see that it was going to be a huge coup because he had world rights.

Max Reinhardt I used to go to Switzerland to see Chaplin once a month, or once every two months – at first he wanted me there every day, but I told him it wasn't possible, I had to run an office. He used to dictate the text to a secretary, then he would read it to me, and I would tell him what I thought and make suggestions, then he would think about it – but he usually put his

21 This first volume of *The Lord of the Rings* trilogy was published in 1954.
22 Early in 1964.

own words in again. After six years we got the book out, and it was a huge success.

Did you ever get impatient about how long it was taking? No, because I knew that we had to go through it like that. That it would be a great success, I had no doubt at all. Everybody had been clamouring for the rights, and when Chaplin announced that the Bodley Head had acquired them, I knew that we were in for a very good thing.

How did you manage to acquire them? Through Graham Greene.[23] We had read in the papers that Chaplin was busy writing his autobiography, and Graham said, 'That must be a marvellous book. Let me write and ask whether we can go and see him.' So Graham wrote, and never got an answer. I then suggested that I should write to Chaplin and say that, as we were going to Switzerland, could we ask if he and his wife would have dinner with us? To my surprise Chaplin replied and said yes. He also told me that if I wrote to him again, I should put my name on the front of the envelope because he never opened letters from people whom he didn't know.

Luckily my wife came to Switzerland with us, and she and Mrs Chaplin discovered that they had both been to adjacent schools in New York. Chaplin had asked us to stay at the house and, after the ladies had retired to bed, he read some of what he had written, to Graham Greene and myself. It was about the early part of his life and described great poverty and the troubles his mother had been through. As he read, tears were flowing from his eyes. He read from midnight until two o'clock in the morning, then said, 'That's as far as I've got.' So we all went to bed. The next day Graham and I told him how marvellous we thought it was. After that we met regularly.

What were your first impressions of him? One was a little bit in awe of him – Chaplin's name was legendary.

What was his manner like with you? He was very polite. Very touchy, too. He didn't like being criticised.

How did you criticise him? I didn't criticise him. We got on very well.

Belinda McGill The book was actually published the first September I was at the Bodley Head, and it was terribly exciting to be caught up in that. Most of my work during that first year was soothing Chaplin and saying, 'Yes, we'll change "and" to "but" in line three from the bottom of page 248.' Whatever he wanted went. He was quite a difficult man, Chaplin, you had to really spoil him and let him have his own way. But Max was diplomatic to the nth. He really was very clever at coping with Chaplin, because he so much wanted the book. If Chaplin dug his toes in, Max would let it go for a bit, then he would come back and say, 'You remember you suggested the

23 The writer, who became a director of the Bodley Head in the late 1950s.

other day . . .' Chaplin would say, 'Did I?' And Max would say, 'Yes, I think you're right. I think we should do it that way.' When really it had been Max's idea in the first place. A persuasive man, Max. Very cultured, very able to make other people see his point of view.

He later sold Chaplin's serial rights to *The Sunday Times*. The owner, Roy Thomson, went to Moscow to meet Khrushchev, whose son-in-law happened to be the editor of *Isvestya*. He said, 'I would like to serialise the book. Can you do anything about it for me?' So Max was asked, and he asked Chaplin, 'What price do we ask from them?' Chaplin said, 'Let's have some caviar.' So *Isvestya*, who had never paid a copyright fee in their lives before, sent six kilos of caviar over in three two-kilo pots, one of which Max was told by Charlie to take home: 'Try it out, make sure it's Beluga.' And the caviar was served at the launch party, which was held at the Savoy.

Max Reinhardt When the book was finished, his wife told me she was amazed that a potentially difficult relationship between publisher and author should have ended in real friendship.
Do you think it is a difficult relationship? I don't think so. I got on very well with my authors.
Do you think there's any particular reason for that? I respect the author, and I respect what they write, and I respect what they do. Graham Greene was another close personal friend. A lot of people write, asking for information about Graham Greene, but I don't think it's for me to give personal information about somebody I knew, and I think one must respect the wishes of people who are close to an author.
How important was it for you to be friends with your authors? I wasn't friends with all my authors. But I looked after them very well.

Diana Murray We did an enormous number of things for authors. For instance, whenever Axel Munthe came to London in the summer, Jock[24] had to find him a flat in central London within sight of trees, where he could hear birds sing and where there would be plenty of wine waiting for him.

He was a difficult author, Axel Munthe, but immensely interesting. He wrote a bestseller called *The Story of San Michele*, and was supposed to have psychic powers. Women were tremendously excited when they heard he was coming to London; he's probably quite forgotten today. The moment his visit was announced in the paper, invitations would pour in from all sorts of people, such as the Asquiths, who wanted to have him to dinner, and my husband would answer some of those for him. There were also letters from people wanting his help, because of this psychic gift. He once had a letter from a lady saying, 'I am the wife of a clergyman. We have a happy marriage, but we don't seem to get on in bed together at all. I know that you

24 John (Jock) Murray, publisher, and husband to Diana.

have mysterious powers. Please can you help?' When Jock showed him this letter, Axel Munthe said, 'You're the more recently married, Jock. You are the one who must answer this letter.'

And who did? Jock did. But it may have gone back to Munthe to be signed. Relations with authors were always very close at Murrays. I think that personal relationship was all-important to the business – you draw the best out of people if you're friendly with them. Jock was lucky in that he could be quite a strict censor from a book point of view, but he could do it in a friendly way without offending people.

What would you say he expected from his authors? I think he expected loyalty. But it was easier then, because someone who became our author was probably our author for life. Nowadays we can't expect that. As a very small firm with limited resources, we can't compete if someone is offered enormous sums elsewhere.

John R. Murray, elder son of Diana and John (Jock) Murray became the seventh John Murray in the family firm.

John Murray My great uncle – old Sir John Murray – didn't have a very creative list. He very much published First World War memoirs and memoirs by his old friends – characters such as Lord Cadogan – who used to come in and chat to him. He also edited the *Quarterly Review*, and he would sit there and dictate review after review to his secretary without a note. He had a very good mind, but his relationships with authors weren't particularly close, as far as I know. Whereas my father's authors were all friends of the family: Osbert Lancaster and Francis Younghusband were godfathers to my sisters; John Piper was my brother's godfather; Freya Stark was my godmother. Then there was Kenneth Clark and Patrick Leigh Fermor and Betjeman. My father had terrific charisma. When he joined the firm, authors started coming to Murrays again.

Diana Murray The story of how Betjeman came is delightful. Jock had only just left Oxford, done his spell at the printers, and gone into Murray's. At Oxford he had made friends with John Betjeman, and was very interested in his early poetry. The only Betjeman poems to have been published at that time were in a small hand-printed edition called *Mount Zion*. Jock went to old Sir John and said, 'There are some poems here by a friend of mine called John Betjeman. You never will have heard of him, but I'm anxious to publish them.' 'Publish them? Certainly not. Poetry doesn't pay. We haven't published any poems since Henley[25] – he didn't pay. Betjeman? Probably a German. No, no, no.' Jock said, 'Supposing I paid for the publication. Would that be all right?' 'That would be different,' said his uncle. 'But how could you do that?' Jock said, 'I have a few Bovril shares. They are all I've got,

25 William Ernest Henley, 1849–1903.

but I'll sell them out if you let me publish Betjeman here.' So Jock paid for the first Betjeman himself. It was immensely successful straight away, and Betjeman remained one of Jock's closest friends all through.

Andrew Franklin People give you ideas and you follow them up; people suggest names and you follow them up; you read an article in the newspaper and you think, that's brilliantly written, I wonder what that person's doing?

Ian Chapman That particular afternoon it was bitterly cold and raining cats and dogs. Unusually for me – because I was not a great letter-writer – I was sitting at the dining room table writing a letter, and unusually for her – because she was not interested in newspapers in those days – Marjory[26] was reading *The Glasgow Herald*. At one point I looked across at her. She was sitting in a high-backed, button-studded, horsehair chair with *The Glasgow Herald* spread across her knees, and there were tears in her eyes. I got up. 'Darling, what is it?' She said, 'Read that.' It was a short story entitled *The Dileas*, and it had won the first prize in *The Glasgow Herald* short story competition. It was about a Western Highland fishing family and the tragedy for them of a loss at sea – an enormously evocative, wonderfully descriptive and very moving story, by a young Glasgow schoolmaster called Alistair MacLean.

That evening, as we were having supper, Marjory said, 'Why don't you try to get in touch with him and see whether he would perhaps write a novel for Collins?' I said, 'I have no authority to do anything like that.' 'Well,' she said, 'you should show a bit of initiative.' So on the Monday morning I rang up *The Glasgow Herald* and said I had read this with great interest and could I have Mr MacLean's address, or, better still, his phone number? They said, 'No, he doesn't have a phone.' But to my surprise they gave me his address in King's Park Avenue. So I wrote a letter, saying how much we had enjoyed the story and that I would very much like to meet, so perhaps he would give me a call. When he rang I could hardly understand what he was saying – his voice was low pitched and very Scottish, but not Glaswegian – but I established that he was fairly newly married, and said, 'Why don't you bring your wife and I'll bring mine and we'll meet at the Royal Restaurant in Glasgow for dinner?' 'How will I know you?' he asked. I said – very originally, I thought – 'I will carry a Collins catalogue.'

We arrived at the appointed hour, and I was holding the catalogue up like a flag. Alistair arrived alone because Gisela, his wife – who was expecting a baby – wasn't well. During the evening we established that he had been in the same honours English class at Glasgow University as Marjory, and also that he had served during the war as a torpedo man on the lower deck of a navy destroyer whose company was on the infamous Murmansk

---

26 Marjory Chapman (née Swinton) later became a prominent editor at William Collins.

convoy run. He was now teaching English at Gallowflats School in Ruther-glen, for a pittance – the £100 prize money from *The Glasgow Herald* was a fortune to him. I said, 'I understand you're writing for publications like *John Bull* and so on. But what about a novel?' 'Oh, no, no, no. No chance,' he said, 'I could'nae write a novel.' I said, 'Just think about it.' We continued to meet once a month or so, and we were having a drink one night when he suddenly said, 'I think I'm going to have a go.'

That was the second week in September. The first week in December the telephone rang in my office in the Collins bible department: 'Ian? This is Alistair. I've done it.' 'What have you done, Alistair?' 'I've written it.' 'What? You've written your book?' 'Yes. Would you like to come and collect it?' At that time I was the proud possessor of a third-hand Ford Popular, which I had at the office that day because it was bucketing rain – again. 'I'll come out this evening.' I drove to King's Park Avenue and rang the bell. Alistair opened the door. 'I've come to collect it, Alistair.' 'Oh, yes.' And he pushed the door to, leaving me outside in the pouring rain. He finally emerged and handed me a brown paper parcel tied up with string. I got back into my Ford Popular and drove back to our digs, thinking, heavens above, what have I done? This poor guy has burnt the midnight oil writing this stuff every night after getting home from work, and probably on jotters that he's got from school. It can't possibly be any good. I have no authority to commission anything anyway. When I got back, Marjory said, 'Let's have a cup of tea and then we'll have a look.' So we took off the string, undid the parcel, and found a beautifully typed-up manuscript – and there on the title-page it said: '*HMS Ulysses* by Alistair S. MacLean.'[27]

Tim Rix Apart from the novels of Mary Renault and Francis King, Long-man published a fair amount of rubbish; books like *Big River - Big Man*, *The Hands of Esau*, *Chocolates for Breakfast*, *I'm Coming Virginia*. We published the whole of James Gould Cozzens, who was a well known American novelist. In order to get a book called *By Love Possessed*, which had been a bestseller in America, Mark Longman had agreed to buy the rights to all his previous books, which completely wasted any benefit that might have come from the bestseller.

Michael Turner The *Tintin* books were offered to Methuen because of our children's list, and they were drawn to my attention by an editor, Leslie Lonsdale-Cooper. I had been given a couple of the albums in the 1930s when I was learning French at school, and seeing them again was like meeting an old friend. Leslie and I thought it would be marvellous to publish them, but it didn't go down with the brass at all. Libraries wouldn't buy strip cartoons, and the books had been turned down by a number of publishers for that

---

27 *HMS Ulysses*, published by Collins in 1955, launched MacLean's career as a bestselling novelist.

reason. Methuen's general editor, John Cullen, was a great Francophile and as keen on the books as we were, but felt he couldn't overrule the children's editor, who was definitely against them. It looked as if *Tintin* was going to be refused. The excuse was that it didn't add up in financial terms – they would cost too much to translate. So Leslie and I said, 'We'll have a go at translating a couple, and we'll do it for free.' Then John overruled the protests, and we went ahead.

The first two books – *King Ottokar's Sceptre* and *The Crab with the Golden Claws*[28] – went out, and nothing much happened until, on the front page of the *Times Literary Supplement*, there was a rave review – and for the *TLS* to give a lead review to a children's strip cartoon was unheard of. It was by John Willett, another fervent Francophile, and not only did he bring out the beauty of the drawings, but also the fact that these were really adult books for children, in that the text did not talk down to them. Leslie and I were stunned. Overnight, *Tintin* became respectable, which gave us exactly what we needed – the entrée to libraries. From then on our *Tintin* list grew and grew until it included the whole canon.

The translation was very much a joint effort: Leslie produced the first draft, I worked on it, then we would get together and fight over the final version, which had to be matched to fit the speech balloons, so the word count was crucial. The text would go to the letterer – occasionally we would have to make revisions so it fitted – then Hergé would read it and maybe make one or two minor suggestions. I can't recollect a disagreement with him, ever. He trusted, to a remarkable degree, that we understood his style and what he did and didn't like. He used to say, 'I want you to convey the spirit, and you can depart from the text. If you get the spirit right, I shall be happy.' That was marvellous, because it gave us almost total freedom.

The one disagreement between Leslie and myself was over Milou's name, but we accepted that we couldn't agree, and said, 'Let's just find one that's harmless.' We both felt – wrongly, I think – that the dog should not have a French name in the English edition, and Hergé himself encouraged us to use an English name – as he also did for Tintin, although we kept that. But he had to be a white dog, and children's publishers used to instruct writers to use simple words. So 'Snowy' was *faute de mieux*. In fact, Hergé never condescends to children. I remember him saying, 'There are dictionaries – even in France.'[29]

Peter Mayer Someone called me and said, 'Now that you're no longer at Penguin, you might want to publish the books of an author you have probably never heard of.' I said, 'Tell me who you have in mind.' 'Walter Brooks.' I said, 'Of course – the *Freddy the Pig* books.' He said, 'Did you

28 Both were first published in English by Methuen in 1958.
29 Hergé (pseudonym of Georges Rémi, 1907–83) was a Belgian.

know that Walter Brooks came from this area?' This was in Woodstock, New York. I said, 'No.' 'Did you know that they're all out of print?' I didn't. He said, 'And did you like them?' 'I loved them.' 'So maybe you'd like to come and join the Friends of Freddy next Saturday? We're 600 strong and we're meeting thirty miles from here.' I said, 'I'm sorry. I am divorced and I have my daughter next weekend.' 'Bring her along – she'll love it.'

So we went to this annual meeting of the Friends of Freddy. The MC got up and said, 'We have a very distinguished guest here this evening.' He looked at me. I thought he was going to say, 'the former head of Penguin Books.' He said, 'From Woodstock, New York, we have Peter Mayer, the publisher of the Overlook Press' – the Overlook Press was about as big as a pea – 'and he has undertaken' – which I hadn't – 'to re-publish all the *Freddy the Pig* books. Will you come up here and say a few words?'

My daughter put her elbow into my tummy. 'Papa, did you?' I said, 'No, I didn't. I have to get out of this.' So I went up there and said, 'Well, I have agreed to *consider* publishing the *Freddy the Pig* books. We are going to start with one or two and see how it goes.' I thought, not many publishers get to publish the books of their childhood. So all right, I'll lose a little money doing this – that's OK.

Overlook Press has now published all twenty-six of the *Freddy the Pig* books. They have been an enormous success: the film rights have been sold, we've sold about 300,000 in hard covers, the paperback rights were sold to Penguin, and the Friends of Freddy have given me a great plaque to hang up: 'For Services to Walter R. Brooks.' And I still go to every one of their meetings.

Michael Turner On Hergé's first visit to London we arranged a signing session at Hamley's toy shop. It stopped the traffic. We had to call the police to control the crowds of children; so many came that they were blocking the pavement, queuing to get into the store, and Hergé had to speed up his signing to reduce the size of the crowd. He did a number of appearances in this country, but I felt strongly that he shouldn't be over-burdened.

Robert Clow The best signing session we had at John Smith's was with Edward Heath,[30] when Sidgwick & Jackson published *Sailing*.[31] We did a lot of advance publicity and took about 750 orders before he came up to Glasgow, then we sold another 750 copies on the day. Sidgwick & Jackson assumed we had ordered too many copies, so they diverted them to another bookshop and we ran out, but Heath walked down the queue and said, 'It's all right. Just leave your name and address and your money, and we'll get more copies up from London straight away.'

30 British prime minister from 1970 to 1974.
31 In 1975.

Before Ted Heath arrived we had a visit from the CID, who ran through the standard procedure of how to prepare to receive famous people. They said, 'Find out whether he minds people smoking in his presence and what he likes for lunch, if you're taking him for lunch. And don't worry, because we will look after security. You won't know we're there, but we will be.' When it came to the actual day, a man in a dirty mackintosh stood at the front of the queue, and when the signing session was finished after about three hours, he turned to me and said, 'There you are. I told you we would be here.'

Meanwhile, following their advice I had phoned up Ted Heath's house-keeper – in those days they gave you home phone numbers – and asked, 'What would Mr Heath like to eat?' 'Oh,' she said, 'he loves whitebait.' I thought, right, we'll start with Eggs Florentine and have whitebait as the main course. So I rang up the Malmaison and booked lunch at one thirty for five of us: Ross Higgins,[32] Heath, a guy from Sidgwick & Jackson, myself and Katrina.[33] When Heath had eventually signed the last copies at three o'clock, he turned to me and said, 'I'd like a bloody great steak.' I said, 'I'm very sorry, Sir, but we've organised whitebait.' He said, 'My God! Not whitebait again.' And it dawned on me that the CID ran though the same procedure with every bookshop – 'Give his housekeeper a ring, find out what he likes to eat' – so everywhere he went he got this ruddy whitebait. But I couldn't change the order by then.

We left the hotel about half past four, and he said, 'Oh dear, I was supposed to be starting a signing session in Edinburgh at four o'clock.' 'Don't worry, Sir,' I said, 'it's only Edinburgh.' It was a Thursday, the day when the building workers in Glasgow got paid, and as the five of us walked abreast up the pavement there were two of them strolling towards us who had obviously been to the boozer. One said to the other, 'Hey look, there's Ted.' And the other said, 'Good old Ted! Great to see you.' Heath turned to me and said, 'There you are. It's just what I've always felt – they like me in Glasgow. Not like those frosty buggers in Edinburgh.' Then off he went. I don't know what happened when he got to Edinburgh. He was going to John Menzies, and he couldn't have got there before half five.

Diana Murray There were certain times when Jock was anxious not to meet authors. If he was making a long train journey, for instance, he would want time to read without having to talk. He kept a false beard and make-up, which he sometimes wore when he was leaving the office in a hurry and there was a visitor waiting in reception who he thought might try to nobble him.

32 A director of John Smith's.
33 Katrina Clow, wife of Robert.

Gordon Graham joined Butterworth Publishers as chairman and chief executive in 1974.

Gordon Graham At that time, Butterworth still reflected its 19th-century roots. It had its own bookshop and printing company, and ninety lawyers on the staff. On budget night the tax editors would sit in the board-room and listen to the chancellor's speech on the radio, taking notes. Then they would write up the whole budget, get it to the printer by midnight and distribute it the following morning. Also, whenever a new edition of *Halsbury*[34] was published, one copy, which was known as 'the Queen's edition', was bound in red leather and the pages were gilt-edged, and a messenger would take it to the palace. I don't suppose Her Majesty was ever too conscious of it, but it was always delivered personally, and received by the librarian.

Charles Clark When I joined them in 1957, Sweet & Maxwell had recently taken over the law publishing firm of Stevens & Sons. Hilary Stevens himself had come to work at Sweet's, where he was instrumental in acquiring the Tavistock Press, a psychiatric imprint with a strong Jungian element. I had always been interested in Jung, so I did an evaluation of the backlist and forthcoming books, and then worked with John Harvard-Watts, the very clued-up psychiatric publisher who came with the imprint. One book in particular caught my attention because of its title. That was *The Divided Self* by R.D. Laing. Then I met the author and was bowled over by him. The first time I met Laing was in the lift – I think we were giving a drinks party to authors to assure them the Tavistock imprint was going to continue and they would be all right – and I remember hearing this strong Glasgow accent. By that time, Laing had cultivated a faintly demonic Glaswegian manner, which I enjoyed enormously.

I then left Sweet & Maxwell for Penguin, so I didn't see the book again until it was published by Tavistock. I thought it was marvellous, which was hardly a unique opinion. Laing took a very patient-oriented view of mental illness at a time when there was a kind of *de haut en bas* view of the patient from doctors, and I think he helped to change that attitude. I then published *The Divided Self* at Penguin, where I don't think it has ever been out of print. *Had it had the same appeal in hardback?* No, because it wasn't known to the 'intelligent layman' – the traditional Penguin audience – until I had acquired the rights, which I did for the unbelievable sum of £250.
How did you do that? I just rang John Harvard-Watts and told him I would like to buy them. He was pleased to hear from me again. I offered 250 quid for world rights – you always start low – and got them. Then I sold them on to America, to an old friend called André Schiffren.[35] I charged him rather more than 250 quid, and he acquired from me the American hardback and paperback rights. He then sold the paperback rights on to Penguin in

34 *Halsbury's Laws of England* (an encyclopaedia of English and Commonwealth Law).
35 American publisher, then at Random House.

America for a fortune, so my American colleagues weren't at all pleased with me. But it was the right thing to do for the book.

Why? I wanted it out in hardback first, in the States. It was important to establish its credibility in professional circles, and the way to do that was to have it published by a good, reputable firm in hardback – which would get reviewed – before it went into paperback.

I also commissioned a lot of original books in psychology and psychiatry for Penguin, because of my interest in the field. In psychiatry, I worked above all with Professor G.M. Carstairs at Edinburgh University, with whom I developed a whole series of books.

What were you aiming at? A coverage of the field, and books I would enjoy myself. That's one of the great secrets about commissioning: you don't do it for an audience; to some extent you do it for yourself. I also worked a lot with Hans Eysenck, who was then at the Maudsley.[36] I deliberately published a book by him called *Know Your Own IQ*, because the whole grammar school entrance system was based on IQ assessment[37] and I thought it was a nonsense. The book was a tremendous success. It was the first time that the average parent could get to grips with what IQs were about, and it meant you could practise, to improve your own IQ.

What were Eysenck's views about IQ tests in the Eleven Plus? He was quite traditional. I don't think he ever quite realised why I was so keen on publishing the book.

What did you read for ideas about books to commission? The broadsheets, particularly the Sunday papers. Journals such as *The Listener* and, to a lesser extent, the *New Statesman* and the *Spectator*. Also the professional literature in the field – *The British Journal of Psychiatry* and some of the law journals.

But the law list at Penguin was really informed by my dissatisfaction with the way law was taught at Oxford as a very technical subject with little attempt to relate it to changes in society. So I began to develop a list with the help of allies such as Bill Wedderburn, who was then at the LSE, as was Bill Cornish, another early author of mine – people with left-wing views who were naturally attracted to ideas about the interaction of law and society. That led to books such as *Freedom, the Individual and the Law*, by Professor Harry Street – now written by Geoffrey Robinson QC. And, outstandingly, Wedderburn's *The Worker and the Law*. These books began to have an influence on the way law was perceived as a subject at university level. *Freedom, the Individual and the Law* had an impact on the way law was taught, and *The Worker and the Law* affected what was taught, as people began to develop courses and seminars round the book because it was the only one available.

When you published 'The Worker and the Law', how important was it that you

36 Hans Eysenck was Professor of Psychology at the Institute of Psychiatry at the Maudsley Hospital from 1955 to 1983.
37 IQ (Intelligence Quotient) tests formed the basis of the Eleven Plus exam.

looked ahead to gauge how well the book would be received? Not at all. I published it because I thought it was needed. You had that sort of freedom at Penguin. As I said to you before, I published what interested me.

That sounds like an extraordinary freedom these days. Oh, yes. The world has changed totally. Obviously a political book like a Penguin Special would have its day, but we weren't dealing with a world dominated by focus groups. I published books because I thought they should be published.

Margaret Busby Publishing is a political activity, because information is power. If you take on books because you believe they are saying something that the world – or anybody – ought to know about, then the process of making that happen is important. Allison & Busby published books that wouldn't have been published otherwise, because everybody else had turned them down. We had a political series called *Motive*, in which we published C.L.R. James, for example. He was somebody I had known all my life, because he had been at school with my father in Trinidad. His magnum opus was *The Black Jacobins*,[38] which had been first published in 1938 and was long out of print. In fact, most of C.L.R. James's work was out of print, apart from his cricketing memoir *Beyond the Boundary*. So in the 1970s we began to re-publish him, including three volumes of his selected writings. C.L.R. James is now recognised as an important figure, but at that point he was very little known. It was an uphill task getting any reviews for his books, but we managed it.

What made you want to publish his work? Because he was significant and deserved to be read. *The Black Jacobins* dealt with the revolution in Haiti; this was a key book, which should not have been out of print. He was putting forward ideas that should have been accessible to everybody. But we were not under the illusion that we were going to publish books like that and become rich on them, which is why we had to publish books like *Love, Sex and Astrology*. It's a juggling act: you publish books that you believe in – which may be contributing something intellectually, but often lose money – and try to subsidise them with books that you hope are going to provide some commercial stability.

What happened to these writers after you had given them a start? Many – Roy Heath, for instance – stayed with us, and won prizes with us. But there was also the classic small publishing situation where you take on unknown writers, they become successful with you, then move to another publisher who pays bigger advances. Everybody has a story of 'the one that got away', but there's no point dwelling on those. You have to concentrate on making a success of the authors whom you do publish.

38 C. L. R. James, *The Black Jacobins: Toussaint L'Ouverture and the San Domingo Revolution*, Dial Press (New York), 1938.

Andrew Franklin Trade publishing[39] is all about taking risks. You believe in a writer and you publish them, and if you're right you'll make money and if you're wrong you'll lose money, and all that matters is that you make a bit more money than you lose. So you back your hunches – some make money, some lose money. The problem is that over the last ten years the losses have become bigger on those that lose money, and the profits have become smaller on those that make money, because booksellers are taking more and more of the total retail price, so the margin – the amount the publisher gets – is getting less and less.

Therefore it's very difficult indeed to set up as an independent trade publisher from scratch, because the risks of the failures are too great and the possibilities of the successes are too small. So you have to have some other activity, and we at Profile had the *Economist* books and our business books, which are inherently profitable, to cover those greater risks.

One book which was not a financial success, but I do think it was and remains a very important book – is *Biological Exuberance* by Bruce Bagemihl, which I bought from America. It's a work of gay activism in which he sets out to show that non-heterosexual activity is widespread in the animal kingdom. So, species by species, it charts the extent of homosexual activities, then brilliantly explains why there was such hostility among early etholo-gists to seeing this. That book had a lot of press coverage and attention and was slated in some quarters. Not many people bought copies, but it has become influential. I think the argument that homosexuality is not found in the natural kingdom is unsustainable since its publication. So I'm proud of having published that book.

A lot of the books I feel passionately about haven't worked. But I didn't buy them expecting that they wouldn't work; I bought them expecting that they would work, and that they would make money. But they didn't. That's OK. What's not OK is to buy books knowing that they will lose money – that way madness lies. There are lots of small publishers who never make a profit, and they have to go back to their owners again and again for more money. That makes you terribly vulnerable, because the time will always come when the owner says, 'I think I'd rather buy a race horse this year.' Then you're finished.

Philippa Harrison The editorial director of a company is the person who shapes and creates the list, and their list is what you judge them on. And, lest it sounds as though I don't think making money is important, I firmly believe that you can't have an editorial director who doesn't also understand about money – I am not suggesting they should be somebody with their head in the clouds who says, 'This is literature, so we will print 100,000 copies' and then sells ten; I am talking about somebody who, if they do

39 As opposed to educational, scientific, technical, medical or otherwise specialist publishing.

think, this is literature, cares enough to find a way of selling as many copies as possible.

At Michael Joseph we published *The Periodic Table*. It had been offered to all the proper up-market publishers and nobody had taken it. Primo Levi was not a natural Michael Joseph author, but two of my young editors – Henrietta Heald and Max Eilenburg – thought the book was phenomenal. I read it, as did Sheila Murphy, who was in charge of publicity. And we bought it. We knew what that book was, but we also knew that Primo Levi had been published elsewhere some years previously and hadn't sold, so we weren't going to be able to subscribe many advance copies to booksellers. So Sheila spent a whole year going through archives to find every single person who had ever said that they admired Primo Levi's work, and sent proof copies to them all, and we didn't publish the book until nearly a year and a half after buying it.

Within a month it had sold 7,000 copies – it became electric. And at that moment Primo Levi became 'discovered', even though he had been known for years. That was wonderful, because apart from being good, he is important. *The Periodic Table* became an enormous commercial success because we did what a hardback publisher was meant to do: we created the market, which we did through the infinite care of Sheila, and giving her the time to make sure that advance copies went to all the right people. It was a really beautiful piece of work.

Andrew Franklin Another book which I think was important – of course, it failed to change policy – was *War on Iraq* by Scott Ritter, the maverick weapons inspector who said there were no weapons of mass destruction. We bought it from America, published it in eight days flat, and it went on to sell 50,000 copies, including at the big anti-war demonstration in February 2003.

Neil Astley Bloodaxe published *No, I'm Not Afraid*, a collection of poems by Irina Ratushinskaya, a Russian Christian activist who had been arrested for distributing Christian literature in Red Square and sent to a labour camp for seven years. Several years after she had been imprisoned, I read a couple of her poems in an American magazine and was struck by her story and by the power of what was not lost in translation. I asked David McDuff, who had translated other Russian work for us, what he knew of Irina Ratushinskaya and whether he could get hold of any more of her work, and I also got in touch with Amnesty and other human rights organisations. David McDuff and I then put together a book which combined translations of her poems with documentation about the camp that she was in, which was actually a labour camp unit for women political prisoners.

This book, *No, I'm Not Afraid,* was used by the people who were campaigning for Irina's release. Candlelit vigils were held, and in

Birmingham the Reverend Dr Dick Rodgers set up a cage in a church and sat inside it for months, living on effectively the same rations as Irina in the labour camp. I was involved in helping to organise a writers' demonstration outside the Russian Embassy in London, where a copy of the book was handed in to the Russian ambassador. We made contact with the Foreign Office and MPs – including David Owen, who is himself a poetry anthologist – and sent copies to figures such as Gorbachev and Reagan. At that time we had a wonderful publicist called Karen Geary, who had a background in London publishing, and she brought her professionalism and experience to that book. *No, I'm Not Afraid* got a lot of publicity, and it became a source of embarrassment to the Russians that the story of this woman's imprisonment was being splashed around the newspapers. Eventually, as a result of David Owen's intercession at the Reykjavik Summit in October 1986, Irina Ratushinskaya was released.

We later discovered that the KGB had gone to see her in the camp and threatened her with a further period of imprisonment because of her poems being published. Until then, she hadn't known that they had reached the West, and it was a great source of inspiration to her, to hear that the poems had got out and that something was happening. She used to write them on strips of thin paper torn from the backs of bibles – the Bible being the only book allowed in the camp – rolled them up tightly and put them inside ball point pens, which would change hands when visitors arrived. That's one way they were taken out of the camp. Also, like other Russian poets, Irina Ratushinskaya knew her poems by heart, so when other prisoners were due for release they would memorise them, and recite them later to someone who would write them down.

What does it mean to you for Bloodaxe to have been involved in that way? If that particular book had not been published, Irina Ratushinskaya might have stayed in the camp for longer. Other people died there, and she could well have died. There is a line from Auden that is often quoted against poetry, which says that 'poetry makes nothing happen'. What was wonderful here was that it was Irina's own poetry that brought about her release.

Mark Barty-King We started the Bantam Press imprint[40] by gradually building up titles, and had one or two successes but nothing amazing. That's the point when you need a bit of luck. The luck in this case was a book called *A Brief History of Time*, which materialised at the American Booksellers Convention in Chicago when I was talking to an American agent called Al Zuckerman, who had the rights. The book was being written by a lecturer at Cambridge called Stephen Hawking – an Englishman with motor neurone disease.

40 Hardback imprint of Transworld, launched in 1985.

Paul Scherer[41] was in Chicago with me, and I remember saying to him, 'I think it's time Bantam Press did a serious book which will tell people that Transworld isn't just into popular publishing.' So we found ourselves making an offer for this book, which dealt with momentous questions such as the beginning of the world and the nature of time. It was already under contract to Bantam in America, which was a bit of luck because there was an editor called Peter Guzzardi working on it there whom we could rely on to do that sort of work. I wouldn't have known where to go for somebody to edit a book like that.

So we bought *A Brief History of Time*, and eventually met Stephen. It was obvious that he was somebody of quite exceptional ability in his own field – that goes without saying. He was also exceptional in that you wouldn't have dreamt anybody with that kind of disability could manage to write. But we didn't realise the book would have the reputation it later acquired, and the first printing was a rather cautious 5,000 copies – not bad for a book of great technical difficulty.

As it turned out, it was a bookseller in the north – I wish I could remember his name – who alerted us. He said, 'Something is happening in my shop. People are very interested in this book that's coming out. There's more to it than you think.' So we put the printing up by 2,500 and approached publication day with a good deal of apprehension. And the book just took off. It zoomed to the top of the bestseller list and stayed there for the longest period of any hardback there has ever been. I take no credit whatsoever for that book, because I didn't understand the first thing about it. But that is the sort of luck that you need. It was totally unpredictable and came completely out of the blue, from no more than my desire to have an important, interesting book. We had never published a science book, and we didn't have a clue, frankly.

Did you ever tell Stephen Hawking that you didn't understand it? Yes, I'm sure I did. There was no secret about it. Lots of people couldn't understand it. On the other hand, there are people in the trade who have read it four or five times.

Science has become a popular subject since then. How popular was it at the time? It wasn't, really. Some other science books did manage to be quite successful, but *A Brief History of Time* became the most famous science book there was. We kept it in hardcover for about eight years before publishing it in paperback. It transformed the fortunes of Bantam Press.

Carmen Callil Virago started by publishing non-fiction. The first list came to me through friends, chance encounters and the many writers and journalists I knew. Ursula Owen, whom I had hired as a freelance editor when she was working at Barrie & Jenkins – she later joined us full time – knew many

41 Managing director and chief executive of Transworld.

feminist academics who advised us, and they suggested this marvellous idea of publishing autobiographies and memoirs and books from the past that illustrated women's lives. And journalists were important – we published Mary Stott of *The Guardian*, and Women in Journalism wrote a book for us. Then Michael Holroyd, a good friend and a great help with Virago, gave me *Frost in May* by Antonia White to read. I couldn't get over it – I identified with it so much – and that weekend I thought, I'm going to start a fiction list, and I'm going to make the books look gorgeous so everybody will want to read them.

I went to Mick Jarvis, who was number two to Dave Larkin, the art director of Panther – where I had worked before – and said, 'I want to do these paperbacks, and I want full colour paintings on each cover, and I want them to be green and to have washed tops and strings.' He said, 'All right.' Then Harriet Spicer – who had begun as my assistant years beforehand but, by the time I started Virago, was teaching herself book production and everything else I couldn't do – said, 'There's absolutely no way we can afford washed tops and strings.' But I got my full colour covers, and Mick did the design, and they were a tremendous success from the beginning.

Why green? Because it's not blue and not pink – blue for a boy, pink for a girl. Or is it the other way around?

You were publishing these in? Paperback. After that, I just read and read and read – I was a terrible insomniac in those days – and soon we were publishing about twenty or thirty titles a year. The books came from all sorts of places: I went to the London Library, and people suggested titles to me. Some – Willa Cather, for instance – came from my mother's reading, whereas *The Weather in the Streets* had been passed around between women of my generation in the '50s and '60s – it was the book that everybody had read. So the moment I started Virago Classics, I wrote to Collins – and I wrote every year for years – asking if I could publish Rosamond Lehmann. And every year they said no, that Penguin had plans. Basically they didn't want their books to be published by a feminist publishing company. Then my friend Christopher MacLehose went to work at Collins – Christopher was also a great help to me in Virago – and as soon as he arrived, he told the rights department to stop being ridiculous and sell the books to me. Virago published them, and they were a tremendous success – I think they were among our bestsellers. We did everything except *Dusty Answer* and *The Echoing Grove*, because Penguin did bring those out at that time. Other publishers got very ratty when they saw that all these books they had on their backlists were selling.

What do you think Rosamond Lehmann thought about Virago? I know exactly what she thought: she said Virago was her saviour. She didn't at all like the idea of feminism. She was very keen on Margaret Thatcher; I was not keen on Margaret Thatcher. But she just loved what happened to her books, and she was grateful and happy. People beat a path to her door; she was on the radio and television again, and interviewed by all the journalists of the day.

But she didn't like it when people droned on about her love affairs, particularly with C. Day Lewis. People differ in their interpretation of that. My view is that Rosamond wasn't heartbroken about Cecil Day Lewis; I think she just always arranged to have hopeless love affairs because they fed her life. But her biographers don't see it like that. You find, in my experience, that people like Rosamond engage in hopeless love affairs because they have a steely centre to them that wants to go in another direction. With her, I think there was a gap between romantic desire and the practical, tough-as-boots desire to have her own life.

What do you think she thought about feminism? She didn't like any 'isms'. It's hard to describe what it was like: by calling yourself a feminist in those days you were putting a bell jar on your head; you were labelled like that for the rest of your life. Which I was. As if you didn't eat and drink and – what are Shakespeare's words? – bleed like others.

Did you have specific conversations with her about it? Not much. We talked much more about life – we talked about everything that friends talk about.

How did I find Antonia? As I said, Michael Holroyd gave me *Frost in May* and I read it. Then I think I used the Society of Authors to try to track her down, but she was so forgotten that even her agent had died. She had been living in Courtfield Gardens SW7 for a decade or longer by that point, so I might have found her in the phone book, and I would have written a letter saying I would like to publish. Then I met her. She lived up thousands of stairs in a little flat; she opened the door, and there she was – small, blondish hair, a face that would have been pretty when she was young. She was very clever and very human, just like Rosamond. Not as grand as Rosamond. But, I would say, cleverer than Rosamond.

In what way cleverer? Sharper. She had a very good and sharp mind, Antonia. We laughed just as much. We talked about this and that, and men and books. She gave me books to read, too. Antonia and Rosamond would both recommend writers to me, and that's often how books came along.

Do you know what Antonia White felt about being published by Virago? Yes. Absolutely thrilled. Happy, happy, happy. Although I would say that some-body like Rosamond – in a perfect world – would have preferred a company like Penguin to say, 'We're going to publish your entire work.' But because it was Virago, her work reached a market that Penguin couldn't get to. It may be that those authors realised we did this – I just don't know. The people who did realise, were the body of women – and male – academics, who started writing about some of these writers. Antonia Byatt wrote all the introductions to Willa Cather; Sally Beauman wrote all the introductions for E.H. Young. There are so many academics – women and men, but mostly women – who started researching these writers and making connections, and a whole world grew up of women writers who were writing about other women writers.

Elaine Showalter's book *A Literature of Their Own* – about the writers of the 1890s up to the 1930s – was another tremendous influence on the list. I may have found May Sinclair from Elaine Showalter. But I also found her from Rosamond, because Rosamond admired May Sinclair a great deal. It was a whole mish-mash of connections and readings and explorations.

Barbara Comyns came to me from Graham Greene. He wrote and said he had served in the Secret Service with her husband and he thought her novel, *The Vet's Daughter*, was quite remarkable. So I read *The Vet's Daughter*, and published it, then we published all her rest. Her real name was Barbara Comyns Carr. She wrote slightly surreal family stories, in the tradition of Stevie Smith, Beryl Bainbridge, Elizabeth Taylor, with their irony. Partly Jane Austen, but wickeder. There's a wonderful wickedness running through the women's writing that I love.

Philippa Harrison Many people of my generation were affected by the concept of Virago – there was a mutual female pleasure in seeing those spinners of green books in a bookshop. The idea of lost, excellent, occasionally great, literature by women – lost, you could argue, *because* they were women – coming back into the stream, gave us a sense of our own history. The books were often about love and loss; they were always funny, always sophisticated. It wasn't a strident part of feminism – it was a celebration of who we were as women, so the vibes it gave off were really good ones.

Gradually we all began to publish the sort of books that would have gone to Virago. Then it was argued: 'Now that publishers understand that women like to read books about themselves, they are all doing them.' That made me irritated. Put differently: if you had female editors with any power, of course they were going to publish women writers. And, as you will have found, there weren't many female editors with power until my generation. That was the difference.

Carmen Callil I had a lot of friends in publishing who were women, and we had all grown up in the business at the same time. Take two of them, Liz Calder and Philippa Harrison: Philippa went on to be important in all sorts of publishing houses, and ultimately saved Little, Brown. Liz is a legend, as you know: she was at Jonathan Cape for years, then went off to start Bloomsbury. It certainly wasn't just me. A lot of other women out there did the same thing.

13 | BLOCKED ZLOTYS

John Prime You wouldn't think anybody could make a success of a chain of left-wing bookshops, especially during the coldest days of the Cold War. But Eva Reckitt did. It really was an astute piece of commercialism applied to socialist beliefs. She started Collet's with Olive Parsons in the early 1930s, and the business continued until the beginning of the '90s.

The first Collet's shop was in the premises of the old 'bomb shop' in Charing Cross Road, which Eva had bought from Mr Henderson, the an-archist, when it was about to close, because she and Olive wanted to save what they saw as a main source of left-wing literature. Eva went to Russia on several occasions and talked to the state import-export agency, Mezh-dunarodnaya Kniga,[1] and hit upon the idea that there was a growing demand for Russian, especially in the American universities, so perhaps she could get East-West trade working in books. She negotiated various con-tracts and got Collet's Russian Bookshop going in Museum Street, then set up the Multi-lingual Bookshop in Great Russell Street.

This wasn't long after the war and there were bomb-damaged properties around on which you could often get a lease quite cheaply. Eva had a nose for that sort of thing. She subsequently opened a Chinese shop, also in Great Russell Street, and started a general bookshop in Hampstead, which was eventually sold to Ian Norrie.[2] Later there were Collet's shops in Manchester, Leeds and Hull, where Reckitt & Coleman, the business owned by Eva's family, was based. They were wealthy people and Eva had worried how they would react to her starting this left-wing bookshop. That is why she called it Collet's, after her middle name, rather than Reckitt's. Apparently they found out very quickly, because soon after she opened she was doing a window display – or rather, I think Olive was doing the window display, and Eva was outside saying, 'A bit this way and a bit that way' – when she suddenly looked up and there, walking towards her down Charing Cross Road, were several of her close relatives. She thought, Oh dear, now I've got to start explaining. But when they arrived, they didn't comment on the politics at all. What they said was, 'Oh, Eva. Going into the retail trade? How could you?'

1 International Books.
2 Bookseller latterly at the High Hill Bookshop, Hampstead.

Collet's Multi-lingual Bookshop occupied the ground floor of one of the terraced houses opposite the British Museum. It was a narrow shop, and shelved up to the ceiling, so we climbed ladders to get to the top. A remarkable amount of stock was held in that small space – initially mainly classical and modern literature, but we gradually began to notice increasing demand for scientific and technical books, because there was research going on in Eastern Europe which universities here wanted to know about.

We also imported Albanian books, although there was nobody working in the shop who knew anything about the language. But there was a small Albanian community in London, and we got to know one particular customer quite well. He was obviously knowledgeable, so we used to show him the Albanian catalogues that came in – they were printed on something that looked like toilet paper – and he would tell us what he thought we might sell. Also, several staff in the nearby School of Slavonic Studies would give us advice about the catalogues we produced ourselves. One in particular, a Dr Cushing, would occasionally come in and say gently, 'There is a mistake on such and such a page.' Looking back, I think we were jumping in where angels fear to tread.

The books often arrived from Russia in such large quantities that there wasn't room for them, so we stored them in the crypt of St George's Church round the corner – it was strange to think that these books from an atheist regime were being handled there. But we also had an account with the Russian Patriarchy, and when they published a new translation of the Bible – it was almost the size of a lectern bible – there was quite a demand from the Russian Orthodox churches here, and at that time there were still many refugees from the Revolution living in London who simply had to have the new Bible. Even in the darkest days of the Cold War the Patriarchy had its own import-export operation, and they were very shrewd business people. They wouldn't accept pounds; we had to pay in dollars.

Collet's did a lot of mail order business with universities abroad. The bulk of it was with the United States, because there was a terrible nervousness on the part of American universities about importing books directly from Eastern Europe. Towards the end of my time at Collet's,[3] we started to get quite large orders from Japan. I don't know why they weren't importing direct, but at that time the Japanese universities were rapidly building up collections of Russian and Eastern European books.

Collet's also acted as a clearing house for sales of British books to Russia. Institutions there would place their orders through Mezhdunarodnaya Kniga, which found it easier to order through Collet's than from individual publishers. We would sort out the bibliographical work, get the books together, then send pallet loads to Mezhdunarodnaya Kniga. Collet's always had a stand at the Leipzig and Prague book fairs. Not many British publishers

3 John Prime worked for Collet's until 1964.

thought they could sell enough books there to justify having a stand themselves, but they would pay us so much per copy to display them on their behalf. A few of them took their own stands at the Eastern European fairs. Oxford University Press, which published books for students of English, used to send Tony Pocock[4] out to man theirs.

Tony Pocock It was easy enough to make those countries want our books – much more difficult to get paid for them. Until 1958 or thereabouts the whole of Eastern Europe was closed to us; they had no sterling and we wouldn't take any blocked Eastern currency. They hit on all sorts of bizarre trading schemes – 'Can we swap you 500 bottles of wine for 100 dictionaries?' – all of which, sadly, we had to decline. But the laughter this engendered made us good friends, which was important, because there had been silence and stand-offishness since the war. Now we were friends. How could we sell more books?

Yugoslavia was the most obvious market. There was a huge demand there for the learning of English. That, with a particularly imaginative British Council in place, led to the British Books for Export Scheme, which meant that embassies and consular offices in Yugoslavia were paid in local currency,[5] and the sterling which that liberated was devoted to the sale of books. This was a tremendous step forward, something we had urged the British embassy to do. Sterling was at last available to the Yugoslavs, and they used it – they bought and bought and bought.

There was also a very important demand for books in Poland, where we set up a similar scheme for our Teaching of English list, whereby the Poles bought it and we agreed that they could bank their zlotys in our favour. We said, 'We know you can't pay us in sterling. Just make sure we have an account in Poland and keep the money there in zlotys for the moment.' Then we agreed that they should print our *Advanced Learner's Dictionary*, and we paid them in their own currency, using the blocked zlotys in ways which enabled us to save money on printing our English language dictionaries. We had similar schemes in Hungary and Czechoslovakia, but we failed with Russia, though the Russians somehow got hold of sterling from other directions so they spent something with us. Not as much as they should have done.

John Prime Tony certainly gave Oxford University Press good value for money. He just was never still for a moment at those fairs. I think it was in Belgrade where I met him first. Apart from the main import-export agency there – Jugoslovenska Knjiga – there were also smaller agencies, one of which was managed by a really fearsome lady with the reputation for always

---

4 Sales manager of OUP from 1955 to 1975.
5 Dinars.

beating people down: 'You don't understand the difficulties we have here. We cannot possibly pay this price for this particular product.' She was the only woman I've ever known Tony Pocock admit he was terrified by. I can still hear him saying, 'I *have* to see this woman. I cannot think of another excuse to postpone my visit with her.'

Tony Pocock Sometimes I dreaded visits to Eastern Europe, because one of us was going to get entangled in trouble sooner or later. We were always heavily inspected at the border, and one day our rep was made to open the boot of his car and out hopped a girl whom he was smuggling out. Not, I can assure you, for his pleasure, or for the pleasure of OUP, but because he had been asked to smuggle her out.
What happened to him? To my astonishment – this was the narrative, and I have never understood it – he was told he could take her out provided he married her. So he married her on the border, took her out, then said goodbye to her at the other side. Quite a nice story, but I don't know any more about it than that. Things like that happened much of the time.

John Prime When British publishers went out to Eastern Europe they would generally be recommended to go to either the Foreign Office or the Board of Trade to be told what they should and shouldn't do. How they should steer clear of any women hanging around the hotel lounges, for example, because they might be up to no good. Also, publishers were sometimes invited for a de-briefing when they returned. I think that's getting near the edge of what is espionage and what isn't. If you are asked for a de-briefing, it seems permissible to go back and tell your own government what you've done, but from the point of view of the Czechs, for instance, that could be interpreted as espionage. I was never invited to one of these de-briefings when I was working for Collet's; they obviously counted me as being to some degree sympathetic to the other side.
How do you know about British publishers being de-briefed? Because one or two of them told me.
Are you willing to say who it was? I don't think I could without asking their permission. But it is pretty general knowledge amongst British publishers that this went on.

Lynette Owen When I had a chance to go to Warsaw, which I did for Cambridge University Press[6] in 1970, it was my first experience of what was then communist Central Europe, and a real eye-opener. It was the one showcase for western books in Poland, and people would travel from all over the country just to get a glimpse of western books, which they would put their names down to buy, although they didn't have much hope of

6 Lynette Owen worked for a number of publishers before joining Longman in 1976.

actually securing them. The books would be bought at the end of the fair by the state importers, who chose where they ended up – whether in state libraries or whether any were available for private purchase.

Sometimes people would order the same book year after year and never get it, and people would come and sit and copy books by hand. On one occasion someone had been copying a book day after day – I didn't think he was going to get through it by the end of the fair – then he came one day and the book had disappeared. 'You've taken it off the shelf,' he said. 'I haven't,' I told him. 'It must be here somewhere.' I went and checked; it was a medical book, and it had obviously been stolen. He just collapsed, broke down on the stand, and accused of me of having removed it. I said, 'I really, really haven't. Someone must have stolen it.' 'But I've been copying it.' I said, 'I know you have, but I haven't got another copy. I'm very sorry.'

One year two young doctors came from Poznan wanting to buy a book on hand surgery. They'd seen a review of it somewhere, they'd got money, and they hoped that they could place an order for it at the fair. They asked how much it was, and it was one of our American medical books, a huge three-volume large-format book of diagrams and photographs. It was nearly £300. When they translated that into zlotys, they obviously hadn't got anything like enough to pay for it. They'd made the journey specially, and they were devastated. That's a most terrible thing to see. It wasn't as though they wanted books for fun; they wanted a specialised, practical book and they had no means of getting it. I eventually took a card from one of them and said I would put them on the mailing list for a catalogue. I managed to find a bashed set that had come back from someone who had been examining it, and sent it to them, and after that they came to see me every year. You can do that once in a while, and it's a nice feeling. Your instinct is, I'd give away all these books if they were mine to give – but I can't.

It would be very difficult to explain what it was like to anyone who didn't see these countries at that time. These are people with a great love for books; if you go into homes in that part of the world you will find a far larger family library than you would in an average British flat. People would come three years running, trying to get an English dictionary, and would say to us, 'Why haven't you supplied it?' and we would say, 'But we never got the order. The order has to be processed through the central state agency; we will gladly supply it if we get the order.' There would be a restricted amount of hard currency available and priority would go to state libraries and university libraries. The individual came last on the list. Now it's not a problem: they can come and pay in cash at the fair, and if the book is there, the distributor will pass it to them. Some of them are the same people who used to come in the old times, but now they actually go away with a bag of books.

In the early '90s when everything started to open up, I used to get phone calls from trade publishers saying, 'You've been going to Poland for a long time. I hear they're starting to ask for rights.' It was almost as though they were saying, 'The Poles have learnt how to read.' They had discovered Poland as a market. In a way it *was* like that, because Poland had suddenly opened up to Dorling Kindersley-type books, which had never been seen there before. I would say that this actually produced a negative effect during the early part of the 1990s, when these markets were flooded by huge-scale translations of western books at the expense of local literature, and it was very tough to publish original books. Now, I would say, the balance has started to be redressed. It was the novelty: either of authors who hadn't been allowed, or of genres of literature that hadn't been available there previously.

But I went to these fairs to sell rights. That was also an interesting experience, because at the time when the Polish book publishing trade was entirely state controlled, it was impossible to remit hard currency out of the country. So if you did sell rights to a Polish state publisher, they could only pay in currency which had to remain within the country. For many years we were not allowed to hold a bank account in Poland, so the money was actually held for us in the publishing houses themselves, and one would go and collect it from them in local currency and try to find some way to spend it while one was in Poland. This situation persisted until around 1990, when it became possible for publishers to remit money out of the country.

I think those conditions very much influenced the attitudes of some western publishers. Those of us who went to Poland – primarily academic publishers – saw the visit as a means of recycling the money; we would pay for some expenses within the country with those royalties. But for publishers who didn't want to exhibit in Poland there would be no particular incentive to do the deals. So a lot of trade publishers not only didn't visit Poland, but would actually refuse copyright licences because they saw no means of recycling the money. Our view was, the books were needed, and if we could use some of the money we would continue to go there.

John Prime Collet's sales to Russia worked largely on a barter basis. Generally, there was no exchange of currency until the end of the year, when we would see how we were in balance with Mezhdunarodnaya Kniga, and settlement would be made. During my time, when the Russians owed us money at the end of the year they would always pay it by the agreed date. But it seems that in the last few years of the Soviet Union, long after I had left Collet's, the Russians began to default on their payments and the debt got bigger and bigger. The Russian universities had been ordering lots of books, and when the Soviet Union collapsed they simply said, 'Sorry. We haven't got any money to pay for them.' And that was the end of Collet's.

Lynette Owen The Soviet Union didn't join the Berne Copyright Convention[7] until 1973, so in the '60s one would occasionally get wind through an author that their book had been translated into Russian. Usually the author was extremely angry and wanted to know what we were going to do about it. There wasn't anything that could be done about it in law, but there were possibilities with one or two of the publishers – all of whom were state owned – to say, 'Might you be prepared to make a local payment, in local currency, that the author could pick up if he ever went to Moscow?' Later, when I went to Longman, I was able to go round and collect deposits of money scattered all over Moscow in post office and bank accounts, which related to unauthorised translations of books that had been done when the Soviet Union wasn't required to recognise copyright, but for which particular publishers – I'm thinking of Nauka and Mir, both of whom were scientific publishers – had been prepared to deposit money in case the author ever turned up to collect it.

Betty Graham Before I arrived, Butterworths hadn't thought it worthwhile to try to sell language rights. But with my background in languages, it seemed the ideal thing to do – and I did it with great pleasure. Then Russia joined the Berne Copyright Convention, which meant we could start selling there, so we took a little stand at the first Moscow book fair. Many British and American publishers didn't really trust the Russians. They said, 'What's the point of signing contracts? They won't pay us.' But we always got paid. We were very friendly with the Russians, and just as open as we were with anyone else. The first year after they joined the Copyright Convention, we were visited at the Frankfurt Book Fair by Yuri Gradov, who was in charge of the copyright agency in Moscow, and Yuri, Gordon[8] and myself between us wrote out the contract which all the other publishers used afterwards.

How did you go about selling rights in Russia? We had an interpreter on our stand, and the Russians had interpreters on theirs. They would examine the books and we would talk about them, then they would make their decision. Butterworths' technical books sold well there, as did some of our medical titles, which they translated into Russian. But their contractual terms were completely different from what we were used to. The Russian didn't pay royalties; they would pay a lump sum no matter how many copies they produced, and the book distribution agency told them how many copies of each particular book to print. I remember at one stand going through the whole spiel of what we were selling, and afterwards the man in charge of that firm said, 'We don't know anything about doing business and we really want to learn from you.' It was not big business, by any means. But it was a start.

---

7 The Berne Copyright Convention, which many European countries signed in 1887, guarantees that the copyright of books published within one signatory state will be upheld within the others.

8 Gordon Graham, then chairman and chief executive of Butterworths.

Lynette Owen There wasn't a great deal of controversy about selling scientific or technical books in Poland, but in areas like modern history and politics, a lot of books would be non-starters. An obvious example would be a book I still have with my present company, Peter Calvocoressi's *World Politics Since 1945*.[9] This was banned for many years in all communist countries, including Poland. If you tried to exhibit it in its original English edition, it would be removed the night before the fair opened, and you would get a delegation the following day, saying, 'One of your books has been removed because it's not suitable for the Polish public.'

The first time, I put it up not realising what would happen, but after that I would take it quite regularly to see whether it would be removed – it would be gone before the fair opened to the public. You never got it back; you were never paid for it. It probably went on the privileged shelves in one of the libraries – certainly in the Soviet Union some people were given access to books which were not allowed to the general public. That situation persisted until the 1990s, when the political environment changed and the book became acceptable both for exhibit and also for translation. It has now gone through two editions in translation.

I can think of sillier removals elsewhere. Raymond Briggs' *When the Wind Blows*[10] was removed as being a pro-nuclear war book in Moscow. Most people suspected it was because they didn't like the pictures of the Russians – there's a point when a Russian soldier appears and menaces someone with a bayonet. But that became such an issue that our Publishers Association representatives went to the highest level to have it returned.

Clive Bradley was secretary and chief executive of the Publishers Association from 1976 to 1997.

Clive Bradley On one occasion vast numbers of books which the Russians apparently claimed were pornographic were seized, so my members said, 'We can't have this, Clive. You'll have to go off and protest to the minister. Freedom to publish, and all that. We're not going to come to the Moscow book fair if they won't allow us to exhibit the books that we want to exhibit.' So I trotted out to see Boris Stukhalin, who received me with a great gang of people and listened carefully to all I had to say. Then he grinned, and said, 'Did you say these books were pornographic, Clive?' I said, 'Well, I think some of them had sexual content. And they may have contained political material.' 'Ah,' he said, 'I think you'll find that they were pornographic and that the customs officials seized them so they could have a look at them themselves. I think you'll see them back on the stands by this afternoon.' And that's indeed what happened.

9 First published by Longman in 1968.
10 First published by Hamish Hamilton in 1982.

Betty Graham The year I started at Butterworths, the total rights income was £9,000. When I left twelve years later it was £120,000.

How did you learn about rights? By experience. And I must mention Lynette Owen of Longmans, who is the doyenne of rights managers. I didn't know Lynette at all, but she called me up one day soon after I took over and asked if she could come and visit me at Butterworths. She knew that I hadn't handled rights before, and she came out of goodness, without my asking, to try to teach me something about rights. And I joined a group of rights people who used to have lunches together once in a while.

Lynette Owen There was a rights group then in the United Kingdom, which met from time to time over a buffet lunch. We used to take turns to organise it, and maybe thirty or forty people would turn out. Latterly we would have a speaker. One of those occasions was organised by the rights person at Pergamon Press when Robert Maxwell was still running it, and there was great speculation on whether he might appear at the event. The whole lunch proceeded without any sign of him, then towards the end he suddenly materialised and made a short speech in which he more or less said, 'If you little girlies stick at it, you might get somewhere one day.' We were almost all women, and relatively young, so I don't know whether he thought we were all assistants or something. But since a good dozen people were on the boards of their companies at the time, it didn't go down very well.

14 | A QUESTION OF TIMING: NET BOOK AGREEMENT 1995

David Whitaker In 1890 Frederick Macmillan wrote a letter to *The Book-seller* making a very strong case for a net book agreement. The editor, who was then Vernon Whitaker, added a long editorial saying it would mean that the trade would have to reduce the prices of books, because if you were no longer going to discount books, you couldn't artificially inflate the price in the hope that you could discount them and still make money. And indeed, book prices did come down. The first net book was published in April 1890, and it was an economics book by Alfred Marshall.

Clive Bradley The Net Book Agreement was an agreement between publishers that if they chose[1] to publish a title as a net book – that is, a book on which booksellers were not allowed to offer discounts against the fixed retail price – then they would all agree to work together to enforce the net price, should a bookseller try to reduce it. They used the Publishers Association[2] to administer this. Such an agreement had to be registered with the Office of Fair Trading, and if the Office of Fair Trading thought it was sufficiently significant, it would be referred to the Restrictive Practices Court for an investigation as to whether or not it operated in the public interest. That's what had happened to the Net Book Agreement in 1962.

The arguments were still running when I joined the PA as secretary in 1976. Some people in publishing – and, indeed, in bookselling – argued that: if there were no Net Book Agreement publishers would still be free to publish titles, and booksellers would be free to set the prices at which they wanted to sell the book; supermarkets, which are accustomed to dealing in discounted goods, would be more willing to sell books, and this would widen the market; there would be greater opportunity for innovation and enterprise. Other people saw the Net Book Agreement as being fundamental to the viability of the book trade.

1 Many titles, including most educational books, were published non-net, but most books sold through general bookshops had a fixed retail (net) price.
2 The Associated Booksellers of Great Britain and Ireland was established in 1895 in order to persuade publishers to issue books at net prices and to guarantee discounts to booksellers. The Publishers Association (PA) was established in 1896 to represent the publishers in negotiations with booksellers. The two associations, together with the Society of Authors, reached an agreement which was implemented on 1 January 1900 and still operated in the early 1990s.

Philippa Harrison The NBA had been administered by the Publishers Association for nearly a hundred years, and there were three sorts of people who opposed it: during my youth and middle age there was a radical chic opposition, personified by people like Matthew Evans at Faber.[3] Then there was another view, personified by Richard Charkin at Oxford University Press:[4] academic publishers felt the Net Book Agreement was nothing to do with them and were fed up, with considerable justification, with the amount of time the Publishers Association spent defending and administering it. And when Charkin was in the position of running a general publishing list he chose to de-net the books in May 1991. The third view was represented by Terry Maher, who started the Pentos bookshop chain. He felt passionately that he would be able to make more money if he used price as a marketing tool, and he referred the NBA to the Office of Fair Trading in 1989. This led to a time-consuming and expensive battle which the PA won.

Clive Bradley When I went to work at the PA, I looked at the Net Book Agreement. Should this be something that we sacrificed in view of Britain's new competition legislation and the European law environment? I decided we should not, for all sorts of reasons – one of which was that support for it was so strong in the trade that, had I gone to the PA council and said, 'I am the new boy here and my advice is to get rid of the Net Book Agreement', it wouldn't have been the Net Book Agreement that went, it would have been Clive Bradley. So one had to recognise that one's job was to defend the thing as best one could – and I quickly realised that it had benefits for book buyers as well as for the trade.

Terry Maher founded Pentos in 1972 and was responsible for the expansion of Dillons Bookstores.

Terry Maher Publishers are the suppliers. In other areas of retail activity it is very clear who is the boss: the suppliers are anxious to please and to stay on good terms with their customers, who are the retailers on the high street. If you went into any area of activity there and said, 'Where does the balance of power lie?' you would see very quickly that it lay with the retailers. In the book trade it was the exact opposite. That's the thing which struck me at the outset.

Clive Bradley We faced many investigations by the Office of Fair Trading into whether or not they should mount a new action against the Net Book Agreement. Before they could do so, they had to show that circumstances had changed significantly since the judgement in 1962.

---

3 Matthew (later Lord) Evans became managing director of Faber & Faber in 1977.
4 Richard Charkin ran OUP's reference division from 1980 to 1984, when he became managing director of its academic division. He joined Reed in 1988 and became chief executive of Reed Consumer Books in 1991.

By the 1980s there were substantial changes in the industry. Book clubs had become more dominant – and they had always been a sore thumb within the Net Book Agreement argument. There was more competition from the United States; conglomeration was already happening, and new bookshops, such as Dillons and Waterstone's, were coming along. Dillons was founded on what in effect had been London University Bookshop – a classic large independent bookshop in Malet Street, which carried a wide range of stock to meet the needs of students. It had been run by a splendid woman called Una Dillon, who was certainly a great supporter of the NBA. Dillon's[5] was bought by a firm called Pentos, whose chairman was Terry Maher. He acquired other bookshops around the country and established the Dillons chain.

Terry Maher When Pentos started it was very much an investment company. My idea was: we will buy something, we will improve its fortunes, then we'll sell it on to somebody else who has an long-term interest in that kind of business. About halfway through my time with Pentos I became more interested in developing things for the longer term. We would certainly have been more financially successful if I'd stuck to the first idea, but I would never have got involved in book retailing to the extent that I did. I loved bookselling, I loved having made an obvious difference to book retailing, and I was passionately concerned about what we were doing.

I had got into the book trade in a rather odd way: through having acquired the religious publisher Marshall, Morgan & Scott, then, through an introduction by Peter Lock of Ward Lock to the Hudson family, buying Hudson's bookshop in Birmingham in 1972. I was then distracted from developing the bookshop idea further until Dillon's University Bookshop came onto the scene in 1977 and I was able to buy it from the University of London.

The astonishing thing about bookshops at that time was that there wasn't a national chain – the trade mostly consisted of independent businesses. Some of them certainly had a good reputation: Blackwell's, Hatchards, Heffer's, John Smith's, Thin's. But the rest were tiny shops, most of them in poor situations. Often they were run by proprietors – many of whom were eccentric – who closed at lunchtime or on Saturday afternoons when most people did their shopping. And there was Foyle's, belonging to a different era.

At that time, book retailing was fragmented and clearly wasn't doing what other areas of retailing were doing. First and foremost I was a businessman – I understand the financial implications of things very well – so I start from that position. A businessman looks for opportunities and the book trade seemed an obvious opportunity.

5 The apostrophe was dropped when Pentos re-branded the business.

You were asked to go and speak at a BA conference?[6] I was asked to make the key-note speech, on a subject of my own making. I talked about how I saw the book trade, and how it was going to change. Well, price control was going to go. I said the kind of thing I'd been saying to different audiences for quite a while – there was nothing new in it whatsoever – and it was in the Sunday papers: 'Here's a bookseller wanting to get rid of price control; it's like a turkey praying for Christmas.' And that got the whole thing going. It was pushed along pretty well by newspapers.

I didn't mount a campaign; I just thought the Net Book Agreement was stupid – it was an irritant. When we had a few shops, it didn't matter that much, but once we had a national chain and we were branding Dillons nationally, it became more of an irritant. We were the best-known bookshop brand in the country, and we were doing market research on the success of our branding: 'Where do people think the cheapest books are?' They were the same price everywhere, we all knew that. But what used to come through strongly, do you think? W.H. Smith. Most people out in the street didn't know about a Net Book Agreement, and they actually thought books were cheaper in Smith's. So we were at a competitive disadvantage there.

Are you saying that it's not that the NBA was incompatible with bookselling, but that it was incompatible with a particular kind of bookselling? You know my political views: I am a Liberal, I happen to believe in free markets, and to have price control in any area, seems to me to stop things developing. We will sell more books if we can use every promotional tool which is available to us. And one of them was not available to us.

Clive Bradley The economists who advised the Office of Fair Trading certainly argued – as they still argue now – that any restrictive practice was bad for trade. In times of recession, people were more keen to sell books come what may. When the market was going well, people were more confident. But when you were having difficulty earning the profits that you earned last year, you said, 'I might be able to sell more books if I allow discounting' – although history showed the pressure which that put on your margins.

Terry Maher If you're to have a business that is going to grow, or even sustain itself, then you have to earn profits to finance the capital investment that you need. The problem with book retailing is that it's both capital intensive and labour intensive – a terrible formula. It requires a lot of money to set the business up. It still costs roughly £100 a square foot to set up a bookshop, because of the special fittings that you need. So if you want to open a 10,000 square foot bookshop – which is quite large – it will cost you a million pounds, just to fit it out. Then you've got the stock. Publishers will say, 'Oh, we finance that.' Well, they don't; they finance about half the stock.

6 Bournemouth, 1988.

So why do it? Because there is a formula that works – but you've got to get it right. You have to make at least forty per cent gross margin, and you have to keep your occupancy costs down. If you're not profitable, you don't stay in business.

Philippa Harrison The early 1990s were tough years for publishers and for booksellers. In an attempt to make a bit more margin and turnover, large publishers had been selling thousands of special editions in outlets that didn't support the NBA – mega-promotional sales of fantastically cheap books. That unsettled the public and unsettled booksellers, and put the whole concept of fixed prices up for grabs. And in August 1994 the Net Book Agreement was referred back to the Restrictive Practices Court through the Office of Fair Trading.

I am told that there was a major discussion about whether to go through this whole process again, how expensive and time-consuming it would be – good, soul-searching stuff – and the decision was that the Publishers Association would defend the Net Book Agreement. That was announced in September, and the day afterwards, Tim Hely Hutchinson[7] announced that he was going to de-net Hodder Headline's books on Boxing Day. And that was the next big chequer on the changing board. W.H. Smith publicly reaffirmed their support for the NBA, but with the interesting proviso that it was the publishers' responsibility to make the decision. At Little, Brown's December 1994 sales conference, I was telling my reps that I truly didn't know whether it would stay or go – although we hoped it would stay.

Terry Maher I found publishers, by and large, frustrating and – in my dealings – not to be relied on. Most of them would tell me they wanted to get rid of the Net Book Agreement. But they didn't want to be the first person to say so publicly, apart from Paul Hamlyn.
How much contact did you have with your fellow booksellers? Very little. I don't believe in belonging to organisations. We were members of the Booksellers Association, but that was for one reason only – Book Tokens. I was always a great believer in doing things for myself and with my colleagues. OK, it might make sense for the individual small bookseller to belong to the Booksellers Association. But I could never see what the Booksellers Association could do for us that we couldn't do for ourselves. We would never have belonged to it if we hadn't had to, in order to participate in Book Tokens – another monopoly practice. Outrageous.

Clive Bradley My experience was that if you met a radical publisher at a dinner party, they would be likely to rubbish the Net Book Agreement. If

7 Then group chief executive of Hodder Headline.

you met them at a Booksellers Association annual conference, they'd be supporting the Net Book Agreement very strongly indeed.

Why? Because booksellers liked the Net Book Agreement. As a publisher, you probably wouldn't want to be seen as an opponent of the Net Book Agreement, because that might make you less popular with booksellers.

What period are you talking about? The Net Book Agreement was formed in the late 19th century and lasted about a hundred years. I think attitudes changed as we got towards the end of that period partly because, as we moved towards conglomeration, market share became an important managerial concept. This meant using price to a greater extent as a marketing tool, which would be against the Net Book Agreement. There was an increasingly tough competition law environment, as the Office of Fair Trading changed from being mildly sympathetic to being strongly against the Net Book Agreement and the European Commission became influenced by American anti-trust laws. But the discussions that took place on the PA council – however radical they were – tended to conclude that the benefits of the NBA outweighed any disadvantages.

Terry Maher One of the things we wanted to do was to use price as a promotional tool in the way that every other retailer does. Take the Booker shortlisted titles: if you wanted to package them all together, you couldn't do it. If a bank came along and wanted to do a promotional campaign on television saying, 'Any young person who opens an account with us will have a £10 voucher they can spend at Dillons', you couldn't do it. Any new approach to book retailing – you couldn't do it. Price is crucial. It's not the most important thing, but it is important.

And what arguments were offered against that? The fact that in 1962 a judge had ruled . . . It always went back to 1962.

Philippa Harrison In May 1995 there was a vicious rise in paper prices – which was going to make life extremely tricky for an already threatened publishing trade. In June, Asda[8] began to use the fact that Hodder Headline had de-netted, and gave a fifty per cent discount on Le Carré – never before in the history of the last hundred years had such a thing happened. Around that time – in the private conversations that heads of houses have with heads of bookshops – Smith's, who historically had always thought that profit came out of decently highly-priced books, began to say that they had changed their minds, and they now thought price was a crucial selling tool.

Clive Bradley The early 1990s recession was biting deep into the book trade. The Net Book Agreement went, not by decision of the PA council, but by a group of big publishers and booksellers meeting privately to consider

8 Supermarket chain.

whether they wanted to defend it. Random House, HarperCollins and W.H. Smith agreed in one momentous week that they would no longer enforce it. And if they were no longer going to operate the Net Book Agreement, there was no point in anybody else trying to do so.

Philippa Harrison On the 26th of September 1995, two days before the meeting scheduled by the PA council – which had the official right to take a general position – Random House and HarperCollins announced that they would de-net their books from the 1st of October. Two hours after that, Smith's announced a major de-netted promotion with Random House and HarperCollins. Jeremy Hardie[9] argued – and, I think, fairly – that the way net pricing had recently operated had allowed publishers to use non-traditional outlets and special editions to reach price-sensitive consumers – i.e. not bookshop customers – while keeping higher margins in sales to 'price-insensitive' buyers. The reason Smith's changed their position was that they didn't want publishers to have control of pricing; they wanted retailers to have control of pricing. That was the beginning of the colossal shift of power from publishers to retailers which has happened from then onwards.

Clive Bradley We had the most contentious meeting of the PA council I have ever attended, with the rest of the PA council up in arms that these particular publishers had unilaterally, so to speak, withdrawn from the Net Book Agreement – which they were quite entitled to do, but others felt should more properly have been the decision of the PA council and argued out in that forum.

Philippa Harrison At a certain level, you could say the meeting was just a matter of accepting a done deal by the big publishers. 'OK, it's gone. Big publishers, they win. All right, give up.' But what actually happened made that meeting as good an exercise of democracy in action as I have seen in my life. Everybody knew that we all had to be at our most serious and effective. It was a fine meeting in which people behaved very well, I thought. You could say it was silly; you could say that in a way we had no power. But it didn't feel silly; it felt important. This was a hundred years of history and it needed to be finished, we thought, properly.

Trevor Moore There it was – bang – the deal had been done, and HarperCollins, Random House, and W.H. Smith were the bad boys. And I was one of them. I took a long time to recover credibility with quite a few booksellers, small booksellers in particular. I called on one buyer who said, 'I didn't cancel your appointment, because I wanted to see you face to face. I wanted to say that there's nothing personal in this decision at all, because we

9 Chairman of W.H. Smith.

like you and we like to see you. But I'm afraid you're no longer welcome here after the way that Random House has behaved. In future we will buy Random House books very reluctantly and very sparingly, and when we buy them, we'll buy them through a wholesaler. I wanted to tell you to your face, so I do apologise for troubling you and causing you to make this fruitless call.' And I thanked him very much for his courtesy and said how sorry I was that I wouldn't be calling there any more.

Suddenly I was representing the big battalions who were determined to push the small operator out of business – that was the context in which it was seen by a lot of booksellers I liked and respected. And I knew that it would indeed be at least partly instrumental in putting some of them out of business, or making life very difficult for them. Of course, you adapt or die, don't you? And in the fullness of time people did.

Philippa Harrison What we all had to do was not just make central deals with each chain and each bookshop, but make individual deals per important book. There were deals where we walked out: in our case, Little, Brown didn't have a single book in the Menzies catalogue, because we would have lost money on them. Each deal was new: no history, no practice, no nothing. You might think the book market would have expanded that Christmas. Did it hell. October, November, December – the three months after Random House and HarperCollins joined Hodder Headline in leaving the Net Book Agreement – had lower growth than the first nine months of the year. That was pretty shaking for everybody. And 1996 was indeed a bad year for the book trade.

Trevor Moore And I got it in the neck from Barbara Gaskin, manager of Jarrolds[10] book department. She said straight away, 'Do you realise that Jarrolds has got a price promise? That means that if anyone can obtain a product in Norwich cheaper than at Jarrolds, we will refund the difference. With every book I now buy from you, I'm going to have to think, how much is Smith's going to be selling it for? How much are Waterstone's going to be selling it for?' And indeed, that was happening. So if she had sold a new Maeve Binchy at the publisher's recommended price on the cover, back it came: 'Smith's are selling this at £3 off.' They were having to refund the money.
What happened to that book department? They survived, and are enthusiastically trying to do deals with publishers to make offers themselves. As I say, it's adapt or die.

Clive Bradley If you're a small bookshop in Nuneaton, market share is not something you greatly worry about. It's, 'Do we make a profit at the

10 Long-established Norwich department store.

end of the year or do we make a loss?' But if you are a shareholder-driven outfit, then profitability and market share become terribly important criteria. Those were the real nails in the coffin of the Net Book Agreement.

Philippa Harrison So there we are, it's gone. Bright new world, black new world – who knows? But a new world. And what that created initially was just the most enormous amount of work for every poor bookseller and every publisher. It was an absolute killer. I went to talk at the Irish Book-sellers Association conference the following March, I think. The whole point about the Irish conference is that everybody disagrees and they stand up and argue. I made my speech; other people made their speeches. Not a word from anybody. Everyone was too fucking tired to argue about anything. We'd all had it.

Clive Bradley My predecessor, Ronald Barker, said that working with Gerry Davies to fight and win the NBA case in 1962 had been his first act as secretary to the Publishers Association, and he had always believed that his last would be to preside over its ending. In fact, Ronald Barker died in 1976, and the Net Book Agreement didn't go until nineteen years later, so it still had quite a lot of life in it. I think for Gerry Davies it was something of a life mission; it was the big issue of his time.

We had other issues to deal with as well at the PA, such as copyright legislation and VAT on books. But if you are employed to lobby for, and legally defend, an issue which has values attached to it, it's difficult not to become personally identified with it. My personal view would be that with the ending of the Net Book Agreement certain values have been lost. Support for smaller bookshops, smaller publishers and short-run literary titles is an important part of publishing. But I think it was inevitable that it went, given the globalisation of trade in the last ten years.

Carole Blake I was on the committee of the Association of Authors' Agents when the Net Book Agreement went. The association and the PA took it in turns to take each other out to dinner and talk about issues of common concern, and the NBA went on a day when one of these dinners had long been planned. It was held at Durrants Hotel. An incredibly hot evening, I remember. Clive Bradley, the chief executive of the PA, arrived first. I was the next to arrive and found him sitting at this long table set out for sixteen people. He had a glass in his hand and he said, 'I'm not speaking to half of my committee; half my committee aren't speaking to the other half, and this is not water that I'm drinking.'

It was a tumultuous evening. Whatever agenda we'd had went out of the window, and all that anybody talked about was this new landscape where none of us knew what the rules would be. The very next morning – I think I'm right in saying – I got a phone call from a publisher saying,

'We've got a chance to do a high discount deal with a chain. Will your author accept a lower royalty than the one in the contract?' And I thought, 'Ah, it's the Wild West. Contracts no longer mean anything.' It really was as fast as that.

Then we had to start negotiating clauses for what authors' royalties would be on high discount deals. That was the beginning of the slippery slope. The royalties in the contracts were no longer royalties that you could rely on. Because, even with these newly agreed clauses, there are publishers who ring up, perfectly legitimately, to ask if this big new deal they're doing with Tesco can carry a ten per cent of price-received royalty. I have to put that to my author and in many cases the author will think, 'Well, if Tesco are going to do a really big promotion, which means a really big order, it's worth it.' And I agree, occasionally. I'd rather not, but there is no other way of getting those big deals from the supermarkets.

Philippa Harrison The diminution in margin had to be shared between the author, publisher and bookseller. Therefore one had to change contracts with authors, whereby they got royalties on the price we received from bookshops, rather than the published price. After a bit, we – publishers and booksellers – got used to it, but the whole author constituency – the primary progenitor of this whole business – felt out on a limb.

What kind of reactions were you getting from authors? 'No, you can't have a different royalty from the one you negotiated. I don't care if you can't sell to Smith's; I don't want my books sold cheap.' They thought they were being cheated, they didn't understand it, they were really unhappy. And, as I said in my speech[11] at the 1998 booksellers' conference, there is something dangerous about a bookselling revolution that doesn't have its primary producers wanting to share it. The NBA going was extremely good for the bestselling author, but it could never have been good for the broad variety of people who write books.

Now, of course, it's horrible. People who may have had a respectable, decent, middle-selling writing career for twenty years are just being dropped all over the place. There is not much of a future for fiction writing that doesn't make it in larger quantities than used to be commercial. I very much regret that. The great argument on my side, would be, how long did it take George Orwell to make his publisher a profit? How many books was it? If George Orwell started today, I do not believe a publisher would support him through that number of books.

It may be sentimental – or it may be because I'm an editor primarily, so that is what I care about – but it seems to me there are real dangers of losing a great writer from publication. But I think I'd be in a minority position on that. And you have to be fair: a book like *The Curious Incident of the Dog in the*

11 As president of the Publishers Association.

Night-time[12] – that terribly good book – sold in infinitely greater quantities than it would have done, I think, before the NBA went. It's a question of whether you think it more important that more people read one book of real quality, or that there are ten books of real quality available. I think that the availability of quality is more important, because a book's longevity can never be fully known by a first generation.

Carole Blake I think the NBA going has made it much more difficult for authors to sell a book in the first place, whether it's literary or commercial. If you have an auction for a very commercial novel, you sometimes get an indescribably large amount of money because every publisher wants things that look sure fire. Yet you can offer them what you think is a very good quality book and no one will touch it.

It is so expensive to launch a new writer. People outside the book trade are astonished to hear that every three-for-two promotion and every front-of-store display costs the publisher money. The retailer will say, 'You're very lucky; we have chosen one of your titles to be in our upcoming promotion. We'll buy a lot of copies of the book. So we will, of course, need an extra five per cent discount. And in order to put your book into the promotion, you will pay us x thousand pounds.'

What happens to that book if a publisher isn't able to contribute? It might sink without trace. And very few unusual books get picked for these promotions. That's why it's wonderful when one comes along that is successful, like Lynne Truss's book on punctuation,[13] published by a small, independently-owned publisher, Profile, which doesn't have bucket loads of money to fling at marketing. That book was reviewed by everybody because it was such an idiosyncratic idea and so very well done.

That's a thing I continue to love about the publishing business, that you can still see oddballs like that selling a million copies. And good luck to Andrew Franklin who runs Profile; he published it beautifully. A bestseller like that can sometimes sink a small publisher if they can't keep up with it: you can end up doing your reprints so fast that you get ahead of yourself and are left with a lot of copies in the warehouse when demand begins to slow down. But he neither ran out of stock nor over-stocked. You need to be very clever to get that right.

Brigitte Bunnell I was a firm supporter of the NBA. I think that's because of my German background and training. Since it was abolished, a lot of time, energy and money has been spent on the price war. But it hasn't meant more book buyers, it hasn't meant more profit. Take the latest *Harry Potter*.[14] The discounting started on Amazon, then people panicked, and by

---

12 Mark Haddon, *The Curious Incident of the Dog in the Night-time*, Jonathan Cape, 2003.
13 Lynne Truss, *Eats, Shoots and Leaves*, Profile Books, 2003.
14 J. K. Rowling, *Harry Potter and the Order of the Phoenix*, Bloomsbury, 2003.

the time publication day arrived, everybody in this country was discounting the title – when you had eight million people guaranteed to rush in at midnight to buy it at the full price.

I talked to friends who have independent bookshops in Britain, and they all set out not to discount. Instead, they had their midnight feasts ready and little goody bags for the kids. Then, the day before, they discounted because they panicked: 'I've ordered 500. What if they buy it down the road at Smith's or on Amazon, and I'm left with my 500 copies?' The trade has given away £16 million so far this year,[15] in discounts to the public. That shows how crazy it has become.

Peter Mayer In my job[16] at Penguin I travelled all over the world, and particularly between Britain and the United States. The US was a free enterprise society. Britain was the same, but with restrictions in some areas, books being one of them. In those early years, America seemed to me a more involving, peppier society – more dynamic than Britain. So I thought that to improve the situation in Britain it would be a good thing if some of those American ideas came over. But the longer I made comparisons the more I saw that selling on price made books like oranges, and in cultural terms they are not. If one grocer is selling four oranges for £1, and another grocer is selling five oranges for £1, you would normally buy from the latter, because all oranges look pretty much the same. But with books, price is not the only issue. Do you want to read this book over and over again, or is it ephemera? Is it an author who everybody's reading, or one you have always meant to read? Book reading and book buying – and book publishing – are more complicated than oranges, but in the absence of the Net Book Agreement it's as though they are the same.

Carole Blake To the supermarkets, for the most part, it doesn't matter which books they stock. They have a choice of hundreds coming out in any one month. So if an author says, 'No, I won't accept such a low royalty per book', the supermarket will often say, 'Never mind, I'll buy something else.' There is no perceived author loyalty amongst the supermarkets, and they offer a very small range. Independents are expected to hold a larger range, but they cannot buy sufficient quantities to demand the same discounts as the supermarkets, so they cannot discount their retail prices to the same level as the supermarkets. That is most violently demonstrated with the *Harry Potter* books, which supermarkets will sell for less than half price.

Alain Gründ We had that price war in France. When the first hypermarkets arrived in 1968, Editions Gründ were among the first to supply them with

15 This was recorded in 2003.
16 Chief executive of the Penguin Group.

books, and we suffered badly from the price competition they led. Lille was the first place where Auchan[17] developed, in an aggressive way. They were selling our books at about twenty-five francs, with a forty per cent discount on the recommended price, while in small bookstores the same books sold for fifty francs. Result: in the region of Lille no bookstore wanted to carry our books, and they were sold only in Auchan. Which, of course, sold a lot. But not as many as we would have sold if all the outlets had stocked them.

Trevor Moore The brave new world – where books were going to be suddenly available in a way they had never been before, to huge numbers of new readers – simply hasn't happened. What *has* happened is that booksellers and supermarkets are using special offers as a means of doing their competitors down. It hasn't brought the price of books down. I think customers are well aware that if they see a new hardback at £3 off, it probably could – or should – have been published not at £17.99, but at £14.99 in the first place.

Alain Gründ In 1981 we managed to get a law[18] which says the publisher has to fix the price and everybody must respect it – with a possible maximum discount of five per cent to the consumer, and that's it. That means the price of books in France is maintained by law, whereas in England the Net Book Agreement was a trade agreement between booksellers and publishers. Of course, in Britain you could always publish books as non-net, which was the case with Paul Hamlyn's books. Paul Hamlyn was against the Net Book Agreement; he thought that books should not only be sold in bookstores. And he was right. But the only way to sell them everywhere is to sell them at the same price. Otherwise, one category of shops drops the line because they want to be safe from the risk of selling a book at a more expensive price than it is sold elsewhere. They do not want to be called thieves by their customers.

Peter Mayer Paul Hamlyn became a friend of mine. He built his empires on the back of what normally-constructed publishers could not do. Paul was a decent man and a brilliant merchant, and if he had been only looking out for his self-interest he should not have argued against price maintenance. I don't think Paul would have been so successful in a free-trading British marketplace, because there would have been many Paul Hamlyns. But because he was a very decent man and cared a lot for publishing itself – and was a socialist millionaire, it has to be said – he believed it would be better for Britain if it got rid of the Net Book Agreement.

I don't think he was right, because I think immense cultural damage has

17 Hypermarket retailer.
18 Loi Lang (10 August 1981).

emerged from that. He was right in that getting rid of the Net Book Agreement did unleash entrepreneurial and merchant thinking in publishers who had been somewhat protected from that. But I saw a jungle in America when I went backwards and forwards, and I saw that the retailers would soon dominate the publishers, which is now increasingly the case.

Andrew Franklin The *Harry Potter* phenomenon – or indeed, the Lynne Truss phenomenon – could not have happened before the abolition of the Net Book Agreement. Titles perceived as most likely to succeed are now heavily discounted by booksellers; they will take a third off the price or do 'bog offs' – buy one get one free – but only on a limited range of titles. That pushes consumers to those titles, which then become important in terms of volume of sales, so booksellers advertise those books more and it becomes a self-reinforcing circle.

The corollary is that sales of other books go down. So publishers complain about the decline of backlist sales and of problems with the midlist – good, solid, important books, which may to all intents and purposes be indistinguishable from the frontlist, but which have never broken out as bestsellers. And, as economic theory would predict, that gap is getting bigger and bigger.

Another consequence has been that independent bookselling is a fraction of what it was before the abolition of the Net Book Agreement. Independent booksellers buy from publishers at a discount of, say, forty per cent. That means that on a £10 book the publisher keeps £6 and the bookseller makes £4. But the big chains, like Smith's and Waterstone's are buying at fifty or even sixty per cent, so the publisher is keeping £4 and the bookseller is keeping £6. Obviously a Waterstone's shop has a vast competitive advantage, so it can afford to discount its books. Independents will survive in areas where people are sufficiently rich or sufficiently demanding that they're not price sensitive – bookshops like Heywood Hill in Mayfair, or Daunt's in Marylebone High Street. Otherwise they will disappear.

Robert Clow Borders must have moved into Glasgow about the same time that the Net Book Agreement went. They were in Buchanan Street, around the corner from John Smith's in St Vincent Street, in a building that had been totally renovated and sat on a beautiful T-junction, in a dominant position which is said to be one of the best retail sites in Britain. They just vacuumed customers out of us and into them, so our sales went down. Every month there was hope amongst some members of our board that things would change, but it was pretty obvious that we had to sell the company. Eventually the lawyers advised us that John Smith's senior managers wished to buy out those shareholders who wanted to sell their shares. The nice thing is that the company still continues to trade. One has to be grateful for that.

Terry Maher Book retailing has changed dramatically – look at all these swish shops on the high street – although the change that has come about as a result of the abolition of the Net Book Agreement has been extremely disappointing, with a lack of imagination in terms of marketing and promotion. It's all 'three for two'. What's 'three for two'? All the shops are the same, there's no originality. Ten years ago we were doing interesting, innovative things, including television advertising and a lot in the newspapers. Posters as well. And we had fun. Some people might not have seen the joke, but even Christina said, 'It was fantastic. I loved your poster outside Foyle's: "Foiled Again? Try Dillons".'

Christina Foyle I think the more bookshops the better, don't you? I'm always glad to see them open. My father used to say, 'Never worry what people do – see what happens to them.' I'd much rather have bookshops in Charing Cross Road than these awful chemists' shops selling birth control stuff.
Ian Norrie Were you a supporter of the Net Book Agreement? Not really. I don't like restrictions. I was glad to see it go. Foyle's had been put on the black list[19] several times. Not that we ever tried to break rules, but sometimes staff do without your knowledge. Then you get into trouble over it.

Brigitte Bunnell Hatchards wouldn't discount for quite a while because our customers were suspicious – if a book was discounted, they thought there was something wrong with it. What we did was to have special offers, as if we had chosen to offer some books at a certain price specially for the customers. Our customers did not associate Hatchards with the word discount. A special offer is different.

Peter Mayer I thought for a while that I might publish a novel about a *ménage à trois* called *Three for Two* and then it would be visibly displayed.

Andrew Franklin There has been a reduction in the price of bestsellers – that's the good thing. And the sale of books into supermarkets encourages some people to read books, so you could argue that it's more democratic. But a good independent bookshop might stock 50,000 titles, whereas the supermarkets might only stock up to a hundred. So the disappearance of the independents means a reduction in choice and variety, and a concentration of power into fewer people's hands. Personally I feel that's a great cultural loss. It doesn't make a difference to Profile, because if you can get your books into the front of the bookshop and they become bestsellers, then you're going to be fine. It's not easy – you have good years and you have bad years – but we've managed to do that enough.

19 By publishers, for breaking the Net Book Agreement.

Michael Seviour I always passionately defended the Net Book Agreement, although I thought it would probably go. I don't think we yet know the full effect. I felt it could mean that a lot of publishers wouldn't have the money to subsidise new authors. When Graham Greene wrote his first books, how many copies were printed, and how many copies were sold? Peanuts. On the other hand, I have just been looking in the British Library bookshop and seen several imprints there that I have never heard of, including one that is reviving classics such as Emma Smith's *The Far Cry*, which MacGibbon & Kee once published. I think that's very enterprising – they're printing work that might not have seen the light of day again, and as very elegantly produced books. I hope the publishers[20] will be successful.

Ainslie Thin I still think that the Net Book Agreement was a good scheme. More and more of the trade is now going into the hands of a very small number of very large retailers. They're not just big national companies, they're big global companies. This is happening not just in bookselling, but in many spheres of business. If we finish up with two or three similar types of outlet, the public won't be well served, and it will miss the special service you get from some small bookshops, or from some small chains. The character is being taken out of bookselling. I deeply regret the loss of the small business, where I believe life can be so much more satisfying. Just purely from a social point of view, I think there should be lots of small firms run by people being able to make their own decisions. But that's not the way of life just now; it's heading in the other direction.

Maureen Condon I think there is a dichotomy between business and bookselling, because the very nature of bookselling – where you expend so much energy and time promoting whatever book you're trying to promote or helping people gain access to information or knowledge – means it is difficult to make it *really* profitable, so that one has a luxurious lifestyle. Maybe if you have centuries of bookselling behind you, as Blackwell's does, wealth will accumulate. But we[21] were first generation booksellers – small booksellers – so there had been no time to accumulate any wealth. But we had an interesting life, and the fact that we had a bookshop enabled us to educate our children – our three children all went to university. I think it was sufficient unto our needs.

Michael Seviour I did notice a shift in attitude; I think the trade has generally become more money orientated. As a bookseller, I would say, 'I'm in this for various reasons. I have to make a profit, so I need to be a good businessman. But there is another thing pushing me, which is that I

---

20 Persephone Books.
21 Maureen Condon and John Prime, who ran bookshops together in King's Lynn.

want to do a good job as a bookseller. I could make more money for my shop by selling books which I think are a blot on the landscape, but I won't do it. So I might be prepared to take a little less profit, in order to run a business that I consider is doing a decent job for society.

Do you think there is a social function for booksellers? I think there's a social function for everything. Any business has a duty to its shareholders, a duty to its customers, a duty to its staff – and a duty to society.

What would the duty to society be? If you are a general bookshop it is to provide a good, general selection of books, and to try to get books for people if you haven't got them in stock. If somebody wants a rare Sanskrit text, for example, to be able to recommend another bookseller, who could get it for them. You would say, 'Well, we would have trouble finding it. But if you wrote to Probsthain's or Luzac's in Great Russell Street, they could order it for you.' If a customer wanted a book that turned out to be from an obscure little publisher, I would explain, 'If we got it for you, they'd only give us twenty per cent discount, and we'll have to pay the cost of the posting and the packing – so we'd have to charge you another £1.50 just to break even. And if I send the order, they'll just chuck it in the in-tray and we might eventually get the book in four weeks' time. But if I gave you the address and you wrote to them yourself, you'd probably get it back by return.'

As a bookseller, you would try to do the best job you could for customers – which I would see as a way of building up the reputation of your business.

Peter Mayer If you go into a large retailing establishment today, the assistants often know less about the books than the readers who come in to buy them – they have a computer keyboard in front of them; they don't really have to know anything. There is a great risk to these retailers from Amazon, because when you access Amazon, you get more information than you will from any assistant. So you have cheaper and cheaper labour, you have less and less training in retailing, and you will increasingly attract only the reader who goes in just to buy the new bestseller. I think it's not impossible that knowledgeable independent booksellers, having almost been wiped out, will raise their heads again. Or that the most important book customers – the real readers – will buy all their books online. Then the large emporia that sell books would become mass-market outlets which just stock a small range of titles. People would deny that this could happen. But I think it is happening now.

Gerry Davies I felt passionately about the Net Book Agreement. Although we didn't have a major bookshop in East Ham, where I grew up, there was a stationer's with a good bookselling section where I bought the early Penguins. When I was working in a library, I read *The Spectator* and the *New Statesman*, and always the book reviews. I could see how important it was to have a stable system. As a librarian, I felt that good bookshops backed up good libraries. I was, you might say, a believer in bookshops. I also believed that publishers would not so easily publish marginal books if they felt that there wasn't a good system of outlets for them. Now that the Net Book Agreement has gone by the wayside, many things I thought would happen have come to pass. It will be after I'm dead, but if I'm anywhere, I will welcome the news that the Net Book Agreement has been re-invented. In a contemporary form, of course.

15 | A CERTAIN CACHET

Efric Wotherspoon Not many of the reps come. Because, as one said to me, you can't sell books to sheep. There would be that forty miles from Tarbet to Campbeltown, and he couldn't sell a single thing on the way.

Bert Taylor When I became a rep for Simpkin's in the late 1930s, I was given a Morris Ten and they would leave me to plan my own journeys. I started off in the southern half of England – including Devon and Cornwall, where I used to get good orders – and after a while I was asked to go further afield. Eventually, just before Simpkin's was blitzed, I was covering the whole of the British Isles with the exception of London.

I used to go to Ireland twice a year. I would go on the boat from Heysham to Dun Laoghaire, and stop at the same hotels every time in Dublin, Limerick, Cork and Belfast. Each time I booked a hotel, I told the boots[1] there that I was due, and they would be waiting at the dock with a barrow, on which my cases were put. I used to take three great cases, because I was carrying remainders and some really big art books. These barrow men – which is what we called them in those days in Ireland – would call for you at the hotel in the morning and load your bags onto a barrow. 'Where are you going to first, Mr Taylor?' You'd tell them the bookshop you wanted to visit, then they'd wheel your bags there and carry them in. Whenever the boots at the Hotel Metropole in Cork knew I was going home, he'd say, 'You're away on the *Innisfallen* tonight, Mr Taylor? Then I'll be round for you.' Sure enough, he was down there half an hour before the boat was due to sail, and he'd bring my cases on board. Everywhere in Ireland I used the barrow boy. Quite different from here or in Scotland or Wales, where you carried your bags in yourself from the car.

It was such a vast territory, people wouldn't believe me when I told them that I was travelling so far afield. I used to go up to Perth and Inverness in Scotland, down to Penzance in Cornwall, and cover the whole of Wales. *What were the difficulties of being a rep?* The great difficulty, my dear, was being away from home so much. I was away from Monday till Friday in most cases, and when I was in Ireland or Scotland I was away for three

---

1 The employee who cleaned guests' shoes.

weeks at a stretch. Your children grow up and you don't really know them as most people do; sometimes I only saw my family at the weekend. If they knew you were on commission, booksellers would post the order to you instead of direct to the publisher, so you could send it in as one of your orders. That meant you were busy working all the weekend when you got home, and preparing to go off on the following Monday.

When I went to Ireland, I left at midday Sunday and caught the train from Euston so that I was in Belfast for Monday morning. Going to Scotland, I used to drive up from Virginia Water in Surrey, where we lived then, and – particularly in the winter – sometimes leave home about six o'clock in the morning and be up in Glasgow by early afternoon. In those days that was quite something.

Other than that, I can't say there were any difficulties. Booksellers are wonderful people to call on. Often I would stop away weekends because I was so far from home. One bookseller I got to know, Bridges of Penzance, always used to see me Saturday afternoons, which fitted in beautifully with me. I would show him a book and he'd say, 'Yes. Good book, Mr Taylor. Cheap as chips. But I don't want any.'

When you've been calling on booksellers for years, they become your friends. Jock Currer, for instance, who was a buyer at the Midland Educational Company in Birmingham – I would often go up on a Friday with the car and meet him when he'd finished work, then we'd pootle off to the Lake District and do a bit of mountain scrambling over the weekend. And I would be invited to booksellers' homes, which was very pleasant indeed. Some of the Scottish bookshops were marvellous.

Are there any particular shops you remember there? Thin's of Edinburgh, obviously.

I've heard that Ainslie Thin[2] was quite fierce with reps. Indeed he could be. He was a well-educated man, was Ainslie Thin. But there you are. He was a bookman, and I respected him as that. Just because I didn't match up to his learning and erudition . . . Well, that was that. After all, we're all human.

What was his manner like as a buyer? Curt, actually. Not a chap you could have a lot of banter with. The other bookshop I used to like in Scotland was Smith's of Glasgow. I got very friendly with the chappie there and his daughter; I used to go home to them in the evenings and play bezique.

In the first two years of the war I still used to go over to Ireland – I had to get a special permit from the Passport Office. Belfast was blacked out, but when you went down to Dublin the lights were all ablaze, and they told me there were Germans walking about there. It was wonderful to go again into a city that was full of life at night, after the wretched blackout conditions that we had on the mainland in Britain. Often you had to adjust your itinerary because of air raids; you'd be going to a city like Coventry, then

2 Ainslie Thin senior.

overnight you heard it was bombed. I think I told you previously[3] that Simpkin's was blitzed in 1940. A month earlier I'd had my call-up papers and was due to go into the RAF the following February. After being demobbed I contacted my old chief, Charlie Robertson from Simpkin's remainder department, who had gone to Odhams Press. He said, 'There's a job as a rep here, if you want it.' So I then became a rep for Odhams.

That was a good list – anything from Odhams, you could sell. Books like *The British Countryside*, which was full of pictures, were selling like hot cakes. No problems at all with Odhams. After the war, books were rationed. You went around with a book like that and a bookseller had to order fifty to get ten. Booksellers had no idea how many they were going to get. If they ordered ten, they might just get two or three – whatever the publisher could let them have. So to counterbalance that, a bookseller would order a hundred of something he thought he could sell, knowing that if he got fifteen or twenty he would be lucky.

Did you earn commission on sales? As a traveller, yes.

So did the rationing affect your salary? Yes, it did. You still got something out of it, but probably not what you would have got in normal times. But you got a basic salary, so you didn't worry unduly.

Did you ever find yourself selling books because you needed the commission, rather than because you believed in the books? I was doing my job, and that was it. I did it to the best of my ability, and I was happy in doing it. I didn't sell just for commission. I was glad to have it, mark you. But I don't think that was what motivated my selling.

What did motivate your selling? A love of books, and a liking for booksellers. And I wanted to see them do well.

Stephen Dearnley The winter of 1947 was one of the worst on record; Glasgow was virtually cut off for three months. The place was miserable. We had Stafford Cripps as Chancellor of the Exchequer and the outlook was all doom and gloom. I'd had about a year as a Collins' trainee, so I went to Ian Collins[4] and asked, 'What next?' He said, 'What do you want to do?' 'Probably go onto the sales side,' I said, 'but it would have to be overseas. I'd rather like to go to America or Canada.' 'No,' he said, 'there's nothing there.' 'What about Africa?' 'No, nothing there.' We scouted around possibilities, then Ian Collins said – slowly, as though nobody in their right senses ever would – 'You could go to Australia.' I said, 'OK. Anything.' So Jo[5] and I embarked on the *Orion*, and arrived in Australia five weeks later to join the Collins office in Sydney.

In January 1948 I had four days of driving lessons; on the fifth day I got the test, and on the sixth I picked up a Morris Ten. I was given a map and a

---

3 *See* Chapter 1.
4 Brother of Billy Collins and a director of William Collins.
5 Stephen Dearnley and Josephine Irwin had married in December 1945.

list of customers – none of whom had seen anybody since before the war – and I had the whole of New South Wales as my territory, including the Darling Downs district of Southern Queensland.

Could you describe a typical visit? Let's say you were calling on a bookshop in a town like Gunnedah. You'd probably driven at least fifty, possibly a hundred, miles from the previous call, generally on dirt roads, so it might have taken a couple of hours or more. I used to send a postcard ahead to these people to say I was coming. You'd go in with two great heavy suitcases – they'd nearly pull your arms off – and ask to see the owner, hoping he or his deputy would settle down with you for a couple of hours to go through the catalogue. That was quite a business. You'd go right through the children's books – Collins had a big children's list – adult fiction and non-fiction lists. There was a series of reference books – *Gem* dictionaries, atlases. The *Rubáiyát of Omar Khayyám*. White Circle paperbacks – before Fontana started. And bibles. Each bible had a different catalogue number, so you had to remember which they were – that was quite an expert thing. 'OK. You want six of F2400C', which was hardcover with illustrations. Or you might have one with yapped edges, or a gold edge. Those orders would be sent from Glasgow in wooden crates through the nearest port of entry: generally Sydney for New South Wales; in Queensland it could be Maryborough or Bundaberg.

What kind of books were selling at that time? That depended on the type of local agricultural economy. In dairying districts the people were very conservative and often fundamental Christians, so you'd always do well with the bibles and Sunday school reward books. If you went into a wealthier grazing area, or mixed wheat and sheep, you'd get a more interesting spread of people – they would actually buy novels. They would even buy picture books and you might, occasionally, sell an art book. In those days we were doing the *Britain in Pictures* series.

What did you enjoy about it most? Discovering the countryside. It was pretty wild, some of it. The roads were very rough. The Morris Ten only lasted about three months before it fell to bits. I got a Ford after that.

When our first child was born early in 1950, I had a stand-up-and-sit-down with my boss and said, 'Listen. I'm not going to go country travelling and be away two or three weeks at a time, leaving my wife on her own with a small child.' I virtually put in my resignation. And very grudgingly I was told, 'All right, we'll give you the Sydney suburbs. But you won't have a car.' So for two months I did the whole of the Sydney suburbs by public transport, lugging these bloody great cases around.

In 1953 I was transferred to Brisbane and had the whole of Queensland as my territory. There you have monsoonal autumn rains, or summer rains, and you used to try to be the first rep to get through to the north after the wet season finished. You would have already done the area between Brisbane and Rockhampton, which was about 500 miles in all. That wasn't so bad. But from Rockhampton you had the major towns: there was Mackay about 250 miles beyond; then Proserpine, then Townsville – that was another 250 miles – then another 400 miles or so on to Cairns. You'd set out and try to get through, and there'd be your mate from Cassells and your mate from Heinemann trying to get there first, because the first person who got through would often get the best orders. Those towns on the Queensland coast were virtually mini-capitals, because they supplied a huge inland area.

We would also get cut off by floods. I remember once having a hell of a time trying to get back from Cairns to Brisbane. The Burdekin River was up at Ayr, so I went to Charters Towers and tried to get down inland along a bush track to the next town at Emerald, about 200 miles further south. Just two wheel-tracks with grass in between, so you weren't going very fast. I asked at the police station, 'Do you reckon I can get down?' and the policeman said, 'The Belyando's up. You might get through; people have already been camped there for about a week.' I did get through on that one.

You'd go all day and it was lonely as hell. I remember driving along this track and what looked like a pig got up and ran in front, then suddenly flew off. It was a great big bush turkey – you would almost hit them. Thirty miles short of Emerald you'd suddenly see telephone wires. 'Ah, civilisation.' If you broke down you were stuffed. It was quite frightening.
Did you ever break down? No, fortunately. A few times I had to leave the car and take the train because of floods, then come back and get it a week or two later. Another time, right out in the west in the black soil country . . . This is soil which can be seven feet deep; black, sticky stuff which is fine when it's dry – hard as anything – but once any rain gets on it, it's a total bog, and if an inch of rain falls, that road can be out for a week. I was at Charleville, right out in the west, when it started to rain. Six hundred miles from Brisbane. I just got in the car and drove all day and all night and got back to Brisbane ahead of the rain. You had to do that, otherwise you would be stuck there.
What idea did Collins in Britain have of the conditions you were working in? Not a clue, I don't think. I remember Billy Collins once sending out a cable to Freddy Howe: 'We've had a complaint from somebody at Cairns. Could Dearnley go up one afternoon and fix it?'

Trevor Moore In the early 1960s I was covering the north west for Hamish Hamilton, a territory which included Liverpool. I remember being in the Kardomah coffee bar, which was bang next door to Philip, Son & Nephew's bookshop and right opposite NEMS – Brian Epstein's North Eastern Music Stores. I heard this strange music coming out from their loudspeakers, and I thought, that's a bit different, what is it? It was a local group called the Beatles and within months they were having this extraordinary freak success.

Cape got in very early with a Beatles tribute book, a collection of photographs of a young Paul, George, John and Ringo. It was essentially a picture book for the fans, but stylish, smart, large format, very well produced. Their rep had an advance copy, and was telling anyone in the Kardomah who would listen – which included quite a few employees of Philip, Son & Nephew – 'What a ridiculous load of rubbish. Look at the crap that Cape are publishing now. This is never going to sell. This idiot rock group. What are we doing, publishing this?' I said to him, 'You are going to sell thousands of that, in Liverpool alone.' And boy, was he wrong, because that book did sell. And he was certainly wrong about the Beatles.

Cape was on the crest of a wave, at the forefront of the most interesting general publishing that was going on at that time.[6] It was really buzzing. They'd published Joseph Heller's *Catch-22*; they were publishing Len Deighton, having previously published Ian Fleming with great success. But that wasn't the only reason I wanted to work for them. Yes, I was joining Cape at that exciting time in their development, but also I was doing the West End. There was a certain cachet in those days to being the London rep.

Trevor Moore joined Jonathan Cape in 1964.

The sales department was in a little street behind 30 Bedford Square. I used to go in at lunchtimes to write the orders out because Norman Askew, the sales director, liked to keep track of what was happening in the shops. Sometimes I would go across the road into the publicity department at the front of 30 Bedford Square, to see what proof copies they might have. One occasionally saw authors in there – Len Deighton was someone I met quite early on in Cape's publicity department.

Cape was in the forefront of experimental literary developments and there were booksellers in London who would be keen to see the list: Ted Hall, fiction buyer in Dillon's University Bookshop; Michael Seviour, manager of Better Books in Charing Cross Road. When I first knew Better Books, it was an exciting shop, but it was later bought by Hatchards and became less interesting. Shortly before the demise of the old regime, I received an order from Michael Seviour for one copy of Malcolm Lowry's *Hear Us O Lord from Heaven Thy Dwelling Place*, with a note attached: 'Souvenir. This is the last order I shall write out from Better Books.' It was written with a certain kind of bitterness, I always felt. When Michael was manager, the shop front of Better Books was stuffed with literary novels, biography and criticism and politics, and there was a room at the back crammed with experimental literature of one kind or another. They used to do very nicely with the Cape Editions – it was under that imprint that Cape published European writers such as Havel, and various American writers.

6 Mid-1960s.

During my time at Cape they published Tom Wolfe. I have a copy of *The Kandy-Kolored Tangerine-Flake Streamline Baby*, signed by him in a flamboyant hand: 'To Trevor, Yeah! Remembering kandy-kolored hours on the Charing Cross Road'.

What was he referring to? To the signing session-cum-appearance that he did in Better Books. It was great fun, but we didn't sell a lot of books, because not that many people turned up. It wasn't the big occasion that we had hoped it would be – I think this was after Hatchards had bought the shop.

Not long after I'd left Cape for Collins, Philip Roth's *Portnoy's Complaint* was published. I had seen a proof and I knew how big that book was going to be. When that happened – it was as big as I thought it was going to be, and bigger – yes, I did feel nostalgic for Cape. I felt that I ought to have been selling that book. And to a degree, I still was. There's a lot of selling of other people's books in this business. One finds oneself constantly talking to booksellers about books, and every now and again I would hear myself saying, 'How many have you ordered of that? Oh, I think you've under-cooked it. I had a proof of that, and I think it's probably the best book that Le Carré's written. In your position I would have taken a few more.' In a funny kind of way – not that I did it for this reason – it seemed to underline your objectivity if you were able to express an opinion about another publisher's book.

Sylvia May In the summer of 1977 I saw an advertisement in *The Bookseller* for trainee reps at William Collins Sons & Co Ltd. I wrote off, and I got an interview with the redoutable Mr Iain Ogston and Mr Ted Collins.

What were they looking for? Enthusiasm, I think. It was a trainee scheme; they were looking for raw material. I was certainly that. Under this scheme they would take on three youngsters every year. You would spend one month with every rep on the road, learning on the ground. Then you'd spend a month in the warehouse, and a month in the manufacturing plant, learning about the different kinds of paper and how books were made. Then hope-fully a vacancy would come up and you'd get a job. I was told afterwards that Iain Ogston had to fight to get them to take me, because I was a girl. They hadn't hired any women before.

The first month I spent with a man called George Howe. He still wore a bowler hat; I'm sure he'd started at Collins before the war. His territory was Surrey, so he was calling on bookshops in Guildford, Epsom, Esher, Godalming, and he was also doing Heathrow airport – that was his big account. We would call on four bookshops a day; two in the morning and two in the afternoon. After George retired, a friend of mine took over some of his accounts. He told a story about going into a bookshop and saying to the buyer, 'But you took ten copies last time we published this author.' And the bookseller beckoned him to the back of the store and opened a cupboard. It was piled high with Collins books that he had never sold and that George had refused to accept as returns.

Then I went up to central London to do Christmas car stock. I'd never driven in London before and my job was to drive round delivering books. I think I had a Marina, a horrible little car. But it was free, a company car. Collins' offices were down in St James's, so I'd be in there first thing in the morning, then off driving round bookstores. Boy, did I get lost and honked at. But I learned my way. In those days I used to double park in Piccadilly, run in to Hatchards with my boxes and run out again. It was much easier; there was no clamping and you rarely got a ticket. When I was a rep later on, I was constantly being towed away. It was a very expensive business.

The first time I went into a bookshop on my own to sell books was when I was training with Alan Trimble, who covered Lancashire and North Wales. He took me to a bookstore in the middle of nowhere and said, 'I'll wait in the car.' Alan had known that bookseller for years; he'd obviously set it up, and it was fine. When you look back on it now, it was so old-fashioned: you walked into a bookshop with a bag, and you just pulled out the jacket of the book: 'How many of these would like?' 'Oh, I'll take one.' So you wrote 'one' on a piece of paper and eventually came out with an order for maybe fifteen books, which wasn't going to pay for the fuel that had got you from Manchester. But what was important was building the relationship between the rep and the bookseller.

Every new title had a target – which doesn't happen any more. Each territory would be given their individual target, and the reps would divide it up: 'If I've got to sell 1,500, that means that Foyle's will have to buy 350.' Then you looked up what Foyle's bought of the last book by that author. If it was only 300, you'd think, I'm going to have to get round this somehow. In Foyle's case you'd take them to lunch. But you would go in knowing not only what the bookstore had previously bought, but also what they had sold. And you were supposed to get there half an hour before your appointment and physically check stock, so you could say, 'You had two of these last time I was here. Now you've only got one. May I put another one in for you?' It's laughable to think of that, because today everything is computerised.

I've heard that Collins was known for its rigorous training of sales reps and also for hardselling. Yes, it was. There would be lots of excuses to put off taking returns. 'Actually, could we deal with them next time I'm here? Would that be all right?' And the bookseller would inevitably agree. 'What about more discount?' 'Well, I'll have to refer it to my boss.' The reps had stiff targets.

I'd been training for about ten months when Reg Fisk retired and I was offered his territory. That was fondly called Wessex, and included Hampshire and the Isle of Wight. I was the first lady rep that Collins employed, and Reg was deeply upset that his life's work should be taken over by this mere slip of a girl. He'd load up his bags with the heaviest books he could find and say, 'Right, bring those into the house.' That's a big part of being a rep; you have to carry a bag. When I was training, the reps had expressed concern that I wouldn't be strong enough. But by then I'd had a lifetime – up to my tender twenty years – of riding horses, carrying buckets of water and hay bales. I was quite strong. Which they hadn't quite anticipated.

So I took over from Reg and started planning my journey cycles – you just get a map out and look at what works where: 'OK, I can do those two shops together.' You would try to visit every store, and I'm pretty sure that territory was monthly, but there may have been stores you saw once every three months if they were small. In Bournemouth there were about four or five accounts, so that took a whole day. Worthing was the furthest call from my home in Swindon, so I'd stay overnight there. It was easy once you'd got the cycle underway, because the final thing you did when you called was to say, 'OK for this time in four weeks? Good. Thank you very much.' And that was your next appointment made.

Most of those shops in Wessex were independent, family run, piled high with books on the floor and shelves. I used to go to the White Horse Bookshop in Marlborough, run by Jimmy Glover. That was a lovely bookshop, full of his own personal taste. We would have proof copies to give out, and ideally you should know what kind of books your bookseller liked. Some of the reps used to keep notes; they'd even keep notes of the bookseller's birthday and what their children were called – and their dog. I never went quite that far, I'm afraid.

What did you enjoy most? The freedom. Driving about the country all day, music on the radio, going to see nice booksellers. Normally I'd grab a sandwich for lunch and eat it in the car. There were certain guidelines, yes. But it was up to you – and the bookseller – when you called on bookshops.

Trevor Moore There's a story I heard from Bob Kemp at Weidenfeld about a bookseller in the West Midlands who had seen the Collins hardback rep by appointment. The rep had spent an hour and a half hard selling, then said goodbye. Then the Fontana rep – the Collins paperback rep – turned up out of the blue. 'Could you give me a few minutes?' So he duly saw the Fontana rep. Then a gentleman he hadn't met before came in and said, 'Collins diaries.' And the bookseller said, 'Look. I've had your hardback colleague in from nine until eleven, then I had the bloody Fontana rep. I just cannot see any more Collins reps.' And this man said, 'No. I want to buy one.' That was the reputation Collins had in those days. They prided themselves on covering every section of the market, and selling harder and more efficiently than anyone else.

Sylvia May I got to know other Collins reps later on, but not in Hampshire. I don't think I even knew who the Fontana rep was, when I was there. You never really saw your colleagues in the bookshops. It was extraordinary, when you think how many of us there were. You would miss them by just a few hours sometimes.

Michael Seviour My grandfather was a bible salesman for Eyre & Spottiswoode, then later moved to Collins. He eventually committed suicide. My father said, 'One of the things that upset him was that he had been persuaded by Godfrey Collins' – who was Billy Collins' uncle – 'to go and be a rep for Collins. And Collins were great publishers but very pushy, whereas at Eyre & Spottiswoode it was more of an occupation for gentlemen.' Apparently my grandfather couldn't stand the pressures in Collins.

Sylvia May I became a central London rep in 1981. That's where all the glamour was, potentially. Talk about journey cycles – that was definitely a journey cycle. Monday morning, nine o'clock, you weren't worth your salt if you weren't in Foyle's. That's where everybody was on a Monday morning, every Monday morning. You turned up as soon as the shop opened and did your departments, checking the stock and taking orders for all your new books. I was representing Collins hardbacks, so I sold fiction, biography, history, military and kids' books. The buyer in my day was Vic Stimac. At ten thirty he would open his door, and you queued to see Mr Stimac. You would hear the noise of the stamp going as he was stamping orders, and if you heard that, you knew he was in a good mood. There were days when you would queue for half an hour – after you'd done all that work – and he would go, 'No' and shut the door, and that was it. Without the order being stamped you couldn't put it through. That was a really entertaining way to start the week.

Brigitte Bunnell The reps came in all shapes. Tall ones, charming ones . . . Jim Leppard from Batsford, the Hamlyn rep, the rep from Mitchell Beazley, Sylvia Graham[7] from Collins, Gillian Hawkins from Weidenfeld . . .
How usual was it to deal with women reps at that time? They were in the minority. But in both those cases they were so hands-on. Sylvia herself had been a bookseller at Hammick's before she became a rep. She was the one you wished every rep would be like: she would do stock checks that you could totally rely on, she would answer the phone if you were busy at the till, she would serve customers, she would fill your shelves, she would unpack parcels – quite apart from the knowledge she brought with her visit. She's still with Collins – now HarperCollins – as sales director for the European market.[8]

7 Maiden name of Sylvia May.
8 Subsequently international sales director.

Sue Butterworth and Jane Cholmeley opened the independent Silver Moon Women's Bookshop on Charing Cross Road in 1984.

Sue Butterworth When we opened Silver Moon we had a shop dog called Biff. I had found her in a local rescue home when she was three months old. She was a cross between a Staffordshire bull terrier and an Alsatian, and looked like she would have your leg off. In fact, she was the most gentle dog. Her favourite spot was the Virago section, which was a nice little corner where she could go to sleep. But to start with, Biff was in the office with a kiddy-guard across the doorway to keep her in. And believe me, if the rep had given you any trouble, you didn't undo it for him. We had a few who were a bit uppity because they weren't sure how to deal with us, and we made them climb over it – with their bags. But most of the reps couldn't have been kinder to us when we were opening. We were pretty wet behind the ears.

Margaret Hughes I appreciated seeing a rep, because you could ask them about a book and they would know. In fact, you wouldn't even need to ask; they would tell you what the book was about, how they were expecting it to sell, what they were doing about publicity. The Penguin reps we have seen recently – young women – have been wonderful, and they've read the stuff, very often. But when other publishers stopped sending reps, we tended not to have their books on the shelves, because you don't think to unless you see the publicity.

Couldn't you have received written information? Well, you could, and you did. And we used that for Collins' books to a large extent, for a number of years. *So why was that relationship with a rep valuable to you?* They are a human face between you and this enormous firm that's churning out stuff and wanting you to buy it. I appreciate a person saying, 'I wouldn't bother with this book.' Or, when the rep comes the next month, you say, 'You said we should have this, but we haven't sold a single copy.' 'Don't worry. Send it back.' It's old-fashioned, I know, but I prefer to have a human being to complain to or congratulate.

Sylvia May There was a café opposite Foyle's called the Book Caff. Looking back, I equate it to a Fleet Street bar of journalists, except it was the old hacks of the book trade huddled in there, drinking undrinkable coffee, eating toast and peanut butter and swapping car stories. And of course, they were all men, weren't they? Then there was me. But gradually over the years – because I did that job for five years – more women reps appeared in the Book Caff.

Brigitte Bunnell There were reps who just looked upon it as a social call to meet other reps. We had the Friday mafia, who would go off to coffee for an hour, instead of selling us books. We would have done the order, so it didn't really matter, because they always went back to their publishing houses with orders from Hatchards.

Where did they go for coffee? To a place in Jermyn Street, then it moved to the Piccadilly Arcade. They would all gather in the front shop. 'Where's So-and-so?' 'On the second floor.' 'Give him a ring. We're off.' And they would all go out together. I remember Kay Stocker, Peter Giddy's[9] secretary, having to go round to the Thirty-Nine – that was the café in Jermyn Street – to get him out of the mafia meeting whenever somebody wanted him urgently. They were all one big club. And to hear them talk was entertaining, the way they put the book trade in order. If one of them had a bestseller, the others would say, 'I didn't realise that crap sells.' If you wanted some news spread, you told certain reps, and they would pass it all round the book trade. Even before *The Bookseller* came out on a Friday, you would know about it, because someone had popped in to tell you. 'Have you heard? And do you know the latest? So-and-so is leaving. And So-and-so is going bankrupt.'

Karl Lawrence Everybody always knew how much everyone else was earning in the book trade. They don't now, but they did then. The accounts department would tell a rep, and the reps would spread it all over the place. Collins paid me £2,000 a year in 1965, which was a lot of money then. I had lunch with Alewyn Birch of Heinemann, and he had heard about it from his rep, Bob Waite, before I even started work. Somebody must have read the letter of appointment and told a rep about it.

Brigitte Bunnell When the Net Book Agreement was going and we had all the hoo-ha – who was putting what nail in and working against it – or when we had threat of VAT on books,[10] the reps may not have had exactly the right information, but they always had something. Then, on a Friday, you would read in *The Bookseller* either confirmation of what you already knew from a rep, or a slightly different version.

Reps were vital for communication and networking. From the social history point of view they were an expression of the intimacy of the book trade. That world has become bigger with the takeovers and corporations, but it is still a small world, and in those days it was a highly intimate world: we all were members of this one big family – or one big club. And with jobs, definitely a lot of headhunting went on – the reps had an important function in alerting others to what was happening. Good people weren't lost to the trade – in fact, they went from strength to strength – thanks, not to an advert, but to the networking of the reps.

9 General manager of Hatchards.
10 Having heard that the British Treasury intended to remove the zero VAT rating from printed matter, the Publishers Association organised a major campaign that culminated in the government's announcement in the 1985 budget that it did not plan to impose VAT on books.

Ian Miller All right, you'd all meet for coffee in the Kardomah on Fridays. But you were sitting down with other buyers from other shops and a mixture of reps, and talking about the book trade. It was social, but it achieved a good rapport between individuals. As a bookseller, the relationship with a rep was important. They probably knew as much about your business as you did, and most would have a shrewd idea what it could sell. When I became manager of Mowbray's in Birmingham,[11] the first rep who came in was a bloke called Bert Hutchins who worked for Collins. He was the doyen of the Midland reps. He brought a book to me called *Anglican Attitudes* by A.J. Cockshut – it was about ten and sixpence in a hardback – and I said, 'Oh, I'll have a dozen.' In London, Mowbray's would have had fifty, probably. And he said, 'It's not for me to say, but I think you'll find two is enough.'

Eric Norris I made a mistake with *Gone with the Wind*.[12] When the rep subscribed it to me, I said, 'All right, Mr Dunwich, I'll have one copy.' Three weeks later he came in again. 'We can't believe it at the firm that you have ordered one copy.' He waffled on and on. I said, 'All right, my friend, I'll have two copies.' How wrong I was.

Trevor Moore Bob Kemp pulled some terrible strokes on his customers. There was a nice bookseller called Joe Prendergast at Combridge Jackson[13] in Birmingham. Weidenfeld had published a book by Harold Wilson – *The Governance of Britain*, or maybe it was one of his earlier ones. Bob was the local rep for Weidenfeld. He had tried very hard to persuade Joe Prendergast to take a large quantity of this book, but Joe had ordered a miserable number. Shortly before publication, Bob phoned Joe Prendergast and said – in his impeccable Harold Wilson voice – 'I'd like to speak to Mr Prendergast, please.' 'Joe Prendergast speaking.' 'This is Harold Wilson here. I'm in Birmingham tomorrow for a lunch, and I'd like to sign fifty copies of my book. Could you get them round to the Midland Hotel?' 'Oh, well, er, well, we might have a little bit of a problem with that. Er, you see, er, oh, we don't . . . I'm sure we could.'

The conversation went on for some time before Bob relented and said, 'Yer can't bloody send the books round, because you 'aven't bloody ordered enough, have yer?' 'Kemp? Is that you Kemp? You bastard. You bastard.' That was the story that Bob told. It was a bit naughty to do that to customers. But what a wonderful way of making it clear to somebody that they hadn't ordered enough copies of a book.

Elizabeth McWatters I don't think you get the same characters in the book trade today. And you don't seem to have the same contact with companies. I

11 Ian Miller took up this appointment in February 1959.
12 Margaret Mitchell, *Gone with the Wind*, Macmillan, 1936.
13 Library suppliers.

can remember people coming in and addressing you by name, then things became more computerised, and at the London Book Fair you would be introduced as 'One of my accounts'. That never would have happened earlier; I was never an 'account'; I was 'a customer from Belfast' – even 'a favoured customer from Belfast'. It started changing towards the late '70s. If you had rung a publisher to put an order through, you would have said, 'I'm So-and-so' and where you were from. Now if you ring, they say, 'What's your account number?'

What made people characters? What was it about those reps that you're thinking about? They were all individuals. Now you're a company person: you have to think how the company perceives you; you go through such rigorous training that you have to think 'company', you don't think of yourself as a person. Would that maybe not be true of booksellers, too? Are they not a Waterstone's person, or whatever the company is? But in those days most bookshops were small companies; there weren't the big multi-nationals that there are today. I had reps in the 1970s who were probably in their sixties and had never worked for a different company. Nowadays, if you hold on to a rep for a couple of years, you think you're doing well.

Why was it important to have that kind of continuity? The reps knew the company before your time, and you always dealt with them. But you don't really get to know a rep in the same way now. It takes a long time to establish confidence in somebody – I know who I could ask to do something, and who I would trust to carry it out.

What kind of thing would you ask a rep to do, that you would need to trust them? To submit an order, and to do it in time. If I give someone an order for a hundred books and I want them by a certain date, I know that person – if it's somebody I trust – will get them to me, come hell or high water. But if it's somebody that I don't know, I say to myself, 'I wonder, will they come? Have they put that order through?'

Brigitte Bunnell For me, the reps have always been a very important link between the bookseller and the publisher. No computer system so far has had the ability to replace the rep. Through the rep you get to know about the publishing house, about the authors, the books that are coming, which are going into reprint, whether the publisher is putting money into a marketing campaign – information that is important to help you to sell the books. When you phoned through an order from Hatchards, you let the rep know, because you wanted to make sure that it didn't get delayed – speed was important for replenishment. And if you had a customer order for a book that was out of print, the rep would move heaven and earth to find you a copy.

16 | THE MARKED PAGE

Carole Blake The word 'editor' encompasses many different kinds of jobs. Copy-editing is doing the punctuation and getting the text into paragraphs and sentences. Structural editing is changing the story line around, and dealing with pace and character. The commissioning editor, on the other hand, is the book buyer, and they hand the books to a desk editor for editing. But most editors these days – certainly those in big companies – are expected to buy books but not necessarily to edit them.

Bruno Brown At the Oxford Press we would read the proofs very carefully, which authors are generally not good at, and check references and facts. We reckoned we could produce a really good book by attention to detail like that. On the whole, other publishers didn't attempt to deal with the detail, so the Oxford Press had a big advantage. Hawkins[1] was extremely good at editing books. He was a bachelor, and spent a lot of time at home reading his proofs and checking them up. He made us do that too.
Where did you do it? I did it at home, in my flat. It was very agreeable. And authors generally appreciated this attention.

Philippa Harrison When I stopped running Little, Brown and became non-executive chairman,[2] I began to work on my own books again. That meant that I could check the manuscripts after they had been copy-edited by the staff or by freelancers, which I hadn't had time to do for some years. And I'm afraid I thought some of the copy-editing was shocking. It wasn't just that the copy-editors missed things, it was that they interpolated themselves quite improperly, I thought, into the writer's style.
How could you tell? You saw the marked page. These people had, I suspect, been trained, and very badly. They were imposing what was 'right' on somebody else's writing, which, in my view, is not the business of the editor. The business of the editor is to help the writer produce the most authentic thing that he or she can produce, and copy-editing should merely be about capital letters, spelling, punctuation – that sort of thing. I had been saying for

---

1 General manager of OUP India when Bruno Brown joined the Press in 1937.
2 In 2000.

ten or fifteen years that I thought the quality of editing coming out of publishers was very much worse than it had been, but I then felt, from looking at some of the copy-edited manuscripts, that some books were being *damaged* by copy-editing.

What did you do? I rubbed the marks out and explained why I had done it.

What did people say? They would argue for it in terms that were, in my view, completely inappropriate – that it is more correct grammatically to have 'he' rather than 'Ted' in that phrase. There's no such thing as 'more correct grammatically'; it's to do with the cadence of a paragraph, the flow of the way the person is talking, what emphasis the writer wanted. They seemed to be tone deaf to that.

This does raise questions about what an editor's role is. Yes. And there is an absolute distinction: in my view, a copy-editor's role is to check facts, and to make punctuation and capitalisation clear to the printer. I think it's legitimate for a copy-editor to break up paragraphs or combine paragraphs, but it should be done extremely rarely. But an editor's job is entirely different: it is about getting the argument in the right order and to point out if there are missing links or if the author skips something.

Andrew Franklin Nobody ever told me how to edit, and I wouldn't begin to know how to tell somebody else – I just do whatever seems instinctually right. In fiction, the two things that seem most apparent and easiest to put right are when a character is left hanging in the air so you don't know what happens to them, or when there is an unseemly rush to close things at the end of a book.

To what extent would you intervene with fiction? I don't publish fiction now, but when I did, I would take the author out to lunch, and I would try to judge, as far as I could, the extent to which they would work on ideas, then say, 'What do you think about doing a bit more here or there?'

What if they weren't receptive to ideas? Well, there's nothing you can do, is there? It's their book. I really do feel that tremendously strongly. I think all you can do is put forward suggestions and ideas and if they reject them that is absolutely their prerogative. There were one or two sections in Barry Unsworth's *Sacred Hunger*,[3] for instance, where I suggested editing it: there was a very interesting section in the middle, and I wanted him to expand it a little bit and cast it a little differently, but he didn't want to. I was wrong and he was right: *Sacred Hunger* won the Booker Prize.

Philippa Harrison The first time I edited non-fiction was at Cape, and for me it worked like this: you had to read the book once – or maybe twice – with absolute concentration, writing down nothing at all. Then at the end, what always happened to me – and this is what I have always been

---

3 Barry Unsworth, *Sacred Hunger*, Penguin, 1992.

frightened of losing, because it appears to be some intuitive gift not involved with conscious thought – was that my mind went click: 'Ah, that's the only bit of the structure that's wrong.' Or, 'Actually they're trying to say this, but the balance goes that way.' That click was the product of real concentration, and it always happened. I would go back and do the moving and – thank God – the intuition was always right and everything got moved into the pattern the author was aiming for or had been muddled about. But I have always been frightened that the intuition would be wrong.

Emma Hargrave became managing editor of Tindal Street Press in 2001.

Emma Hargrave You work out, or find out, what kind of relationship you are going to have with an author. For me, a lot of the pleasure of the job comes from building – or rather, earning – those relationships. That's why I think responsibility is important in an editor, because if we are talking about relationships, we are also talking about trust. An author doesn't come because they want to be friends with you; they come because they want somebody to publish their books and to be a good editor for their books. This goes back to your earlier question: 'How do you choose to take on an author?' In fact, you are choosing to take on a book, and the book is the reason for having a close relationship with the author.

Why is trust important in that relationship? Because the author is entrusting you with their manuscript, and they have to have faith that your agenda is to do the best for the book, rather than, for example, to distort it into a particular kind of book that you might want to publish. Many of the authors we work with at Tindal Street Press are first-time authors, so they haven't been though an editorial process before, and they are trusting you to have the book's best interest at heart.

Neil Astley started Bloodaxe Books in the late 1970s.

Neil Astley Brendan Kennelly and I had a great working relationship when I was editing *The Book of Judas*.[4] He gave me a pile of around 1,000 poems and I had to hack them down to 400 pages, so there was a sense in which I was involved authorially in a way that I wasn't with other books. When it came to proof stage, I found that there was a blank page between the end of one section and the start of the next, so, without telling him, I wrote a poem in the voice of the book, and stuck it in. Brendan didn't spot it at first, because it's such a huge book. I said – on the telephone – 'Do you like the way in which the poem has come out on such and such a page?' He turned to it and straightaway read the poem to me – so I heard his discovery of the poem, which I had written in his voice, and I knew it had worked, because he loved every part of it. It's a poem in which the author is kidnapped from the action by Judas, who then takes over. But I wouldn't have done that to any other

4 Brendan Kennelly, *The Book of Judas*, Bloodaxe, 1991.

poet; it's simply that I'd had the kind of relationship with Brendan over the years which made it possible to do that. There are also some mischievous entries in the index – which I compiled and he didn't proof read – such as, 'The Lost Poems of Judas', where you turn to the page and find that it's blank. Or piss-takes in the index of first lines, like: 'The first time I slept with Madonna, she . . .' and when you turn to that page, it's blank as well. Little tricks like that were also part of the fun of that book.

Jessica Kingsley started Jessica Kingsley Publishing in 1988.

Jessica Kingsley I think the reason that it's so important for an author to trust their editor – and why they often have very oddly close relationships – is because you have seen inside their head. You have seen the first draft – the unfinished product and the unformed thought. That includes their mistakes, and part of your job is to help them sort them out. They also have to trust you to provide an objective view of what it is a reader wants and of what should go in the book. You are the first reader. And it's important to keep the freshness of the first reading as a manuscript develops, because it's quite unusual to get a manuscript in finished form – there's often something that needs to be done to it.

That's one of the things that makes it fun, that you are relying on your judgement. If you let that get to you, it becomes onerous and grim. But I think it is also something that people are inclined to be a bit too casual with – you do get very inexperienced people making quite crass judgements on manuscripts. It is part of the learning process in my company that you will introduce junior editors to books at an early stage, and listen to what they have to say about them, and it's quite a nice moment when they become less confident, because it means they are starting to understand how tricky it is to really listen to the author's voice and to what they are trying to say.

How can you afford to spend the time doing that? Sometimes you just *have* to do it. That's one reason we publish a lot of books that are much more straightforward – professional books for professionals – where the author's voice, on the whole, is not intended to be very evident. One's critical judgement there will be: has the book got a proper introductory chapter? Has it got too much on the literature review? Is the structure right? Did we get what we agreed in the way of a manuscript? If not, what are we going to do about it? Those books are much easier to deal with, because the authors aren't baring their souls, whereas at the other end of what we publish, they may be.

Some of our best books have been ones where you darn well better have judged them right. One of my favourites is *Freaks, Geeks and Asperger Syndrome: A User Guide to Adolescence*, which was written by Luke Jackson when he was thirteen. He wrote it to help other kids with Asperger syndrome, so it was a book written with the best of intentions, where he could have exposed himself horribly and produced something that would have made him squirm when he looked back on it five years later. Actually, I think he wrote a book that he can look back on and be really proud of. It won the Special Needs Children's Book Award last year, and really deserved to – that book has changed a lot of people's lives. We have sold 50,000 copies, because people understand what an important book it is. This was one book that was vital to get right – and it was, in fact, nearly right when it came in.

Emma Hargrave I think the job of an editor is to ask questions: 'For me, this paragraph has this effect.' 'This character feels like this for me; is that what you intend?' 'Why have you introduced Mr X at this point?' Or if you don't understand a turn of phrase, you query it. But you're not saying that you want the writer to change it; you are just saying, 'As an editor, I would like to know.' It's not about giving advice, but about saying, 'I'm not clear why you are choosing to do this.'

To what extent are those personal questions? I think they are very personal, because you're talking about somebody's novel or short story. You need to explain to the writer that you are not asking the questions because they have got something wrong. They might be questions that a reader would ask, and you don't want your reader to be asking questions in that way.

How did you learn that? Just through practice. Also, a friend of mine, Helen Cross, wrote a stunning book called *My Summer of Love*, which Bloomsbury published extremely successfully. She praised her editor,[5] and what she said was that her editor asked questions rather than told her to do things. And I liked that. Even if you are telling somebody something, you can think about it in the context of a question. You have to work to the author's agenda, not to your own. You have to think, what is this author trying to achieve? How can I, as a reader, ask the questions that will help them achieve it more clearly?

There must be editors who are prescriptive. I think you can be, if you are very confident and know exactly what you're doing. We have an author called Clare Morrall, whose first published book[6] was on the Booker shortlist. Her editor in Canada is Ellen Seligman, who works at McClelland & Stewart and is famous for building an impressive list. She has already bought the rights to Clare's second book, which hasn't yet been published here. I suggested that Clare could have her second book published in Canada first, which would mean that she could work directly with Ellen Seligman as an editor, rather than as a publisher who was buying her book in its finished form. And – I have to admit – I thought it might also be an opportunity for me to ask Clare, 'How did Ellen work with you?' Because it is hard to learn how other

5 Alexandra Pringle.
6 Clare Morrall, *Astonishing Splashes of Colour*, Tindal Street Press, 2003.

editors work – editors from a different place, or of a different generation, for example. I'm always interested in that. It would be fantastic to spend a week sitting near Ellen Seligman and see how she operates. Or to see the editor of Austin Clarke – the Canadian writer whom Tindal Street published last March[7] – work with someone of such stature and with such clear ideas about what he wants to do as a writer. You think, how can I talk to this person and understand what they are trying to achieve, and dare to suppose that I might improve their work? But I imagine that even authors at the height of their game would want somebody who is able to say, 'Actually, Mr Clarke, this chapter has gone on for too long.' I would love to see how people do that. To have the vision to recognise what someone could do to improve as a writer is, I think, very interesting.

Andrew Franklin There isn't a single publisher that I'm aware of who has any formal guidelines defining how the relationship between editor and author should be – it is entirely left to the editor to pursue it in the way they feel appropriate. So people have to wing it, or observe it as assistant editors, or learn it on the job. Which seems to me quite interesting, because the relationship between the author and publisher is such a fundamental part of publishing.

I don't know how you would train somebody up. It's really a sort of apprenticeship system: people start as assistant editors, then they become junior editors, then they become editors, then senior editors, then editorial directors and then publishers. There are no rules, and I think personality plays a large part in it. But there is, of course, a job to get done, which is to acquire the book, then to ensure that you get the best possible manuscript, then to publish it in the best possible way.

What can go wrong? Almost anything. Your author can be so alienated they choose not to publish the book with you and go elsewhere – I've had that. Or they deliver the book that you didn't want, rather than the book you did want – I've had that. They refuse to co-operate with you when you come to market and publicise it – I've had that. So instead of smoothing the process so that author and publisher work together in perfect harmony for the success of the best possible book, they work antagonistically, or not at all.

How would you approach a manuscript with an author? That's not something you can easily teach, either. Of course, I never see what other British editors do, but I do see what American editors do, because if we buy a book from an American publisher, they might write one of their editorial letters, or maybe I read the book in its first draft, and again later. One of my authors at Penguin, Redmond O'Hanlon, is the most meticulous writer I have ever known. He writes everything out longhand in the most extraordinary detail and then crafts it sentence by sentence. When he delivers the manuscript it is

7 Austin Clarke, *The Polished Hoe*, Tindal Street Press, 2004.

letter-perfect; there are no repetitions or awkwardnesses, and not a single thing to be changed. But with hasty writers you may find words like 'synoptic' or 'valetudinarian' turning up twice in two paragraphs. Odd things that are irritating. American editors are very good at picking up that.

Occasionally you go further and say, 'I really think you ought to drop those two pages of dialogue, which don't advance the story at all.' But I would be amazed if authors accepted all my suggestions. In a way, I would be a bit distressed if they did, because some suggestions would be wrong. You might say, 'I would really like to know more about this character', then twenty pages later he pops up in sufficient detail. So then you ask, 'Do you want to bring this forward, or would you just like to refer to him tangentially?' And very often the answer is 'No. I'm happy with it as it is.' That's fine. Some authors don't accept any suggestions at all and then I'm just irritated that I've put all that time in. It's a very slow way of reading a book – it takes hours.

Philippa Harrison The essence of the editorial relationship with a writer of fiction is the longevity of your knowledge of each other – the way that you can recognise, in somebody's fourth novel, something that is particularly important to them, because you remember them referring to it in their first. Whereas non-fiction, even if it involves a lifetime's thought – like that of Eric Hobsbawm – describes something that is objectively real, and much more accessible, both to its creator and to an editor.

In either case, I think that the most productive thing an editor can do is to explain why they love something, and then ask the sort of question which shows the writer that they have understood it right through. Then the writer thinks, ah, they've got it. And then they relax and feel they trust you. If you fail to ask – deeply as opposed to superficially – appropriate enough questions or to express appropriate enough thoughts, there will always be this sense of distrust from the writer, of having to watch out and guard their writing from this outsider, and you will never get the best editorial work done in that atmosphere. Obviously you can do all the changing of commas and repetitions. But really creative editorial work, which helps the author unlock something they didn't know that they had, only comes from trust. And the way that trust is earned is through serious attention to the text.

Kingsley Amis and I had become very fond of each other and had a friendly, jokey sort of relationship – until he came into Hutchinson for my editorial suggestions for *Jake's Thing*,[8] when a completely different person arrived in the room. By that stage he was rather shuffling his feet because of various physical problems, and he would normally shuffle towards me with his arms open. But that day he stood at the door, absolutely erect, with his coat balanced over his shoulders, and said, 'Mrs Harrison, will you take

8 Kingsley Amis, *Jake's Thing*, Hutchinson, 1978.

my coat?' Whoops, I thought, this is going to be tricky. 'Certainly,' I said. I went and took his coat, then he came and sat down, absolutely unsmiling, brushed, just shaved, not aggressive exactly, but with a completely defended hostile manner.

I can't remember what I first tried, but he wasn't having that. So I went on – because it was Kingsley, who was very keen on grammar and facts – to something small but, as it were, perfect. And he said, 'Mrs Harrison, I think you've put your tiny little finger on something.' Then gradually it became a Kingsley and me conversation and all was just fine. But it was so interesting, that absolute change of personality and marking of boundaries, the first time we were embarking on an editorial relationship as opposed to a friendly author/publisher relationship.

And how had he addressed you previously? 'Philippa' of course, and arms out for a hug.

So was there a sort of tongue-in-cheek sense about it? No. It was a theatre we both recognised. And I never referred to it, nor did I ever laugh about it.

Carole Blake Many companies today would prefer their editors to buy a manuscript that doesn't need editorial work. Most agents will have received rejection letters from editors that say, 'I really like this, but it needs an awful lot of work, and I can't take it on.'

What do you think is behind that change? I believe that, as publishing has become bigger business and shareholders are involved, companies want books to be published more quickly in order to get a faster return on investment. It's understandable: a big chunk of money goes out on signature of a contract, then the publisher has to wait for the manuscript. When it does arrive, they hope they can send it to the printer pretty quickly. That is partly why agents edit their clients' work – it makes it easier to sell the book.

What effect has that had on what is published? I think it's raised the bar, in that publishers expect authors to perform enormously well from the word go. Nobody is allowed a learning period any more. I touched on this earlier,[9] when I said that Dick Francis was able to write his way into his career, gaining a little bit more in sales with each book, until suddenly one book took off, and then they all did.

I think there's a lot more pressure on editors: they have to do much more preparation of figures and estimates than previously, because they have to get the sales and marketing department on board before they're allowed to buy the book. There is also a big overhead built into the cost of publishing every book – and the bigger the company, the greater the overhead. It's a more professional world than it was when I first entered the business, but it's a harsher one. That can make for shorter careers for authors: one failure and it's 'Don't come back.' Sometimes it isn't even real

9 *See* page 148.

failure, but if a publisher pays an author a lot of money for a book, the expectations are huge and the book is expected to become a bestseller straightaway, which may be unrealistic.

What effect has that had on agents? It means you have to be so much more careful when you take on a client, and you have to do whatever editorial work you believe is necessary to get the manuscript to look as good as possible before you show it to anyone. Now that so many different imprints are owned by the same group, if you get a rejection from one of them, in some cases the group will say, 'Don't send it back here to anyone else.'

Philippa Harrison It occurs to me that, in the big shift towards marketing – as opposed to editorial choice – being the essential weight in modern publishing, perhaps the respect for the writer is less primary than it used to be. If that were right, it would, I think, be a very serious indictment of modern publishing. And I do think that, in general, companies now give more time and attention to how books are marketed and packaged, than to the detail of the content.

What you think is behind that? I think the great change – cliché, cliché – was October 1995, when the Net Book Agreement went. Once discounting became a primary marketing tool and the power of marketing was unconsciously handed over to the retailers, the fight to make your book one that all the chains promoted became infinitely more essential.

The other significant thing is the change in how paperback rights are acquired. In my early career, most books bought by hardback publishers were sold on to a variety of paperback publishers. But when[10] most books started to be bought simultaneously by a hardback imprint and a paperback imprint owned by the same group, that may have changed the importance of editing because, as the paperback imprint was buying at the same time on the basis of the unedited manuscript, the publisher no longer had to get the editing perfect to sell paperback rights.

Elizabeth McWatters In my early days in bookselling, if you found a mistake in a Penguin book you got £1 if you pointed it out. I don't know when that stopped, but I remember the reps saying, 'If you ever find a mistake in a book you get £1.' They'd be bankrupt by now if they'd kept it up.

And did you? I never did. If there was a printing error in it, surely somebody else would have noticed it. They wouldn't be waiting for me to point it out.

10 In the early 1980s.

17 | THE CIRCLES MAKE THEMSELVES

Michael Turner You can't say, 'There is somebody who is likely to be one of us. Let's bring him in.' It doesn't work that way at all. The circles make themselves.

Gordon Graham returned to Britain from the US in 1963 to run the American publishing firm of McGraw-Hill in the UK and Europe.

Gordon Graham Book people think this business is different from all other businesses, and that those within it understand this and the rest of the world perhaps doesn't. A sense of mission enters into this – they belong to this special occupation which is benefiting mankind. They wouldn't articulate it that way, but that's what it is. And it leads to all sorts of manifestations like the Garrick Club and the Society of Bookmen, which you don't get in other businesses in the same sense.
What was that society like when you came back to the UK in 1963? I was not part of it, and because of whom I was working for it took quite a long time to be accepted. There was a considerable degree of xenophobia at that time; the book business was very nationalistic. Nobody ever said anything insulting; it was just that the door didn't open; you had to knock on it quite persistently. The way I did it was quite simple: I made myself useful to the industry; I served on committees, I volunteered to run functions, I had ideas.

Michael Geare I suppose it is true to say that for a good many years – and certainly all the years of the family businesses – the publishing trade was, to a surprising extent, run from the Garrick Club, of which I have been a member for thirty years. But it was a personal, clubby, genial, civilised trade, without much back-stabbing. Let me give you an example. My senior rep at Dent's told me that when he started work as a raw sales rep, he stayed at a small hotel in East Anglia where publishers' reps tended to stay, and a senior rep from Hodder said, 'Haven't seen you before, young chap. You'd better come along with me and I'll introduce you to all the buyers.' And jolly well took him round and eased his path. Presumably if a rep did that today he would get fired for assisting the competition.

Tim Rix From 1960 onwards, the trade steadily became more competitive in almost every way. I think the disappearance of family firms had a big effect. Previously, a group of publishers would lunch together at the round table in the corner of the Garrick Club dining room every Friday and exchange information about matters affecting the trade: issues of tax and royalty rates, what the government was up to, and how to deal with American publishing.

Mark Barty-King The Garrick? Oh, Lord, no. It's a strange English invention, the club. It does nothing for me at all.

Per Saugman The others belonged to the Savile or the Garrick, but I joined the RAC club because I was told the food was very good, you could stay there nearly always, and they had a swimming pool.
Why didn't you join a club where there were a lot of fellow publishers? Because I didn't want to meet them. They would have seen who I was having lunch with and talk about it all. They were beginning to get slightly worried by my activities. They had been sitting on their bums, never going out of their offices to find an author, and I was buzzing round like a spring hare. When I first visited Birmingham, they hadn't seen a medical publisher there for years.
How do you know that they were beginning to get worried? I could see it when I went to meetings at the Publishers Association. They were anxious about me. I disturbed their rest.

Michael Geare Let me be very clear about the Garrick. The difference between the Garrick Club and the Groucho – then and now – is that I imagine at the Groucho you could get thrown out if you're not discussing business, but at the Garrick, if you are found discussing business of any kind, you really do get thrown out. Nevertheless, there were a great many senior members of publishing who were close chums because of their membership, so they got together off the premises, and did make little mutual arrangements between various publishing groups in a quiet way.
Could you talk a little bit more about how that network worked? I will just give you one example. Before he became notorious, Robert Maxwell got control of a famous wholesaling firm called Simpkin Marshall. Does it ring a bell? Simpkin Marshall had been a wonderful wholesaler for heaven knows how long. If a chap came to you asking for a job in the trade and had spent some years at Simpkin Marshall, you knew that he knew his business. Maxwell got hold of it, and – at that stage perfectly sensibly, I think – said they needed a certain degree of discount from publishers to carry the expenses of their operation and leave them with a modest profit. And all the old publishing boys said, 'Oh no, don't like the look of this fellow. And he's asking too much money. No, no.' And of course, in two or three years, Simpkin

Marshall simply went bust. One of the rare occasions when Maxwell was plumb right and the old guard were quite, quite wrong. Simpkin Marshall did a great service to the trade, and would have continued to do so. But they just let it die.

Sue Thomson joined the Hamlyn Publishing Group in 1966. In 1971 she and Paul Hamlyn set up Octopus Books.

Sue Thomson I remember going to a Book Publishers Representatives Association dinner way back – it would have been late 1950s or very early '60s – and the 'foreigners' were on a table on their own. I remember Paul being there with a party from Hamlyn. It was very much, 'That's Paul Hamlyn, you know.' He was regarded as an opportunist. This would have been at the time of Books for Pleasure and his remainder business. He sold books that other people had failed to sell, and the establishment didn't like that. Paul was a great success the minute he laid hands on his first barrow, as the saying goes. But he wasn't a barrow boy. He bought up publishers' remainders and sold them successfully in all sorts of unlikely outlets as well as through the conventional book trade, and it was somewhat resented.

This goes back to the difference between publishers and booksellers, because the publishers had had it comfortable for a long time. With the war and paper rationing, a publisher could sell whatever he printed. So publishers had become, in my view, quite arrogant about their place in the world, and I think some of them resented the incursion of these 'foreigners', not because they were foreigners, but because they were doing things that conventional publishers were not thinking of. They weren't hide-bound by the concept that had built up in the war years that you could sell whatever you could print, and that people would come to you cap-in-hand for your wares.

After the war, when paper became plentiful again, publishers had no idea how to discipline their stock control, so stuff was printed and they couldn't sell it. This was a new phenomenon. Then along came people such as Paul Hamlyn, who said, 'I'll buy it off you for a knock-down price', then went out and sold it. This was really bad news for these people. Who are these upstarts? It was resented, I think. And the fact that he didn't conform; he wouldn't join the Publishers Association, he didn't want to become part of the club.

Michael Turner At any time there are newish publishers going against the grain. And a good thing too – they are breaking the mould, and the fact they are doing so gets them known in the trade. It's even better if you are slightly eccentric, because then you become a figure. Somebody like Tommy Joy, for instance: not only was he a terribly hard worker and deeply caring about what he did, he couldn't help being Tommy at his most eccentric. I think he is rather typical of some people in the business, in the way his career incorporated his personality. People who follow convention in the trade may be perfectly decent operatives but they aren't really highly rated – they tend to be seen as hangers-on. Publishing loves movers and shakers and, to an extent, so does bookselling.

Ian Norrie The book trade is a marvellous world of misfits. We accept one another, shall I say? Don't forget that it is a very sociable trade. Publishers have always liked holding parties, partly in the mistaken belief that this sells books, and partly because it's always fun to celebrate a new book or a new author. There was a time when you could go to a publisher's party every night of the week, and some people did.

Per Saugman The fiction publisher has to go to an awful lot of cocktail parties. In medical publishing it was usually a cup of coffee at eleven o'clock.

Michael Geare One also met publishing people through meetings and conventions and, of course, the great annual Booksellers Association conference, which is essentially a publishers' conference with booksellers playing a comparatively small part.

David Whitaker There is a story from Edmond Segrave[1] about a BA conference held at Gleneagles. The booksellers would always arrive first at the conference, then the publishers would join them a day later. By chance, Edmond Segrave arrived early. He was taking an early morning walk, when he happened to meet the barman, who was clearing up the bottles from the back of the bar. Segrave asked him how it was going. 'Very quiet,' said the barman. 'These booksellers don't drink much. Not like the boilermakers, who were here last week. The boilermakers could certainly drink.' 'Right,' said Segrave. 'But the publishers will be arriving tonight.' The barman looked sceptical. That night, the publishers did arrive, and the following morning Edmond Segrave met the barman hauling out the empties. 'How did it go?' he asked. 'Oh gawd,' said the barman, 'the boilermakers were nothing like this lot.'

Robert Clow When the BA conference was held at Aviemore, we followed the Scottish Mod – the Gaelic equivalent of the Eisteddfod – which has a reputation for being a hard-drinking body. But we were told afterwards that our alcohol consumption was infinitely greater than theirs. I have to say, I was slightly astonished to find that the booksellers and publishers had drunk more than the Mod.
Who would have paid? The publishers, mainly.
Even though it was a Booksellers Association conference? Yes. The booksellers

---

1 Editor of *The Bookseller* from 1933 to 1971.

would finance their own accommodation, but the publishers would entertain.

How important do you think that socialising was for doing business? I think it was very important. Around 600 people would turn up, and virtually all the major publishing houses would attend. If they didn't think it was important, they wouldn't have bothered. Apart from being three or four days' high living, it was also very stimulating. I suspect that's probably fairly rare in trades. I can't imagine that the stationers are as exciting and excitable as publishers and booksellers, can you?

And in terms of how important that was for business . . . It was important to John Smith's, because if you liked the individuals, you tended to like their firms, and the firms tended to be favourably disposed to you.

Tony Pocock There was always much dancing and partying attached to the BA conference. Singers were brought in to entertain us, wine was drunk. Nobody ever drank too much, as I remember. Oh dear, no. Yes, we drank a lot of wine, and whisky. It was unbelievable. In the '50s and '60s socialising was much more of an affair in the trade than it later became.

How important do you think that socialising was for business? It produced remarkable friendships in the trade, and I think that was very important indeed. It wasn't long after the war had ended, and the book trade hardly existed in the way that it did ten years later. It was a marvellous way of helping the business to cement itself and reassure itself that it was going in the right direction.

How did the socialising do that? As you get to know people, on the whole you like them better, therefore you are prepared to talk to each other about matters that concern your work.

Robert Clow Ross Higgins introduced me to Richard and Marguerite Blackwell, and also to Reuben and Esther Heffer, and that's how one started to mix with the Blackwells and Heffers. Richard was always going on about 'chums' in the book trade – you either were a chum or you weren't, and God help you if you weren't. So, later in life, as chairman of the Scottish branch of the Booksellers Association, I adopted a similar attitude, which is why I wouldn't ask particular publishers to a booksellers' dinner in Glasgow. I wouldn't ask Maxwell, for example, because he was beyond the pale even in those days. Again, it comes back to personalities. I'm sure that was equally important in Richard's mind. He either liked people or he didn't.

So what made somebody a chum? If they were supportive of you and you liked their company, that made them a chum.

What qualified you for being a chum? Personally? The introduction from Ross Higgins, I suspect, to that particular coterie within the book trade.

What would disqualify somebody? If they hadn't got the overall interest of the book trade at heart, and were out for themselves.

Tony Pocock We at OUP got to know Blackwell's very well, partly because we were both Oxford-based firms, but also because we had an annual mixed hockey match which was taken very seriously indeed, with some competition to get into the side. And I got to know the Blackwell's side as much through hockey as I did through having a glass of wine with them.

Who was in the Blackwell's team? Toby Blackwell played. Hugo Brunner[2] was on our side – do you remember him? Spirited girls played as well. They were much fitter than the men, which was good for their morale and ours, because it was clear they were much better than us. The match was played with great rivalry and many sneaky fouls, which was quite fun.

What happened after the match? We had drinks, there was a bit of partying, then we drove back to London in the coach. It was a serious occasion, the great match.

Stan Remington I was introduced to the book world Lodge, which met at the Central Temple in Great Queen Street, next door to the Connaught Rooms. The members were mainly marketing and sales directors, and the meetings were always at three thirty on a Friday afternoon, when they knew they wouldn't be called on as their reps would be travelling home. I wasn't too keen, I must say, when I was on the inside. It wasn't my world.

How important do you think it was in the book trade? Not very. Nearly all this bunch were dining mates or committee meeting mates, so there were links between them anyway. Marketing and sales people do socialise; it's something they have to do for their job. They lived in one another's pockets; doing favours, letting one another know about openings coming up in publishing houses that were bigger or better than theirs. This was going on all the time; they didn't need the Masons for it.

Tony Pocock Certainly in those days, we did spend a lot of time and money getting to know others in the trade. Talking about problems helped to expose some of the things that we were doing right or wrong – although I was careful not to give away money questions. The freedom of expression was a good thing, I think. It made people concerned for the trade as a whole – was it as efficient as it should be? – which in due time led to the Book Trade Working Party,[3] and did away with petty jealousies. You wanted the best for others as well as oneself. I don't think that is an exaggeration or a sentimental view of the trade at that time.

Tim Rix I remember Tony Pocock quite well. He was terribly naive and ignorant – like me – when he became sales manager of OUP, so he was

2 Of OUP, later of Chatto & Windus.
3 A committee set up by the Publishers and Booksellers Associations to examine key trade issues, which was jointly chaired by Tony Pocock and Julian (Toby) Blackwell. It produced the Book Trade Working Party Report of 1972.

terrifically dependent on the Longman sales manager, a man called Arthur Stanton, who had been in the business for years. Tony used to ring up Arthur all the time – 'These people are asking for x discount, what on earth do I say?' – and Arthur gave him a lot of help. Also, OUP and Longman shared a warehouse in Kenya at one point, and I remember going round to OUP to talk about it. In those days Longman and OUP swapped information about anything from the credit-worthiness of overseas booksellers to what the problems were with distribution or exchange rates.

But you were competitors. Yes. But in those days we did try to help each other. It sounds pious, but it's true.

Was there any subterfuge? In terms of being competitive? If so, I wasn't aware of it. We were all very secretive about our sales figures, ludicrously so. But everything else could be talked about.

Tony Pocock It was obvious that Longmans were going flat out to win the English language teaching race, and they had to be stopped.

How did you do that? By being more efficient than they were. Or trying to be. No, we were good friends with Longmans. We had to be. I'm sure that at first we were rivals – we did our best to be. Then we got better and better at what we were doing, by giving more generous discounts, and having better reps, and moving into markets like South America. And suddenly we realised that we were competing with them.

How did Longmans react? I think they thought we were a bit impertinent, wading in with our courses and our dictionaries. We had tremendous success with the *Advanced Learner's Dictionary.*

Who was your counterpart at Longmans? A girl whose name I can't remember,[4] who specialised in English Language Teaching books. We met every year at the Frankfurt and Warsaw book fairs.

How did it work when you met each other socially? We were very happy with each other: dancing at trade dos, laughing and . . . How else does one do with an, as it were, enemy, quote, quote?

Was there ever any sense of enemies? Yes, of course there was. All the time you were looking for weaknesses in the conversation – a remark dropped which would betray some secret about discounts given, or the name of a person I didn't know and ought to get to know.

How would you compete over discounts? You couldn't, really. You just had to make sure that you were giving the same terms to a great wholesaler that they were.

Could you not find that information out from the wholesaler themselves? Yes. But they weren't necessarily prepared to give you the whole truth. All rivalries are like that, but once you let spite come in you're lost. You have to remain as friendly as you possibly can.

4 Doris Bendemann.

Did spite ever come into it? Not in my case, no. But a kind of theatrical cunning, I think. The training in the theatre helps; you're putting on an act much of the time.

How useful was your training in the theatre for you as a salesman? Hugely important. I have tried to explain that most of one's selling, or relationships with people in the trade, is a question of theatre, drama, pretence. Of saying as much as one can without telling the whole truth. It's all theatre, that.

Tim Rix Tony slightly exaggerates the extent to which OUP was competing successfully with us. It was not until the mid to late '80s that it began to take over from Longman in the way that he describes. At the time, it was quite a long way behind. But he's right that OUP had certain things: the *Advanced Learner's Dictionary* was completely dominant in those days.

Willie Kay Menzies used to be quite friendly with W.H. Smith. The head buyer there, Reggie Last, was a contemporary of mine, and when Tom Hodges succeeded him, I knew him well, too. As opposition we got on fine. The two families got on well, too. The Smiths might come up to Scotland on holiday, and they would stay with the Menzies.

Would you not worry about competitors finding out business information? I think there would be that worry nowadays.

Wasn't there then? I don't think so. If there was anything happening on the newspaper side – maybe strikes coming, or industrial unrest in the printing trade – I think Menzies and Smith's kept each other informed.

Robin Hyman There were organisations such as the Galley Club – which is still going strong – for printers and publishers, and the Society of Young Publishers, which I joined in 1958, which organised lectures, discussions and outings. There was the Book Production Managers' Group, where about twenty-five of us met in different publishers' offices once a month for an informal chat – there were no minutes – and compared notes, within reason. You got to know quite a lot of people through these networks.

Diane Spivey I remember Charles Clark[5] giving new staff a pep talk when I first arrived at Hutchinson. He told us that he very much believed in training because, although people moved on quite quickly, it was a small industry, and we all had a duty to train for it. Also, because it was small, people might go somewhere else for a few years, then come back to Hutchinson in later life. And it was certainly a mobile industry. After working in one company for a couple of years, you would know people who had gone off to work elsewhere, so your network would start to spread.

5 Charles Clark was managing director of Hutchinson when Diane Spivey joined in 1977.

Charles Clark The book trade keeps meeting itself very happily. There are endless lunch clubs and dining clubs, and by and large those invited as guests are also in the trade. There's the Society of Bookmen, isn't there? There was also a group of educational publishers who met for lunch at Kettner's. There's a lot that kind of clubbiness around. David Roy,[6] for example, who was both respected and much liked in the trade, was forever going off to meet people socially in the Scottish book trade because he was very fond of it. It may be a characteristic of all media worlds, but the book world is fairly incestuous in that way. Perhaps that is a better word than 'clubby'.

Were there any discomforts to do with that closeness? I wasn't conscious of any real discomforts. I think there was an insufficiently rigorous grip on some of the features of the book trade, which is why we had the Book Trade Working Party. But that's no real way to run a trade – to depend on a number of chaps getting together and enjoying themselves drafting reports over a year or two. I don't think you can make progress in the trade like that; it needs a more regular nurturing. Part of Clive Bradley's success as chief executive at the Publishers Association was in getting people to think all the time about where the trade was going, and not wait for a ten-yearly review.

Clive Bradley The past presidents of the Publishers Association all sat together at the far end of the council table – I remember these rather elderly, severe gentlemen like Easter Island statues, looking stoney-faced at any new idea.[7] They turned out to be very pleasant people but, my God, they were reluctant to see change. The PA had done things this way for eternity; why should it do them any differently now?

The council was a dignified body – members were regarded as the senators of the industry – and the tradition was that you didn't speak at your first meeting. That changed when Hamish MacGibbon,[8] who had just been elected to council, commented on the minutes of the previous meeting, which took some nerve. The president was a bit startled by this: 'But were you here, Mr MacGibbon?' Eventually meetings became freer and easier. The industry itself was changing – there was more competition between publishers and with other media. And whereas in the old days most of the members of council all owned their companies, by the time I went to the PA, the majority may have been managing directors or chairmen, but they were mainly salaried employees.

Robin Hyman In my production days at Evans Brothers, I could have phoned an opposite number in any one of a number of firms to ask for

---

6 Sales manager at Hutchinson.
7 Clive Bradley had arrived at the PA in 1976.
8 Managing director of Heinemann Educational Books, son of James MacGibbon of MacGibbon & Kee.

advice. 'I'm considering using printer x. I have never worked with them before. What do you think?' This would all be in confidence, of course. And they would say, 'Terrific' or 'Don't touch them with a bargepole.'

Did you see that kind of co-operation change during your time in publishing? As publishing companies got larger and were run more by accountants and business people, the climate did change. Fredric Warburg[9] called his autobiography *An Occupation for Gentlemen*, and that encapsulates the spirit of what publishing was in my early days: small firms run by people who were not motivated particularly by profit but by the wish to publish 'good books'. Most of those firms have now been eaten up by larger ones, which still want to publish good books, but profit is crucial because they are public companies with large amounts of City money invested in them – or American or German money, in the case of the multinational conglomerates. That doesn't mean you couldn't still ring up a friend in another firm to ask a question, but there is probably a bit less socialising.

We live in a rougher, tougher world, where more heads fall, and there are more job losses through takeovers. In the days that I'm talking about, things seemed more settled, and you didn't expect firms like Chatto or Murray ever to change. Murray is now part of Hodder Headline, and Chatto is part of Random House. They haven't necessarily lost their identity, but they are different animals today.

The phrase 'an occupation for gentlemen' occurs a lot in the course of these recordings. What does it represent for you? Firstly, publishing was a male-dominated industry with virtually no women in senior positions. Two of the most powerful people in British publishing today[10] are Marjorie Scardino, chief executive of Pearson, and Gail Rebuck, head of Random House. That would have been undreamt of in the 1950s.

Secondly, it implies a staid and slow-moving business. Not too much stress, long lunch hours, long holidays, not a lot of work on a Friday afternoon or a Monday morning. A house in the country, to which you retreated. The owner of the firm probably being Oxbridge-educated, highly cultured and not as interested in profit as in continuing a tradition of good, literary publishing – fiction, belles-lettres, poetry, biography – and earning enough to keep the firm afloat, or, if he had a lot of private money, it could run at a loss. And indeed, the council of the Publishers Association for many years tended to be general publishers of that nature, rather than those in the more commercial end of publishing, such as legal, technical, scientific, medical, school book publishing. I won't say these were treated with contempt, but they were regarded by the 'gentlemen' as of a different order – not quite in the same world.

9 Of Secker & Warburg.
10 This recording was made in 2003.

Trevor Moore Sales conferences at Hamish Hamilton were pleasant and civilised affairs that took place in Jamie's[11] office, sitting in armchairs and talking about the forthcoming books. Jamie would say, 'There's a very interesting little book of memoirs here in our belles-lettres section. I think you have something to say about this, Roger?' And Roger Machell[12] would say, 'Well, it's a most delightful autobiography by a frightfully interesting woman who was a close friend of Virginia Woolf.'

Tim Rix I don't think there was a single woman on the PA council when I joined in the early 1970s, and the members were very much 'gentlemen'. Nobody would have appeared without a tie, and we were referred to as 'Mr this' or 'Mr that'. When I arrived for my first meeting – the PA was still in Bedford Square – I put my briefcase down on a chair for a moment, in order to take my coat off, and a voice said, 'That's Bruno's chair.'[13] There were no names by the places, so you didn't know whose chair was which. I picked up my briefcase and nervously wondered which chair to sit in next.

The council business combined great formality with a high degree of collegiality. People wanted to help each other and they wanted to help the trade. Now the council is obviously informal, but less collegial – the members are from big companies, and very conscious of the fact that they compete with each other.

Do you have any ideas about why there was that collegiality at that time? There was a famous saying in publishing back in the '50s and '60s: 'A man should serve the trade he lives by.' A man, mind you. This was still quoted in the early '70s after I joined the council, and it applied to the companies themselves, because there were still a lot of family companies, and many of the heads felt that you had a duty to do what you could for the good of the wider trade. Everyone on council took trouble over every issue, whether it was about relations with booksellers or copyright or European legislation for VAT, and they were willing to serve on the council's committees, such as the training committee or the industrial relations committee. And attendance at the BA conference – as much a publishers' conference as it is a booksellers' – was *de rigeur*. You went because it was right that you should be there, not just for your own company, but to help publishing relate to bookselling. It was certainly felt that Longman should play an important part in the PA. Longman was always a great supporter of the Net Book Agreement, and the PA was there partly in order to keep that going.

Diane Spivey In 1980 I was working at Hodder, which was in Bedford Square, right in the heart of old-fashioned publishing. Jonathan Cape was there, and the Publishers Association; Chatto & Windus, Edward Arnold and

11 Hamish Hamilton himself.
12 Editorial director.
13 Sir John (Bruno) Brown.

Thames & Hudson were nearby. So it was quite a smart place to be. This was just before the early Lady Di days and there seemed to be quite a lot of debby young girls who wore pie-crust collars, coloured tights and print dresses, and cycled in from Fulham on bicycles with big baskets on the front, which they left chained to the railings in Bedford Square. Nice girls worked at Hodder. I was a little out-classed, I think.

Rosemary Goad There was a lot of starry-eyedness about publishing, so there were always more applicants than there were jobs, and you had to explain very carefully that the money was extremely poor and they might not be able to live on it. It wasn't just Fabers – publishing in general was really badly paid. It was traditionally seen as a gentleman's profession, and certainly the assistants and the secretaries were expected to have private means.

When I arrived at Fabers in 1953 this attitude still lingered. You could not have lived on the salary, if you were really paying for everything. A lot of people lived at home; others moonlighted – some pulled pints in the evenings. You could do it if you scraped and saved, but there was nothing left over at all. Women in Publishing, the Publishers Publicity Circle and the Society of Young Publishers were always fighting for better salaries, and once we had a union, they did become much fairer at Fabers.

Eventually it was realised that most people did not have private means – in fact, the most talented in publishing probably didn't – and that you needed to pay them properly. It changed, of course, when the conglomerates came and there was more money about. To be fair to Fabers, they weren't making huge profits. Everybody thought they were, but they weren't.

Diane Spivey People kept saying that publishing was a 'gentleman's profession'. I think the expression is used nostalgically today, but in the early 1980s it was seen as a damning thing to say. Many of the junior or middle management staff were women, but they were really having trouble making the next step up. Women in Publishing almost had an underground feel to it. It was very exciting; there was a strong sense that there was a lot to be done. In those days you wouldn't necessarily have wanted your boss to know that you were going to a Women in Publishing event – it was considered quite radical.

There were a lot of these 'Women in something or other' groups starting up and the papers were full of 'Why do we have to have these women-only groups? What's wrong with women joining other groups?' But there was a huge difference. I occasionally went to meetings of the Society of Young Publishers, which seemed to be full of earnest young men with an eye to the main chance. The meetings were incredibly formal, with questions to the chair, an official speaker, questions afterwards, and a vote of thanks to the speaker. There was a very male, Rotary Club feel to the meetings. And I remember being taken to the Paternoster Club's Christmas dinner, which was the only time women were allowed. It was very much a dinner for the ladies, where the person chairing it would say, 'Gentlemen . . . Oh, ho ho, I mean, Gentleman *and* Ladies.' I remember one of the speakers completely ignoring the fact that there were any women present, and saying, 'You gentlemen will understand this.'

Women in Publishing had a less formal approach. Committee members took it in turns to chair meetings, and – whether you were good at it or not – you had to stand up to welcome guests and announce forthcoming events. My time on the committee turned my self-confidence around. Women in Publishing gave huge numbers of women the confidence to run things. And it was through being involved in Women in Publishing and the Publishers' Pantomime that I really got to know people. Thinking about it, one reason the Publishers' Pantomime was so ground-breaking was because it was a social environment within the trade that didn't involve men in suits.

Carole Blake It's surprising how many men in British publishing like to get into a frock. The first Publishers' Pantomime I appeared in was *Alice in Blunderland*, in 1994. We are not talking high art, here. The pantomime used to be at Christmas time, but when the London Book Fair began to be held in March, it seemed a good idea to move it so that those of us appearing could make fools of ourselves in front of the international trade. Overseas publishers love to watch it, but are horrified at the thought of doing something similar.

SB Do you know of anybody who went for auditions and didn't get a part?
Diane Spivey I don't. But there was a distinction between those who were invited because they were somebody the organisers wanted to have in the pantomime so a role would be made for them, and the rest of us who were there because we liked acting or singing or dancing. There were, if you like, the workers and the stars. But after the second pantomime they began to cross over because some people were outstandingly good. Toby Roxburgh, an editor at Futura, was an excellent actor. He wasn't a grand person within publishing, but after the first pantomime you wouldn't have had another one without Toby in one of the main roles.

Peter Mayer was in one of the pantomimes, I remember. He was running Penguin at that time, and he played the scarecrow in *The Wizard of Oz*, singing, 'If I only had a brain'. He had been drafted in, and I think he was having trouble explaining to his colleagues what it all entailed. He was a good sport. I think that was it: there was a feeling that everybody, even from the senior levels of publishing, were being good sports. Looking back, there was an element of the great and the good in publishing being prepared to let their hair down and be seen on stage doing silly things.

But you weren't one of the great and good. No, exactly. I wasn't. And I think I benefited from it hugely in terms of getting to know people and feeling part of a greater publishing community. I loved the pantomime. I had always loved acting anyway, and this felt like one thing I knew I could do alongside these people.

I remember a moment at the beginning of *Dick Whittington* . . . The shows were held at the Golden Lane theatre behind the Barbican. It's an old-fashioned Victorian theatre, a little one, all gilt and red velvet, but pretty shabby. And in that one, Toby Roxburgh and I opened the show – he was King Rat and I was Dick. There was a wonderful feeling of companionship: being on this darkened stage, hearing the audience on the other side of the curtain – everybody was flooding in – and lots of noise and gossip and laughter, and knowing that you had to begin the show and you were waiting behind the curtains for it all to start.

Carole Blake The Publishers' Pantomime has the longest interval in theatrical history because a cut of the bar takings goes to charity. One year, Jane Gregory,[14] who was organising it, said to the people who managed the bar at the Golden Lane, 'You must open the bar a long time before the performance. The interval will be three quarters of an hour. Then keep the bar open for a long time after the show. And stock up on alcohol.' The Golden Lane theatre people said, 'No, that's far too long. We've had advertising and television people in here. We know about this.' But Jane insisted. And of course, each night the bar was drunk dry. Why? The book trade likes to drink.

Diane Spivey In the last week of rehearsals we would pitch up – probably about fifty of us – at an Indian restaurant and take over the whole place. This would be quite late at night. There would be singing and shouting and jokes – it was really quite riotous. For somebody as young as I was, it was fun to feel involved – it was almost like being in with the grown-ups. But I did have the experience once of inviting my boyfriend to one of the performances and really wishing I hadn't, because it was completely incomprehensible to somebody outside the publishing industry – so full of in-jokes and everybody knowing everybody else. I suddenly saw it through his eyes and thought, my God. I think one or two senior American publishers were brought along and never quite understood what it was all about.

Carole Blake The American book trade is more competitive, and they do stand on their dignity. And, as a German publisher once said to me, 'Carole, it would never happen in Germany.' They enjoy the fact that it is not just publishers or agents or authors, but all of us in it together – also that we

14 Literary agent.

perform for charities, including BTBS, the Book Trade Benevolent Society, which runs a subsidised housing scheme at Kings Langley in Hertfordshire.

John Prime The Booksellers' Retreat was established around 1845 by a number of publishers, so that booksellers who were retiring with nothing and nowhere to go could be offered homes. A member of the founding committee was related to the paper maker John Dickinson, who had mills by the Grand Union canal near the village of Kings Langley. Mr Dickinson had a spare piece of land in a field which had been cut up by the building of the railway to Liverpool and Manchester. It was a strangely elongated field on a slope, and unkind people have suggested that he hadn't got much else to do with it. Another story is that Mr Dickinson's wife, who was a well-known philanthropist, had said, 'We have made a tremendous amount of money from the book trade by supplying them with paper. Now we ought to return thanks in some way.'

Carole Blake BTBS has accomplished a lot, on a shoestring and with a small number of staff.[15] It also runs a grants programme, but it is hard to mention specific instances, because when everybody knows everybody to the extent that they do in the book trade, individuals are easily recognisable. I think the British book trade can be proud of the fact that we have a charity, but I wish that its members would take more notice of BTBS, particularly the big companies – rant coming up here – because it is the big companies that spit people out, make people redundant or end someone's career by finding them unemployable after a certain age. Publishers are diminishing their rep forces year on year, and booksellers are made redundant as groups are put together. The trade gives a lot of us a rather nice standard of living, and if we think of it as a family, we need to look after the rest.

John Prime After the Second World War there were more applicants than there were places – including an unusual number of single women – so it was decided to build some bed-sitting bungalows. I chose this one because of the view. You can see about fourteen different species of tree from this window – that one in the centre is an incense cedar, with a western red cedar on each side – and it's good to sit underneath them in the summer, once you've got accustomed to the continual hum of the M25 and the noise of the railway line. All tenants have a key to the gate onto the station platform and, although we're in the foothills of the Chilterns, I can get from my door to Euston station in half an hour.

Everyone here has had a job handling books one way or another. Bert Taylor, whom you have interviewed, was a publisher's representative. Several people worked in publishers' despatch departments. Within two

15 Carole Blake was chairman of BTBS from 2004 to 2007.

days of my arriving here, someone knocked at the door and said, 'I know you're John Prime, but you don't know me, do you?' It turned out that she had worked in the old 'bomb shop' at Collet's when I was there.

Carole Blake Not long ago, all the residents of The Retreat were older people. But the average age has become much younger. We find that we don't only have to help people at the end of their career, we also need to help people at the beginning, because this 'family' in the book trade doesn't pay newcomers enough for them to be able to afford to live in London, which is where most of the work is. So we try to offer a few people short-term housing while they get themselves on their feet.

Maybe the book trade is becoming less of a family as years go by. As big business controls more and more of it, many of the biggest publishers – and some of the biggest booksellers – are not British owned. Maybe the executives don't feel as emotionally connected to people in the trade as did the families which once dominated the British book trade. The Unwins paid for one of the original bungalows at The Retreat, and the most recent addition – the Foyle Building – was largely paid for by a donation from the Foyle Foundation. But it's hard to make the executives of big companies feel that there is any reason to give money to BTBS.

Is it to do with their accountability to shareholders? Yes. And accountability to people who are not British. Why should Bertelsmann or Hachette Livre support the British book trade? Although I'm delighted to say that there has been a good response to one recent initiative, whereby large companies agree to donate a specific amount on a regular basis. And one small, privately-owned publishing company has recently offered to give BTBS £2,500 a year, which is huge in relation to its turnover – and compared with larger companies that give nothing.

Jessica Kingsley The Independent Publishers Guild – which has been supported by the Arts Council – has grown enormously, from 320 to 480 members in about three years. The IPG has been extremely important to me because of its collegiality.

Why is that important? Because otherwise you are inventing the wheel on your own. Obviously people from larger companies can be hugely helpful, but there are certain problems that only somebody from a company similar to your own will have an answer to. I spent a lot of last Saturday talking to another independent publisher about the sales role in a company of our size, and how you would appoint someone appropriate. I'm not sure anybody from a large company would understand what the problems were. That's why friendships with people who are doing similar things to yourself are not just nice because you have so much in common, but also important.

I think independent publishers are all eccentric in our own particular ways because we are doing something odd and different, and it's very hard work and not terribly well paid. Also, we tend to be generalists – when you build up a company, you have to do everything. The IPG naturally collects together a group of people who do that sort of thing, which means friendships are easier to make. I have found it harder to make friends in the traditional part of publishing, although belonging to the PA has helped, as has being on PA council, because you do gradually get to know those people, and friendships grow from that. I also belong to the Society of Bookmen, which is a dining club that attracts senior people from the book trade – publishers, booksellers, agents, librarians, some authors. It is useful for networking, but also very enjoyable. I am a member of the Society of Academic Publishers, which is another dining group. And there is the Dining Club, which is a group of senior women in publishing who meet maybe five times a year.

Andrew Franklin It is staggering how few people there are in senior managerial roles in British publishing who are not white and upper-middle class – particularly editorially, but also in sales and marketing. It's really shocking. Sonny Mehta[16] is a formidably notable exception. I bet you haven't interviewed anyone who is not white.
What does the British book trade look like to you, as a world? Grey, white, middle-aged, upper-middle class. Complacent. What else? But I really don't think the book world exists in that way. I think it's lots of overlapping little worlds: booksellers and publishers and agents and large companies and tiny companies, and people in marketing and people in publicity. They are all slightly separate and different. The publishing world is not a closed community where everybody knows each other. There are many strong relationships, and a lot of the people you have interviewed will know each other in different capacities – but each will know some and not all of the others.
It's more usual for somebody to say that the book trade is like a community, that everybody knows each other . . . Well, they do say that, but it's complete nonsense. If you asked me to name the board members of the Publishing Association, I couldn't tell you a single one. Partly because I'm not interested. But there is a lot of overlap.

This was very striking at a reception the Queen gave for the book trade about three years ago.[17] There were perhaps about 600 people there: publishers, authors, booksellers, agents and librarians. Apparently, Buckingham Palace said afterwards that it had been spectacularly successful by the standards of these things. The previous reception had been for the emergency services – ambulance workers, firemen and policemen – who surely deserve to be invited to Buckingham Palace more than a bunch of drunk publishers, but they didn't know each other, so they all just stood around, no

16 Sonny Mehta was editorial director and then publishing director of Pan Books between 1972 and 1987, when he left to head Alfred A. Knopf in New York.
17 This recording was made in 2004.

doubt looking very smart in uniform, but having rather stiff, formal conversations. So it was not a good party. Whereas this was. It wasn't a good publishing party, but it was an OK party.

Margaret Busby I probably know every black person involved in publishing in any significant role, and you don't need two hands to count them. I still go to literary events where I'm the only black person. I first met Ellah Allfrey, who is now an editor for Cape at Random House, at a book launch a few years ago – hey presto, there was another black woman – so we ended up talking. Another black editor is Elise Dillsworth at Virago. Alison Morrison, who was marketing manager at Walker Books, came into the industry through an Arts Council scheme by which African or Caribbean candidates spent time as trainees in a publishing company.

In the mid-1980s, I was involved in setting up a group called GAP – Greater Access to Publishing – in order to campaign for more diversity in the publishing industry. It was started by a few of us who were concerned by the situation, including Jessica Huntley of Bogle L'Ouverture Press – a small, autonomous black company – and Lennie Goodings at Virago. Women, mostly – it always seems to be women behind these initiatives. But it's a perennial problem, so efforts to promote diversity continue today with the Arts Council's Decibel scheme and DIPNET – Diversity in Publishing Network – set up by Alison Morrison and Elise Dillsworth.

Publishing needs to draw on a wider pool of talent. Yes, a good editor can work with any writer, but writers themselves should be allowed preferences. Also, if your job is to look for new writing but you don't have any access to whole areas of the population, then your list will be the poorer. Many young black people have an image of writers as celebrities, such as Maya Angelou. When they talk to me about becoming a writer, I'm forever trying to say, 'Think about publishing as well. You can do both. Toni Morrison has been a publisher as well as a writer; so has Alice Walker.' So many people want to be writers because they think that's a route to being rich and famous. I wish there were equivalent numbers of black people saying, 'I want to be a publisher.'

Gloria Bailey I'm guessing, but I think it's partly because if you're going to go to university, you want a job that will make you money. Many West Indians like their children to become doctors and lawyers, so that's where they head off.

Margaret Busby I have a family full of doctors and lawyers, and in Africa, as in the Caribbean – as in parts of this country, I'm sure – that's what people want their children to be. Publishing is not a well-paid industry, by and large, and if you have that level of education, maybe you will be attracted to a field where you'll earn a better livelihood. But I try to get over the power that publishing represents, because it has the ability to influence what information is out there. There is an African proverb: 'Until the lions have their say, tales of victory will be told by the hunter.' What's going to happen if you opt out and don't try to participate in the decision-making process?

Did I tell you the story about Derek Walcott? Derek Walcott is a renowned black writer, but when he won the Nobel Prize, my phone was going every minute – 'Have you read Derek Walcott? Can you write something on him by four o'clock?' It was almost as though nobody had bothered to read him before – he had just been 'black literature'. The next year, the same thing happened with Toni Morrison. These are writers who were important enough to win the Nobel Prize, but they had been ignored by most of the British literati. I remember talking to one particular journalist about Toni Morrison, shortly before she won the prize, and they said, 'Who's he?'

Somebody must have been reading them, in order for them to win. Yes. But not very widely in Britain. The literary world here is very, very circumscribed. I'm sure it's more of an old boys' network than we might imagine. At times, I feel I am invited to things because someone has suddenly thought, Oh, we'd better get a black person – or a black woman. So I am the proverbial 'twofer' – two for the price of one: black, and a woman. I don't mind playing that role sometimes, because I realise that otherwise, a particular perspective will be missing.

That was what Rosemarie Hudson[18] *said to me, when I expressed exactly that reservation about asking you to make this recording.* But if we don't, in fifty years' time, when we have all died, there will be nothing official to say that we were ever here, and it will look as though there were no black people in publishing. Which is clearly not the case. Just think of John La Rose, Jessica Huntley, Ellah Allfrey, Rosemarie Hudson, Verna Wilkins[19] . . . The list goes on.

I mentioned earlier that Boyd Tonkin[20] recently asked me to review a new book from Ayebia Books. That may well be the only broadsheet review that title will get. How do you persuade shops to stock the books if there's going to be no press coverage to create demand? How many black people work on the book pages of newspapers? Those who are there today have probably never heard of Ayebia Books or Black Amber – or Bogle L'Ouverture. That is the problem.

---

18 Founder of Black Amber Press.
19 John La Rose founded New Beacon Books; Jessica and Eric Huntley founded Bogle L'Ouverture Press; Verna Wilkins founded Tamarind (publishing company). For Rosemarie Hudson and Ellah Allfrey, see above.
20 As literary editor of *The Independent*.

18 | CHANGING HANDS

Per Saugman When I came to England in 1949 as a trainee, I told John Grant at Blackwell Scientific Publications that I would like to meet some London publishers, and he arranged this for me. One of these visits was to J. & A. Churchill, who had been publishers for 150 years. A butler showed me in to the managing director, Mr Rivers, who sat – with the usual ink pot – at one end of this enormous room with a glorious view of Gloucester Place, while his son sat behind a much smaller desk at the other end. Mr Rivers was a man who took himself very seriously. He pressed a little button on the desk: 'Would you like a cup of tea, Mr Sorgman? That is how you pronounce your name, isn't it?' I said yes. No point in trying to explain to him that it's pronounced like 'ploughman'. 'Do you take milk with your tea?' 'Yes, please.' 'I thought so.' He was very charming, and I could see him sitting there, playing with his gold pencil on a chain, clearly waiting for books to be submitted to him.

It was a great help to have seen these people at – almost in inverted commas – work. They were just thinking about going to the club, while young Saugman here, who had to build up a publishing firm, was buzzing round the country, seeking out authors and inviting them to write books on this, that and the other. That, of course, didn't build many friendships with my colleagues, because if they ever had an idea and wrote to an author about it, the chances were that they had already signed up with Blackwell's.

Michael Turner I was demobbed in October 1950 and worked for Dent until I went up to Cambridge. The first time I met Martin Dent was the day I left the company, when I was called up to see 'Mr Martin'. He said he was sorry he hadn't been able to meet me before, but would like to wish me all the best, and he thanked me for what I'd done for the company. Then he said something which has remained with me ever since: 'Wherever you go in all the world in future, you have something that is very important to you. You can say to anybody, "I have worked for Dent".' It was rather touching in a way. There was this feeling that heads of companies were something rather special. I saw this later on when I became involved with the Publishers Association. They led extremely comfortable lives and lived very high on the hog and felt they should be accorded a great deal of respect. I once paid a visit to Billy Collins. I went into the building – Collins was then behind the Royal Academy – and was eventually told, 'Mr Collins will see you now.' There was a staircase, so I started walking up. 'Stop! Stop! Only directors of the company are allowed to use the staircase.' So I went up the back staircase.

Gordon Graham When I arrived in Britain from the US in the early 1960s, British publishing and bookselling were very inward-looking and tended to be dominated by revered figures like Sir Stanley Unwin and Sir Basil Blackwell. Many of the traditional British houses, such as Collins, Heinemann and Butterworths, had been established in the 19th century, and felt that it was their destiny to command the market for books. But in the Jewish diaspora from Europe immediately before the Second World War, a lot of experienced or would-be publishers arrived in the UK – Paul Hamlyn, Robert Maxwell, George Weidenfeld, the Neuraths of Thames & Hudson, and many others. When Andor Kraszna-Krausz of Focal Press arrived in 1938, he had been a photographic publisher in Berlin for nearly twenty years. He went round all the publishers asking for a job and nobody would give him one, so he started his own publishing house, which gradually dominated photographic publishing. These new publishers did not regard themselves as heaven anointed. They started from nothing and built their own businesses, and by the 1960s they were beginning to shake the establishment.

How? Quite simply by eating into their markets. These publishers were successful, and this was part of the social change that shook the traditional British publishers out of their complacency. Because they *were* complacent. And don't forget one non-immigrant, who was also regarded as an outsider: Allen Lane. Penguin was one of the most successful British companies, and it was new – it only started in 1935.

When people talk about these people today, they talk about them with admiration. How were they regarded at the time? As outsiders. They were not liked at all. But the background to this was much bigger than publishing; it was part of the post-imperial evolution of Britain. This was a time of great inner turbulence, and it can probably be seen more clearly in publishing than in other businesses, because publishing is at the heart of the culture. Publishers talked about 'British books' as if there was something special about British books. Actually, they were just books. Paul Hamlyn was definitely regarded as someone who had no sense of tradition, and who regarded books as a commodity. The traditional publishers tended to be their own editors and were often close to their authors, but this new wave had a much more practical, commercial attitude to the business.

What about André Deutsch? Yes. André, I think, was different. He was also a lot less commercially successful. There's some kind of a lesson there.

But the change was manifested by the sale of the family firms, which began in the '60s. That was, in some form, a flag of surrender: these ancient companies were not inviolate, they would not last forever. Very often the sales had to do with estate duty – or that was the real reason. And perhaps the children didn't want to go into the business.

Tim Rix I remember hearing my mother at a dinner party tell the assembled company how sad it was that there were no Longmans left in Longman. I said, 'Where do you think I'd be if the place was full of Longmans? I certainly wouldn't be the chief executive.'

Gordon Graham One of the first family firms to go was Butterworths, which was sold in 1967 to the International Publishing Corporation, supposedly to save it from falling into the hands of Robert Maxwell, who had made a bid. There was also an American bid, and there was much murmuring – and indeed publicity, on television and in the press – that a premier English law publisher should not fall into the wrong hands. So it was bought by IPC in an absent-minded moment on the part of Cecil King.[1] Penguin was sold in 1970, as soon as Allen Lane died, to Pearson, which had already bought Longmans. The so-called conglomerates were just beginning. Maxwell and Hamlyn were part of this. Maxwell wanted to build his own corporation, and he did. It came to a sorry end. Hamlyn built his companies, then sold them – he sold his first to IPC soon after it bought Butterworths.

There was a lot of sentimental talk about the value of independence and the way that family companies had higher values than publicly owned corporations. Some family companies had very high standards of business practice and dedication to the cause of the book, but others did not. A lot of these smaller family-run houses lived pretty close to the bone. They are now all part of large corporations, which have a very different approach to the business from that of the families. It's too easy a generalisation to say that a business was better when it was family owned – it varied according to the individuals within the corporations. It was certainly cosier. Some of the family firms held out into the '90s. But now you only need one hand to count the survivors.

Michael Turner Stockbrokers began to hold regular luncheon meetings for potential investors to meet owners of publishing houses, and publishers began to hold lunches in their own boardrooms for institutional shareholders – as ABP[2] did. It then became important for publishers to produce results on a much shorter time scale, because institutional shareholders were not concerned with what we were publishing, they were concerned with the results. They regarded an expanding company as a wise investment, but if you comfortably produced the same profit, year after year, you were suspect

1 Chairman of International Publishing Corporation (IPC).
2 Associated Book Publishers (which included Methuen, Eyre & Spottiswoode, Chapman & Hall, Sweet & Maxwell, Stevens & Sons, Spon, Tavistock Publications and W. Green).

– you should be striking out and getting larger. Growth was the call – growth in the sense of size and profit. So a number of publishers took that particular route. ABP was one of them.

In the early 1980s, the performance of publishing companies came under scrutiny from journalists who often had no idea of the nature of publishing or of the enormous differences in types of publishing. Compared with paperback publishing, the time scales in scientific, medical or legal publishing are immensely long. ABP came under considerable pressure from investors and commentators who claimed that we didn't have sufficient overseas interests, and that we were concentrating on long-term projects which would not produce a return for some time. We produced the *Dictionary of Organic Compounds*, which was a twelve-year project. It was published more or less on time, helped by the fact that ABP was one of the first to use electronic publishing. But your standing in the City determined your ability to borrow money to invest in new technology, and something that was going to be delivered in twelve years' time was of little interest to the City. Yet if you were not investing in something new, you were failing in your duty to march into the new world. All publishers with public holdings found themselves in an increasingly difficult position at that time, and tended to be encouraged – perhaps a bit more than encouraged – to follow what the City wanted.

On one occasion in the late 1970s, ABP gave a boardroom lunch where a cabinet minister was present. Over coffee, the talk turned to the future. He said, 'I'm afraid you're far too conservative. You're not showing enough initiative. Somebody – whom you know perfectly well – is going to wreck you all because he will lead the whole publishing industry, and you will be nowhere. And that person is Robert Maxwell.' Despite what was said afterwards, Maxwell was the most admired man in the City at that time, and many financial journalists were tipping him as the future. It was a very dangerous period indeed. And it is interesting now to see how publishers are increasingly trying to find a way out of this short-termism. An article in the current *LOGOS*[3] points out that, apart from blockbusting paperbacks, it looks as though trade publishing – which was still very much the love of some investors until recently – will in future have to return to individual, private companies.

Gloria Bailey I remember opening *The Bookseller* each week and seeing large numbers of staff being made redundant – and I mean hundreds. I think that was the first time the industry had seen such large numbers of people losing their jobs. *The Bookseller* used to carry massive headlines on the front page – you couldn't miss that something different was happening.
Roughly when was that? I would have thought this was late 1980s, early '90s.

3 International quarterly journal for the book professions.

Things settled down after that. It was a shock because publishing hadn't seen anything like that before. It had always been described as a profession where things were done in a gentlemanly way – people stuck to agreements and business wasn't as cut-throat as people felt it became later.

Philippa Harrison My generation all say that publishing was great fun until about 1985.
What happened then? Companies were getting much bigger, everything was becoming more corporate – or more monolithic – and you no longer sold your own paperback rights, so you weren't taking your own risks. That was the first big change. The end of the NBA was the second big change. Neither, in any way, increased the fun. But the young probably think it was terrific fun until about 2000.
So maybe it was just about . . . Getting old. Exactly.

In 1986 the CVBC group – Chatto, Virago, Bodley Head and Cape – was sold to Random House.

Carmen Callil I experienced a period of absolute uproar in publishing, as Chatto changed from being a small, hardback literary publishing house and became part of a big corporation. When Gail Rebuck took over as c.e.o of Random House UK,[4] she had tough, hard, vile decisions to make and, I think, painful times in cutting, cutting, cutting, the staff and the lists of these old companies. But she did it. Virago had left and gone off on its own. Chatto was amalgamated with Christopher Sinclair-Stevenson's company, which Random House bought, so it became a bigger entity and therefore profitable. And Gail now has this great empire of small, editorial groups, serviced by a big successful machine.
Do you remember any authors feeling disgruntled about the company being owned by an American company? Yes, certainly I do. That would have been aired. There was a lot of unhappiness about what happened to British publishing in the '80s, when many of the old imprints were sold or folded. It was one era gradually changing into another. People didn't like it being Americans, but subsequently it became all sorts of people, whether Germans or Dutch. A global world. I think it had to happen. But it's not the end of the world. I did something else.
What did you do? I became a writer.

Carole Blake I fear that authors are being marginalised. Each author is an individual, and no matter how famous or how bestselling they are, and no matter how strong their agent is, they are always at a disadvantage in negotiating with a huge corporation. For example, as an agent, I can find myself negotiating a contract for an almost indefensibly tightly-worded

4 In 1991.

warranty clause and instead of talking through the issues I am trying to bring up, the contracts director will say, 'I have no power over that, it's group policy. If we don't get exactly that wording, our insurance company won't back us if we're sued for libel.' More and more clauses in publishing contracts are becoming set in stone because the companies are so big they just don't want to re-negotiate them individually. What power do authors have in that?

Max Reinhardt Trust between author and publisher was very important. You should have the author's interests as much in mind as your own – and if you are loyal to the author, the author is loyal to you. But that seems to have gone now. Publishing is changing completely.

Were there any times where the interests of the author might have been different from the publisher's? There may have been, but amiable discussions solved them. What I see in publishing today is very distressing. That is why I have always refused to sell the Nonesuch Press,[5] although I have had many approaches from people wanting to buy it. We don't publish any books under that imprint now, but I still treasure it.

What kind of advice would you give to a young person setting up a publishing company today? Don't be mean to the author. Look after their interests as much as if they were yours. And remain friendly. But in a conglomerate, the personal touch disappears. That's what is really lacking in publishing today.

Peter Mayer Three years ago, after Max had died,[6] Joan Reinhardt called me: 'Peter, do you know about the Nonesuch Press?' 'Yes, of course I do.' 'Well, it's still alive, although it doesn't publish. I was just thinking that Max would like it if you had some interest in it. I don't know if it's of any value' – she was very modest – 'but would you like to have a talk about it?' I said, 'I would love to, if only to see you again' – because I hadn't seen her in quite a few years. I had recently bought Duckworth because I like trying to preserve something of value, and because I wanted to maintain a personal connection with British publishing. Nonesuch, which had been founded by Francis Meynell, was also quintessentially British. That interested me. The fact that it was dormant also interested me. I am more interested in buying an old house than a new house, and I feel that way about publishing houses, too.

So, after not too much conversation, I acquired the Nonesuch Press. I was glad to do so for a continued association with the Reinhardt family, and for reconnection with Max. I had first met him in my twenties, when we

---

5 The Nonesuch Press was founded by the poet Francis Meynell in the 1920s. In 1953 Max Reinhardt agreed to become responsible for producing books under the imprint, with Meynell continuing as designer.

6 Max Reinhardt died in 2002.

were introduced by Roger Straus,[7] and – for whatever reason – Max liked me. I certainly liked him.

When I had gone to work at Avon Books in the US in the early '60s, Roger was one of the few people I knew in American publishing, and there were about five people in British publishing whom he thought I should meet. They were very grand figures, and I was not only very young but I was only the head of a tiny mass-market paperback publishing company which was more commercial than literary – I was an unlikely person to meet these people. But they were all very nice, and Max particularly so. He didn't just see me in his office, he invited me to his home. That was one of the peculiar charms of the Reinhardts, and of others at that time. I think that publishers' lives were integrated in a way they aren't today, when the private lives of corporate executives are separate from their office lives. Once private ownership disappears, everybody survives by how well they are doing in the eyes of the management or shareholders, which drives one into public stances rather than private behaviour.

Tell me about that visit to Max's home. He was only seeing me because Roger Straus had written a note to him, but he was warm and welcoming. He wanted to know as much about who I knew and what I liked, as about any books that I was publishing. He wanted to know about *me*. I think he would have done this with any younger person.

Max was interested in the publishing world, and very interested in publishing gossip from New York. He was a publisher who sought to make a good, sustainable business out of literary books, for the most part. That was also pretty much what Roger sought to do, but perhaps Roger had the keener nose for colleagues and connections in Europe, so he put together a list that resulted in, I think, twenty-three Nobel Prizes. I don't think that Max was quite so culturally acquisitive; he was more interested in his life and his friends. And Joan, with her Anglo-American background, was absolutely part of that. Max lived in a very glamorous world of famous actors and actresses, directors and producers, some of whom found their way into his publishing.

Clearly, I didn't have much to offer Max, but he gave me personal attention and time. And time is, I think, central to your question about that era, not of more 'gentlemanly' publishers, but of more leisurely and less driven publishers than today. I believe that, aside from changes in technology and retailing, the main engine driving this tougher publishing period is the change from private to public ownership. Many of these publishing companies had no known value; they had either been created or inherited by the principals who worked in them. These owners were not interested in 'return on investment'; their interests were either cultural or about status. They had private means, so they weren't dependent on publishing for their living. Or, in the event that they *were* dependent on it, their concern was not

---

7 Co-founder of Farrar, Straus & Giroux Inc.

'return on investment', but 'I need £50,000 to live on. Can I get that out of the business?'

Only when a company is sold does anybody know what its actual value is. And when you have paid £x for a company, you drive your employees to produce a return that makes that investment viable. External ownership is one of the great thieves of time, because it means we must perform to someone else's expectation: 'We have done a budget which calls for one hundred books to be published every year and, my God, we're behind, we have to publish more books to get the return on investment or else we have to raise the average cost of every book.' You kill yourself to perform, so that you are not found wanting by the holding company, which itself doesn't want to lose its position *vis à vis* the shareholders. But it was more important to Max to do what his friend Roger suggested, than to squeeze out one more book. And this is not just the story about Max meeting a kid from New York, but one about the industry in general.

You mentioned the word 'gentlemanly' just now. I don't think all these people were of a superior virtue. The style was more gentlemanly, people were more gracious. But I'm not sure that they didn't try to serve their self-interest. Everybody in business has to survive.

Philippa Harrison In the 1970s and early '80s, the first person any intelligent editor from America would come to see in England was Sonny Mehta at Pan. He was in a tremendous position as a broker of knowledge because he would have read and known about all the books coming up here.

Was it because it was Pan or was it because it was him? It was both. These things are always both. Without Pan, Sonny wouldn't have been the person to see – and somebody less good at Pan wouldn't have been worth seeing.

Would you make that kind of statement about a corporation today? No. The whole situation is different. I certainly think corporations can be both improved and damaged, but I think individuals are a lot less important than they were.

Are there individuals today whose names will have the same resonance as Sonny Mehta – or André Deutsch? I think there will be a few people who will exercise as much personal choice – it's likely that Jamie Byng[8] will, at Canongate – but I don't think that there will be names of the same weight in larger companies. And the weight we give to André, you could argue, isn't proportional – there will have been editors in large publishing houses who probably controlled a bigger list with more turnover. So maybe we are looking at *éclat*. With the exception of some smaller publishers, I can't think of anybody who would be commonly agreed as being a 'famous' editor in the same way today. Liz Calder, of course, still publishes her own authors. But that was an 'our generation' thing, and it's about structure. In the 1970s

8 Publisher at Canongate.

there were so many small, individual publishers – Cape, Bodley Head, William Heinemann, Secker & Warburg and so on – then gradually they all became part of groups. That changes things colossally. Hutchinson lived or died according to decisions made by individuals. If they were bad, you fired the person who made them, and if they were good, the individual became famous. That's how it worked in a small company, and it gave you great freedom. But if you are part of a corporation within which six publishing houses are competing for the same book, and there are rules about which one it goes to as opposed to the other, sales and marketing become more powerful, and you don't live or die in the same way.

Do you think publishing is considered to be as glamorous as it used to be? I've no idea. The press still talks about it quite a lot, doesn't it? I think there are now perhaps more marketing people being talked about. Caroline Michel, who was a brilliant marketer at Vintage, is famous in the press.

So were publishers written about more, before the '80s? I would have thought so, yes. And very often in connection with a writer or a book.

So they were recognised as being important in the phenomenon of whichever book was being talked about? Precisely so.

And would have been? I think so. But it's an unfashionable thing to say. The line now is, 'How could you describe anyone as "one of our authors"?' We are *their* publishers.'

Rosemary Goad If you read about Canongate – which we have all been doing recently, since Yann Martel won the Booker[9]– it sounds as if they work extraordinarily like Fabers in the old days. I think that once you increase your list, you no longer have the time and energy to give to individual authors and titles – although some of the big corporates *have* managed it. I'm terribly impressed by the way Helen Fraser has turned round Penguin, and I think Cape are happy within Random House. I believe it is possible. I think there are a lot of good people out there still, all enjoying themselves and publishing a lot of good books. I also think there's a lot of standardised pap published in the belief that everybody wants it.

Mark Barty-King I think what's recently happened to John Murray[10] is very sad. But why should it be? John Murray's authors are now benefiting from having the Hodder Headline sales force go out and sell the hell out of their books. The conglomerates have, by and large, just as good and devoted editors as the small publishers; the difference is that they have the marketing to get books across in ways the small publisher can't. It's sad when people don't understand that the same care and passion are devoted to books in a conglomerate as anywhere else.

9 Yann Martel, *The Life of Pi*, Canongate, 2002.
10 John Murray Ltd was bought by Hodder Headline in 2002.

Why are conglomerates often cast as bogeymen? Because it's easy. It's so romantic to think of the little peel-away publisher: somebody leaves a company and starts up on their own, and – wow! – they get something exciting and they're off. But it is a very costly business to keep a company going and do the kind of marketing and distribution a book needs in order to be published properly.

Louie Frost[11] As a bookseller, I like to deal directly with a publisher. But now, instead of just being able to phone a publisher and say, 'What's happened to this book?' you have to find out who distributes for them, and get on to whoever that is. It's probably childish to mind; it's just that I was used to things being small. And I was used to certain publishers, but now they're all changing hands like mad. Collins, Longmans, Oliver & Boyd, Schofield & Sims, E. J. Arnold, Stanley Thorne . . . These were all school publishers. Most of them have been taken over or their distribution has been taken over. Collins isn't Collins any longer – it's HarperCollins; Blackie doesn't exist any longer. It's sad as far as I'm concerned. But that's business.

Mark Barty-King I think the book trade is a cottage industry, and I think it always will be. We may like to imagine it's a big business, but it isn't. Sales haven't really increased that much over the last ten years. There is only a certain amount of reading that people can do, and I think we have probably reached the limit of what's possible with books in the UK. But it is a very congenial business, and there aren't many places in it where people can walk off with £50 million and hide it – people know each other too well, and spend too much time together, so there are very few secrets.

Peter Mayer If you call up someone in another publishing house with a question, they invariably do everything to help you, even though they may be your competitor. Why? Because the genius of publishing lies in judgements based on instinct, so the real competition between us is one in which mystery prevails.

Profile here in Britain has just published a book on punctuation, called *Eats, Shoots and Leaves*.[12] A very interesting and energetic young publisher, Andrew Franklin, who once worked for me at Penguin, is the man who bought that book. It has now sold, I understand, something like a million copies in two months. Apparently he heard Lynne Truss on the radio and said to himself, 'I should contact her and get her to write a book.' If I had listened to the same radio programme, I wouldn't have had the sense to do that. But perhaps there is another book, which I am publishing, that Andrew would not have picked. That's where the real competition takes place. So you might as well help your colleagues, because when it comes to the

11 Louie Frost worked for Thin's, Edinburgh from 1948 to 2002.
12 Lynne Truss, *Eats, Shoots and Leaves*, Profile Books, 2003.

creative side, you are out there on your own in the universe, choosing between shooting stars.

Andrew Franklin *Eats, Shoots and Leaves* has been a triumphant success and we have had hundreds and hundreds of letters from the public about it. I don't know what a large publisher would do – I guess they would expect the author or agent to answer them – but we took the decision to answer every single letter, just as a service to the author. One was from a person who wrote some pompous letter, and we replied, saying, 'Thanks very much, we're very grateful to you for taking the trouble to write, but Lynne gets so many letters that unfortunately it's not possible for her to answer them one by one.' And this person wrote back: 'How dare you answer that? It was addressed to Lynne Truss, it wasn't addressed to you. I insist that you send it on to her, and that you write a grovelling apology, and you should know that I'm a published author.' So I just wrote back: 'Dear . . .' whatever he was called, 'you may be a published author but you are also a fool. Yours sincerely.' And sent it off. Then I told Lynne, and she was thrilled. It's a mildly chivalrous thing to do, isn't it? Sort of protecting her from trouble. You can get away with that in a small company because you're not answerable to anybody. But you can't do it in a big company because all hell would break out.

Mark Barty-King When I first went to Transworld[13] we decided we would be very cheeky and ring up Hodder. I said, 'Look, we're coming into this business – we're going to be your competitors – and we don't know a damn thing about it. Could we have a look at your warehouse and distribution operation in Dunton Green?' And they said, 'Oh, do. Come and look around, tell us what you want to see. We'll give you lunch.' They knew we would be directly in competition with them, but that was the sort of business it was in those days. You had your friends, who were ready to share information with you.

I remember another situation way back at Heinemann,[14] with one of the first books I ever bought. I asked the agent what this particular author had been paid for his previous book, which had been published by another publisher. He told me, but he added on something like £250, which was quite a lot of money in those days. It was palpably untrue, and I never really trusted that agent again.

How did you know that it wasn't an accurate figure? It was simple – you knew James Hale at Macmillan, so you rang up and asked him. Nobody would expect you to do anything else. I think there is still a lot of shared information, and I think that is good for the trade as an entity. But as the conglomerates

13 In 1984, to establish its new hardback imprint, Bantam Press.
14 Mark Barty-King worked at Heinemann from 1966 to 1974.

have grown, barriers are obviously put up. You are reporting to somebody who is reporting to somebody else in New York or Europe, so you get a general insecurity about what is right and what is not right to do. Whereas if you are running your own small operation, you can say what you like.

Carole Blake It seems normal to us in publishing that so much business is done by word of mouth and on trust, but others are amazed that huge deals are done on a phone call, and that you regard it as a done deal before signing the contract. There is very little breaking of faith in publishing, even these days. We all know that if we give our word on something and that turns out not to stick, then we will not only lose the trust of that particular person, but of others who will hear about it. Publishing is the most gossipy business imaginable and, even internationally, we pretty much all know each other.

Philippa Harrison One of the attractions for editors of my generation was that our relationships with American editors were as personal and as vital as the relationships we had with paperback editors in Britain. You got to know some people well, and others not so well, but other minds you really clicked with. Alice Mayhew – the great political editor in America from the '70s until now – became a close friend. She was at Simon & Schuster and had previously been at Random House. We would often ring each other up, because when we saw a book, we just knew: 'Alice would love that' or 'Philippa would love that'. Friendships like that were about creating shared experiences – and publishing a book that you really cared about with somebody on the other side of the Atlantic whom you really liked was great fun.

Carole Blake Very little of import happens that doesn't fly round the world fast, and that was true even before email. In the early days of my rights-selling career, stories would abound of the social life at Frankfurt, as well as the deals.
It's very difficult to get anybody to tell me about what really went on behind the scenes at Frankfurt. I wonder why? There were an enormous number of affairs in publishing in my early days. People talked about them a lot, but were careful never to let them reach the ears of non-publishing spouses. When I first became an agent, I used to say to my assistants, 'It's very important that you know who used to be married to whom and who's slept with whom, because you have to be careful when telling people stories about others.'

But it's human nature to be fascinated by who is fascinated by whom, isn't it? And if you tell me something interesting that I didn't know, I will offer you a titbit in exchange. In the same way, if a British editor tips off an American editor about a book they are chasing, that favour will be returned later. That happens in a formal way through literary scouts, who tell overseas publishers what's coming. It also happens in a friendly way between editors with similar taste who work in different markets. When companies joined international conglomerates, the owners tried to say, 'Synergy – that's what it's all about. If the UK company publishes a book, its sister company in the States will want it, too.' In fact, that doesn't work, because you can't force an editor to like a book. But if you have an editor in the UK and an editor in the US who like each other, trust each other, and have similar taste, they will buy books together.

Yesterday I was talking to Drenka Willen at Harcourt Brace in the States – a highly respected editor who has published many prize-winning literary authors and publishes my author Joseph O'Connor. She had been talking to Geoff Mulligan of Secker, who is Joseph's UK publisher. Drenka said, 'Geoff says he's seen an outline for Joseph's new book. I wonder if I could see it, too?' Secker and Harcourt are not owned by the same group, but Drenka and Geoff have such parallel literary taste, that if either of them hears about a book that sounds as though it will appeal to someone who publishes André Brink, Louis de Bernières and Joseph O'Connor – as they both do – they will probably tip the other off. There are many networks of relationships in publishing, formal and informal, and those that work least well are the ones that companies try to impose.

19 | ARE YOU WORKING OR ARE YOU JUST CHATTING?

Gloria Bailey Have you ever been to a book fair? I love the atmosphere – it feels like Christmas. In this industry you make friends around the world, so even if you're in a different country, people know each other. You walk down the aisles and people say, 'It's nice to see you. How have you been since the last fair? Have you had an invitation to our party? You should come along.' And it's not necessarily because of business. People in this trade are very friendly: once you've seen a face twice, if that person recognises you, they'll smile.

Lynette Owen As soon as you go into the exhibition hall at a book fair, you get a strong impression of crowds and of having difficulty moving down the aisles, and of people stopping and talking. My own company has over a hundred staff at the Frankfurt Book Fair – it's a people-intensive industry.

At the London Book Fair recently we had hired a young man and woman to provide drinks to customers when they came to the stand, and on the second morning they arrived early, while I was putting my papers together. The young man said, 'Tell me, what are you people doing here at the fair?' I said, 'What do you mean?' He said, 'Are you working or are you just chatting?' I thought that was a very interesting perception. All the customers I was seeing, I know very well and, because it's a fairly tactile industry, when people arrive they will hug you. And this is what he was seeing. I said, 'No, actually I've done a lot of business here.' He said, 'Oh. I was just puzzled about how it worked.' Maybe he'd seen books and he thought we should have been reading them. Very often I would not be showing books; what I would be doing is talking about ones that don't yet exist – I would have information, and be talking about books that are coming next year. He could see it was a publishing fair, but he couldn't work out how it was functioning. From the little kitchen at the back of the stand it just looked like a lot of friends chatting.

Peter Mayer At the London Book Fair this week,[1] for the first time in many years, I was there as a British publisher again – albeit the smallest one in the

1 This was recorded in March 2004.

room. I stood in the Duckworth stand with the Duckworth staff, in front of my wares, greeting people walking down the aisles. 'Harry, I haven't seen you in a long time. What are you doing now? How's your wife? Come take a look at this book.' I've been doing it for a thousand years at Overlook; I've done it before at Penguin. 'This is a book we're publishing in July; this is a book we're doing in May . . .' I was really enjoying myself.

David Young I remember walking round the Frankfurt Book Fair with Melvin Powers of the Wilshire Book Company, Sunset Boulevard, Los Angeles – he's still in publishing, now in his eighties. A most elegant man. It was 1972, and the first time I went – I was then working at Thorsons. Melvin could sell a book to anybody – he had more front than Brighton – and he was walking me round, showing me how you did a deal. When he was buying he would pick the book up and weigh it in his hands and flick through it, then he would talk to the person – a little bit of blarney. The most suave man. I admired him hugely. You'd just look at this guy operating in his element, enjoying publishing. That's what I revel in: the enjoyment of publishing. It's a fantastic business to be in. There are very few bad people in the book trade – and we know who they are.

Carole Blake When I go to the Frankfurt Book Fair with my colleague Isobel Dixon, we have a sheaf of invitations for each evening, and before we leave the fair each day we plan which ones to go to: 'I'll go to this one and that one and this one.' 'Right. I'll go to the first one with you, but then I'll go to a different one and meet you back at the third one. We can separate after that – go to different dinners – then I'll see you in such-and-such a bar afterwards.' We have the evenings booked like a military campaign. And if we plait our evenings together so we see each other occasionally, we can swap stories about who we have been dancing with and what books we've been talking about while we've been dancing. Frankfurt is so book-intensive that you do sometimes track a deal back and find that the first conversation was on a dance floor.

David Young A lot of people moan about going to Frankfurt: 'Oh no, it's my fortieth Frankfurt.' I do that myself, but I actually love seeing so many friends from around the world in that concentrated way.
I hear wild stories about Frankfurt, but they're always off-tape. The apocryphal tale is that the Frankfurt prostitutes all go home (a) because there's no business as everybody in publishing sleeps together, and (b) to get fit and ready for the forthcoming Motor Show, where their services are required. A number of people do have longstanding liaisons at Frankfurt – it's a very friendly business. But I don't think that's anything like as widespread as people make out. Maybe it was rocking 'n rolling more in the '70s and '80s.

Carole Blake You really need your wits about you at a Frankfurt party because you have to be sure you can instantly match name with face, with company, and with language. If you are dropping into a casual conversation, people will always say, 'What have you sold today?' or 'What's hot?' or 'What have you bought today?' and you want to be able to think immediately of something to give them a hint on. So you have to remember not just who they are and where they work but what language they buy in – and which of your authors are free for that market. It is an extraordinary mental test. Plus you're drinking at the same time, plus it's very noisy, plus most people aren't wearing their labels. But it really does keep your energy levels high, and it's vital that you are working on pure adrenalin at Frankfurt otherwise you'd realise just how exhausted you are. You're running on practically no sleep, far too much booze, too much excitement, brain spinning like a top, so when you do eventually wind down at the end of the fair, it's 'Oh, my goodness, I'm so tired' and 'Oh, my goodness I feel ill'. Having an appointment every thirty minutes, then party after party, dinner after dinner, drinks dates, sometimes only two hours sleep, day after day . . . that is tiring. And, as I said, some of these parties involve dancing. For years, Goldmann – the paperback imprint of Bertelsmann – used to have a party in Die Fabrik, an old factory in Saxenhausen, on the other side of the river, in the middle of nowhere. It was always pitch dark inside, spotlights on the dance floor, music pounding . . . For some reason it always seemed to be great fun.

Anthony Blond If you get publishers together drinking in Frankfurt, they'll always be talking about the books they've turned down, but with huge guffaws of laughter. Nobody gets very bitter about it at all. You got it wrong – so what? There are lots of other books.

Gloria Bailey Friendships tend to last, I think, in publishing. When I first came into the industry, I used to say to a friend who worked elsewhere, 'They look after each other.' If someone lost their job, half of the time they'd be back in work simply because someone knew that they were looking and would recommend them for a job before it had even been advertised.

Willie Kay You asked me what made me so fond of books. I would only repeat a famous saying: 'A book is a man's best friend.' I may be able to tell you where it's from – I'll look it up before you go.
What does it mean to you to have spent your life working with books? That I have been working with friends.

Tim Rix For years I didn't have anything to do with books really, apart from reading them – as a chief executive you don't have anything to do with them day to day. But I would still get a kick out of the finished books – all the ones we published came across my desk. It's an incredibly satisfying field to be in. Many of us don't analyse the importance of publishing. It's becoming different now, partly because of technology. But at one time, the practice of medicine relied on medical publishing; without medical books, doctors would have been nowhere. The same applied to the law and to education – they couldn't operate without books. And you could go on. So if you had a sense of what publishing was about, you couldn't help but feel that you were in an activity or industry or trade – whatever you like to call it – that was of social importance. There are other activities, of course, of social importance, but that's what being in publishing meant to me. I feel very fortunate that I didn't end up doing something else.

Louie Frost It's not just that I've always loved books, but I've met so many fine people – teachers, children and students – that I would never have met in my life if I hadn't worked in that bookshop. I feel that's reason enough to have been there.

Tommy Joy I just loved being in a really first-class bookshop. If I had my life again, that's what I would do – go into a really first-class bookshop. You've not only got all the most interesting people coming in all the time, but you've also got books coming in all the time. Those two things make life very interesting. I only wish that my memory was better than it is. Because these things are not forgotten. You can wake up in the night and find you have been dreaming about something that you didn't even know was in your thoughts.

Trevor Moore Publishing was my whole life for most of my life. Since I stopped work last September I've adjusted very well. If I go into a bookshop I can now look at the books objectively, rather than think about the last time I went into that shop as a rep. I've done that successfully at Jarrolds in Norwich, at Ottakar's in Lowestoft, Norwich and Bury St Edmunds, at the Orwell Bookshop, Southwold and at the Aldeburgh Bookshop. I can even look at Random House books almost as a customer. But I cannot get those bloody sales conferences out of my mind when I'm dreaming: the number of times I wake up and I'm in Brighton or Birmingham having conversations with members of the one-time sales force. I even dream about reps that are no longer with us – people like Ken Griffiths and Bob Kemp, from the old days.

Karl Lawrence As we talked, I wondered whether I ought to have differentiated more clearly between perception and fact. But I think the nature of what we've been doing is to record perceptions. And they were all very real perceptions, recollected 'in tranquillity'.

Emma Hargrave I haven't planned what I've said, and I'm concerned that some of the things will be indicative of the mood I happened to be in when we spoke. I find that slightly frustrating, because there isn't a chance to go back over it and say, 'Well, actually . . .' It's an emotional perspective as much as anything else.

Andrew Franklin Witness statements – which is in effect what these are – are problematic sources of evidence, I think. And conversations are even more problematic, because naturally I'm guided both by the questions you ask and by the relationship I have developed with you as my interlocutor. So if I was conducting research, I would never use these on their own; I would go and look at other things as well. I would look at the trade press and at contemporary newspapers, which comment on the state of independent publishing interestingly, if erratically, from time to time. And there are some thoughtful books about publishing. I would certainly go and interrogate the financial statements. Profile is a £5-million company and Random House is, I think, a £160-million company. That difference in scale has vast consequences which are not easily conveyed on a tape. I'm sure that you've covered British publishing from all sorts of angles, but I still think you have to contextualise it with concrete information.

Diane Spivey I think people do see their time within publishing in very different ways. I don't think I've said anything major about the nature of publishing, but I hope I've given a flavour of what it felt like to work in those individual companies at that particular time.

Elizabeth Burchfield There aren't many university presses, and there is none as big as OUP, and they are different in many ways from any other kind of publishing. So I think that I have told you about a rather particular world, although it was a world of its time – a particular world, in its own time.

Carmen Callil Virago is now owned by Little, Brown, and publishes as it ever did, but such books are not seen as shocking or different today. The agenda is the same, but it's not noticed so much; the books are reviewed just like any others. Virago has become a mainstream publishing house with a special slant. Virago has had different periods of history – which is what happens to all publishing houses – and you have just interviewed me about mine.

Maureen Condon I don't think I expected, ever, that anybody would want to record my history. But I think the recordings are important, because you're talking to people who worked for years in the trade and whose impulses and expectations would otherwise never come into the public domain. I hope listeners will recognise that we lived by a code of behaviour that was part of our moment in time – and that you shouldn't put today's values on what happened in the past.

What I most fear is that I may have been inaccurate. I'm used to writing my ideas down, and with the written word you can always say, 'I'll re-write that bit.' And memory plays tricks with everyone. But I'm glad I made the recording, because it somehow puts things into perspective. I do feel incredibly privileged to have been part of the book trade at that time.

Michael Geare There used to be road signs which, as you approached them from one direction, said one thing, and as you turned and looked round after you'd passed, said something quite different. And this is true: people say, 'The summers were always wonderful when I was young and *Punch* isn't what it used to be.' Well, it isn't. But for somebody like me, who has led an extremely happy life, looking back simply enhances cheerfulness. Actually, by the time people start to listen to this, their mindsets will be so totally different from mine that it will seem incomprehensible. Yet if they listen carefully, they may get the idea that there were views and opinions held which, although they now appear totally absurd, at the time were held sincerely and in good faith. When you read 17th-century letters, the quality of the sentiment still comes through, even if it's very oddly expressed. I shall never know about it, anyway. [*indicates tape recorder*] Off!

BIOGRAPHICAL NOTES

The purpose of these notes is to give context to the extracts in this book. They provide only partial accounts of each career, and their style and format vary (information about education, for instance, is just given when relevant to material in the text). Fuller details can be found in the interview summaries on the online catalogue of the British Library Sound Archive (www.cadensa.bl.uk). Although every attempt has been made to give accurate information here and in the summaries, we recommend that it is cross-checked with other sources.

Neil Astley started Bloodaxe Books in the late 1970s. Bloodaxe is now considered to be Britain's leading publisher of new poetry.

Gloria Bailey joined the Publishers Association in 1983 as an exhibitions assistant, and became manager of its international division in 1990. In 2000 she set up Turnkey Exhibition Services, which she runs alongside her work administering international trade fairs.

Mark Barty-King worked for Abelard-Schuman in New York from 1962 to 1964, and at John Howell Books, San Francisco from 1964 to 1965. He joined William Heinemann, London in 1966, became editorial director of Granada Publishing in 1974 and set up Bantam Press at Transworld in 1984. Mark Barty-King was managing director of Transworld from 1995 until his retirement in 2003.

Elsie Bertram and her elder son Christopher (Kip) Bertram started out in the book trade by supplying Hamlyn's children's books and Pan paperbacks to retail outlets throughout Norfolk in the late 1960s. They soon established a wholesale business, Bertram Books, that was crucial to the book trade. The company was sold in 1999 for around £50million.

Carole Blake started in publishing in the 1960s at George Rainbird, where she became rights manager. She was the first rights and contracts manager at Michael Joseph, from 1970 to 1974, and also at W.H. Allen, from 1974 to 1975, when she left to become marketing manager at Sphere Books. In 1977 she founded the Carole Blake Literary Agency, which merged with the Julian Friedmann Agency to form Blake Friedmann in 1983.

Anthony Blond started his first publishing company in 1958 after running a literary agency. In 1962 he set up Blond Educational. From 1971 to 1979 he ran Blond & Briggs in partnership with Desmond Briggs. In 1982 he bought the firm of Frederick Muller with Anthony White, and published under the imprint of Muller, Blond & White until 1987.

Clive Bradley read law at Clare College, Cambridge and at Yale. He is a barrister and journalist, and was Labour's broadcasting officer for the 1964 election, IPC Group Labour Adviser, Deputy General Manager of the Daily and Sunday Mirror, and director of The Observer. He was chief executive of the Publishers Association from 1976 to 1997.

Sir John (known as Bruno) Brown joined OUP in 1937 as deputy manager of the Indian branch. In 1941 he was commissioned into the Royal Artillery. After his regiment was captured at the fall of Singapore in 1942, he spent three and a half years as a prisoner of the Japanese. When the war ended he returned to London, where he became OUP's sales manager. In 1956 he succeeded Geoffrey Cumberlege as OUP's London Publisher.

Brigitte Bunnell served a three-year apprenticeship in her family's bookselling business, Buchhandlung Determann, in Heilbronn, Germany. She worked briefly for Hachette's London bookshop before joining Hatchards in 1977. She became manager of the art department the following year, and general manager of Hatchards in 1989.

Elizabeth Burchfield came to England from New Zealand in the early 1950s and joined Penguin Books as a secretary in the production department. She moved to OUP in 1954 as secretary to the Publisher (initially Geoffrey Cumberlege, and from 1956, John Brown). She became promotions manager of OUP in 1968 and remained with the Press until her retirement.

Margaret Busby became Britain's first black woman book publisher when she co-founded Allison & Busby with Clive Allison in the late 1960s. She was editorial director of the company until it was sold in 1987, and subsequently became editorial director of Earthscan. She is now a writer, broadcaster, editor and consultant.

Sue Butterworth was a secretary, first at Phoebus Partworks and then at Macdonald Educational, before becoming an editorial assistant at Book Club Associates in the late 1970s. With Jane Cholmeley, she opened Silver Moon Women's Bookshop, London in 1984. She was a long-serving committee member of Women in Publishing.

Carmen Callil founded Virago in 1972. Ten years later she became managing director of Chatto & Windus and the Hogarth Press. She moved with the company in 1987 when the CVBC group (Chatto, Virago, Bodley Head and Cape) was sold to Random House. She is the author of *Bad Faith: A Forgotten History of Family and Fatherland*, Jonathan Cape, 2006.

Ian Chapman joined William Collins Sons & Co. in 1947 as a management trainee. After his appointment as sales manager in 1955 he worked closely with Billy Collins (chairman) and became an integral member of the board. Ian Chapman was chairman and chief executive of William Collins plc from 1981 until 1989 when the company was acquired by News International.

Charles Clark read law at Jesus College Oxford, and joined law publishers Sweet & Maxwell as an editor in 1957. He was an editor and director at Penguin Books from 1960 to 1966, and managing director of Penguin Education from 1966 to 1972, when he became managing director of the Hutchinson Publishing Group. He was copyright adviser to the Publishers Association between 1984 and 1999. Charles Clark was the author of *Publishing Agreements* (first published in 1980), which now appears as *Clark's Publishing Agreements*, edited by Lynette Owen.

Robert Clow joined the Glasgow bookselling business of John Smith & Son in the mid-1950s. He trained at Bumpus in London, the Librairie Payot in Geneva, and at André Deutsch, before returning to Glasgow in 1961. He succeeded John Knox as managing director of John Smith's in 1968 and retired as chairman of the board in 2000. The following year, after 250 years as an independent bookselling firm, John Smith's was sold to library suppliers, Coutts Information Services.

Peter Cochrane read law at Wadham College, Oxford and served in the Second

World War with the 2nd Queen's Own Cameron Highlanders (his account of this, *Charlie Company*, was published by Chatto & Windus in 1977). After the war he became a reader at Chatto & Windus. He was made a partner in the firm, but left to work for the printing firm of Butler & Tanner in order to support his family. Peter Cochrane continued to work as an editor throughout his career and in his retirement.

Maureen Condon and John Prime (*See* below) ran bookshops in King's Lynn in partnership from 1968 to 1982. Their Broad Street premises, which opened in the new Vancouver shopping centre in 1973, were designed to promote accessibility, and included a separate children's bookshop planned with the child's eye-view in mind.

Laurence Cotterell served with the Middlesex Yeomanry in the Middle East, North Africa and Italy during the Second World War. Afterwards he joined Harrap, where he became publicity manager. He moved to Longman in 1953, and subsequently worked as public relations and publicity adviser to companies that included the Bodley Head, Book Club Associates and W.H. Smith. In the mid-1970s Laurence Cotterell was chairman of the Poetry Society.

Gerry Davies worked as a librarian in East Ham, Bury St Edmunds and Cambridge (where he was deputy city librarian) before becoming general secretary to the Booksellers Association (BA) in 1955. He left in 1965 to work for Bowker, and subsequently moved to Whitaker's (both companies being publishers and suppliers of information to the libraries and the book business). In 1970 Gerry Davies returned to the BA, where he was director until his retirement in 1981.

Stephen Dearnley joined William Collins Sons & Co. in 1946 as a publishing trainee. He transferred to their Australian company in October 1947, and started work as their New South Wales country representative in January 1948. He retired from Collins in 1978.

André Deutsch came to England from Hungary shortly before the Second World War. He launched his first firm, Allan Wingate, with his friend Diana Athill in 1945, and his second firm, André Deutsch, in 1952.

Ronald Eames joined Allen & Unwin in 1932 as an office boy, then worked on publicity and promotions until succeeding John Freeman as typographer in 1935. He served as a conscientious objector during the war and returned afterwards to Allen & Unwin, where he became production manager. He remained with the firm until his retirement in the mid-1970s.

Julian Fall joined his family's long-established business of Goulden & Curry, Tunbridge Wells as an apprentice in 1948, and succeeded Thomas Raywood as manager of the book department in 1955. When Anthony Goulden retired the following year, Julian Fall became a co-director with Anthony's son, John Goulden. They closed the business in 1986.

Klaus Flugge became an apprentice bookseller at Volksbuchhandlung Theodore Körner in Grabow, East Germany in 1949. In 1953 he left East Germany and found work at Lingenbrink (book wholesaler and distributor) in Hamburg before emigrating to New York. There he worked in a bookshop owned by Doubleday before joining the publishing firm of Abelard-Schuman. In 1961 he was sent to develop Abelard-Schuman's business in London, which he ran until selling it to Blackie & Son in 1975. Klaus Flugge set up Andersen Press in 1976.

Christina Foyle was seventeen when, in 1928, she joined the London bookselling business established in 1903 by her father, William, and uncle, Gilbert. In 1930 she started the Foyle's Literary Luncheons, which continue to this day. Christina and her husband, Ronald Batty, took over the running of Foyle's when William Foyle retired in 1945. She ran and chaired the firm until her death in 1999.

Christopher Foyle joined Foyle's in 1962 as a trainee bookseller at the behest of his aunt, Christina Foyle. He gained experience of the book trade in Tubingen, Berlin, Helsinki and Paris before returning to work at Foyle's until 1972, when he left to become a partner in Emerson & Dudley (financial advisers). In 1978 he founded Air Foyle, an executive air charter and cargo company. Christopher Foyle succeeded his aunt as chairman of Foyle's after her death in 1999.

Andrew Franklin joined Faber & Faber as an editorial assistant in 1982 and later worked briefly at Methuen (Associated Book Publishers) before joining Penguin Books in 1984 as commissioning editor on the Pelican list. From 1989 to 1995 he was director of Penguin's Hamish Hamilton imprint. Andrew Franklin and Stephen Brough set up Profile Books in 1996.

Louie Frost joined booksellers James Thin of Edinburgh in 1948, and later ran the branch of Thin's at Fettes College for sixteen years before becoming head of Thin's school department. She remained with the firm until retiring when it was sold in 2002.

David Gadsby joined A. & C. Black in 1955 as an editor in the educational department, where he started a children's list aimed at primary schools. He became joint managing director of A. & C. Black in 1973, and served on the Bullock Committee of Enquiry into Reading and the Use of English.

Michael Geare worked for C.H. Johnson, manufacturer of Foudrinier wires for the paper industry, before becoming sales director of Four Square around 1958. He was sales director of J.M. Dent from 1962 to 1971, and editorial director of Dent from 1970 to 1971. He was deputy editor of *The Bookseller* from 1971 to 1989.

Rosemary Goad worked for various publishers, including Evans Brothers, before joining Faber & Faber as a secretary in 1953. She assisted the editor Charles Monteith from his arrival in September that year until his retirement in the early 1980s. She became an editorial director of Fabers and was responsible for personnel until her retirement in 1989. She continues to edit the work of P.D. James.

Betty Graham (née Cottrell) worked as a translator at bankers J.P. Morgan until joining McGraw-Hill, New York in 1956 as personal secretary to Gordon Graham (*See* below). She moved to McGraw-Hill in the UK in 1963. In 1974 she joined Butterworths, where she developed the company's rights business. Since retiring from Butterworths in 1990, she has been associate editor of *LOGOS*, the journal of the international book community.

Gordon Graham started in the book business in 1946 as a representative for Odhams Press in India. He was a rep for McGraw-Hill in Asia from 1950 to 1956, and from 1956 to 1963 was international sales manager of McGraw-Hill in New York. For the next twelve years he was managing director of McGraw-Hill in the UK and Europe. From 1974 until retiring in 1990 he was chairman and chief executive of Butterworths. Since retiring he has published the journal *LOGOS* (*See* Betty Graham above).

Alain Gründ joined his father (Michel Gründ) at Librairie Gründ (later Gründ Editions) in 1963. This publishing house had been established by Ernest Gründ (Alain Gründ's grandfather) in 1880. In developing its publication of international co-editions, Alain Gründ built long-term business relationships with firms that included Octopus Books, Walker Books and Macmillan. He was president of the International Publishers Association from 1996 to 2000.

Emma Hargrave is publisher of Tindal Street Press, an independent, Birmingham-based publisher of contemporary regional fiction. She was previously a freelance editor for Faber & Faber, Transworld and the Women's Press, and has been involved in running Tindal Street Press since 1998 when it evolved from the long-established Tindal Street Fiction Group.

Philippa Harrison started in publishing at Associated Book Publishers (ABP) in 1963. She joined Longmans in 1966, moved to Jonathan Cape in 1967, became editorial director of Hutchinson in 1974, joint editor-in-chief at Penguin in 1979, editorial director of Michael Joseph in 1980, and managing director and publisher of Macmillan, London in 1986. She left publishing in 1988, but returned in October 1991, and the following March she and Charlie Haywood created Little, Brown UK out of Macdonald, the Maxwell company which she had put into administration. After resigning as chief executive in May 2000, she became non-executive chairman until August 2001. Philippa Harrison was the first woman to serve as president of the Publishers Association, from 1998 to 1999.

Nicholas Heffer qualified as a chartered accountant before joining Heffer's bookselling firm in Cambridge in 1965, following his father (Reuben) and grandfather (Ernest) into the business founded in 1876 by his great-grandfather, William Heffer. Nicholas became a director of Heffer's in 1969 and remained with the firm until its sale to Blackwell's in 1999.

Marni Hodgkin joined Viking in New York in 1940 to work for the children's editor May Massee. She moved to Britain in 1944. She was editor of children's books at Rupert Hart-Davis from 1960 to 1966, and at Macmillan from 1966 to 1978.

Margaret Hughes became a bookseller in 1962 when she joined Haigh & Hochland in Manchester. In 1969 she and her husband, Dan Hughes, bought Sam Read's bookshop in Grasmere, which they ran until selling the business in 2000. This firm, established by Sam Read in 1887, is the oldest bookshop in the Lake District.

Robin Hyman joined Evans Brothers in 1955 and became production manager in 1957. He was made a director of the firm in 1964, became deputy managing director in 1967, and managing director in 1972. He left Evans Brothers in 1977 to form his own company, Bell & Hyman, after buying the long-established firm of George Bell. In 1986 Bell & Hyman merged with Allen & Unwin to form Unwin Hyman, which was sold to HarperCollins in 1990.

Tommy Joy left school in 1918 at the age of fourteen and worked in the Bodleian Library before becoming apprenticed to Thornton's University Bookshop in Oxford. In 1935 he became senior assistant at Harrods Circulating Library, which he ran, along with the book department, during the war. He became head book buyer at the Army & Navy Stores in 1945 and deputy managing director in 1956. He was managing director of the Hatchards Group from 1965 to 1985. Tommy Joy was president of the Booksellers Association from 1957 to 1958.

Willie Kay joined John Menzies Wholesale in Glasgow in 1934 at the age of sixteen, and became assistant buyer in the book department. In 1954 he moved to Menzies head office in Edinburgh as assistant book buyer, and eventually became the firm's chief book buyer. After retiring from John Menzies in 1972, Willie Kay and his wife Margaret ran their own bookshop in Edinburgh.

Ian Kiek joined Simpkin Marshall in 1932, at the age of sixteen, for eighteen months before entering the business established by his grandfather, Sidney Kiek & Sons (nonconformist booksellers and publishers) in Paternoster Row. When the firm collapsed in the mid-1930s Ian Kiek returned to Simpkin Marshall until 1940, when he was dismissed for being a conscientious objector. Apart from a brief spell at Hamish Hamilton in the early 1950s, he worked as a publisher's representative for Michael

Joseph from 1949 to 1961, when he became senior representative for Hutchinson until his retirement in 1982.

Jessica Kingsley set up Jessica Kingsley Publishing in 1988. This company, which specialises in books on social and behavioural sciences, is the pioneer publisher in the field of autism and Asperger Syndrome.

Reginald (Reggie) Last began his bookselling career with W.H. Smith in Woburn Sands in 1917, and worked in Bath, Oxford, Goring-on-Thames, Sevenoaks and Ealing, before becoming manager of Smith's flagship shop, Truslove & Hanson in Sloane Street, London in 1946. He became head of W.H. Smith's library department in 1951, and was the company's head book buyer from 1957 until retiring in 1965.

Karl Lawrence joined Simpkin Marshall as a graduate trainee in 1952. From 1953 he ran the Island Bookshop, Nassau and built a bookselling and news agency business in the Bahamas. In 1965 he returned to Britain, where he worked for Collins, André Deutsch, Collier Macmillan and HarperCollins. Karl Lawrence became a leading figure in the development of book distribution systems, including ISBNs, tele-ordering, bar codes and RFID (Radio Frequency Identification).

Cherry Lewis worked at The Economist Bookshop in 1955 and in 1956, when the business was run by Gerti Kvergic and owned by the London School of Economics, where Cherry Lewis qualified in Social Science Administration. She later worked for Evans Brothers, Fleetway Press (an Odhams company later acquired by the International Press Corporation) and as a sub-editor on *Woman* magazine. In 1977 she joined the publishing firm Antique Collectors Club, where she became senior editor.

Belinda McGill joined the Bodley Head as personal secretary to Max Reinhardt in 1964, left in 1969 to bring up her family, and returned to work as personal assistant to Max and Joan Reinhardt in the late 1990s.

Elizabeth McWatters worked in the book department of J.P. Gardner & Son in Belfast from 1961 to 1968, before moving to the University Bookshop, where she became deputy manager. When it was bought by the university in 1972, the shop was re-named Queen's University Bookshop.

Terry Maher founded the investment company Pentos in 1972 and was its chairman and chief executive until 1993. Pentos bought Hudson's bookshop in Birmingham in 1972, and Dillon's University Bookshop in 1977. As chief executive of Pentos, he was responsible for developing Dillons Bookstores into a national chain and challenged the book trade's system of retail price maintenance upheld by the Net Book Agreement.

Sylvia May (née Graham) worked in Hammick's bookshop in Windsor before joining William Collins as a trainee representative in 1977, becoming the firm's first woman rep. After representing Collins in Wessex, she became central London rep in 1981. She became sales manager of Collins' hardback division in 1987, European sales manager of HarperCollins in 1994, and international sales director in 2002.

Peter Mayer began his publishing career in New York in the early 1960s as an editor, first at Orion, then at Avon Books. He was publisher and president of Pocket Books from 1976 to 1978, when he became chief executive (and later chairman) of the international Penguin Group, based in London. Since leaving Penguin in 1997, Peter Mayer has run the American independent Overlook Press (which he and his father set up in 1971) and Duckworth (which he acquired in 2003). In 2005 he bought the Nonesuch Press from Joan Reinhardt (*See* Max Reinhardt below).

Ian Miller began his bookselling career in 1949 at Mowbray's (Anglican booksellers) in London and became manager of Mowbray's in Birmingham in 1959. In 1964 he moved to Hudson's Bookshops, Birmingham, where he became personnel and training manager and a director and, after its acquisition of Hudson's in 1972, an employee of Pentos Bookselling Group.

John Milne trained at James Thin Ltd., Edinburgh before taking over his father's bookselling business, Bisset's of Aberdeen, where he was managing director from 1954 to 1987.

Trevor Moore worked in the sales department of Hutchinson from 1958 to 1960, when he became a representative for Hamish Hamilton. He was London representative for Jonathan Cape from 1964 to 1969 and, subsequently, for Collins, Deutsch and Hodder & Stoughton. In 1984 he joined Transworld as sales manager of their new hardback imprint, Bantam Press. He then represented Century Hutchinson (later Random House) until retiring in 2002. From 1964 to 1965 he also worked part-time in John Sandoe's bookshop, Chelsea.

Victor Morrison joined Michael Joseph's production department in 1950. He was managing director from 1975 until he left the company in 1980.

Diana Murray (née James) read for various publishers before marrying the publisher John (Jock) Murray in 1938. She worked on the staff of Murrays during the Second World War, and afterwards remained closely involved with the firm, reading and editing typescripts, and entertaining authors at home.

John R. Murray elder son of Diana and John (Jock) Murray, became the seventh John Murray in the business when he joined John Murray Publishers in 1964. He succeeded his father as chairman, and remained with Murrays until it was sold in 2002 to Hodder Headline (then part of the W.H. Smith Group).

Ian Norrie began his bookselling career in 1948, working for Martyn Goff in St Leonard's-on-Sea and later in Seaford. He worked at Foyle's from 1949 to 1950, at William Jackson Books from 1950 to 1955, and at Alfred Wilson Ltd. from 1955 to 1956. He ran the High Hill Bookshop, Hampstead from 1956 to 1988. Ian Norrie has been a publisher, journalist and book trade historian.

Eric Norris began his bookselling career at Miller & Gill in Charing Cross Road in 1931. He then worked in Simpkin & Marshall's remainder department, at the Bodley Head as an invoice clerk, and at the Students' Bookshop, Tottenham Court Road, where he was dismissed in the Second World War for being a conscientious objector. He was subsequently employed at Truslove & Hanson, then in Denny's bookshop and, from 1954, at The Pioneer Bookshop, Woolwich, of which he became joint-owner.

Lynette Owen worked in the rights department of Cambridge University Press from 1968 until 1973, when she became rights manager at Pitmans. In 1976 she succeeded Doris Bendemann as rights manager at Longman. Lynette Owen is an international authority on rights and the general editor (following Charles Clark) of *Clark's Publishing Agreements*.

Charles Pick joined Victor Gollancz Ltd. as an office boy in 1933 and became a salesman, initially for Gollancz and later for the newly-established firm of Michael Joseph. After war service with the Royal Artillery, he returned to Michael Joseph, where, following Michael Joseph's death in 1958, he became joint managing director with Peter Hebdon. When the Thomson Organization bought the firm in 1961, Charles Pick, Peter Hebdon, and editorial director Roland Gant, resigned. After their plan to buy Jonathan Cape collapsed, Charles Pick became managing director of William Heinemann until his retirement in 1985, when he established the Charles Pick Literary Agency.

Tony Pocock read English Literature at St Edmund Hall, Oxford, then trained as an actor at the Maddermarket Theatre, Norwich before war service in the Royal Marines. He joined Oxford University Press in 1951 as assistant editor on the *Oxford Junior Encyclopaedia*, and succeeded Bruno Brown as sales manager in 1955. From the mid-1970s until his retirement in 1987 he was sales director, and later vice-chairman, of Faber & Faber.

John Prime worked for the International Union of Students in Prague from 1952 to 1953. After returning to Britain, he ran Collet's Multilingual Bookshop and then became general manager of Collet's bookshops. He left Collet's to run the bookshop at the 1964 World Book Fair, after which he became manager of Willshaw's bookshop in Manchester. From 1968 to 1982 he ran bookshops in King's Lynn in partnership with Maureen Condon (*See* above). He subsequently worked briefly as sales manager for Educational Publications Ltd., before joining Austick's of Leeds, where he was manager of the general bookshop. After retiring in 1994, John Prime moved to the Booksellers' Retreat in Kings Langley, Hertfordshire.

Max Reinhardt began publishing in 1947, with the acquisition of accountancy imprint HFL Ltd. (H. Foulks Lynch). The following year, encouraged by his friends, the actors Anthony Quayle and Ralph Richardson, he set up the general list of Max Reinhardt Ltd. He acquired the Nonesuch Press from Francis Meynell in 1953 and bought the Bodley Head from Sir Stanley Unwin in 1956. In 1973 the Bodley Head joined forces with Chatto & Windus and Jonathan Cape to share distribution and warehousing. This company (CBC) expanded in 1982 with the purchase of Virago to become CVBC. Max Reinhardt resigned as joint chairman in March 1987, and later that year CVBC was sold to Random House. He continued to publish under the Reinhardt Books imprint until 1998.

Stan Remington graduated from the London School of Economics in 1946 as a Bachelor of Commerce, and worked as an accountant for Cromer Works (printers) until joining the book department of Odhams Press in 1949. In 1963 Odhams was merged with the Mirror Group to form International Publishing Corporation (IPC). A year later, IPC purchased Paul Hamlyn Books and Stan Remington became deputy chief executive of the Hamlyn Group's mail order division. In 1971 he was appointed marketing manager of Book Club Associates. The following year he became manager of all its book operations. In 1976 he became chief executive. Stan Remington retired in 1987.

Tim Rix joined Longman in 1958 and worked as an overseas educational publisher. In 1961 he became publishing manager for the Far East and South East Asia, based in Kuala Lumpur. He returned to the UK in 1964 and worked as a senior ELT publisher until becoming managing director of the ELT division in 1968. He was chief executive of the Longman Group from 1976 until he retired in 1990. Tim Rix was chairman of Book Aid International from 1994 to 2006.

Per Saugman served an apprenticeship at Munksgaard's bookshop in Copenhagen and continued his training in Switzerland and Britain, where he worked for Blackwell's bookshops in Oxford and Bristol. He became sales manager of Blackwell's Scientific Publications in 1952 and was managing director from 1953 until 1987.

Michael Seviour joined Bumpus as a collector (calling at publishers' trade counters for customer orders) in 1951, before joining Chatto & Windus, where he worked in the warehouse. He returned to Bumpus in 1955 as stock assistant (later stock manager), and became manager of Bumpus when it moved to Baker Street in 1958. He was manager of Better Books from the early to the mid-1960s, then ground floor manager and literature buyer at Dillon's University Bookshop. After leaving Dillon's in 1974, he ran Webster's in Winchester, Boate's in Kingston-upon-Thames, and branches of Hatchards in Richmond and Kingston-upon-Thames.

Diane Spivey read English Literature at York University before joining Hutchinson in 1977, initially as export sales assistant and later as contacts assistant. She was rights assistant at Hodder & Stoughton from 1979 to 1981, then joined Methuen as rights manager, becoming rights director in 1983. She was subsequently rights director at Harrap from 1987 to 1992, Cassell from 1992 to 1996, and, after a brief spell as UK sales director at Quarto, contracts and rights director at Simon & Schuster UK from 1997 to 2003. She has been rights and contracts director of Little, Brown (UK) since 2004. Diane Spivey served on the main committee and training committee of Women in Publishing in the 1980s and 1990s.

Frank Stoakley left school in 1920 at the age of fifteen and worked briefly at Deighton, Bell & Co. (booksellers) in Cambridge, before joining Heffer's, where he later built and ran a science department of international repute. He remained with Heffer's until his retirement in 1980.

Bert Taylor started work at Simpkin Marshall in 1920 at the age of fifteen. He served in the RAF during the Second World War, then worked as a publisher's representative for Odhams, Staples Press and Evans Brothers.

Judy Taylor worked at the Bodley Head for thirty years from 1951. She became a director of the Bodley Head in 1963, deputy managing director in 1971, and a director of Chatto, Bodley Head and Cape in 1973. She was the first woman to serve on the council of the Publishers Association (from 1972 to 1978). In 1971 she was awarded an MBE for services to children's publishing. She is now an expert on the work of Beatrix Potter.

Ainslie Thin trained at Blackwell's in Oxford and George's in Bristol before starting at James Thin in 1958, joining J. Ainslie Thin (his uncle) and Jimmy Thin (cousin) in the Edinburgh bookselling business established in 1848 by the original James Thin (his great-grandfather). He soon became a partner. When Thin's became a limited company in 1973, Jimmy Thin and Ainslie Thin became joint managing directors. On Jimmy Thin's retirement in 1989, Ainslie Thin became sole managing director until his own retirement in 1999, when he handed over to his daughter, Jackie Taylor. The business of James Thin Ltd. was sold to the bookselling firms of Blackwell's and Ottakar's in 2002. Ainslie Thin was president of the Booksellers Association from 1976 to 1978.

Sue Thomson began her book trade career at Foyle's in 1956. She went on to work at Thames & Hudson, at Condé Nast and for the *Law Society Gazette*. In 1966 she joined the Hamlyn Publishing Group, where she became production director. In 1971 she and Paul Hamlyn set up Octopus Books, of which she was managing director, then deputy chairman. She was instrumental in the flotation of Octopus in 1983. Sue Thomson served on the Council of Almoners of Christ's Hospital for sixteen years from 1987, and was non-executive chairman of Quadrille Publishing Ltd. from 1994 to 2002.

Michael Turner worked for J.M. Dent as a re-writer on *Everyman's Encyclopaedia* from 1950 to 1951 before reading English Literature at Trinity College, Cambridge. He joined Methuen as a publisher's reader in 1953 and later combined editorial work with developing Methuen's publicity and promotions. He became sales director, then group marketing director of ABP (Associated Book Publishers, created from the merger between Methuen and Eyre & Spottiswoode in 1954) and was group managing director and chief executive of ABP from 1982 to 1988. Michael Turner and Leslie Lonsdale-Cooper have been the translators of Hergé's *Tintin* books into English since 1958.

Carol Unwin (née Curwen) trained and worked as a children's nurse before her marriage in 1952 to the publisher Rayner Unwin, second son of Sir Stanley, founder of George Allen & Unwin Ltd. Carol Unwin created a remarkable garden at the family home in Buckinghamshire, where their son Merlin (himself a publisher) and daughters Camilla, Sharon and Tamara spent their early lives.

Martha van der Lem-Mearns was an assistant in John Smith's antiquarian bookshop in Glasgow before joining Blackie & Son as an editor in 1955. In 1962 she became a children's book editor at Nelson's in London for five years before moving to Holland, where she worked in publishing. Since returning to Britain with her family, she has worked as an editor of medical publications.

Anne Walmsley joined Faber & Faber in 1955 as secretary to Peter du Sautoy and left in 1959 to teach at Westwood High School in Jamaica. She returned to Britain in 1963 and worked for the BBC before being appointed Longman's Caribbean publisher in 1967. In 1975 she became humanities publisher for Africa and the Caribbean then, in 1976, publishing manager with Longman Kenya, in Nairobi. She left Longman on her return to Britain in 1978, took an MA in African Studies, then worked as a freelance consultant and editor while doing part-time research for *Index on Censorship*. Since completing a PhD in 1993 on the Caribbean Artists Movement, Anne Walmsley has worked on Caribbean art as a writer and teacher. She is the author of *The Caribbean Artists Movement, 1966–72: a literary and cultural history*, New Beacon Books, 1992.

David Whitaker joined his father Haddon Whitaker at J. Whitaker & Sons in 1953. He was the fourth generation to enter this family firm, which was the main supplier of business information and bibliographical data to the book trade, and publisher of its weekly journal, *The Bookseller*. David Whitaker was editor of *The Bookseller* from 1977 to 1979 and succeeded his father as chairman of Whitaker's from 1985 until retiring in 1997. He has been a leading figure in the development of bibliographic data and distribution systems, including ISBNs and electronic data interchange.

Ronald Whiting joined the Bodley Head (then owned by Sir Stanley Unwin) as a post boy in 1943. After volunteering for the RAF, and being placed in the Grenadier Guards, he returned by means of an army training scheme to work for Allen & Unwin and the Bodley Head as a sales representative. He left in 1951 to became sales manager at the publishing firm of Dennis Dobson. He was co-founder and joint owner of Whiting & Wheaton (publishers), and later joined Georg Rapp to create Rapp & Whiting, publishing poetry, science fiction, children's and general books. After working for the British Publishing Corporation, Ronald Whiting became managing director of Hamlyn Publishing until he retired in 1985.

Efric Wotherspoon trained and worked as a children's nurse, then gained experience in several Glasgow bookshops before returning in 1950 to work with her mother in the family bookselling business of K. & J. Martin in Campbeltown. Efric Wotherspoon continued to run the shop until the end of her life in 2000.

David Young began his career in publishing in 1970 at Thorsons Publishing Group, the company established by his grandfather, Leonard Woodford, in 1930. When HarperCollins acquired Thorsons in 1989, David Young was appointed to the HarperCollins board; he became manager of their trade division in 1993. In 1996 he joined Little, Brown (UK) as managing director; he became chief executive in 2000. Little, Brown was renamed Time Warner Book Group UK in 2000, and in 2005 David Young moved to New York to become chairman and ceo of Time Warner Book Group. The company was bought by Hachette Livre in April 2006 and renamed Hachette Book Group.

SUGGESTIONS FOR FURTHER READING

Histories, biographies and memoirs about the book trade

Adamson, Judith, *Max Reinhardt, A Life in Publishing*, London: Palgrave Macmillan, 2009.

Athill, Diana, *Stet: a memoir*, London: Granta Books, 2000.

Blond, Anthony, *The Book Book*, London: Jonathan Cape, 1985.

Briggs, Asa, *Essays in the History of Publishing*, London: Longman, 1974.

Briggs, Asa, *A History of Longmans And Their Books*, London: British Library, 2008.

Carpenter, Humphrey, *The Seven Lives of John Murray*, London: John Murray, 2008.

Davies, Gerry, and Barker, Ronald, *Books are Different: An Account of the Defence of the Net Book Agreement*, London: Macmillan, 1966.

de Bellaigue, Eric, *British Book Publishing as a Business since the 1960s*, London: British Library, 2004.

Duffy, Maureen, *A Thousand Capricious Chances: A History of the Methuen List 1889–1989*, London: Methuen, 1989.

Elliot, David, *A Trade of Charms*, London: Bellew, 1992.

Epstein, Jason, *Book Business: publishing, present and future*, New York: Norton, 2001.

Feather, John, *A History of Book Publishing*, London and New York: Routledge, 1996 (reprinted).

Finkelstein, David, and McCleary, Alistair (eds.), *The Edinburgh History of the Book in Scotland: 4: Professionalism and Diversity, 1880–2000*, Edinburgh: Edinburgh University Press, 2007.

Finkelstein, David, and McCleary, Alistair (eds.), *The Book History Reader*, London and New York: Routledge, 2002. [An introduction to the academic field of the History of the Book.]

Graham, Gordon, *As I Was Saying: Essays on the International Book Business*, East Grinstead: Hans Zell, 1994.

Gordon, Giles, *Aren't We Due a Royalty Statement?* London: Chatto & Windus, 1993.

Gründ, Alain, *Une affaire de famille*, Paris: Editions Gründ, 1999.

Hare, Steve (ed.), *Allen Lane and the Penguin Editors 1935–1970*, Harmondsworth: Penguin, 1995.

Hill, Alan, *In Pursuit of Publishing*, London: John Murray, 1988.

Holman, Valerie, *Print for Victory: book publishing in England, 1939–1945*, London: British Library, 2008.

Howard, Michael, *Jonathan Cape, Publisher*, London: Jonathan Cape, 1971.

James Thin Ltd, *James Thin: 150 Years of Bookselling 1848–1998*, Edinburgh: The Mercat Press, 1998.

Joy, Thomas, *Mostly Joy: A Bookman's Story*, London: Michael Joseph, 1971.

Lambert, Jack Walter, and Ratcliffe, Michael, *The Bodley Head, 1887–1987*, London: The Bodley Head, 1987.

Lewis, Jeremy, *Kindred Spirits*, London: HarperCollins, 1995.

Lewis, Jeremy, *Penguin Special: the Life and Times of Allen Lane*, London: Viking, 2005.

LOGOS: The Forum of the World Book Community, Marlow: LOGOS International Publishing Educational Foundation, 1990—

Maher, Terry, *Against My Better Judgement*, London: Sinclair-Stevenson, 1994.

Miles, Barry, *In the Sixties*, London: Jonathan Cape, 2002. [Includes an account of Better Books.]

Mountain, Penny, and Foyle, Christopher, *Foyles: A Celebration*, London: Foyles, 2003.

Norrie, Ian, *Mentors and Friends: short lives of prominent publishers and booksellers I have known*, London: Elliott & Thompson, 2006.

Norrie, Ian, *Mumby's Publishing and Bookselling in the Twentieth Century*, London: Bell & Hyman, 1982.

Owen, Peter (ed.), *Publishing: The Future*, London: Peter Owen, 1988.

Owen, Peter (ed.), *Publishing Now*, London: Peter Owen, 1996.

Reinhardt, Max, *Memories*, 1998 (privately printed for the author).

Rolph, C. H. (ed.), *The Trial of Lady Chatterley: The Transcript of the Trial*, London: Penguin, 1961.

Saugman, Per, *From the First Fifty Years: An Informal History of Blackwell Scientific Publications*, Oxford: Blackwell Scientific Publications, 1989.

Sinclair, Iain (ed.), *London: City of Disappearances*, London: Hamish Hamilton, 2006. [Impressions of a different London book world.]

Sutcliffe, Peter, *The Oxford University Press: an informal history*, Oxford: Oxford University Press, 1978.

Sutherland, John, *Reading the Decades: fifty years of the nation's bestselling books*, London: BBC Books, 2002.

Unwin, Rayner, *George Allen & Unwin: A Remembrancer*, Ludlow: Merlin Unwin Books, 1999.

Unwin, Stanley, *The Truth about a Publisher: an autobiographical record*, London: Allen & Unwin, 1960.

Unwin, Stanley, *The Truth about Publishing*, London: Allen & Unwin, 1960.

Warburg, Fredric, *An Occupation for Gentlemen*, London: Hutchinson, 1959.

Wynne-Tyson, Jon, *Finding the Words: A Publishing Life*, Norwich: Michael Russell (Publishing) Ltd., 2004.

Practical information about the publishing industry today

Writers' and Artists' Yearbook, London: A. & C. Black. [annual publication.]

Blake, Carole, *From Pitch to Publication: everything you need to know to get your novel published*, London: Macmillan, 1999.

Turner, Barry (ed.) *The Writer's Handbook*, London: Palgrave Macmillan. [annual publication.]

Oral history

Courtney, Cathy, and Thompson, Paul (eds.), *City Lives: the Changing Voices of British Finance*, London: Methuen, 1996. [Edited from interviews in the *City Lives* collection recorded by National Life Stories.]

Oral History: the journal of the Oral History Society, vol. 1, no. 1, 1969 – *See* also: Oral History Society (UK) www.ohs.org.uk

Parker, Tony, *Studs Terkel: A Life in Words*, London: HarperCollins, 1997. [An iconic American oral historian interviewed by a legendary British colleague.]

Perks, Robert, and Thomson, Alistair, *The Oral History Reader*, London and New York: Routledge, 2006 (2nd ed.). [A comprehensive introduction to the theory and practice of oral history.]

Thompson, Paul, *The Voice of the Past: Oral History*, Oxford: Oxford University Press, 2000 (3rd ed.). [A classic.]

INDEX

Numbers in bold type indicate pages with extracts from the subject's *Book Trade Lives* recording.
A lower case n following a page reference (e.g. 52n) indicates a footnote.

Batsford, B. T. & Co. 15 252
Batty, Ronald 114
Baum, Louis 75
Beacon Books 152
Beatles, the 247–8
Beauman, Sally 214
Beckett, Samuel, *Waiting for Godot* 25
Beddingham, Roy 133
Beginner's Guide to Sex 177
Bell, George & Co. 308
Bell & Hyman 45–6 308
Belowski, Mr (Librairie Payot) 178
Bendemann, Doris 272 311
Benedictus, Roger 97
Bennett, Arnold 61
Bennett, Mrs (Bumpus) 60
Bennett, Mr (Blackie & Son) 94
Beoty's restaurant 163 164
Berne Copyright Agreement 222
Berne, Eric, *Games People Play* 145
Berkhout, Joop 41–3
Bertelsmann 300
Bertram, Elsie 125 **126–8 179** 304
Bertram, Kip 126 304
bestseller lists 74–5
bestsellers 5–6 9 17–18 35 41 46 61 62 80
    100–8 *passim* 117 143 146 147 154 178–85
    passim 192–210 *passim*
Betjeman, John 200–1
Better Books 62–3 76–8 116 248–9 312
Bevan, Aneurin 131
Biafran War 42
bibles 54 246
Bim 21
Bingham, Charlotte, *Coronet Among the
    Weeds* 192
Birch, Alewyn 254
Bissett's Bookshop 64 65 310
Bissex, Mr (Simpkin Marshall) 4
Black, Jill 96 100
Black Amber Press 284
Black, A. & C. 57 97 106 158 307
Blackie, W. G. 93
Blackie & Son 2 33 54 92–5 97 294
Blackwell, Basil 47 66–7 171 178 286
Blackwell, Julian, known as Toby 47 66
    271 271n
Blackwell, Richard 47 6
Blackwell's bookshop 48–52 *passim* 64 66
    170 172 173 178 227 271 308 312
Blackwell Scientific Publications 52n 190
    285 312
Blake, Carole **146–9 163 166 177 187
    233–6 257 264–5 278–81 289–90 296–7
    299–300** 304

Blake, Quentin 92
Blake Friedmann Literary Agency 166 187
    304
Bland, Mr (Bumpus) 58 63
Blass, Ron 160–1 180
Blatty, William Peter, *The Exorcist* 187–8
Blitz, the 1 7
Blond, Anthony **180–1 182–3 187–8 300** 304
Blond & Briggs 304
Bloodaxe 210–11 259–60 304
Bloomsbury Publishing 98n 215 235–6 261
Blythe, Ronald, *Akenfield* 146
Bodleian Library 47
Bodley Head 26–7 90 95–104 *passim* 133–4
    154 155 161 165n 197–9 289 293 306–14
    passim
Bogarde, Dirk 72
Bogle L'Ouverture Press 283 284
Bologna Children's Book Fair 105 307
Bolodeoku, Layi 42
Bond, James 9 39
Bond, James, *The Birds of the West Indies* 39
Book Aid International 37–8 312
Book Café / Caff 133 253
Book Centre 7
Book Club Associates 305 306 311
book fairs, *see* Bologna, Frankfurt, Leipzig,
    London, Moscow, Warsaw
Book Production Managers' Group 273
Book Publishers' Representatives
    Association 134–5 268
book tokens 229
Book Trade Benevolent Society 110 123
    280–1
Book Trade Working Party 271 274
Books for Pleasure 268
Bookmen, Society of 46 170 266 274 282
Bookseller, The 38 56 75 127 140 159 163 164
    175 249 254 288 307 313
Booksellers Association 66 108 109 111 119
    120n 122 126 144 159 167–76 *passim* 228
    230 269–70 271n 276 306 308 312
Booksellers' Retreat 110 123 280–1 311
bookselling / bookshops 47–84 107–38 142
    167–80 *passim* 216–17 226–9 231–3
    236–43 245–55 *passim*
Bookselling and Stationery Trades Wages
    Council 112
BookTrack 74–5
Boon, Alfred 131
Boon, John 158
Boothe, John 144
Borders Bookshops 238
Boston, Lucy 96
Bowen, Elizabeth 121

Clark, Kenneth 200
Clark, Margaret 96 97–8 101 165
Clarke, Austin 262
Clow, Robert **54–61** *passim* **67 143–4 178–9
204–5 238 269–70** 305–6
Clowes, Jonathan 166
co-editions 102 104
Coady, Frances 154
Cobbing, Bob 77
Cochrane, Peter **15–17** 306
Cocking, Miss (Bumpus) 58–9
Cockshut, A. O. J., *Anglican Attitudes* 255
Code-Holland, Robert 158
Cold War 216–24
Cole, Teddy 70
collectors 53–4 56–8
Collet's bookshops 153 216–18 221 281 311
Collier Macmillan 309
Collins, Godfrey 252
Collins, Ian 16 245
Collins, Ted 249
Collins, William (Billy) 70–8 112 247 286
305
Collins, Wm. Sons & Co. 1 2 16 38 54 57
70 74 76–8 99 116 142 152 162 177n 213
231 249–55 *passim* 286 294 305–14 *passim*
Colwell, Eileen 96
Comber, Leon 35
Combridge Jackson 255
Comerford, Tony 124
commissioning editors, *see* editing
Comyns, Barbara 215
Concise Oxford Dictionary 117
Condon, Maureen **78 80 81 108 240 302–3**
306
conscientious objectors 4 6 306
Constable & Co. 91
contracts 28 104
Cooke, Geraldine 150
Coombs, Robert 39
Cooper, Diana 113
Cooper, Jilly 71
Cooper, Leo 19
Corgi Books 141 146–7 151–3
Cornish, Bill 207
Cortie, Ron 131 135
Costain, Thomas, *The Silver Chalice* 9
Cotterell, Laurence **13–15** 19 306
Courtney, Cathy 110
cover design 142–5 147
Coward, Noel 62
Cozzens, James Gould, *By Love Possessed*
202
Crane, Walter 88
Crick, Michael 186

Crook, Arthur 145
Cross, Helen, *My Summer of Love* 261
Cullen, John 203
Cumberlege, Geoffrey 21 28 35 157
Currer, Jock 244
Curtis Brown 17
CVBC (Chatto, Virago, Cape & Bodley
Head) 154 289 305 311

Dahl, Roald 101–2
Dallah, Mrs (OUP) 31
Daunt's bookshop 238
David, Dick 158
David, Elizabeth 121 122; *French Provincial
Cooking* 122
Davies, Gerry 107 127 **158 167–76** *passim*
180 233 241–2 306
Day Lewis, Cecil 214
de Beauvoir, Simone, *The Second Sex* 141
de la Mare, Walter, *A Child's Day* 88
Dearnley, Stephen **16** 99 **245–7** 306
Deighton, Len 151 248
Deighton, Bell & Co. 47 312
Denny's Bookshop 310
Dent, Martin 285
Dent, J. M. & Co. 4n 95n 97 100 142 161
285 307
Depotex, George 117
Determann, Franz 73
Dettmer, John 116
Deutsch, André **10 12–13 17–18** *passim* 65
73 144–5 158 160 161 195 286 292 305
306 309 310
Dial Books 105
Dickens, Monica 136 191–2
Dickinson, John 280
Dictionary of Organic Compounds 288
Dignum, Reg 131
Dillon, Una 108 117–20 227
Dillon's University Bookshop 108 117–20 ;
Dillons Bookstores 226 227 228 309 312
Dillsworth, Elise 283
Dining Club, the 282
DIPNET (Diversity in Publishing
Network) 283
discounts *see* Net Book Agreement
distribution 1–11 75 126–8
diversity in the publishing profession
282–4
Dixon, Isobel 166 187 299
Dobson, Dennis & Co. 313
Donne-Smith, Basil 172–3
door-to-door bookselling 82–4
Doran, Hart 6
Dorling Kindersley 221

Geare, Michael **107 137 139 140–2 156 159–61** *passim* 164 **266–9 303** 307
Geary, Karen 211
Geoghan, Mr (OUP) 157
George, Mabel 96
George's bookshop 67
Ghana 43
Gibbs, Philip 171
Giddy, Peter 60 71 73–4 133 254
Glasgow 53–6 143–4 204–5 238
Glasgow Herald 179 201–2
Glover, Jimmy 251
Goad, Rosemary x **21–3 25 156–7 183–4 185–7 277 293** 307
Godwin, Tony 62–3 76 77–8 144 145
Goff, Martyn 310
Goffin, Raymond 20–1 23 31–2
Gold Medal Books 142
Golding, William, *Lord of the Flies* 183 184
Goldsack, Sydney 16 116
Gollancz, Victor 57 103 129 130 131 156 182 190 311
Gone with the Wind ix 171 255
Goodings, Lennie 283
Gordon, Giles 163
Goulden & Curry 68–9 134 306
Gradov, Yuri 222
Graham, Betty **222 224** 307
Graham, Gordon **206** 222 **266** 286–7 307–8
Graham, Herbert Maxwell 53
Graham, Sylvia, *see* May, Sylvia
Granada Publishing 147–8 151 304
Grant, John 285
Green, Bryan, Canon 180
Green, Jenny 72
Green, Miss (Bumpus) 60
Greenaway, Kate 88
Greene, Graham 9 27 155 165 198–9 240
Greene, Graham C. 185
Greene, Hugh Carlton 165
Greer, Germaine, *The Female Eunuch* 147
Gregory, Jane 279
Grey Owl, *The Adventures of Sajo and Her Beaver People* 55
Griffiths, Ken 301
Groucho Club 267
Grove Press 145
Gründ, Alain **236–7** 307
Guinzberg, Harold 90–1
Guyana 24–5 40
Guzzardi, Peter 212
Gwynne, Felicité 121

Haddon, Mark, *The Curious Incident of the Dog in the Night-Time* 234–5

Haigh & Hochland 164 308
Hale, James 295
Hall, Henry S. & Samuel R. Knight, *Algebra* ix 171
Halsbury's Laws of England 206
Hamilton, Hamish 10–11 62 91 97 103 134 136 150 166n 195 247 276 307 308
Hamlyn, Paul 84 126 137–8 158 170 174 229 237–8 268 286 287
Hamlyn Publishing Group 268 304 311 313 314
Hammick's bookshop, Windsor 252 309
Handprint Press 106
Hansluck, Mr (Economist Bookshop) 124
Harcourt Brace 15 297
Hardie, Jeremy 231
Hardy, Patrick 91
Hargrave, Emma **259 261–2 302** 308
Harlock, Miss (Bumpus) 60
Harper & Row 100
HarperCollins *see* Collins
Harrap, George & Co. 14 57 132 306 312
Harrap, Walter 14
Harris, Gerald 134
Harrison, David 131
Harrison, Philippa **153 166 183–9** *passim* **209–10 215 229–35** *passim* **257–9 263–5** *passim* **292–3** 308
Harrison, Miss (Bumpus) 59–60
Harrods 52 62 122 134 139 308
Hart, Gilbert 130–1 135
Hart-Davis, Rupert 17 91 97 101 147 308
Harvard-Watts, John 206
Hatchards bookshop 69–74 77 112 133 197 227 239 250 254 305 308 312
Hatier, Editions 102
Hawking, Stephen, *A Brief History of Time* 154 211–12
Hawkins, Gillian 252
Hawkins, Roy 28–34 *passim* 257
Haywood, Charlie 308
Heald, Henrietta 210
Heaney, Seamus x 25 26
Hearne, John, *Voices under the Window* 23
Heath, Edward 204–5
Heath, Roy 208
Hebdon, Peter 56 118 122 311
Heffer, Ernest 47 48 52 308
Heffer, Nicholas **47 49** 308
Heffer, Reuben 47 270 308
Heffer's bookshop 47–52 *passim* 64 131–2 172 173 227 308 312
Heinemann, William 35 43 111 116 131 136 192 254 274 286 293 295 304 311
Heller, Joseph, 183; *Catch-22* 154 248

Knox, John, known as Jack 54–6 67 179 305–6
Körner, Theodore, Volksbuchhandlung 86
Krazna-Krausz, Andor 286
Kvergic, Gerti 108 122–4 309

La Rose, John 284
Lacey, Robert, *Majesty* 62
Laing, R. D., *The Divided Self* 206–7
Lamb, Tommy 130
Lancaster, Osbert 200
Landsborough, Gordon 141
Lane, Allen 16 62 77 119 139 145 152 153 286 287
Lang, Andrew 88
Last, Reggie **50 69** 273 309
law publishing 206–8 222 287
Lawrence, D. H. 9; *Lady Chatterley's Lover* 179–81
Lawrence, Karl **1 7–11 37–8 39 74 76–7 144–5 161 177 254 301** 309
Lawrence, T. E., *Seven Pillars of Wisdom* 61
Le Carré, John 230
Leaf, Munro & Robert Lawson, *The Story of Ferdinand* 89
Leary, Timothy 77
Leckie, Mr (John Menzies) 53
Lee, Laurie 195
Leech, Iris 123
Lehmann, Rosamond 213–15
Leigh Fermor, Patrick 200
Leipzig Book Fair 217–18
Lennon, John, *A Spaniard in the Works* 108
Leppard, Jim 252
Lessing, Doris 183
Lever, Harold 46
Levi, Primo, *The Periodic Table* 210
Lewis, Cherry **123–4** 309
libraries 52 67 95 98–9 101 130 155 174 202 220 223
Lines, Kathleen 95 101
Lingard, Ann 23
Lingenbrink 91
Listener, The 25 26 207
Little, Brown 215 229 232 257–8 302 308 312 314
Littleton, Peter 175–6
Livingstone, E. & S. 64
Lock, Peter 227
Lofthouse, Alex 10
LOGOS 288 307
London, Freddy 132
London Book Fair 256 278 298–9
London bookselling 56–63 68–78
Longman, Elizabeth 40

Longman, Mark 20 40–1 43 202
Longman, Michael 20
Longman, William 20
Longman family 170 287
Longman Caribbean Ltd 40
Longmans Green & Co. 1 19–20 29–45 *passim* 103 167 192 222 223 272–3 287 294 306 311–12 314
Lonsdale-Cooper, Leslie 202–3 313
Ludlum, Robert 147
lunch 156–68
Luscombe, William 177
Luzac's bookshop 241
Lynch-Blosse, Mr (Allen & Unwin) 132
Lyons, J. (cafés) 3 156

Macandrew, Rennie 177–8; *The Red Light* 177–8
MacArthur, Brian 75
Macbain, J. Murray, *The Book of a Thousand Poems* 46
McClelland & Stewart 261
Macdonald & Co. 130 308
McDougall/Holmes McDougall Publishers 53–4
McDuff, David 210
MacFarlane, Neil 103
MacGibbon, Hamish 274
MacGibbon & Kee 147 240
McGill, Belinda **26–7 161 197 198–9** 310
McGraw-Hill 266 307
Machell, Roger 276
McKee, David 105; *Not Now Bernard* 101; *Two Can Toucan* 102; *The Conquerors* 106
MacLean, Alistair 201–2; *HMS Ulysses* 202
MacLehose, Christopher 213
Macmillan, Alex ix 170–1
Macmillan, Harold 43 170
Macmillan & Co. 2 29 33 34 35 43 90 97 101 255 295 308
MacRae, Julia 91 97
McWatters, Elizabeth x **26 132 255–6 265** 310
Magliabechi 176
Magnum Paperbacks 149
Maher, Terry **226–30 239** 309
Mailer, Norman, *The Naked and the Dead* 17–18
Malaya 35–6
Malmaison Hotel, Glasow 205
Mamlok, Gwyneth 97
Map House, The 16
marketing/promotions/advertising 139–55 265
Márquez, Gabriel García 183

Octopus Publishing 268 308 313
Odhams Press 57 82–4 126 134 152 190 245
   309 311 312
Odhams Practical Cookery 190
Office of Fair Trading 225 226 228 229
Ogg, George 93 94
Ogston, Iain 249
O'Hanlon, Redmond 262–3
Ojora, Otunda 46
Oliver, John 134
Oliver & Boyd 65 294
Olympia Press 178 179
l'Opéra restaurant 159
Orion Books 309
Orwell, George 130 234
Orwell Press 301
Osborne, John, *Look Back in Anger* 25
Ottakar's Bookshops 150 301 312
Overlook Press 204 299 309–10
Owen, David 211
Owen, Lynette **219–24** *passim* **298** 311
Owen, Ursula 212–13
Oxenbury, Helen 104
Oxford 47–52 *passim* 66–8
Oxford Junior Encyclopaedia 81–3
Oxford University Press 12 18–43 *passim*
   53 57 81–3 95 96 116 120 132 140 157
   158 168 218 226 257 271 272 273 302 305
   311

Paget, Clarence 144–5
Paladin Books 147
Palundi, *Indian Administration* 32
Pan Books 41 141 142–3 148–9 151 179
   282n 292 304
Panther Books 147 152
paper rationing 17 18 268 269
paperbacks 139–55 159–60 213
Parker, Joy 72
Parsons, Ian 15 16 158
Parsons, Olive 216
Partington, Professor (Cambridge) 131–2
Paternoster Club 278
Payot, Librairie 178
Pearson Group 37 275 287 298
Penguin Books 16 20 21 62n 77 119 139–55
   passim 159–63 180 189 195 204 206–8 213
   214 236 253 265 286 287 293 305 307 308
   309; Penguin Classics 21
Pentos Bookselling Group 226 309 310
People's Theatre 77
Pergamon Press 224
periodicals 41
Perrick, Ben 113 115
Persephone Books 240

Philadelphia, restaurant 164
Philip, Son & Nephew 247 248
Phillips, Godfrey Ltd 140–1 153
Phoenix House 96
Picador Books 188
Pick, Charles 122 129 **130 140 156** 158–9
   165 **190 191–2** 311
Pictorial Education 41
Pioneer Bookshop 310
Piper, David, *The Companion Guide to
   London* 80
Piper, John 200
Pitman, Sir Isaac & Co. 158 311
Plath, Sylvia 25
play scripts 25 116
Pocket Books 309
Pocock, Tony **81–2 119–20** 170 **218 219
   270 271 272–3** 311
Poems from Italy 14
poetry 12–13 14–15 19 25–6 61 77 79
   210–11 259–60
Poetry Society 19 306
Poland 218 219–21
Pooley, Mr (Simpkin Marshall) 4–5
Porter, Peter 61
Powers, Melvin 299
Praed, Harry 16
Prague Book Fair 217–18
Prendergast, Joe 255
Priestley, J. B. 61
Prime, John 78 **80** 81 **108–9** 118 119 **122–3**
   153 **216–19 221 240 280–1** 306 311
Pringle, Alexandra 261
Prior, Mr (Deighton, Bell & Co.) 47
Probsthain, Arthur, Booksellers 241
Profile Books 162–3 235 294 302
Publishers Association 98 170 190 223–33
   passim 254n 267–76 *passim* 282 285 304
   305 308 312
Publishers' Pantomime 278–80
Publishers Publicity Circle 277
publishers' representatives 4 30–9 *passim*
   50 65 73 82–4 94–5 124 129–38 151–3
   156–7 164 165 193 243–56 266
Publishers Weekly 90
Puffin Books 79
Puffmore, Henry 176
Pugh, Evelyn 5
Pyle, Howard 88

Quadrille Publishing 313
Quarto Books 312
Quayle, Anthony 27 311

Rainbird, George 150 304

Random House 105 154–5 195 231–2 275 289 293 301 302 305 311
Ranfurly, Countess of 37–8
Ranfurly Library 37
Rapley, Bill 119
Rapp, George 314
Rapp & Whiting 314
Ratushinskaya, Irina, *No, I'm Not Afraid* 210–11
Raymond, Harold 15 16
Raymond, Piers 10
Rayward, Tommy 68–9
Rea, Julian 44
Read, Sam, bookshop 79–80 308
Rebuck, Gail 275 289
Reckitt, Eva 153 216
Reed Elsevier 37
Reinhardt, Joan 290 291 310
Reinhardt, Max 27 95 98 133–4 161 165 **197–9 290–2** 310 311
remainders 4 6
reps, *see* publishers' representatives
Remington, Stan **82–4 152 190–1 271** 311
Renault, Mary 202
Reynolds, Jim 147
Richards, Victor 43
Richardson, Ralph 27 161 311
Ritter, Scott, *War on Iraq* 210
Rieu, E. V. 21
rights 144–5 206 222 289
Rivers, Mr (J. & A. Churchill) 285
Rix, Tim **18–20 35–9 41 43–5** *passim* **193 194 202 271–2 273 276 287 300–1** 311–12
Robbins, Lionel 123
Roberts, John 13
Roberts, Commander 81–4
Robertson, Charles 4 6 245
Robinson, Geoffrey 207
Rodgers, Dick 211
Rose, Francis 115
Rose, Jim 160
Rosemount Press 64
Ross, Tony 104–5; *Goldilocks and the Three Bears* 104
Rosset, Barney 145
Roth, Philip 183; *Portnoy's Complaint* 249
Rothmann, Mr (Deighton, Bell & Co.) 48
Rothschild, Lord 131–2
Rowling, J. K. 98 235–6 238
Roxburgh, Toby 278 279
Roy, David 274
royal family 69 72 73
royalties 28 194–5
Rudd, Katherine 93
Rules, restaurant 165

Rush, Mr (Foyle's) 115
Russia 115 216–23
Rutherford, Ernest ix 51
Ryder, John 95–6

Sabah 36
Salinger, J. D. 141
Salt, Laura 81–2
Sandoe, John 59 120–2 310
Sarawak 35 36
Sassoon, Siegfried 14–15
Saugman, Per 52n **67 85 178 190 191 267 269 285** 312
Saunders, Charles 116
Savile Club 157 267
Savoy Hotel 156 193 199
Sayers, Dorothy L. 141 190
Scardino, Marjorie 275
Scherer, Paul 151 212
Schiffren, André 146 206–7
Schofield & Sims 294
Scholastic Publishing Co. 46
School of the Air 99
Schwartz, Lew 92
science books 49 190 191
Seawright, Miss 173
Secker, Martin 145
Secker & Warburg 18 145 293 297
secondhand books 49 50–1 76 130
Segrave, Edmond 157 175 269
Selby, Hubert, *Last Exit to Brooklyn* 180–1
Selfridges 193
Seligman, Ellen 261–2
Sendak, Maurice, *Where the Wild Things Are* x 100–1
Seuss, Dr, *The Cat in the Hat Comes Back* 80
Seviour, Michael **10 56–63** *passim* **72 76 78 109 116 118 119 240–1 248 252** 312
Seyd, Pat 132
Seymour, Arthur 24–5
Shah, Idries 164
Shaw, Christopher 144
Shaw, George Bernard 110
Shears, Gillian 118
Sheed & Ward 57
Sherlock, Sheila 191
Showalter, Elaine 215
Sidgwick & Jackson 2 204
Sierra Leone 43–4
Silver Moon Women's Bookshop 253 305
Simon & Schuster 312
Simpkin Marshall 1–11 126 127 134 243–5 267–8 309 310 312
Simpson, James 54
Simpson, Stephen 72–3